Gamification and Game-Based Learning

Kruger Brentt
Publishers

Gamification and Game-Based Learning

Keneilwe Molosi | Camilo Mejia

Kruger Brentt
Publishers
2025

Kruger Brentt Publishers UK. LTD.
Company Number 9728962

Regd. Office: 68 St Margarets Road, Edgware, Middlesex HA8 9UU

ISBN: 978-1-78715-312-7

For information on all our publications visit our website at http://krugerbrentt.com/

PREFACE

In recent years, gamification and game-based learning have emerged as innovative approaches to education, harnessing the power of games and game design principles to enhance learning outcomes and engagement. By incorporating elements such as competition, rewards, and narrative into educational experiences, gamification and game-based learning transform traditional teaching methods, making learning more interactive, immersive, and enjoyable for students of all ages. As educators seek to adapt to the changing needs and preferences of digital-native learners, understanding the principles and applications of gamification and game-based learning has become essential for fostering creativity, critical thinking, and lifelong learning skills.

This book, titled "Gamification and Game-Based Learning," is a comprehensive exploration of the concepts, strategies, and best practices in leveraging games for educational purposes. Drawing upon the expertise of educators, game designers, and researchers, this volume offers insights, methodologies, and practical examples for integrating gamification and game-based learning into teaching and learning environments.

From the psychology of motivation and engagement to the design principles of effective educational games, "Gamification and Game-Based Learning" covers a wide range of topics essential for understanding and implementing game-based approaches to education. Through clear explanations, case studies, and actionable strategies, readers will gain a deep understanding of how gamification and game-based learning can enhance student motivation, participation, and achievement across diverse subject areas and learning contexts.

Moreover, this book explores the potential of gamification and game-based learning to promote collaboration, creativity, and problem-solving skills, preparing students for success in an increasingly complex and interconnected world. By examining innovative examples of game-based learning initiatives in K-12 education, higher education, and corporate training, we highlight the transformative impact of games on learning outcomes and student engagement.

As we navigate the opportunities and challenges of integrating games into education, it is our hope that "Gamification and Game-Based Learning" will serve as a valuable resource for educators, instructional designers, policymakers, and researchers seeking to harness the power of games for learning. Whether you are a teacher looking to gamify your classroom, a trainer exploring new approaches to corporate learning, or a researcher studying the impact of games on learning outcomes, this book invites you to explore the exciting possibilities of gamification and game-based learning in education.

Keneilwe Molosi | Camilo Mejia

CONTENTS

PART-I

FOUNDATION OF GAMIFICATION AND GAME-BASED LEARNING

CHAPTER 1

UNDERSTANDING GAMIFICATION AND GAME-BASED LEARNING

1.1 DEFINING GAMIFICATION AND GAME-BASED LEARNING

1.1.1 Defining Gamification

Gamification is the strategic attempt to enhance systems, services, organizations, and activities by creating similar experiences to those experienced when playing games in order to motivate and engage users. This is generally accomplished through the application of game design elements and game principles (dynamics and mechanics) in non-game contexts.

Gamification is part of persuasive system design, and it commonly employs game design elements to improve user engagement, organizational productivity, flow, learning, crowdsourcing, knowledge retention, employee recruitment and evaluation, ease of use, usefulness of systems, physical exercise, traffic violations, voter apathy, public attitudes about alternative energy, and more. A collection of research on gamification shows that a majority of studies on gamification find it has positive effects on individuals. However, individual and contextual differences exist.

Gamification can be achieved using different game mechanics and elements which can be linked to 8 core drives when using the Octalysis framework.

History

The term "gamification" first appeared online in the context of computer software in 2008. Gamification did not gain popularity until 2010. Even prior to the term coming into use, other fields borrowing elements from videogames was common; for example, some work in learning disabilities and scientific visualization adapted elements from videogames.

The term "gamification" first gained widespread usage in 2010, in a more specific sense referring to incorporation of social/reward aspects of games into software. The technique captured the attention of venture capitalists, one of whom said he considered gamification the most promising area in gaming. Another observed that half of all companies seeking funding for consumer software applications mentioned game design in their presentations.

Several researchers consider gamification closely related to earlier work on adapting game-design elements and techniques to non-game contexts. Deterding *et al.* survey research in human–computer interaction that uses game-derived elements for motivation and interface design, and Nelson argues for a connection to both the Soviet concept of socialist competition, and the American management trend of "fun at work". Fuchs points out that gamification might be driven by new forms of ludic interfaces. Gamification conferences have also retroactively incorporated simulation; e.g. Will Wright, designer of the 1989 video game SimCity, was the keynote speaker at the gamification conference Gsummit 2013.

In addition to companies that use the technique, a number of businesses created gamification platforms. In October 2007, Bunchball, backed by Adobe Systems Incorporated, was the first company to provide game mechanics as a service, on Dunder Mifflin Infinity, the community site for the NBC TV show *The Office.* Bunchball customers have included Playboy, Chiquita, Bravo, and The USA Network. Badgeville, which offers gamification services, launched in late 2010, and raised $15 million in venture-capital funding in its first year of operation.

Gamification as an educational and behavior modification tool reached the public sector by 2012, when the United States Department of Energy co-funded multiple research trials, including consumer behavior studies, adapting the format of Programmed learning into mobile microlearning to experiment with the impacts of gamification in reducing energy use. Cultural anthropologist Susan Mazur-Stommen published a business case for applying games to addressing climate change and sustainability, delivering research which "...took many forms including card-games (Cool Choices), videogames (Ludwig), and games for mobile devices such as smartphones (Ringorang)."

Techniques

Gamification techniques are intended to leverage people's natural desires for socializing, learning, mastery, competition, achievement, status, self-expression, altruism, or closure, or simply their response to the framing of a situation as game or play. Early gamification strategies use rewards for players who accomplish desired tasks or competition to engage players.

Types of rewards include points, achievement badges or levels, the filling of a progress bar, or providing the user with virtual currency. Making the rewards for accomplishing tasks visible to other players or providing leader boards are ways of encouraging players to compete.

Another approach to gamification is to make existing tasks feel more like games. Some techniques used in this approach include adding meaningful choice, onboarding with a tutorial, increasing challenge, and adding narrative.

Game Design Elements

Game design elements are the basic building blocks of gamification applications. Among these typical game design elements, are points, badges, leader-boards, performance graphs, meaningful stories, avatars, and teammates. According to Chou, the efficacy of the Octalysis Framework in gamification, shows that experience points (XP), badges, and progress indicators can significantly enhance user engagement and productivity in business learning programs.

Points

Points are basic elements of a multitude of games and gamified applications. They are typically rewarded for the successful accomplishment of specified activities within the gamified environment and they serve to numerically represent a player's progress. Various kinds of points can be differentiated between, e.g., experience points, redeemable points, or reputation points, as can the different purposes that points serve. One of the most important purposes of points is to provide feedback. Points allow the players' in-game behavior to be measured, and they serve as continuous and immediate feedback and as a reward.

Badges

Badges are defined as visual representations of achievements and can be earned and collected within the gamification environment. They confirm the players' achievements, symbolize their merits, and visibly show their accomplishment of levels or goals. Earning a badge can be dependent on a specific number of points or on particular activities within the game. Badges have many functions, serving as goals, if the prerequisites for winning them are known to the player, or as virtual status symbols. In the same way as points, badges also provide feedback, in that they indicate how the players have performed. Badges can influence players' behavior, leading them to select certain routes and challenges in order to earn badges that are associated with them. Additionally, as badges symbolize one's membership in a group of those who own this particular badge, they also can exert social influences on players and co-players, particularly if they are rare or hard to earn.

Leaderboards

Leaderboards rank players according to their relative success, measuring them against a certain success criterion. As such, leaderboards can help determine who performs best in a certain activity and are thus competitive indicators of progress that relate the player's own performance to the performance of others. However, the motivational potential of leaderboards is mixed. Werbach and Hunter regard them as effective motivators if there are only a few points left to the next level or position, but as demotivators, if players find themselves at the bottom end of the leaderboard. Competition caused by leaderboards can create social pressure to increase the player's level of engagement and can consequently have a constructive effect on participation and learning. However, these positive effects of competition are more likely if the respective competitors are approximately at the same performance level.

Performance Graphs

Performance graphs, which are often used in simulation or strategy games, provide information about the players' performance compared to their preceding performance during a game.

Thus, in contrast to leaderboards, performance graphs do not compare the player's performance to other players, but instead, evaluate the player's own performance over time. Unlike the social reference standard of leaderboards, performance graphs are based on an individual reference standard. By graphically displaying the player's performance over a fixed period, they focus on improvements. Motivation theory postulates that this fosters mastery orientation, which is particularly beneficial to learning.

Meaningful Stories

Meaningful stories are game design elements that do not relate to the player's performance. The narrative context in which a gamified application can be embedded contextualizes activities and characters in the game and gives them meaning beyond the mere quest for points and achievements. A story can be communicated by a game's title (e.g., Space Invaders) or by complex storylines typical of contemporary role-playing video games (e.g., The Elder Scrolls Series). Narrative contexts can be oriented towards real, non-game contexts or act as analogies of real-world settings.

The latter can enrich boring, barely stimulating contexts, and, consequently, inspire and motivate players particularly if the story is in line with their personal interests. As such, stories are also an important part in gamification applications, as they can alter the meaning of real-world activities by adding a narrative 'overlay', e.g. being hunted by zombies while going for a run.

Avatars

Avatars are visual representations of players within the game or gamification environment. Usually, they are chosen or even created by the player. Avatars can be designed quite simply as a mere pictogram, or they can be complexly animated, three- dimensional representations. Their main formal requirement is that they unmistakably identify the players and set them apart from other human or computer-controlled avatars. Avatars allow the players to adopt or create another identity and, in cooperative games, to become part of a community.

Teammates

Teammates, whether they are other real players or virtual non-player characters, can induce conflict, competition or cooperation. The latter can be fostered particularly by introducing teams, i.e. by creating defined groups of players that work together towards a shared objective. Meta-analytic evidence supports that the combination of competition and collaboration in games is likely to be effective for learning.

Game Element Hierarchy

- The described game elements fit within a broader framework, which involves three types of elements: *dynamics*, *mechanics*, and *components*. These elements constitute the hierarchy of game elements.
- Dynamics are the highest in the hierarchy. They are the big picture aspects of the gamified system that should be considered and managed; however, they never directly enter into the game. Dynamics elements provide motivation through features such as narrative or social interaction.
- Mechanics are the basic processes that drive the action forward and generate player engagement and involvement. Examples are chance, turns, and rewards.
- Components are the specific instantiations of mechanics and dynamics; elements like points, quests, and virtual goods.

Applications

Gamification has been applied to almost every aspect of life. Examples of gamification in business context include the U.S. Army, which uses military simulator *America's Army* as a recruitment tool, and M&M's "Eye Spy" pretzel game, launched in 2013 to amplify the company's pretzel marketing campaign by creating a fun way to "boost user engagement." Another example can be seen in the American education system. Students are ranked in their class based on their earned grade-point average (GPA), which is comparable to earning a high score in video games. Students may also receive incentives, such as an honorable mention on the dean's list, the honor roll, and scholarships, which are equivalent to leveling-up a video game character or earning virtual currency or tools that augment game success. Job application processes sometimes use gamification as a way to hire employees by assessing their suitability through questionnaires and mini games that simulate the actual work environment of that company.

Marketing

Gamification has been widely applied in marketing. Over 70% of Forbes Global 2000 companies surveyed in 2013 said they planned to use gamification for the purposes of marketing and customer retention. For example, in November, 2011, Australian broadcast and online media partnership Yahoo!7 launched its Fango mobile app/SAP, which TV viewers use to interact with shows via techniques like check-ins and badges. Gamification has also been used in customer loyalty programs. In 2010, Starbucks gave custom Foursquare badges to people who checked in at multiple locations, and offered discounts to people who checked in most frequently at an individual store. As a general rule Gamification Marketing or Game Marketing usually falls under four primary categories;

- **Brandification (In-Game Advertising):** Messages, images or videos promoting a Brand, Product or Service within a game's visuals components. According to NBCNews game creators Electronic Arts used "Madden 09" and "Burnout Paradise" to promote 'in-game' billboards encouraging players to vote.
- **Transmedia:** The result of taking a media property and extending it into a different medium for both promotional and monetisation purposes. Nintendo's "007: GoldenEye" is a classic example. A video game created to advertise the originally titled movie. In the end, the promotional game brought in more money than the originally titled film.
- **Through-the-Line (TTL) & Below-the-Line (BTL):** Text above, side or below main game screen (also known as an iFrame) advertising images or text. Example of this would be "I love Bees".
- **Advergames:** Usually games based on popular mobile game templates, such as 'Candy Crush' or 'Temple Run'. These games are then recreated via platforms like WIX with software from the likes of Gamify, in order to promote Brands, Products and Services. Usually to encourage engagement, loyalty and product education. These usually involve social leaderboards and rewards that are advertised via social media platforms like Facebook's Top 10 games.

Gamification also has been used as a tool for customer engagement, and for encouraging desirable website usage behaviour. Additionally, gamification is applicable to increasing engagement on sites built on social network services. For example, in August, 2010, the website builder DevHub announced an increase in the number of users who completed their online tasks from 10% to 80% after adding gamification elements. On the programming question-and-answer site Stack Overflow users receive points and/or badges for performing a variety of actions, including spreading links to questions and answers via Facebook and Twitter.

A large number of different badges are available, and when a user's reputation points exceed various thresholds, the user gains additional privileges, eventually including moderator privileges.

Inspiration

Gamification can be used for ideation (structured brainstorming to produce new ideas). A study at MIT Sloan found that ideation games helped participants generate more and better ideas, and compared it to gauging the influence of academic papers by the numbers of citations received in subsequent research.

Health

Applications like Fitocracy and QUENTIQ (Dacadoo) use gamification to encourage their users to exercise more effectively and improve their overall health. Users are awarded varying numbers of points for activities they perform in their workouts, and gain levels based on points collected. Users can also complete quests (sets of related activities) and gain achievement badges for fitness milestones. Health Month adds aspects of social gaming by allowing successful users to restore points to users who have failed to meet certain goals. Public health researchers have studied the use of gamification in self-management of chronic diseases and common mental disorders, STD prevention, and infection prevention and control.

In a review of health apps in the 2014 Apple App Store, more than 100 apps showed a positive correlation between gamification elements used and high user ratings. MyFitnessPal was named as the app that used the most gamification elements.

Reviewers of the popular location-based game *Pokémon Go* praised the game for promoting physical exercise. Terri Schwartz (*IGN*) said it was "secretly the best exercise app out there," and that it changed her daily walking routine. Patrick Allen (*Lifehacker*) wrote an article with tips about how to work out using *Pokémon Go*. Julia Belluz (*Vox*) said it could be the "greatest unintentional health fad ever," writing that one of the results of the game that the developers may not have imagined was that "it seems to be getting people moving." One study showed users took an extra 194 steps per day once they started using the app, approximately 26% more than usual. *Ingress* is a similar game that also requires a player to be physically active. *Zombies, Run!*, a game in which the player is trying to survive a zombie apocalypse through a series of missions, requires the player to (physically) run, collect items to help the town survive, and listen to various audio narrations to uncover mysteries. Mobile, context-sensitive serious games for sports and health have been called *exergames*.

Work

Gamification has been used in an attempt to improve employee productivity in healthcare, financial services, transportation, government, and others. In general, enterprise gamification refers to work situations where "game thinking and game-based tools are used in a strategic manner to integrate with existing business processes or information systems. And these techniques are used to help drive positive employee and organizational outcomes."

Crowdsourcing

Crowdsourcing has been gamified in games like Foldit, a game designed by the University of Washington, in which players compete to manipulate proteins into more efficient structures. A 2010 paper in science journal Nature credited Foldit's 57,000 players with providing useful results that matched or outperformed algorithmically computed solutions. The ESP Game is a game that is used to generate image metadata. Google Image Labeler is a version of the ESP Game that Google has licensed to generate its own image metadata. Research from the University of Bonn used gamification to increase wiki contributions by 62%.

In the context of online crowdsourcing, gamification is also employed to improve the psychological and behavioral consequences of the solvers. According to numerous research, adding gamification components to a crowdsourcing platform can be considered as a design that shifts participants' focus from task completion to involvement motivated by intrinsic factors. Since the success of crowdsourcing competitions depends on a large number of participating solvers, the platforms for crowdsourcing provide motivating factors to increase participation by drawing on the concepts of the game.

Education and Training

Gamification in the context of education and training is of particular interest because it offers a variety of benefits associated with learning outcomes and retention. Using video-game inspired elements like leaderboards and badges has been shown to be effective in engaging large groups and providing objectives for students to achieve outside of traditional norms like grades or verbal feedback. Online learning platforms such as Khan Academy and even physical schools like New York City Department of Education's Quest to Learn use gamification to motivate students to complete mission-based units and master concepts. There is also an increasing interest in the use of gamification in health sciences and education as an engaging information delivery tool and in order to add variety to revision.

With increased access to one-to-one student devices, and accelerated by pressure from the COVID-19 pandemic, many teachers from primary to post-secondary settings have introduced live, online quiz-show style games into their lessons.

Gamification has also been used to promote learning outside of schools. In August 2009, Gbanga launched a game for the Zurich Zoo where participants learned about endangered species by collecting animals in mixed reality. Companies seeking to train their customers to use their product effectively can showcase features of their products with interactive games like Microsoft's Ribbon Hero 2.

A wide range of employers including the United States Armed Forces, Unilever, and SAP currently use gamified training modules to educate their employees and motivate them to apply what they learned in trainings to their job. According to a study conducted by Badgeville, 78% of workers are utilizing games-based motivation at work and nearly 91% say these systems improve their work experience by increasing engagement, awareness and productivity. In the form of occupational safety training, technology can provide realistic and effective simulations of real-life experiences, making safety training less passive and more engaging, more flexible in terms of time management and a cost-effective alternative to practice. The combined use od virtual reality and gamification can provide a more effective solutions in term of knowledge acquisition and retention when they are compared with traditional training methods.

Technology Design

Traditionally, researchers thought of motivations to use computer systems to be primarily driven by extrinsic purposes; however, many modern systems have their use driven primarily by intrinsic motivations. Examples of such systems used primarily to fulfill users' intrinsic motivations, include online gaming, virtual worlds, online shopping, learning/education, online dating, digital music repositories, social networking, online pornography, and so on. Such systems are excellent candidates for further 'gamification' in their design. Moreover, even traditional management information systems (e.g., ERP, CRM) are being 'gamified' such that both extrinsic and intrinsic motivations must increasingly be considered.

As illustration, Microsoft has announced plans to use gamification techniques for its Windows Phone 7 operating system design. While businesses face the challenges of creating motivating gameplay strategies, what makes for effective gamification is a key question. One important type of technological design in gamification is the player centered design. Based on the design methodology user-centered design, its main goal is to promote greater connectivity and positive behavior change between technological consumers. It has five steps that help computer users connect with other people online to help them accomplish goals and other tasks they need to complete. The 5 steps are: an individual or company has to know their player (their target audience), identify their mission (their goal), understand human motivation (the personality, desires, and triggers of the target audience), apply mechanics (points, badges, leaderboards, etc.), and to manage, monitor, and measure the way they are using their mechanics to ensure it is helping them achieve the desired outcome of their goal and that their goal is specific and realistic.

Authentication

Gamification has also been applied to authentication. Games have been proposed as a way for users to learn new and more complicated passwords. Gamification has also been proposed as a way to select and manage archives.

Online Gambling

Gamification has been used to some extent by online casinos. Some brands use an incremental reward system to extend the typical player lifecycle and to encourage repeat visits and cash deposits at the casino in return for rewards such as free spins and cash match bonuses on subsequent deposits.

Legal Restrictions

Through gamification's growing adoption and its nature as a data aggregator, multiple legal restrictions may apply to gamification. Some refer to the use of virtual currencies and virtual assets, data privacy laws and data protection, or labor laws.

The use of virtual currencies, in contrast to traditional payment systems, is not regulated. The legal uncertainty surrounding the virtual currency schemes might constitute a challenge for public authorities, as these schemes can be used by criminals, fraudsters and money launderers to perform their illegal activities.

A March 2022 consultation paper by the Board of the International Organization of Securities Commissions (IOSCO) questions whether some gamification tactics should be banned.

Criticism

University of Hamburg researcher Sebastian Deterding has characterized the initial popular strategies for gamification as not being fun and creating an artificial sense of achievement. He also says that gamification can encourage unintended behaviours.

Poorly designed gamification in the workplace has been compared to Taylorism, and is considered a form of micromanagement.

In a review of 132 of the top health and fitness apps in the Apple app store, in 2014, using gamification as a method to modify behavior, the authors concluded that "Despite the inclusion of at least some components of gamification, the mean scores of integration of gamification components were still below 50 percent. This was also true for the inclusion of game elements and the use of health behavior theory constructs, thus showing a lack of following any clear industry standard of effective gaming, gamification, or behavioral theory in health and fitness apps."

Concern was also expressed in a 2016 study analyzing outcome data from 1,298 users who competed in gamified and incentivized exercise challenges while wearing wearable devices. In that study the authors conjectured that data may be highly skewed by cohorts of already healthy users, rather than the intended audiences of participants requiring behavioral intervention. Game designers like Jon Radoff and Margaret Robertson have also criticized gamification as excluding elements like storytelling and experiences and using simple reward systems in place of true game mechanics. Gamification practitioners have pointed out that while the initial popular designs were in fact mostly relying on simplistic reward approach, even those led to significant improvements in short-term engagement. This was supported by the first comprehensive study in 2014, which concluded that an increase in gamification elements correlated with an increase in motivation score, but not with capacity or opportunity/trigger scores.

The same study called for standardization across the app industry on gamification principles to improve the effectiveness of health apps on the health outcomes of users.

MIT Professor Kevin Slavin has described business research into gamification as flawed and misleading for those unfamiliar with gaming. Heather Chaplin, writing in *Slate*, describes gamification as "an allegedly populist idea that actually benefits corporate interests over those of ordinary people". Jane McGonigal has distanced her work from the label "gamification", listing rewards outside of gameplay as the central idea of gamification and distinguishing game applications where the gameplay itself is the reward under the term "gameful design".

"Gamification" as a term has also been criticized. Ian Bogost has referred to the term as a marketing fad and suggested "exploitation-ware" as a more suitable name for the games used in marketing. Other opinions on the terminology criticism have made the case why the term gamification makes sense.

In an article in the *LA Times*, the gamification of worker engagement at Disneyland was described as an "electronic whip". Workers had reported feeling controlled and overworked by the system.

1.1.2 Game-Based Learning

Game-based learning is basically a computerized imitation of a real-world system or process. In the context of business, these games imitate real-world processes in various fields such as sales, training, and development, and allow employees to hone their skills in decision making, strategic thinking, problem-solving, market analysis, teamwork and leadership, operations, and financial analysis.

Game-based learning involves animated programs that have 'humans' and 'opponents' whose interactions have an effect upon each other and on the environment. These games allow employees to control the movements and actions of the animated characters, with the aim to develop some competitive skills.

For example, in the case of game-based training for sales, employees receive an imaginary business situation to make decisions, which can include making decisions on advertising, price, sales tips, meeting targets, etc. These games mirror real business challenges, have an element of competitive challenge, use images and data to enhance the learner experience, and incorporate data and reporting for feedback.

Advantages of Game-Based Learning

Game-Based Learning Helps in Retaining Learning Insights

Enterprises invest heavily in training employees and then struggle to retain the learnings once they retire or leave. Game-based training usually has machine learning built into the systems which allow all colleagues, past and present to benefit from the combined knowledge pool. Besides, game-based learning allows learners to progress at their own pace, thus, making learning a more personalized experience.

Learning through Familiar Devices

Online Game-based learning can be possible through devices which employees are already familiar with, for example, the smartphone. The familiarity with these devices simplifies learning. With apps installed in their phones, employees can use today's digital and machine tools to improve their productivity and enhance their skills to further improve their careers.

Game-Based Learning Stimulates the Imagination

Game-based learning allows learners and instructors to visualize 3D models in real-time and at scale. This helps to make learning more contextual, more real and therefore more enjoyable and relevant to the learners. A virtually enhanced world encourages the learners to use their imagination and discover new possibilities in a fun and interactive way. Interactive learning facilitates deep learning, increasing the possibility of retaining information for a longer time.

Learning to Last a Lifetime

If successfully used, game-based learning can provide a learning experience that can last a lifetime. Let us take the case of an instructor who has to teach the employees about real problems faced every day at the workplace. In a traditional setting, the employees would be presented with a case study to read and understand the difficulties faced on the job and the solutions applied to mitigate the problems. However, using game-based learning, the instructor can actually make the learners experience the situation. Simulation games places participants in realistic, problem-based scenarios, where they have to apply their problem-solving skills to resolve the issues. Simulation is already used in many fields of work, for example, healthcare simulation involves replicating real-life medical scenarios, where learners have to perform a virtual dissection or prescribe appropriate medications. There are flight simulations to train pilot trainees, that are complete with different weather conditions, mid-air scenes and runway take offs.

Games thus help to create realistic situations through simulations and situational role plays to enable employees gain practical knowledge that they are unlikely to forget.

Game-Based Learning Helps in Simplifying Difficult Concepts

Abstract concepts can be difficult to teach. Games can be used to give a tangible shape to such concepts, allowing employees look at them from a different perspective. Take the case of a combustion engine. Using simulated diagrams, the instructor can bring to life the different parts that make up an engine. Then again, to explain how it functions, instructors can use a 3D holograph of an engine in motion to enable the trainees to look at it from all angles and enjoy a highly detailed, immersive exploration of its internal movements and the conversion of energy from one form to another.

Learning by Doing

As digital technology grows, it becomes more and more difficult to keep the employees engaged. Game-based learning helps to bridge this gap and bring them closer to reality. It makes learning multisensory and more alive. The more the learners do, the more they learn, the more they assimilate and the more they retain.

Improving Sales

Sales simulations are unique in the sense that they involve a higher level of customization, and participants can learn at their own pace, with ample time for practice and feedback. Learning involves both individual learning and team learning, and an instructor is also present to solve problems which learners don't comprehend.

Collaborate with the Team

Since game-based learning involves a real-world situation, the entire team can collaborate in the learning environment, brainstorm on the possible outcomes and share their ideas to overcome problems.

Reduce Chances of Failure in the Real World

As mentioned, games resemble the real world, which means that the company benefits by allowing its employees make and learn from their mistakes in the virtual world, rather than making mistakes in actual situations. This in turn helps the company to save both money and reputation. Employees trained extensively in the virtual world are less likely to fail in the real world.

Higher Receptivity to Learning

Game-based learning is multi-sensory learning which greatly enhances a learner's ability to grasp and retain concepts. Sales personnel can learn new sales tips faster, retain them in their memories and remember to use them effectively to close a sale in real-time.

1.2 THE EDUCATIONAL BENEFITS OF GAMES

Games have been a fundamental part of human culture and society for thousands of years, serving various purposes beyond mere entertainment. In recent decades, educators have increasingly recognized the potential of games as powerful tools for learning. From traditional board games to digital simulations, games offer a wide range of educational benefits across different age groups and subject areas.

Games offer a wealth of educational benefits that extend far beyond mere entertainment. From promoting engagement and motivation to fostering critical thinking, collaboration, creativity, and subject mastery, games have the potential to revolutionize education and enhance learning outcomes across diverse contexts. By integrating games into educational settings, educators can create dynamic and immersive learning experiences that cater to the needs and interests of 21st-century learners. Moreover, as technology continues to evolve, the potential for games to transform education and empower learners is virtually limitless. As such, harnessing the educational benefits of games represents a promising avenue for promoting lifelong learning and preparing learners for success in an increasingly complex and interconnected world.

1.2.1 Understanding the Educational Value of Games

Games, in their various forms, possess unique attributes that make them effective educational tools. Unlike traditional instructional methods, games offer immersive and interactive experiences that actively engage learners. By integrating gameplay elements such as challenges, rewards, and feedback mechanisms, games create dynamic learning environments that stimulate cognitive processes and foster deeper engagement.

1.2.2 Engagement and Motivation

One of the most significant advantages of games in education is their ability to captivate learners' interest and sustain their motivation. Unlike passive learning activities, games provide immediate feedback and tangible rewards for progress and achievement. This feedback loop reinforces positive behaviors and encourages learners to persist in their efforts. Moreover, the element of challenge inherent in games motivates players to overcome obstacles and strive for mastery, promoting a growth mindset and resilience in the face of failure.

1.2.3 Problem-Solving and Critical Thinking

Games often present players with complex problems or puzzles that require analytical thinking, strategic planning, and decision-making skills to solve. Whether it's navigating a virtual environment, deciphering clues in a mystery game, or strategizing in a multiplayer competition, players are constantly engaged in cognitive processes that enhance their problem-solving abilities. Moreover, the iterative nature of gameplay encourages players to experiment with different approaches and learn from their mistakes, fostering a deeper understanding of underlying concepts.

1.2.4 Collaboration and Communication

Many games, particularly multiplayer or cooperative ones, require players to collaborate with teammates, communicate effectively, and coordinate their actions to achieve common goals. Whether its coordinating strategies in a strategy game, working together to solve puzzles in an escape room game, or negotiating alliances in a social deduction game, players develop essential teamwork and communication skills. These collaborative experiences not only enhance social interactions but also prepare learners for real-world situations that require cooperation and teamwork.

1.2.5 Creativity and Imagination

Games provide fertile ground for creative expression and imaginative exploration. From designing custom characters and building virtual worlds to crafting intricate narratives and solving creative challenges, players are encouraged to unleash their creativity and think outside the box. In sandbox games like Minecraft, for example, players have the freedom to create and explore limitless possibilities, fostering creativity, problem-solving, and self-expression. Moreover, games that incorporate elements of storytelling and world-building immerse players in rich narratives that stimulate their imagination and emotional engagement.

1.2.6 Subject Mastery and Learning Outcomes

Beyond the cognitive and socio-emotional benefits, games can be powerful tools for teaching specific subjects and academic concepts. Educational games are designed to align with curriculum standards and learning objectives, presenting content in an interactive and engaging format. Whether it's practicing math skills through educational apps, exploring historical events through simulation games, or learning a new language through gamified exercises, games provide opportunities for active learning and skill development. Moreover, the adaptive nature of many educational games allows learners to progress at their own pace and receive targeted support based on their individual needs and abilities.

1.2.7 Digital Literacy and Technological Skills

In an increasingly digital world, proficiency in digital literacy and technology skills is essential for success in education and beyond. Games provide a platform for developing these skills in a fun and engaging way. Whether it's navigating virtual interfaces, using software tools, or understanding digital content, players gain practical experience with technology while enjoying interactive gameplay experiences. Moreover, the gamification of learning activities can motivate learners to explore and experiment with technology, fostering a sense of curiosity and confidence in their digital abilities.

1.2.8 Cultural Understanding and Global Awareness

Games offer a unique opportunity for cultural exploration and cross-cultural understanding. Many games incorporate diverse cultural elements, historical contexts, and global perspectives, allowing players to explore different cultures and societies from around the world. Whether it's experiencing historical events through simulation games, immersing oneself in the mythology of different cultures through fantasy games, or engaging with characters from diverse backgrounds in narrative-driven games, players gain insights into the richness and diversity of human experiences. These immersive experiences promote empathy, tolerance, and global awareness, fostering a more inclusive and interconnected worldview.

1.2.9 Health and Well-being

While games are often criticized for promoting sedentary behavior and screen time, they can also promote health and well-being when designed with a focus on physical activity, mindfulness, and relaxation. Gamified fitness apps, for example, encourage users to engage in physical exercise by incorporating game-like elements such as challenges, rewards, and progress tracking. Similarly, games designed for stress relief and relaxation, such as meditation apps and puzzle games, provide opportunities for players to unwind and recharge in a digital environment. By harnessing the power of games for health and well-being, educators and game developers can promote holistic development and self-care among learners of all ages.

1.3 HISTORICAL CONTEXT OF GAMES IN EDUCATION

Games have been utilized as educational tools throughout history, dating back to ancient civilizations where they were employed to teach essential skills and knowledge.

Throughout history, games have played a crucial role in education, serving as vehicles for transmitting knowledge, instilling values, and fostering essential skills. From ancient civilizations to the digital age, games have evolved alongside educational practices, adapting to technological advancements and pedagogical trends. As educators continue to harness the power of games in teaching and learning, they unlock new possibilities for engaging, immersive, and effective educational experiences.

1.3.1 Ancient Civilizations: The Origins of Educational Games

Mesopotamia and Egypt

In ancient Mesopotamia and Egypt, board games such as Senet and Royal Game of Ur were not only sources of entertainment but also served educational purposes.

These games involved strategic thinking, mathematical calculations, and even religious symbolism, imparting important cognitive skills to players.

Greece and Rome

The ancient Greeks valued physical education, incorporating competitive sports like wrestling and running into their educational curriculum. The Olympic Games, for instance, not only celebrated athleticism but also promoted virtues like discipline, sportsmanship, and unity.

1.3.2 Medieval and Renaissance Period: Games as Moral Instruction

Chess and Strategy Games

During the Middle Ages and Renaissance, games like chess gained popularity among the aristocracy and clergy. Chess, with its intricate rules and emphasis on strategy, served as a metaphor for life's battles and moral dilemmas. Players learned to plan ahead, anticipate opponents' moves, and make strategic decisions—a valuable skill set applicable beyond the game board.

Moral Allegories and Parlor Games

Parlor games of the Renaissance period often conveyed moral lessons through allegorical narratives. Games like "The Game of the Goose" and "Snakes and Ladders" used symbolic imagery to represent life's journey, teaching players about virtues, vices, and the consequences of their actions.

1.3.3 Industrial Revolution: Emergence of Educational Board Games

Spreading Literacy through Games

The Industrial Revolution saw the rise of mass literacy and the need for accessible educational materials. Board games became a popular medium for teaching literacy, numeracy, geography, and history to children and adults alike. Games like "The Mansion of Happiness" and "Geographical Lotto" combined entertainment with learning, making education more engaging and interactive.

Educational Reform Movements

Educational reformers of the 19th century recognized the potential of games as pedagogical tools. Figures like Friedrich Froebel, the founder of kindergarten, emphasized the importance of play in early childhood education. Froebel's educational materials, including geometric building blocks known as Froebel Gifts, encouraged children to explore mathematical concepts through hands-on play.

1.3.4 20th Century: Rise of Digital and Simulated Learning

Educational Simulations and SimCity

The latter half of the 20th century witnessed the advent of digital technology and computer-based learning. Educational simulations like SimCity allowed students to design and manage virtual cities, fostering critical thinking, problem-solving, and urban planning skills. Simulations provided a safe and immersive environment for experimentation and exploration, supplementing traditional classroom instruction.

Educational Video Games

The rise of video games in the late 20th century spurred the development of educational titles across various subjects. Games like "Math Blaster," "Where in the World is Carmen Sandiego?" and "Oregon Trail" made learning fun and engaging for generations of students. These games combined entertainment with educational content, motivating players to master academic skills while navigating virtual adventures.

1.3.5 21st Century: Gamification and Digital Learning Platforms

Gamification in Education

In the 21st century, educators increasingly embraced gamification—the use of game elements in non-game contexts—to enhance learning experiences. Gamified platforms and apps incentivized student participation, tracked progress, and provided instant feedback, increasing motivation and retention. Elements like points, badges, leaderboards, and quests transformed mundane tasks into engaging challenges, driving student engagement and achievement.

Serious Games and Virtual Reality

The emergence of serious games and virtual reality (VR) technology expanded the possibilities for immersive learning experiences. Serious games tackled complex issues like climate change, global health, and social justice, inviting players to explore real-world problems and solutions in a simulated environment. VR simulations provided hands-on training in fields like medicine, engineering, and military operations, offering experiential learning opportunities without real-world risks.

CHAPTER 2

THE PSYCHOLOGY OF PLAY AND LEARNING

2.1 PLAY AS A LEARNING MECHANISM

Play is a fundamental aspect of human development, facilitating learning, socialization, and creativity across various stages of life. Play is a powerful learning mechanism that transcends age, culture, and context. From early childhood through adulthood, play fosters cognitive, social, and emotional development, cultivating essential skills for lifelong learning and success. Educators play a crucial role in harnessing the educational potential of play by creating environments that support exploration, experimentation, and discovery. By embracing play as a fundamental aspect of learning, we can inspire curiosity, creativity, and a lifelong passion for discovery.

2.1.1 The Importance of Play in Early Childhood Education

Play-Based Learning

Play-based learning is an educational approach that harnesses the natural inclination of children to play as a means of fostering holistic development. Play-based learning offers a rich and dynamic approach to education that honors children's natural inclination to explore, discover, and create. By embracing play as a cornerstone of early childhood education, educators empower children to become active, curious learners who are equipped with the skills, knowledge, and dispositions needed for success in school and beyond. As we continue to recognize the profound educational benefits of play, we pave the way for transformative learning experiences that inspire wonder, curiosity, and lifelong learning.

Understanding Play-Based Learning

- **Definition and Philosophy:** Play-based learning centers on the idea that play is a fundamental vehicle for learning and development in early childhood. It emphasizes child-initiated, open-ended activities that promote exploration, creativity, and problem-solving. In play-based learning environments, children engage in activities that are meaningful, relevant, and tailored to their interests and developmental needs.

- **The Role of the Educator:** Educators in play-based settings serve as facilitators, observers, and collaborators in children's learning experiences. Rather than dictating instruction, they create supportive environments that encourage curiosity, experimentation, and social interaction. Educators scaffold children's play by providing resources, posing open-ended questions, and guiding their exploration while respecting their autonomy and agency.

Principles of Play-Based Learning

- **Child-Centered Approach:** At the heart of play-based learning is a child-centered approach that prioritizes children's interests, strengths, and developmental stages. Learning experiences are tailored to individual needs and preferences, allowing children to take ownership of their learning journey and pursue topics of personal relevance.
- **Hands-On Exploration:** Play-based learning emphasizes hands-on, experiential learning opportunities that engage multiple senses and modes of expression. Children learn through direct manipulation of materials, experimentation with concepts, and interaction with peers and adults, fostering deeper understanding and retention of knowledge.
- **Open-Ended Play:** Open-ended play encourages creativity, imagination, and divergent thinking. Rather than prescribing specific outcomes, play-based activities allow for multiple pathways and solutions, empowering children to explore, innovate, and express themselves in meaningful ways.

Benefits of Play-Based Learning

- **Holistic Development:** Play-based learning promotes holistic development across cognitive, social, emotional, and physical domains. Through play, children develop critical thinking skills, language proficiency, emotional regulation, and motor coordination, laying the foundation for lifelong learning and well-being.
- **Social-Emotional Growth:** Play-based environments provide opportunities for children to develop social skills such as communication, cooperation, empathy, and conflict resolution. Through collaborative play, children learn to negotiate roles, share resources, and navigate social dynamics, fostering positive relationships and a sense of belonging.
- **Motivation and Engagement:** Play-based learning capitalizes on children's natural curiosity, intrinsic motivation, and joy of discovery. Children are actively engaged in learning activities that capture their

interest and imagination, leading to deeper levels of engagement, concentration, and enjoyment.

Implementing Play-Based Learning

- **Creating Enabling Environments:** Play-based learning environments are thoughtfully designed to stimulate exploration, creativity, and collaboration. They feature flexible spaces, diverse materials, and engaging provocations that invite children to play, inquire, and create. Educators organize materials and resources in accessible ways, allowing children to exercise agency and make choices based on their interests.
- **Observing and Documenting Children's Play:** Educators play a crucial role in observing and documenting children's play experiences to inform curriculum planning and assessment. Through careful observation, educators gain insights into children's interests, strengths, and areas for growth, guiding their instructional decisions and individualizing learning experiences.

Types of Play

Play is a multifaceted activity that encompasses various forms and expressions. Understanding the different types of play can provide insights into children's development, preferences, and learning styles. The diverse types of play provide children with rich and varied opportunities for learning, development, and self-expression.

By understanding and supporting different forms of play, educators can create environments that cater to children's individual interests, strengths, and developmental needs. Whether engaging in symbolic play, constructive play, social play, physical play, exploratory play, dramatic play, or games with rules, children benefit from the myriad opportunities for growth, exploration, and enjoyment that play provides.

- **Symbolic Play:** Symbolic play, also known as pretend or imaginative play, involves children using objects, actions, or roles to represent other people, objects, or scenarios. This type of play allows children to explore different identities, roles, and perspectives while engaging their creativity and imagination. Through symbolic play, children develop language skills, social understanding, and cognitive flexibility.
- **Constructive Play:** Constructive play involves using materials such as blocks, clay, or building sets to create objects, structures, or designs. This type of play fosters spatial awareness, fine motor skills, and problem-solving abilities as children manipulate and assemble materials to achieve their goals. Constructive play encourages experimentation,

planning, and innovation, laying the groundwork for future STEM (science, technology, engineering, and mathematics) skills.

- **Social Play:** Social play encompasses a range of interactive activities that involve cooperation, communication, and collaboration with peers. This type of play includes games, role-playing, and group activities where children interact, negotiate, and share experiences with others. Social play promotes social-emotional development, empathy, and interpersonal skills as children learn to navigate relationships, resolve conflicts, and work together towards common goals.
- **Physical Play:** Physical play involves bodily movements, exertion, and exploration of the environment. This type of play includes running, jumping, climbing, swinging, and other gross motor activities that promote physical fitness, coordination, and spatial awareness. Physical play also provides opportunities for sensory exploration and self-regulation as children engage their senses and release energy through movement.
- **Exploratory Play:** Exploratory play focuses on sensory exploration and discovery as children investigate their surroundings and manipulate objects. This type of play involves touching, smelling, tasting, listening, and observing the properties of materials and elements in the environment. Exploratory play stimulates curiosity, curiosity, and inquiry skills as children make observations, form hypotheses, and test their ideas through hands-on exploration.
- **Dramatic Play:** Dramatic play, also known as socio-dramatic or role play, involves children assuming roles, enacting scenarios, and engaging in imaginary scenarios. This type of play allows children to experiment with social roles, norms, and relationships while developing language skills, emotional regulation, and perspective-taking abilities. Dramatic play encourages creativity, empathy, and symbolic thinking as children immerse themselves in imaginary worlds and narratives.
- **Games with Rules:** Games with rules involve structured activities with predetermined guidelines, goals, and procedures. This type of play includes board games, card games, and organized sports that require adherence to rules, turn-taking, and fair play. Games with rules promote cognitive skills such as strategy, planning, and problem-solving, as well as social skills like cooperation, sportsmanship, and rule-following.

2.1.2 Play and Cognitive Development

Piaget's Theory of Play

Piaget's theory of cognitive development, or his genetic epistemology, is a comprehensive theory about the nature and development of human intelligence. It was originated by the Swiss developmental psychologist Jean Piaget (1896–1980). The theory deals with the nature of knowledge itself and how humans gradually come to acquire, construct, and use it. Piaget's theory is mainly known as a developmental stage theory.

In 1919, while working at the Alfred Binet Laboratory School in Paris, Piaget "was intrigued by the fact that children of different ages made different kinds of mistakes while solving problems". His experience and observations at the Alfred Binet Laboratory were the beginnings of his theory of cognitive development.

He believed that children of different ages made different mistakes because of the "quality rather than quantity" of their intelligence. Piaget proposed four stages to describe the development process of children: sensorimotor stage, pre-operational stage, concrete operational stage, and formal operational stage. Each stage describes a specific age group. In each stage, he described how children develop their cognitive skills. For example, he believed that children experience the world through actions, representing things with words, thinking logically, and using reasoning.

To Piaget, cognitive development was a progressive reorganisation of mental processes resulting from biological maturation and environmental experience. He believed that children construct an understanding of the world around them, experience discrepancies between what they already know and what they discover in their environment, then adjust their ideas accordingly. Moreover, Piaget claimed that cognitive development is at the centre of the human organism, and language is contingent on knowledge and understanding acquired through cognitive development. Piaget's earlier work received the greatest attention.

Child-centred classrooms and "open education" are direct applications of Piaget's views. Despite its huge success, Piaget's theory has some limitations that Piaget recognised himself: for example, the theory supports sharp stages rather than continuous development (horizontal and vertical décalage).

Nature of Intelligence: Operative and Figurative

Piaget argued that reality is a construction. Reality is defined in reference to the two conditions that define dynamic systems. Specifically, he argued that reality involves transformations and states. *Transformations* refer to all manners of changes that a thing or person can undergo. *States* refer to the conditions or the appearances in which things or persons can be found between transformations. For example, there might be changes in shape or form (for instance, liquids are reshaped as they are transferred from one vessel to another, and similarly humans change in their characteristics as they grow older), in size (a toddler does not walk and run without falling, but after 7 yrs of age, the child's sensorimotor anatomy is well developed and now acquires skill faster), or in placement or location in space and time (e.g., various objects or persons might be found at one place at one time and at a different place at another time). Thus, Piaget argued, if human intelligence is to be adaptive, it must have functions to represent both the transformational and the static aspects of reality. He proposed that operative intelligence is responsible for the representation and manipulation of the dynamic or transformational aspects of reality, and that figurative intelligence is responsible for the representation of the static aspects of reality.

Operative intelligence is the active aspect of intelligence. It involves all actions, overt or covert, undertaken in order to follow, recover, or anticipate the transformations of the objects or persons of interest. *Figurative intelligence* is the more or less static aspect of intelligence, involving all means of representation used to retain in mind the states (i.e., successive forms, shapes, or locations) that intervene between transformations. That is, it involves perception, imitation, mental imagery, drawing, and language. Therefore, the figurative aspects of intelligence derive their meaning from the operative aspects of intelligence, because states cannot exist independently of the transformations that interconnect them. Piaget stated that the figurative or the representational aspects of intelligence are subservient to its operative and dynamic aspects, and therefore, that understanding essentially derives from the operative aspect of intelligence.

At any time, operative intelligence frames how the world is understood and it changes if understanding is not successful. Piaget stated that this process of understanding and change involves two basic functions: *assimilation* and *accommodation.*

Assimilation and Accommodation:

- Through his study of the field of education, Piaget focused on two processes, which he named assimilation and accommodation. To Piaget, assimilation meant integrating external elements into structures of lives or environments, or those we could have through experience. *Assimilation* is how humans perceive and adapt to new information. It is the process of fitting new information into pre-existing cognitive schemas. Assimilation in which new experiences are reinterpreted to fit into, or assimilate with, old ideas and analyzing new facts accordingly. It occurs when humans are faced with new or unfamiliar information and refer to previously learned information in order to make sense of it. In contrast, *accommodation* is the process of taking new information in one's environment and altering pre-existing schemas in order to fit in the new information. This happens when the existing schema (knowledge) does not work, and needs to be changed to deal with a new object or situation. Accommodation is imperative because it is how people will continue to interpret new concepts, schemas, frameworks, and more. Piaget believed that the human brain has been programmed through evolution to bring equilibrium, which is what he believed ultimately influences structures by the internal and external processes through assimilation and accommodation.

- Piaget's understanding was that assimilation and accommodation cannot exist without the other. They are two sides of a coin. To assimilate an object into an existing mental schema, one first needs to take into account or accommodate to the particularities of this object to a certain extent. For instance, to recognize (assimilate) an apple as an apple, one must first focus (accommodate) on the contour of this object. To do this, one needs to roughly recognize the size of the object. Development increases the balance, or equilibration, between these two functions. When in balance with each other, assimilation and accommodation generate mental schemas of the operative intelligence. When one function dominates over the other, they generate representations which belong to figurative intelligence.

Cognitive Equilibration:

- Piaget agreed with most other developmental psychologists in that there are three very important factors that are attributed to development: maturation, experience, and the social environment. But where his theory differs involves his addition of a fourth factor, equilibration, which "refers to the organism's attempt to keep its cognitive schemes in balance".
- Equilibration is the motivational element that guides cognitive development. As humans, we have a biological need to make sense of the things we encounter in every aspect of our world in order to muster a greater understanding of it, and therefore, to flourish in it. This is where the concept of equilibration comes into play. If a child is confronted with information that does not fit into his or her previously held schemes, disequilibrium is said to occur. This, as one would imagine, is unsatisfactory to the child, so he or she will try to fix it. The incongruence will be fixed in one of three ways. The child will either ignore the newly discovered information, assimilate the information into a preexisting scheme, or accommodate the information by modifying a different

scheme. Using any of these methods will return the child to a state of equilibrium, however, depending on the information being presented to the child, that state of equilibrium is not likely to be permanent.

- For example, let's say Dave, a three-year-old boy who has grown up on a farm and is accustomed to seeing Horses regularly, has been brought to the zoo by his parents and sees an Elephant for the first time. Immediately he shouts "look mommy, Horsey!" Because Dave does not have a scheme for Elephants, he interprets the Elephant as being a Horse due to its large size, color, tail, and long face. He believes the Elephant is a Horse until his mother corrects. The new information Dave has received has put him in a state of disequilibrium. He now has to do one of three things. He can either:

1. turn his head, move towards another section of animals, and ignore this newly presented information;
2. distort the defining characteristics of an Elephant so that he can assimilate it into his "Horsey" scheme; or
3. he can modify his preexisting "Animal" schema to accommodate this new information regarding Elephants by slightly altering his knowledge of animals as he knows them.

- With age comes entry into a higher stage of development. With that being said, previously held schemes (and the children that hold them) are more than likely to be confronted with discrepant information the older they get. Silverman and Geiringer propose that one would be more successful in attempting to change a child's mode of thought by exposing that child to concepts that reflect a higher rather than a lower stage of development. Furthermore, children are better influenced by modeled performances that are one stage above their developmental level, as opposed to modeled performances that are either lower or two or more stages above their level.

Sensorimotor Stage

- The first of these, the sensorimotor stage "extends from birth to the acquisition of language". In this stage, infants progressively construct knowledge and understanding of the world by coordinating experiences (such as vision and hearing) from physical interactions with objects (such as grasping, sucking, and stepping). Infants gain knowledge of the world from the physical actions they perform within it. They progress from reflexive, instinctual action at birth to the beginning of symbolic thought toward the end of the stage.

- Children learn that they are separate from the environment. They can think about aspects of the environment, even though these may be outside the reach of the child's senses. In this stage, according to Piaget, the development of *object permanence* is one of the most important accomplishments. Object permanence is a child's understanding that an object continues to exist even though they cannot see or hear it. Peek-a-boo is a game in which children who have yet to fully develop object permanence respond to sudden hiding and revealing of a face. By the end of the sensorimotor period, children develop a permanent sense of self and object and will quickly lose interest in Peek-a-boo.

Table: Piaget Divided the Sensorimotor Stage into Six Sub-Stages".

#	Sub-stage	Age	Description
1	Simple reflexes	Birth–6 weeks	"Coordination of sensation and action through reflexive behaviors". Three primary reflexes are described by Piaget: sucking of objects in the mouth, following moving or interesting objects with the eyes, and closing of the hand when an object makes contact with the palm (palmar grasp). Over the first six weeks of life, these reflexes begin to become voluntary actions. For example, the palmar reflex becomes intentional grasping.
2	First habits and primary circular reactions phase	6 weeks–4 months	"Coordination of sensation and two types of schema: habits (reflex) and primary circular reactions (reproduction of an event that initially occurred by chance). The main focus is still on the infant's body". As an example of this type of reaction, an infant might repeat the motion of passing their hand before their face. Also at this phase, passive reactions, caused by classical or operant conditioning, can begin.
3	Secondary circular reactions phase	4–8 months	Development of habits. "Infants become more object-oriented, moving beyond self-Preoccupation; repeat actions that bring interesting or pleasurable results". This stage is associated primarily development of with the coordination between vision and prehension. Three new abilities occur at this stage: intentional grasping for a desired object, secondary circular reactions, and differentiations between ends and means. At this stage, infants will intentionally grasp the air in the direction of a desired object, often to the amusement of friends and family. Secondary circular reactions, or the repetition of an action involving an external object begin; for example, moving a switch to turn on a light repeatedly. The

			differentiation between means and ends also occurs. This is perhaps one of the most important stages of a child's growth as it signifies the dawn of logic.
4	Coordination of secondary circular reactions stages	8–12 months	"Coordination of vision and touch—hand-eye-coordination; coordination of schemas and intentionality". This stage is associated primarily with the development of logic and the coordination between means and ends. This is an extremely important stage of development, holding what Piaget calls the "first proper intelligence". Also, this stage marks the beginning of goal orientation, the deliberate planning of steps to meet an objective.
5	Tertiary circular reactions, novelty, and curiosity	12–18 months	"Infants become intrigued by the many properties of objects and by the many things they can make happen to objects; they experiment with new behavior". This stage is associated primarily with the discovery of new means to meet goals. Piaget describes the child at this juncture as the "young scientist," conducting pseudo-experiments to discover new methods of meeting challenges.
6	Internalization of schemas	18–24 months	"Infants develop the ability to use primitive symbols and form enduring mental representations". This stage is associated primarily with the beginnings of insight, or true creativity. This marks the passage into the preoperational stage.

Preoperational Stage

By observing sequences of play, Piaget was able to demonstrate the second stage of his theory, the pre-operational stage. He said that this stage starts towards the end of the second year. It starts when the child begins to learn to speak and lasts up until the age of seven. During the pre-operational stage of cognitive development, Piaget noted that children do not yet understand concrete logic and cannot mentally manipulate information. Children's increase in playing and pretending takes place in this stage. However, the child still has trouble seeing things from different points of view. The children's play is mainly categorized by symbolic play and manipulating symbols. Such play is demonstrated by the idea of checkers being snacks, pieces of paper being plates, and a box being a table. Their observations of symbols exemplifies the idea of play with the absence of the actual objects involved.

The pre-operational stage is sparse and logically inadequate in regard to mental operations. The child is able to form stable concepts as well as magical beliefs (magical thinking). The child, however, is still not able to perform operations, which are tasks that the child can do mentally, rather than physically. Thinking in this stage is still egocentric, meaning the child has difficulty seeing the viewpoint of others. The Pre-operational Stage is split into *two* substages: the symbolic function substage, and the intuitive thought substage. The symbolic function substage is when children are able to understand, represent, remember, and picture objects in their mind without having the object in front of them. The intuitive thought substage is when children tend to propose the questions of "why?" and "how come?" This stage is when children want to understand everything.

Symbolic Function Substage:

- At about two to four years of age, children cannot yet manipulate and transform information in a logical way. However, they now can think in images and symbols. Other examples of mental abilities are language and pretend play. Symbolic play is when children develop imaginary friends or role-play with friends. Children's play becomes more social and they assign roles to each other. Some examples of symbolic play include playing house, or having a tea party. The type of symbolic play in which children engage is connected with their level of creativity and ability to connect with others. Additionally, the quality of their symbolic play can have consequences on their later development. For example, young children whose symbolic play is of a violent nature tend to exhibit less prosocial behavior and are more likely to display antisocial tendencies in later years.
- Egocentrism occurs when a child is unable to distinguish between their own perspective and that of another person. Children tend to stick to their own viewpoint, rather than consider the view of others. Indeed, they are not even aware that such a concept as "different viewpoints" exists. Egocentrism can be seen in an experiment performed by Piaget and Swiss developmental psychologist Bärbel Inhelder, known as the three mountain problem. In this experiment, three views of a mountain are shown to the child, who is asked what a traveling doll would see at the various angles. The child will consistently describe what they can see from the position from which they are seated, regardless of the angle from which they are asked to take the doll's perspective. Egocentrism would also cause a child to believe, "I like *The Lion Guard*, so the high school student next door must like *The Lion Guard*, too."
- Similar to preoperational children's egocentric thinking is their structuring of a cause and effect relationships. Piaget coined the term "precausal thinking" to describe the way in which preoperational children use their own existing ideas or views, like in egocentrism, to explain cause-and-effect relationships. Three main concepts of

causality as displayed by children in the preoperational stage include: animism, artificialism and transductive reasoning.

- Animism is the belief that inanimate objects are capable of actions and have lifelike qualities. An example could be a child believing that the sidewalk was mad and made them fall down, or that the stars twinkle in the sky because they are happy. Artificialism refers to the belief that environmental characteristics can be attributed to human actions or interventions. For example, a child might say that it is windy outside because someone is blowing very hard, or the clouds are white because someone painted them that color. Finally, precausal thinking is categorized by transductive reasoning. Transductive reasoning is when a child fails to understand the true relationships between cause and effect. Unlike deductive or inductive reasoning (general to specific, or specific to general), transductive reasoning refers to when a child reasons from specific to specific, drawing a relationship between two separate events that are otherwise unrelated. For example, if a child hears the dog bark and then a balloon popped, the child would conclude that because the dog barked, the balloon popped.

Intuitive thought Substage:

- A main feature of the pre-operational stage of development is primitive reasoning. Between the ages of four and seven, reasoning changes from symbolic thought to intuitive thought. This stage is "marked by greater dependence on intuitive thinking rather than just perception." Children begin to have more automatic thoughts that don't require evidence. During this stage there is a heightened sense of curiosity and need to understand how and why things work. Piaget named this substage "intuitive thought" because they are starting to develop more logical thought but cannot explain their reasoning. Thought during this stage is still immature and cognitive errors occur. Children in this stage depend on their own subjective perception of the object or event. This stage is characterized by centration, conservation, irreversibility, class inclusion, and transitive inference.
- Centration is the act of focusing all attention on one characteristic or dimension of a situation, whilst disregarding all others. Conservation is the awareness that altering a substance's appearance does not change its basic properties. Children at this stage are unaware of conservation and exhibit centration. Both centration and conservation can be more easily understood once familiarized with Piaget's most famous experimental task.

- In this task, a child is presented with two identical beakers containing the same amount of liquid. The child usually notes that the beakers do contain the same amount of liquid. When one of the beakers is poured into a taller and thinner container, children who are younger than seven or eight years old typically say that the two beakers no longer contain the same amount of liquid, and that the taller container holds the larger quantity (centration), without taking into consideration the fact that both beakers were previously noted to contain the same amount of liquid. Due to superficial changes, the child was unable to comprehend that the properties of the substances continued to remain the same (conservation).
- Irreversibility is a concept developed in this stage which is closely related to the ideas of centration and conservation. Irreversibility refers to when children are unable to mentally reverse a sequence of events. In the same beaker situation, the child does not realize that, if the sequence of events was reversed and the water from the tall beaker was poured back into its original beaker, then the same amount of water would exist. Another example of children's reliance on visual representations is their misunderstanding of "less than" or "more than". When two rows containing equal numbers of blocks are placed in front of a child, one row spread farther apart than the other, the child will think that the row spread farther contains more blocks.
- Class inclusion refers to a kind of conceptual thinking that children in the preoperational stage cannot yet grasp. Children's inability to focus on two aspects of a situation at once inhibits them from understanding the principle that one category or class can contain several different subcategories or classes. For example, a four-year-old girl may be shown a picture of eight dogs and three cats. The girl knows what cats and dogs are, and she is aware that they are both animals. However, when asked, "Are there more dogs or animals?" she is likely to answer "more dogs". This is due to her difficulty focusing on the two subclasses and the larger class all at the same time. She may have been able to view the dogs as dogs *or* animals, but struggled when trying to classify them as both, simultaneously. Similar to this is concept relating to intuitive thought, known as "transitive inference".
- Transitive inference is using previous knowledge to determine the missing piece, using basic logic. Children in the preoperational stage lack this logic. An example of transitive inference would be when a child is presented with the information "A" is greater than "B" and "B"

is greater than "C". This child may have difficulty here understanding that "A" is also greater than "C".

Concrete Operational Stage

The concrete operational stage is the third stage of Piaget's theory of cognitive development. This stage, which follows the preoperational stage, occurs between the ages of 7 and 11 (middle childhood and preadolescence) years, and is characterized by the appropriate use of logic. During this stage, a child's thought processes become more mature and "adult like". They start solving problems in a more logical fashion. Abstract, hypothetical thinking is not yet developed in the child, and children can only solve problems that apply to concrete events or objects. At this stage, the children undergo a transition where the child learns rules such as conservation. Piaget determined that children are able to incorporate inductive reasoning. Inductive reasoning involves drawing inferences from observations in order to make a generalization. In contrast, children struggle with deductive reasoning, which involves using a generalized principle in order to try to predict the outcome of an event. Children in this stage commonly experience difficulties with figuring out logic in their heads. For example, a child will understand that "A is more than B" and "B is more than C". However, when asked "is A more than C?", the child might not be able to logically figure the question out mentally.

Two other important processes in the concrete operational stage are logic and the elimination of egocentrism. Egocentrism is the inability to consider or understand a perspective other than one's own. It is the phase where the thought and morality of the child is completely self focused. During this stage, the child acquires the ability to view things from another individual's perspective, even if they think that perspective is incorrect. For instance, show a child a comic in which Jane puts a doll under a box, leaves the room, and then Melissa moves the doll to a drawer, and Jane comes back. A child in the concrete operations stage will say that Jane will still think it's under the box even though the child knows it is in the drawer.

Children in this stage can, however, only solve problems that apply to actual (concrete) objects or events, and not abstract concepts or hypothetical tasks. Understanding and knowing how to use full common sense has not yet been completely adapted.

Piaget determined that children in the concrete operational stage were able to incorporate inductive logic. On the other hand, children at this age have difficulty using deductive logic, which involves using a general principle to predict the outcome of a specific event.

This includes mental reversibility. An example of this is being able to reverse the order of relationships between mental categories. For example, a child might be able to recognize that his or her dog is a Labrador, that a Labrador is a dog, and that a dog is an animal, and draw conclusions from the information available, as well as apply all these processes to hypothetical situations.

The abstract quality of the adolescent's thought at the formal operational level is evident in the adolescent's verbal problem solving ability. The logical quality of the adolescent's thought is when children are more likely to solve problems in a trial-and-error fashion. Adolescents begin to think more as a scientist thinks, devising plans to solve problems and systematically test opinions. They use hypothetical-deductive reasoning, which means that they develop hypotheses or best guesses, and systematically deduce, or conclude, which is the best path to follow in solving the problem. During this stage the adolescent is able to understand love, logical proofs and values. During this stage the young person begins to entertain possibilities for the future and is fascinated with what they can be.

Adolescents also are changing cognitively by the way that they think about social matters. One thing that brings about a change is egocentrism. This happens by heightening self-consciousness and giving adolescents an idea of who they are through their personal uniqueness and invincibility. Adolescent egocentrism can be dissected into two types of social thinking: imaginary audience and personal fable. Imaginary audience consists of an adolescent believing that others are watching them and the things they do. Personal fable is not the same thing as imaginary audience but is often confused with imaginary audience. Personal fable consists of believing that you are exceptional in some way. These types of social thinking begin in the concrete stage but carry on to the formal operational stage of development.

Testing for Concrete Operations:

- Piagetian tests are well known and practiced to test for concrete operations. The most prevalent tests are those for conservation. There are some important aspects that the experimenter must take into account when performing experiments with these children.
- One example of an experiment for testing conservation is the water level task. An experimenter will have two glasses that are the same size, fill them to the same level with liquid, and make sure the child understands that both of the glasses have the same amount of water in them. Then, the experimenter will pour the liquid from one of the small glasses into a tall, thin glass. The experimenter will then ask the child if the taller glass has more liquid, less liquid, or the same amount of liquid. The child will then give his answer. There are three keys for the experimenter to keep in mind with this experiment. These are justification, number of times asking, and word choice.

4. *Justification*: After the child has answered the question being posed, the experimenter must ask why the child gave that answer. This is important because the answers they give can help the experimenter to assess the child's developmental age.
5. *Number of times asking*: Some argue that a child's answers can be influenced by the number of times an experimenter asks them about the amount of water in the glasses. For example, a child is asked about the amount of liquid in the first set of glasses and then asked once again after the water is moved into a different sized glass. Some children will doubt their original answer and say something they would not have said if they did not doubt their first answer.
6. *Word choice*: The phrasing that the experimenter uses may affect how the child answers. If, in the liquid and glass example, the experimenter asks, "Which of these glasses has more liquid?", the child may think that his thoughts of them being the same is wrong because the adult is saying that one must have more. Alternatively, if the experimenter asks, "Are these equal?", then the child is more likely to say that they are, because the experimenter is implying that they are.
7. *Classification*: As children's experiences and vocabularies grow, they build schemata and are able to organize objects in many different ways. They also understand classification hierarchies and can arrange objects into a variety of classes and subclasses.
8. *Identity*: One feature of concrete operational thought is the understanding that objects have qualities that do not change even if the object is altered in some way. For instance, mass of an object does not change by rearranging it. A piece of chalk is still chalk even when the piece is broken in two.
9. *Reversibility*: The child learns that some things that have been changed can be returned to their original state. Water can be frozen and then thawed to become liquid again; however, eggs cannot be unscrambled. Children use reversibility a lot in mathematical problems such as: 2 + 3 = 5 and 5 – 3 = 2.
10. *Conservation*: The ability to understand that the quantity (mass, weight volume) of something doesn't change due to the change of appearance.
11. *Decentration*: The ability to focus on more that one feature of scenario or problem at a time. This also describes the ability to attend to more than one task at a time. Decentration is what allows for conservation to occur.
12. *Seriation*: Arranging items along a quantitative dimension, such as length or weight, in a methodical way is now demonstrated by the concrete operational child. For example, they can logically arrange a series of different-sized sticks in order by length. Younger children not yet in the concrete stage approach a similar task in a haphazard way.
    - These new cognitive skills increase the child's understanding of the physical world. However, according to Piaget, they still cannot think in abstract ways. Additionally, they do not think in systematic scientific ways. For example, most children under age twelve would not be able to come up with the variables that influence the period that a pendulum takes to complete its arc. Even if they were given weights they could

attach to strings in order to do this experiment, they would not be able to draw a clear conclusion.

Formal Operational Stage

The final stage is known as the formal operational stage (early to middle adolescence, beginning at age 11 and finalizing around 14–15): Intelligence is demonstrated through the logical use of symbols related to abstract concepts. This form of thought includes "assumptions that have no necessary relation to reality." At this point, the person is capable of hypothetical and deductive reasoning. During this time, people develop the ability to think about abstract concepts.

Piaget stated that "hypothetico-deductive reasoning" becomes important during the formal operational stage. This type of thinking involves hypothetical "what-if" situations that are not always rooted in reality, i.e. counterfactual thinking. It is often required in science and mathematics.

- Abstract thought emerges during the formal operational stage. Children tend to think very concretely and specifically in earlier stages, and begin to consider possible outcomes and consequences of actions.
- Metacognition, the capacity for "thinking about thinking" that allows adolescents and adults to reason about their thought processes and monitor them.
- Problem-solving is demonstrated when children use trial-and-error to solve problems. The ability to systematically solve a problem in a logical and methodical way emerges.

Children in primary school years mostly use inductive reasoning, but adolescents start to use deductive reasoning. Inductive reasoning is when children draw general conclusions from personal experiences and specific facts. Adolescents learn how to use deductive reasoning by applying logic to create specific conclusions from abstract concepts. This capability results from their capacity to think hypothetically.

"However, research has shown that not all persons in all cultures reach formal operations, and most people do not use formal operations in all aspects of their lives".

Experiments:

- Piaget and his colleagues conducted several experiments to assess formal operational thought.
- In one of the experiments, Piaget evaluated the cognitive capabilities of children of different ages through the use of a scale and varying weights. The task was to balance the scale by hooking weights on the ends of the scale. To successfully complete the task, the children must use formal

operational thought to realize that the distance of the weights from the center and the heaviness of the weights both affected the balance. A heavier weight has to be placed closer to the center of the scale, and a lighter weight has to be placed farther from the center, so that the two weights balance each other. While 3- to 5- year olds could not at all comprehend the concept of balancing, children by the age of 7 could balance the scale by placing the same weights on both ends, but they failed to realize the importance of the location. By age 10, children could think about location but failed to use logic and instead used trial-and-error. Finally, by age 13 and 14, in early to middle adolescence, some children more clearly understood the relationship between weight and distance and could successfully implement their hypothesis.

The Stages and Causation

Piaget sees children's conception of causation as a march from "primitive" conceptions of cause to those of a more scientific, rigorous, and mechanical nature. These primitive concepts are characterized as supernatural, with a decidedly non-natural or non-mechanical tone. Piaget has as his most basic assumption that babies are phenomenists. That is, their knowledge "consists of assimilating things to schemas" from their own action such that they appear, from the child's point of view, "to have qualities which, in fact, stem from the organism". Consequently, these "subjective conceptions," so prevalent during Piaget's first stage of development, are dashed upon discovering deeper empirical truths.

Piaget gives the example of a child believing that the moon and stars follow him on a night walk. Upon learning that such is the case for his friends, he must separate his self from the object, resulting in a theory that the moon is immobile, or moves independently of other agents.

The second stage, from around three to eight years of age, is characterized by a mix of this type of magical, animistic, or "non-natural" conceptions of causation and mechanical or "naturalistic" causation. This conjunction of natural and non-natural causal explanations supposedly stems from experience itself, though Piaget does not make much of an attempt to describe the nature of the differences in conception. In his interviews with children, he asked questions specifically about natural phenomena, such as: "What makes clouds move?", "What makes the stars move?", "Why do rivers flow?" The nature of all the answers given, Piaget says, are such that these objects must perform their actions to "fulfill their obligations towards men". He calls this "moral explanation".

Postulated Physical Mechanisms Underlying Schemes, Schemas and Stages

First note the distinction between 'schemes' (analogous to 1D lists of action-instructions, e.g. leading to separate pen-strokes), and figurative 'schemas' (aka 'schemata', akin to 2D drawings/sketches or virtual 3D models). In 1967, Piaget considered the possibility of RNA molecules as likely embodiments of his still-abstract schemes (which he promoted as units of action) — though he did not come to any firm conclusion. At that time, due to work such as that of Swedish biochemist Holger Hydén, RNA concentrations had, indeed, been shown to correlate with learning.

To date, with one exception, it has been impossible to investigate such RNA hypotheses by traditional direct observation and logical deduction. The one exception is that such ultra-micro sites would almost certainly have to use optical communication, and recently studies have demonstrated that nerve-fibres can indeed transmit light/infra-red (in addition to their acknowledged role). However it accords with the philosophy of science, especially scientific realism, to do *indirect* investigations of such phenomena which are intrinsically unobservable for practical reasons. The art then is to build up a plausible interdisciplinary case from the indirect evidence (as indeed the child does during concept development) — and then retain that model until it is disproved by observable-or-other new evidence which then calls for new accommodation.

In that spirit, it now might be said that the RNA/infra-red model *is* valid (for explaining Piagetian higher intelligence). Anyhow the current situation opens the way for more testing, and further development in several directions, including the finer points of Piaget's agenda.

Practical Applications

Parents can use Piaget's theory in many ways to support their child's growth. Teachers can also use Piaget's theory to help their students. For example, recent studies have shown that children in the same grade and of the same age perform differently on tasks measuring basic addition and subtraction accuracy. Children in the preoperational and concrete operational levels of cognitive development perform arithmetic operations (such as addition and subtraction) with similar accuracy; however, children in the concrete operational level have been able to perform both addition problems and subtraction problems with overall greater precision. Teachers can use Piaget's theory to see where each child in their class stands with each subject by discussing the syllabus with their students and the students' parents.

The stage of cognitive growth of a person differ from another. Cognitive development or thinking is an active process from the beginning to the end of life. Intellectual advancement happens because people at every age and developmental period look for cognitive equilibrium. To achieve this balance, the easiest way is to understand the new experiences through the lens of the preexisting ideas. Infants learn that new objects can be grabbed in the same way of familiar objects, and adults explain the day's headlines as evidence for their existing worldview.

However, the application of standardized Piagetian theory and procedures in different societies established widely varying results that lead some to speculate not only that some cultures produce more cognitive development than others but that without specific kinds of cultural experience, but also formal schooling, development might cease at certain level, such as concrete operational level. A procedure was done following methods developed in Geneva (i.e. water level task). Participants were presented with two beakers of equal circumference and height, filled with equal amounts of water. The water from one beaker was transferred into another with taller and smaller circumference. The children and young adults from non-literate societies of a given age were more likely to think that the taller, thinner beaker had more water in it. On the other hand, an experiment on the effects of modifying testing procedures to match local cultural produced a different pattern of results. In the revised procedures, the participants explained in their own language and indicated that while the water was now "more", the quantity was the same. Piaget's water level task has also been applied to the elderly by Formann and results showed an age-associated non-linear decline of performance.

Relation to Psychometric Theories of Intelligence

Researchers have linked Piaget's theory to Cattell and Horn's theory of fluid and crystallized abilities. Piaget's operative intelligence corresponds to the Cattell-Horn formulation of fluid ability in that both concern logical thinking and the "eduction of relations" (an expression Cattell used to refer to the inferring of relationships). Piaget's treatment of everyday learning corresponds to the Cattell-Horn formulation of crystallized ability in that both reflect the impress of experience. Piaget's operativity is considered to be prior to, and ultimately provides the foundation for, everyday learning, much like fluid ability's relation to crystallized intelligence.

Piaget's theory also aligns with another psychometric theory, namely the psychometric theory of *g*, general intelligence. Piaget designed a number of tasks to assess hypotheses arising from his theory.

The tasks were not intended to measure individual differences and they have no equivalent in psychometric intelligence tests. Notwithstanding the different research traditions in which psychometric tests and Piagetian tasks were developed, the correlations between the two types of measures have been found to be consistently positive and generally moderate in magnitude. *g* is thought to underlie performance on the two types of tasks. It has been shown that it is possible to construct a battery consisting of Piagetian tasks that is as good a measure of *g* as standard IQ tests.

Challenges to Piagetian Stage Theory

Piagetian accounts of development have been challenged on several grounds. First, as Piaget himself noted, development does not always progress in the smooth manner his theory seems to predict. *Décalage*, or progressive forms of cognitive developmental progression in a specific domain, suggest that the stage model is, at best, a useful approximation. Furthermore, studies have found that children may be able to learn concepts and capability of complex reasoning that supposedly represented in more advanced stages with relative ease. More broadly, Piaget's theory is "domain general," predicting that cognitive maturation occurs concurrently across different domains of knowledge (such as mathematics, logic, and understanding of physics or language). Piaget did not take into account variability in a child's performance notably how a child can differ in sophistication across several domains.

During the 1980s and 1990s, cognitive developmentalists were influenced by "neo-nativist" and evolutionary psychology ideas. These ideas de-emphasized domain general theories and emphasized domain specificity or modularity of mind. Modularity implies that different cognitive faculties may be largely independent of one another, and thus develop according to quite different timetables, which are "influenced by real world experiences". In this vein, some cognitive developmentalists argued that, rather than being domain general learners, children come equipped with domain specific theories, sometimes referred to as "core knowledge," which allows them to break into learning within that domain. For example, even young infants appear to be sensitive to some predictable regularities in the movement and interactions of objects (for example, an object cannot pass through another object), or in human behavior (for example, a hand repeatedly reaching for an object has that object, not just a particular path of motion), as it becomes the building block of which more elaborate knowledge is constructed.

Piaget's theory has been said to undervalue the influence that culture has on cognitive development. Piaget demonstrates that a child goes through several stages of cognitive development and come to conclusions on their own, however, a child's sociocultural environment plays an important part in their cognitive development. Social interaction teaches the child about the world and helps them develop through the cognitive stages, which Piaget neglected to consider.

More recent work from a newer dynamic systems approach has strongly challenged some of the basic presumptions of the "core knowledge" school that Piaget suggested. Dynamic systems approaches harken to modern neuroscientific research that was not available to Piaget when he was constructing his theory. This brought new light into research in psychology in which new techniques such as brain imaging provided new understanding to cognitive development. One important finding is that domain-specific knowledge is constructed as children develop and integrate knowledge. This enables the domain to improve the accuracy of the knowledge as well as organization of memories. However, this suggests more of a "smooth integration" of learning and development than either Piaget, or his neo-nativist critics, had envisioned. Additionally, some psychologists, such as Lev Vygotsky and Jerome Bruner, thought differently from Piaget, suggesting that language was more important for cognition development than Piaget implied.

Post-Piagetian and Neo-Piagetian Stages

In recent years, several theorists attempted to address concerns with Piaget's theory by developing new theories and models that can accommodate evidence which violates Piagetian predictions and postulates.

- The neo-Piagetian theories of cognitive development, advanced by Robbie Case, Andreas Demetriou, Graeme S. Halford, Kurt W. Fischer, Michael Lamport Commons, and Juan Pascual-Leone, attempted to integrate Piaget's theory with cognitive and differential theories of cognitive organization and development. Their aim was to better account for the cognitive factors of development and for intra-individual and inter-individual differences in cognitive development. They suggested that development along Piaget's stages is due to increasing working memory capacity and processing efficiency by "biological maturation". Moreover, Demetriou's theory ascribes an important role to hypercognitive processes of "self-monitoring, self-recording, self-evaluation, and self-regulation", and it recognizes the operation of several relatively autonomous domains of thought.
- Piaget's theory stops at the formal operational stage, but other researchers have observed the thinking of adults is more nuanced than formal operational thought. This fifth stage has been named post formal thought or operation. Post formal stages have been proposed. Michael Commons presented evidence for four post formal stages in the model of hierarchical complexity: systematic, meta-systematic, paradigmatic, and cross-paradigmatic. There are many theorists, however, who have criticized "post formal thinking," because the concept lacks both

theoretical and empirical verification. The term "integrative thinking" has been suggested for use instead.

- A "sentential" stage, said to occur before the early preoperational stage, has been proposed by Fischer, Biggs and Biggs, Commons, and Richards.
- Jerome Bruner has expressed views on cognitive development in a "pragmatic orientation" in which humans actively use knowledge for practical applications, such as problem solving and understanding reality.
- Michael Lamport Commons proposed the model of hierarchical complexity (MHC) in two dimensions: horizontal complexity and vertical complexity.
- Kieran Egan has proposed five stages of understanding. These are "somatic", "mythic", "romantic", "philosophic", and "ironic". These stages are developed through cognitive tools such as "stories", "binary oppositions", "fantasy" and "rhyme, rhythm, and meter" to enhance memorization to develop a long-lasting learning capacity.
- Lawrence Kohlberg developed three stages of moral development: "Preconventional", "Conventional" and "Postconventional". Each level is composed of two orientation stages, with a total of six orientation stages:

13. Punishment-Obedience,
14. Instrumental Relativist,
15. Good Boy-Nice Girl,
16. Law and Order,
17. Social Contract, and
18. Universal Ethical Principle.

- Andreas Demetriou has expressed neo-Piagetian theories of cognitive development.
- Jane Loevinger's stages of ego development occur through "an evolution of stages". "First is the Presocial Stage followed by the Symbiotic Stage, Impulsive Stage, Self-Protective Stage, Conformist Stage, Self-Aware Level: Transition from Conformist to Conscientious Stage, Individualistic Level: Transition from Conscientious to the Autonomous Stage, Conformist Stage, and Integrated Stage".
- Ken Wilber has incorporated Piaget's theory in his multidisciplinary field of integral theory. The human consciousness is structured in hierarchical order and organized in "holon" chains or "great chain

of being", which are based on the level of spiritual and psychological development.

- Oliver Kress published a model that connected Piaget's theory of development and Abraham Maslow's concept of self-actualization.
- Cheryl Armon has proposed five stages of " the Good Life". These are "Egoistic Hedonism", "Instrumental Hedonism", "Affective/Altruistic Mutuality", "Individuality", and "Autonomy/Community".
- Christopher R. Hallpike proposed that human evolution of cognitive moral understanding had evolved from the beginning of time from its primitive state to the present time.
- Robert Kegan extended Piaget's developmental model to adults in describing what he called constructive-developmental psychology.

Vygotsky's Sociocultural Theory

Lev Semyonovich Vygotsky (November 17 [O.S. November 5] 1896 – June 11, 1934) was a Soviet psychologist, best known for his work on psychological development in children and creating the framework known as cultural-historical activity theory.

His major ideas include:

- **The Social Origin of Mind:** Vygotsky believed that human mental and cognitive abilities are not biologically determined, but instead created and shaped by use of language and tools in the process of interacting and constructing the cultural and social environment.
- **The Importance of Mediation:** He saw mediation as the key to human development, because it leads to the use of cultural tools and becomes a pathway for psychological development through the process of interiorization.
- **The Zone of Proximal Development:** Vygotsky introduced the concept of the ZPD which refers to the gap between a child's current level of development and the level they are capable of reaching with tools provided by others with more knowledge.
- **The Significance of Play:** Vygotsky viewed play as a crucial aspect of children's development, as the best sandbox to build and develop practice of mediation.

Lev Simkhovich Vygodsky (his patronymic was later changed to *Semyonovich* and his surname to *Vygotsky* for unclear reasons) was born on November 5, 1896, in the town of Orsha in Mogilev Governorate of the Russian Empire (now Belarus) into a non-religious middle-class family of Russian Jewish extraction. His father

Simkha Leibovich (also known as Semyon Lvovich) was a banker and his mother was Tsetsilia Moiseevna.

Vygotsky was raised in the city of Gomel, where he was homeschooled until 1911 and then obtained a formal degree with distinction in a private Jewish gymnasium, which allowed him entrance to a university. In 1913, Vygotsky was admitted to the Moscow University by mere ballot through a "Jewish Lottery": at the time a three percent Jewish student quota was administered for entry in Moscow and Saint Petersburg universities. He had an interest in the humanities and social sciences, but at the insistence of his parents he applied to the medical school at Moscow University. During the first semester of study, he transferred to the law school. In parallel, he attended lectures at Shanyavsky Moscow City People's University. Vygotsky's early interests were in the arts and, primarily, in the topics of the history of the Jewish people, the tradition, culture and Jewish identity.

In January 1924, Vygotsky took part in the Second All-Russian Psychoneurological Congress in Petrograd (soon thereafter renamed Leningrad). After the Congress, Vygotsky met with Alexander Luria and with his help received an invitation to become a research fellow at the Psychological Institute in Moscow which was under the direction of Konstantin Kornilov. Vygotsky moved to Moscow with his new wife, Roza Smekhova, whom he would have two children with. He began his career at the Psychological Institute as a "staff scientist, second class". He also became a secondary teacher, covering a period marked by his interest in the processes of learning and the role of language in learning.

By the end of 1925, Vygotsky completed his dissertation titled "The Psychology of Art", which was not published until the 1960s, and a book titled "Pedagogical Psychology", which apparently was created on the basis of lecture notes that he prepared in Gomel while he was a psychology instructor at local educational establishments. In the summer of 1925 he made his first and only trip abroad to a London congress on the education of the deaf. Upon return to the Soviet Union, he was hospitalized due to tuberculosis and would remain an invalid and out of work until the end of 1926. His dissertation was accepted as the prerequisite of a scholarly degree, which was awarded to Vygotsky in autumn 1925 *in absentia*.

After his release from the hospital, Vygotsky did theoretical and methodological work on the crisis in psychology, but never finished the draft of the manuscript and interrupted his work on it around mid-1927. The manuscript was published later with notable editorial interventions and distortions in 1982 and was presented by the editors as one of the most important of Vygotsky's works. In this early manuscript, Vygotsky argued for the formation of a general psychology that could unite the naturalist objectivist strands of psychological science with the more philosophical approaches of Marxist orientation. However, he also harshly criticized those of his colleagues who attempted to build a "Marxist Psychology" as an alternative to the naturalist and philosophical schools. He argued that if one wanted to build a truly Marxist Psychology, there were no shortcuts to be found by merely looking for applicable quotes in the writings of Marx. Rather one should look for a methodology that was in accordance with the Marxian spirit.

From 1926 to 1930, Vygotsky worked on a research program investigating the development of higher psychological functions, i.e. culturally governed lower psychological functions such as voluntary attention, selective memory, object-oriented action, and decision making. During this period he gathered a group of collaborators including Alexander Luria, Boris Varshava, Alexei Leontiev, Leonid Zankov, and several others. Vygotsky guided his students in researching this phenomenon from three different perspectives:

- The instrumental approach, which aimed to understand the ways humans use objects as mediation aids in memory and reasoning.
- A developmental approach, focused on how children acquire higher cognitive functions during development
- A culture-historical approach, studying how social and cultural patterns of interaction shape forms of mediation and developmental trajectories

Vygotsky died of a relapse of tuberculosis on June 11, 1934, at the age of 37, in Moscow. One of Vygotsky's last private notebook entries was:

- This is the final thing I have done in psychology – and I will like Moses die at the summit, having glimpsed the promised land but without setting foot on it. Farewell, dear creations. The rest is silence.

Major Themes of Research

Vygotsky was a pioneering psychologist with interests in extremely diverse fields: his work covered topics such as the origin and the psychology of art, development of higher mental functions, philosophy of science and the methodology of psychological research, the relation between learning and human development, concept formation, interrelation between language and thought development, play as a psychological phenomenon, learning disabilities, and abnormal human development (aka *defectology*).

His philosophical framework includes interpretations of the cognitive role of mediation tools, as well as the re-interpretation of well-known concepts in psychology such as internalization of knowledge. Vygotsky introduced the notion of zone of proximal development, a metaphor capable of describing the potential of human cognitive development.

His most important and widely known contribution is his theory for the development of "higher psychological functions," which emerge through unification of interpersonal connections and actions taken within a given socio-cultural environment (i.e. language, culture, society, and tool-use). It was during this period that he identified the play of young children as their "leading activity", which he understood to be the main source of preschoolers' psychological development, and which he viewed as an expression of an inseparable unity of emotional, volitional, and cognitive development. At this time, Vygotsky explored his long-time interest in the philosophy of Spinoza's examinations concerning human emotion. As his work matured, Spinoza's thought became a more central visitation in Vygotsky's later work, increasingly focused on the issue of human emotion and its role in higher psychological functions and development.

While Vygotsky never met Jean Piaget, he had read a number of his works and agreed on some of his perspectives on learning. At some point (around 1929–30), Vygotsky came to disagree with Piaget's understanding of learning and development, and held a different theoretical position from Piaget on the topic of inner speech; Piaget thought that egocentric speech follows from inner speech and "dissolved away" as children matured. Vygotsky showed that egocentric speech became inner speech, and then called "thoughts". Piaget only read Vygotsky's work after his death and openly praised him for his discovery of the social origin of children's thoughts, reasoning, and moral judgements.

Cultural-historical Theory

The hypothesis put forward by Vygotsky was a paradigm shift in psychology. He was first to propose that all psychological functions that govern mental, cognitive and physical actions of the individual are not immutable but have a history of cultural development (in human history and in everyone personally) through interiorization of cultural tools. Therefore, the process of transformation which is happening when current cultural tools are interiorized becomes the focus of psychological research.

- It was assumed before, that individual possess function in well done, half-done or raw form, that function would unfold in the society, become complex, bigger, is enriched or, vice versa - slowed down and suppressed etc. Now we have reasons to believe that in regard of higher mental functions things are opposite. Functions first appear in social group in form of social relations of a child, then they become mental functions of an individual. For example, assumption was that every child is able to think, make arguments and proofs and look for sound reasonings. Debates with others grow from collision of these reasonings. But things are different. Research shows - debates foster

> thinking. Research also leads us to the same conclusions in regard to all other mental functions.

Vygotsky posits the existence of lower and higher mental functions. The latter have social origins and complex system structure, mediated by cultural tools and controlled by an individual. Vygotsky came to the conclusion that consciousness is possible because of the mediated nature of higher psychological functions. Between the stimulus and the reaction of a person (both behavioral and mental), an additional connection arises through a mediating link - a stimulus-means, or a sign. Signs are tools that mediate higher psychological functions and control one's own behavior. A word could direct attention, create personal meaning, form a concept and coordinate.

Vygotsky illustrated his idea of mediation via Buridan's ass paradox. A problematic situation of choosing between two equal possibilities, interested Vygotsky primarily from the point of view of solving it through a coin flip - redelegating decision to the outside object - an example of using cultural tools to govern one's own psychological function of volition.

While developing a method for studying higher psychological functions, Vygotsky was guided by the principle of *ex ungue leonem* and additionally analyzed phenomena such as using a knot in the handkerchief for remembering and finger counting.

Cultural Mediation and Internalization

Vygotsky studied child development and the significant roles of cultural mediation and interpersonal communication. He observed how higher mental functions developed through these interactions, and also represented the shared knowledge of a culture. This process is known as internalization. *Internalization* may be understood in one respect as "knowing how". For example, the practices of riding a bicycle or pouring a cup of milk, initially, are outside and beyond the child. The mastery of the skills needed for performing these practices occurs through the activity of the child within society. A further aspect of internalization is *appropriation*, in which children take tools and adapt them to personal use, perhaps using them in unique ways. Internalizing the use of a pencil allows the child to use it very much for personal ends rather than drawing exactly what others in society have drawn previously:

- The child acts and speaks at the same time, both are intertwined in one continuous operation for him. In this way, a blend of speech and action arises, a peculiar mixture from an adult's point of view, but a completely natural state for the child, who from the very first days of life, due to his helplessness, finds himself in conditions where the path from him to things and from things to him goes through another person.

Zone of Proximal Development

"Zone of Proximal Development" (ZPD) is a term Vygotsky used to characterize an individual's mental development. He originally defined the ZPD as "the distance between the actual developmental level as determined by independent problem solving and the level of potential development as determined through problem solving under adult guidance or in collaboration with more capable peers." He used the example of two children in school who originally could solve problems at an eight-year-old developmental level (that is, typical for children who were age 8). After each child received assistance from an adult, one was able to perform at a nine-year-old level and one was able to perform at a twelve-year-old level. He said "This difference between twelve and eight, or between nine and eight, is what we call *the zone of proximal development.*" He further said that the ZPD "defines those functions that have not yet matured but are in the process of maturation, functions that will mature tomorrow but are currently in an embryonic state." The zone is bracketed by the learner's current ability and the ability they can achieve with the aid of an instructor of some capacity.

Scaffolding:

- According to Vygotsky, through the assistance of a more knowledgeable other, a child is able to learn skills or aspects of a skill that go beyond the child's actual developmental or maturational level. This assistance is defined as 'scaffolding'. The lower limit of ZPD is the level of skill reached by the child working independently (also referred to as the child's developmental level). The upper limit is the level of potential skill that the child is able to reach with the assistance of a more capable instructor. In this sense, the ZPD provides a prospective view of cognitive development, as opposed to a retrospective view that characterizes development in terms of a child's independent capabilities. The advancement through and attainment of the upper limit of the ZPD is limited by the instructional and scaffolding-related capabilities of the more knowledgeable other (MKO). The MKO is typically assumed to be an older, more experienced teacher or parent, but often can be a learner's peer or someone their junior. The MKO need not even be a person, it can be a machine or book, or other source of visual and/or audio input.

Thinking and Speech

In the last years of his life, Vygotsky paid most of his attention to the study of the relationship between thought and word in the structure of consciousness. This problem was explored in Vygotsky's book, *Thinking and Speech*, that was published posthumously in 1934. The book was a collection of essays and scholarly papers that Vygotsky wrote during different periods of his thought development. It was edited by his closest associates Kolbanovskii, Zankov, and Shif. The book established the connection between speech and the development of mental concepts and awareness. Vygotsky described silent inner speech as being qualitatively different from verbal external speech, but both equally important. Vygotsky believed inner speech developed from external speech via a gradual process of "internalization" (i.e., transition from the external to the internal), with younger children only really able to "think out loud". He claimed that in its mature form, inner speech would not resemble spoken language as we know it (in particular, being greatly compressed). Hence, thought itself developed socially.

Inner speech, according to Vygotsky, develops through the accumulation of long-term functional and structural changes. It branches off from the child's external speech along with the differentiation of the social and egocentric functions of speech, and, finally, the speech functions acquired by the child become the main functions of his thinking.

In this work, Vygotsky points out the genesis of the development of thinking and speech and that the relationship between them is not a constant value.

- But since we wanted to express all this in one short formula, in one sentence, we might put it thus: if at the beginning of development there stands the act, independent of the word, then at the end of it there stands the word which becomes the act, the word which makes man's action free.

2.1.3 Play-Based Approaches in Education

Montessori Education

The Montessori method, developed by Maria Montessori, emphasizes hands-on, child-centered learning through self-directed play and exploration. Montessori classrooms are equipped with carefully designed materials that encourage independent learning and sensory exploration. Through activities like practical life exercises, sensorial experiences, and uninterrupted play, children develop autonomy, concentration, and a love of learning.

Reggio Emilia Approach

The Reggio Emilia approach to early childhood education values play as a vehicle for self-expression, inquiry, and collaboration. Inspired by the Italian town of Reggio Emilia, this approach emphasizes the importance of the environment as the "third teacher" and encourages open-ended, project-based learning experiences. Through long-term investigations, artistic expression, and dialogue with peers and educators, children develop critical thinking skills, creativity, and a sense of community.

2.1.4 Play in Lifelong Learning

Playful Learning in Schools

Playful learning approaches have gained traction in formal educational settings beyond early childhood education. Educators recognize the benefits of incorporating playful elements into curriculum design to engage students, promote inquiry-based learning, and foster a culture of creativity and innovation. Playful learning environments encourage risk-taking, experimentation, and collaboration, preparing students for success in an ever-changing world.

Gamification and Game-Based Learning

Incorporating elements of play into education extends to the integration of gamification and game-based learning strategies. Gamification involves applying game design principles, such as points, badges, and leaderboards, to non-game contexts to motivate learners and enhance engagement. Game-based learning utilizes educational games to teach specific concepts and skills, providing interactive and immersive learning experiences across various subjects and grade levels.

2.2 COGNITIVE AND EMOTIONAL BENEFITS OF PLAY

2.2.1 Cognitive Benefits of Play

Play is not merely a pastime for children; it's a powerful tool for cognitive development. Play is not just child's play; it's a fundamental aspect of cognitive development. By engaging in various types of play, children exercise their cognitive abilities, sharpen their thinking skills, and lay the foundation for future academic success. Educators and caregivers play a vital role in creating environments that support play-based learning and capitalize on the cognitive benefits of play, ensuring that children have the opportunity to learn, grow, and thrive intellectually through play.

Understanding Cognitive Development

Cognitive Processes

Cognitive development encompasses a range of mental processes, including perception, attention, memory, language, reasoning, and problem-solving. These processes form the foundation of cognitive functioning and play a vital role in how children perceive, interpret, and interact with the world around them.

Piaget's Theory of Cognitive Development

Jean Piaget's theory of cognitive development posits that children progress through distinct stages of cognitive growth, each characterized by qualitatively different ways of thinking. According to Piaget, play is not only a manifestation of cognitive development but also a catalyst for further intellectual advancement.

Types of Play and Cognitive Benefits

Symbolic Play and Creativity

Symbolic play, such as imaginative role-playing and pretend scenarios, promotes creativity and abstract thinking. By pretending to be different characters or engaging in make-believe situations, children exercise their imagination, develop symbolic representation skills, and explore alternative perspectives and possibilities.

Constructive Play and Spatial Skills

Constructive play, involving activities like building with blocks or assembling puzzles, enhances spatial awareness and visual-spatial reasoning. Through hands-on manipulation of objects and spatial arrangements, children learn about concepts such as size, shape, symmetry, and spatial relationships, laying the groundwork for future math and engineering skills.

Social Play and Theory of Mind

Social play, including cooperative games and group activities, fosters theory of mind—the ability to understand and attribute mental states to oneself and others. By interacting with peers, negotiating roles, and navigating social dynamics, children develop empathy, perspective-taking abilities, and an understanding of others' thoughts, feelings, and intentions.

Physical Play and Motor Skills

Physical play, such as running, jumping, and climbing, promotes gross motor skills, coordination, and body awareness. By engaging in active play, children develop strength, agility, and balance while refining their motor control and spatial orientation abilities.

Exploratory Play and Inquiry Skills

Exploratory play, involving sensory exploration and hands-on investigation of the environment, stimulates curiosity and inquiry skills. Through sensory experiences, experimentation, and observation, children learn about cause and effect, make predictions, and formulate hypotheses, fostering scientific thinking and problem-solving abilities.

Dramatic Play and Language Development

Dramatic play, characterized by role-playing and storytelling, supports language development and communication skills. By engaging in conversations, narrating stories, and expressing thoughts and emotions through play, children expand their vocabulary, practice linguistic structures, and develop narrative competence.

Games with Rules and Executive Functions

Games with rules, such as board games and organized sports, challenge children's executive functions—the cognitive processes responsible for self-regulation, planning, and decision-making. By following rules, strategizing, and adapting to changing circumstances, children develop skills in impulse control, cognitive flexibility, and goal-directed behavior.

Implementing Play-Based Activities for Cognitive Development

Creating Stimulating Environments

Educators can create stimulating environments that encourage play-based learning and cognitive development. By providing open-ended materials, flexible spaces, and diverse play opportunities, educators empower children to explore, experiment, and engage in meaningful cognitive activities.

Facilitating Play-Based Learning Experiences

Educators play a crucial role in facilitating play-based learning experiences that target specific cognitive skills and objectives. By scaffolding children's play, posing open-ended questions, and providing prompts or challenges, educators guide children's exploration and promote deeper levels of cognitive engagement.

Integrating Play into Curriculum

Integrating play-based activities into the curriculum allows educators to address cognitive learning goals while honoring children's natural inclination to play. By incorporating play-based learning experiences across subject areas, educators provide opportunities for children to apply cognitive skills in real-world contexts and make meaningful connections between concepts and experiences.

2.2.1 Emotional Benefits of Play

Play is not only a source of joy and entertainment but also a powerful tool for emotional development. Play is not only a source of fun and enjoyment but also a valuable tool for emotional development and resilience. By engaging in various types of play, children learn to recognize, express, and regulate their emotions, cultivate empathy and compassion, and build positive relationships with others. Educators and caregivers play a vital role in creating environments that support play-based emotional learning and provide children with the tools and resources they need to navigate their emotional worlds with confidence and resilience.

Understanding Emotional Development

- **Emotional Competence:** Emotional development involves the acquisition of emotional competence—the ability to recognize, understand, express, and regulate one's own emotions as well as respond effectively to the emotions of others. Emotional competence forms the basis for healthy relationships, self-esteem, and overall well-being. Erikson's Psychosocial Stages: Erik Erikson's theory of psychosocial development emphasizes the importance of emotional development across the lifespan. According to Erikson, children navigate a series of psychosocial crises that shape their sense of self, identity, and relationships. Play provides a safe and supportive context for children to explore and resolve these psychosocial challenges.

Types of Play and Emotional Benefits

- **Symbolic Play and Emotional Expression:** Symbolic play, such as pretend play and role-playing, offers children a creative outlet for expressing and processing their emotions. By adopting different roles, enacting scenarios, and exploring imaginary worlds, children can experiment with a range of emotions and perspectives in a safe and non-threatening environment.
- **Social Play and Empathy:** Social play, including cooperative games and group activities, fosters empathy and perspective-taking skills. Through interactions with peers, children learn to understand and respond to others' emotions, develop a sense of empathy and compassion, and cultivate positive relationships based on mutual respect and understanding.
- **Physical Play and Stress Relief:** Physical play, such as running, jumping, and rough-and-tumble play, serves as a natural outlet for releasing pent-up energy and relieving stress. Engaging in physical activity triggers the release of endorphins—the body's natural feel-good hormones—promoting relaxation, mood regulation, and emotional well-being.
- **Exploratory Play and Curiosity:** Exploratory play, involving sensory exploration and hands-on investigation, stimulates curiosity and wonder. By exploring their environment, children experience a sense of awe and discovery, fostering positive emotions such as excitement, fascination, and joy.
- **Dramatic Play and Self-Expression:** Dramatic play, characterized by storytelling and imaginative role-playing, allows children to express and explore their feelings, desires, and fears. Through dramatic play, children can act out scenarios, narratives, and emotions, gaining insights into their own experiences and developing a sense of agency and autonomy.

- **Games with Rules and Emotional Regulation:** Games with rules, such as board games and organized sports, provide opportunities for children to practice emotional regulation and impulse control. By following rules, taking turns, and managing frustration or disappointment, children learn to regulate their emotions, cope with setbacks, and exhibit sportsmanship and fair play.

Implementing Play-Based Activities for Emotional Development

- **Creating Safe and Supportive Environments:** Educators and caregivers can create safe and supportive environments that encourage emotional expression and exploration through play. By fostering trusting relationships, establishing clear expectations, and providing opportunities for open communication, adults can create a nurturing context for children to express and regulate their emotions.
- **Modeling Emotion Regulation:** Adults play a crucial role in modeling emotion regulation and coping strategies during play interactions. By demonstrating empathy, validating children's feelings, and offering support and guidance, adults can help children navigate challenging emotions and develop effective coping skills.
- **Encouraging Reflective Play:** Encouraging reflective play involves prompting children to reflect on their play experiences and emotions. Through open-ended questions, reflective prompts, and guided discussions, educators can help children make connections between their play experiences and their emotions, fostering self-awareness and emotional intelligence.

2.3 MOTIVATION AND ENGAGEMENT IN GAMES

2.3.1 Motivation in Games

Motivation lies at the heart of gameplay, driving players to engage, persist, and strive for success. Motivation serves as the driving force behind gameplay, influencing players' engagement, persistence, and satisfaction.

By understanding the intrinsic and extrinsic factors that shape motivation, game designers can create experiences that captivate players' interest, challenge their abilities, and foster a sense of achievement and belongingness.

As games continue to evolve and diversify, motivation remains a central consideration in shaping the gaming experiences of tomorrow.

Understanding Motivation

- **Definition and Importance:** Motivation refers to the internal and external factors that energize, direct, and sustain behavior towards achieving a goal. In the context of games, motivation plays a crucial role in driving player engagement, retention, and satisfaction, ultimately shaping the overall gaming experience.

- **Self-Determination Theory:** Self-Determination Theory (SDT) provides a framework for understanding intrinsic motivation—the drive to engage in an activity for its own sake, out of interest or enjoyment. According to SDT, intrinsic motivation is fueled by three basic psychological needs: autonomy, competence, and relatedness.

Intrinsic Motivation in Games

- **Autonomy:** Autonomy in games refers to the sense of freedom, choice, and control that players experience during gameplay. Games that offer meaningful choices, player agency, and opportunities for self-expression empower players to pursue their goals autonomously, enhancing intrinsic motivation.
- **Competence:** Competence relates to the feeling of mastery, skill development, and progress that players derive from gameplay. Games that provide clear goals, feedback, and challenges that match players' skill levels foster a sense of competence and achievement, motivating players to overcome obstacles and improve their performance.
- **Relatedness:** Relatedness pertains to the sense of connection, social interaction, and belongingness that players experience within gaming communities. Multiplayer games, social features, and collaborative gameplay experiences facilitate social connections, support networks, and shared experiences, enhancing players' sense of relatedness and motivation to play.

Extrinsic Motivation in Games

- **Rewards and Reinforcement:** Extrinsic motivation involves external incentives, rewards, or consequences that drive behavior. In games, rewards such as points, achievements, unlockable content, and in-game currency serve as extrinsic motivators that incentivize players to perform specific actions, complete tasks, and progress through the game.
- **Progression Systems:** Progression systems, such as experience points (XP), levels, and skill trees, provide a sense of advancement and tangible rewards for players' efforts. By offering clear milestones, rewards, and a sense of progression, progression systems motivate players to invest time and effort into gameplay and strive for continuous improvement.

- **Competition and Social Comparison:** Competition and social comparison drive extrinsic motivation by fostering a sense of rivalry, status, and achievement. Leaderboards, rankings, and competitive multiplayer modes encourage players to compete with others, compare their performance, and strive for recognition and social validation within the gaming community.

Game Design Elements and Motivation

- **Clear Goals and Feedback:** Games with clear goals, objectives, and feedback mechanisms provide players with a sense of direction and progress. By setting meaningful goals and providing timely feedback on players' actions and performance, game designers keep players engaged and motivated to pursue their objectives.
- **Challenge and Mastery:** Games that strike the right balance between challenge and skill offer optimal conditions for motivation and engagement. A well-designed difficulty curve, adaptive challenges, and opportunities for skill development ensure that players remain challenged yet capable of success, fostering a sense of mastery and flow.
- **Immersive Narratives and Worlds:** Immersive narratives, rich storytelling, and expansive game worlds captivate players' imaginations and create a sense of immersion. By providing immersive experiences that transport players to fantastical realms, games evoke curiosity, wonder, and emotional investment, sustaining motivation and engagement over time.

Cultivating Motivation in Game Design

- **Player-Centered Design:** Player-centered design involves understanding players' motivations, preferences, and needs and designing games that cater to their interests and desires. By incorporating player feedback, playtesting, and iterative design processes, game developers can create experiences that resonate with players and sustain their motivation over time.
- **Dynamic and Personalized Experiences:** Dynamic and personalized experiences adapt to players' preferences, play styles, and progress, ensuring that gameplay remains relevant and engaging. Procedural generation, dynamic difficulty adjustment, and personalized content recommendations tailor the gaming experience to individual players, maximizing motivation and enjoyment.
- **Community and Social Engagement:** Building a vibrant gaming community and fostering social engagement enhance motivation and

retention among players. By facilitating social interactions, cooperative gameplay, and user-generated content creation, game developers can cultivate a sense of belongingness, camaraderie, and shared experiences within the gaming community.

2.3.2 Engagement in Games

Engagement serves as the lifeblood of gaming experiences, captivating players and immersing them in virtual worlds. Engagement lies at the heart of gaming experiences, captivating players and immersing them in virtual worlds. By understanding the psychological principles, immersive elements, and player interactions that contribute to engagement, game developers can create experiences that captivate players' interest, stimulate their senses, and foster a sense of immersion and enjoyment. As games continue to evolve and diversify, engagement remains a central consideration in shaping the gaming experiences of tomorrow.

Understanding Engagement

- **Definition and Significance:** Engagement refers to the state of absorption, focus, and involvement that players experience during gameplay. It encompasses cognitive, emotional, and behavioral aspects, driving players to invest time, attention, and effort into gaming experiences. Engaged players are deeply immersed in the game world, experiencing a sense of flow—the optimal state of concentration and enjoyment.
- **Flow Theory:** Flow theory, proposed by psychologist Mihaly Csikszentmihalyi, describes the state of flow as a state of complete absorption and optimal experience characterized by intense concentration, heightened focus, and a sense of effortless control. Flow occurs when the challenge of an activity matches the skill level of the individual, leading to a state of "optimal experience."

Elements of Engagement in Games

- **Immersive Storytelling:** Immersive storytelling captivates players' imaginations and draws them into the game world through compelling narratives, rich characters, and intricate plotlines. By creating immersive narratives and interactive story arcs, game developers evoke emotional investment, curiosity, and suspense, sustaining players' engagement throughout the gaming experience.
- **Interactive Gameplay:** Interactive gameplay provides players with agency, choice, and meaningful decisions that shape the outcome of the game. By offering opportunities for exploration, experimentation, and player-driven narratives, interactive gameplay empowers players to become active participants in the game world, fostering a sense of ownership and investment in the outcome.

- **Reward Systems:** Reward systems, such as points, achievements, and unlockable content, incentivize players to achieve specific goals and milestones within the game. By providing tangible rewards and feedback for players' actions and accomplishments, reward systems reinforce desired behaviors, motivate progress, and sustain engagement over time.

Social Interaction

Social interaction enhances engagement by facilitating collaboration, competition, and communication among players. Multiplayer modes, social features, and online communities provide opportunities for players to connect, cooperate, and compete with others, fostering a sense of camaraderie, belongingness, and shared experiences.

- **Immersive Environments:** Immersive environments stimulate players' senses and evoke a sense of presence and realism within the game world. By creating detailed graphics, atmospheric soundscapes, and interactive environments, game developers transport players to fantastical realms, evoking awe, wonder, and emotional immersion.
- **Dynamic Challenges:** Dynamic challenges provide players with opportunities for skill development, mastery, and adaptive learning. By offering a variety of challenges, puzzles, and obstacles that adjust to players' skill levels and progress, game developers keep players engaged and motivated to overcome new challenges and push their limits.
- **Continuous Feedback:** Continuous feedback loops provide players with timely information, updates, and progress indicators that keep them informed and engaged. By providing clear goals, feedback on players' actions, and progress tracking systems, game developers maintain players' motivation and engagement by reinforcing their sense of accomplishment and progress.

Fostering Engagement in Game Design

- **Player-Centric Design:** Player-centric design involves understanding players' preferences, motivations, and needs and designing games that cater to their interests and desires. By incorporating player feedback, playtesting, and iterative design processes, game developers can create experiences that resonate with players and sustain their engagement over time.
- **User Experience (UX) Design:** User Experience (UX) design focuses on creating intuitive, seamless, and enjoyable interactions between players and games. By designing intuitive interfaces, responsive controls, and immersive experiences, UX designers enhance players' engagement and enjoyment, reducing barriers to entry and enhancing accessibility for all players.

- **Community Building:** Building a vibrant gaming community and fostering social engagement enhance engagement and retention among players. By facilitating social interactions, cooperative gameplay, and user-generated content creation, game developers can cultivate a sense of belongingness, camaraderie, and shared experiences within the gaming community.

CHAPTER 3

THE ROLE OF TECHNOLOGY IN GAME-BASED LEARNING

3.1 DIGITAL GAME VS. TRADITIONAL GAME

The debate between digital and traditional games has been ongoing, with proponents on both sides advocating for the unique benefits of each. The digital game vs. traditional game debate underscores the diverse range of gaming experiences available to players. While digital games offer immersive interactivity, accessibility, and cognitive challenges, traditional games provide tangible engagement, social interaction, and opportunities for creativity. Rather than viewing digital and traditional games as competing entities, it is important to recognize the complementary strengths of each and embrace the diversity of gaming experiences that cater to the preferences and interests of players worldwide. Whether enjoying the latest blockbuster video game or gathering around a classic board game with friends and family, gaming continues to evolve and thrive as a source of entertainment, learning, and social connection in our digital age.

3.1.1 Digital Games

Digital games refer to interactive experiences that are played on electronic devices such as computers, consoles, smartphones, and tablets. These games encompass a wide range of genres, including action, adventure, simulation, strategy, puzzle, and role-playing games, and often feature immersive graphics, sound effects, and multiplayer capabilities.

3.1.2 Traditional Games

Traditional games encompass a diverse array of non-digital games that have been played for centuries across cultures and societies. These games include board games, card games, tabletop games, outdoor games, and sports, and typically involve physical components such as boards, cards, dice, pieces, or equipment.

3.1.3 Gameplay Experience

- **Interactivity and Immersion:** Digital games offer high levels of interactivity and immersion, allowing players to control virtual avatars, navigate digital environments, and interact with complex game systems and mechanics. The immersive audiovisual effects and narrative storytelling of digital games draw players into captivating virtual worlds, enhancing the overall gaming experience.

- **Tangibility and Social Interaction:** Traditional games provide tangible components and opportunities for face-to-face social interaction, fostering physical engagement, collaboration, and communication among players. The tactile nature of traditional game pieces, the social dynamics of gameplay, and the shared experiences of laughter, camaraderie, and competition contribute to the unique appeal of traditional games.

3.1.4 Accessibility and Convenience

- **Accessibility of Digital Games:** Digital games offer unparalleled accessibility and convenience, allowing players to access games anytime, anywhere, and on a variety of devices. With the advent of digital distribution platforms and cloud gaming services, players can easily download or stream games, purchase digital copies, and engage in online multiplayer matches with players around the world.
- **Accessibility of Traditional Games:** Traditional games may require physical components, dedicated play spaces, and coordination among players, making them less accessible and convenient compared to digital games. However, traditional games offer the advantage of being low-cost, offline activities that can be enjoyed by individuals or groups without the need for electronic devices or internet connectivity.

3.1.5 Learning and Skill Development

- **Cognitive Skills in Digital Games:** Digital games can facilitate the development of cognitive skills such as problem-solving, critical thinking, decision-making, and spatial reasoning. Many digital games incorporate educational content, puzzles, and strategic challenges that encourage players to think analytically, adapt to changing situations, and explore new strategies for success.
- **Social Skills in Traditional Games:** Traditional games promote the development of social skills such as communication, cooperation, negotiation, and sportsmanship. Whether playing board games with family members, card games with friends, or team sports with peers, traditional games provide opportunities for social interaction, collaboration, and relationship-building in real-world settings.

3.1.6 Creativity and Customization

- **Creativity in Digital Games:** Digital games offer extensive opportunities for creativity and customization through character creation, level design, modding, and player-generated content. Players can express their creativity by designing custom avatars, building virtual worlds, and sharing their creations with the gaming community through online platforms and social media.
- **Creativity in Traditional Games:** Traditional games also foster creativity and imagination through open-ended gameplay, storytelling, and rule modifications. Players can invent their own variations of traditional games, create new game rules or scenarios, and adapt gameplay to suit their preferences, encouraging innovation and personalization within the gaming experience.

3.2 GAMIFICATION TOOLS AND PLATFORM

3.2.1 Gamification Tools

Gamification tools have gained prominence across various domains, offering innovative ways to enhance engagement, motivation, and learning outcomes. Gamification tools offer innovative approaches to enhancing engagement, motivation, and learning outcomes across diverse contexts. Whether in education, marketing, healthcare, or workplace productivity, gamification leverages game design principles to captivate users' interest, drive behavior change, and foster meaningful experiences.

By understanding the principles, types, and benefits of gamification tools and considering key implementation considerations, organizations and individuals can harness the power of gamification to achieve their objectives and engage users in new and exciting ways.

Types of Gamification Tools

- **Points, Badges, and Leaderboards (PBLs):** PBLs are foundational gamification elements that reward users for completing tasks, achieving milestones, or demonstrating desired behaviors. Points accumulate based on users' actions, badges signify achievements or accomplishments, and leaderboards display rankings or standings, fostering competition, recognition, and a sense of achievement.
- **Progress Bars and Visual Feedback:** Progress bars and visual feedback provide users with real-time feedback on their progress, performance, or completion status. By visualizing goals, milestones, or task completion, progress bars enhance motivation, clarify expectations,

and promote a sense of accomplishment as users track their progress towards objectives.

- **Quests, Challenges, and Missions:** Quests, challenges, and missions present users with specific goals, tasks, or quests to complete within a defined timeframe or context. By framing activities as quests or challenges with clear objectives and rewards, gamification tools encourage users to take action, overcome obstacles, and experience a sense of adventure and accomplishment.
- **Levels, Ranks, and Unlockable Content:** Levels, ranks, and unlockable content introduce progression systems that reward users with access to new features, content, or privileges as they advance through stages or tiers of engagement. By providing tangible rewards and incentives for progress, gamification tools motivate users to invest time and effort into achieving mastery and unlocking additional benefits.
- **Social Features and Collaboration:** Social features and collaboration mechanisms facilitate interaction, communication, and community-building among users. Whether through social networks, forums, or multiplayer challenges, gamification tools leverage social dynamics to foster peer support, collaboration, and shared experiences, enhancing engagement and motivation through social connections.

Benefits of Gamification Tools

- **Increased Engagement and Motivation:** Gamification tools leverage game design principles to captivate users' interest, sustain their attention, and motivate them to participate actively in activities or tasks. By introducing elements of challenge, competition, and reward, gamification enhances engagement and fosters intrinsic motivation, leading to higher levels of involvement and commitment.
- **Improved Learning Outcomes:** In educational settings, gamification tools promote active learning, skill acquisition, and knowledge retention by making learning experiences interactive, immersive, and enjoyable. By incorporating game elements such as quizzes, simulations, and interactive exercises, gamified learning platforms facilitate active participation, experimentation, and mastery of educational content.
- **Behavior Change and Goal Achievement:** In behavioral interventions, gamification tools serve as effective tools for promoting behavior change, habit formation, and goal achievement. By providing clear goals, feedback, and rewards for desired behaviors, gamification

motivates users to adopt healthier habits, improve self-discipline, and sustain positive changes over time.

- **Data Collection and Analysis:** Gamification tools offer valuable insights into user behavior, preferences, and performance through data collection and analysis. By tracking user interactions, engagement metrics, and performance indicators, gamification platforms generate actionable data that can inform decision-making, optimize user experiences, and drive continuous improvement.

Considerations for Effective Implementation

- **Alignment with Objectives and Audience:** Effective gamification requires careful consideration of the target audience, goals, and context to ensure alignment with user preferences and desired outcomes. Gamification tools should be tailored to the specific needs, interests, and motivations of users to maximize engagement and effectiveness.
- **Clear Design and Feedback Mechanisms:** Clear design and feedback mechanisms are essential for guiding users' actions, progress, and performance within gamified experiences. Gamification tools should provide clear goals, instructions, and feedback to help users understand expectations, track their progress, and stay motivated throughout their journey.
- **Balancing Intrinsic and Extrinsic Motivation:** Balancing intrinsic and extrinsic motivation is crucial for creating sustainable and meaningful gamification experiences. While extrinsic rewards may initially drive engagement, intrinsic motivations such as autonomy, mastery, and purpose are essential for long-term engagement and behavior change.
- **Iterative Design and Evaluation:** Iterative design and evaluation are key principles of gamification that involve continuous refinement and optimization based on user feedback and data analysis. Gamification strategies should be regularly evaluated, adjusted, and improved to address user needs, preferences, and evolving objectives effectively.

3.2.2 Gamification Platform

Gamification platforms have emerged as powerful tools for enhancing engagement, motivation, and performance across various domains. Gamification platforms offer powerful tools for enhancing engagement, motivation, and performance across diverse domains. Whether in the workplace, education, marketing, healthcare, or wellness, gamification platforms leverage game design principles to create immersive, interactive, and rewarding experiences that drive desired behaviors and outcomes. By understanding the core components, applications, benefits, and considerations for effective implementation of gamification platforms, organizations and individuals can harness the power of gamification to empower engagement, inspire action, and achieve meaningful results.

Definition and Purpose

A gamification platform is a software solution designed to integrate game elements, mechanics, and principles into non-game contexts to motivate, engage, and reward users. These platforms offer a range of features, including points, badges, leaderboards, challenges, progress tracking, and analytics, to create immersive and interactive experiences that drive desired behaviors or outcomes.

Core Components

Gamification platforms typically consist of several core components that enable the design, implementation, and management of gamified experiences:

- **User Profiles:** User profiles store information about individual users, including their preferences, progress, achievements, and activity history.
- **Game Mechanics:** Game mechanics define the rules, interactions, and feedback mechanisms that shape users' experiences within the platform.
- **Rewards System:** Rewards systems provide incentives, such as points, badges, levels, or virtual goods, to motivate users and reinforce desired behaviors.
- **Analytics Dashboard:** Analytics dashboards track user engagement, performance metrics, and behavior patterns to inform decision-making and optimize gamification strategies.
- **Administration Tools:** Administration tools allow platform administrators to configure settings, manage content, and monitor user activity.

Applications of Gamification Platforms

- **Employee Engagement and Productivity:** In the workplace, gamification platforms can boost employee engagement, productivity, and morale by turning routine tasks or training activities into engaging challenges or competitions. By rewarding achievements, recognizing contributions, and fostering friendly competition, gamification platforms motivate employees to excel and achieve their goals.
- **Education and Training:** In educational settings, gamification platforms enhance learning outcomes, retention, and engagement by transforming

traditional coursework or training programs into interactive and immersive experiences. By incorporating game elements such as quizzes, simulations, quests, and leaderboards, gamification platforms make learning enjoyable, memorable, and effective.

- **Customer Engagement and Loyalty:** In marketing and customer service, gamification platforms drive customer engagement, loyalty, and brand advocacy by offering interactive experiences, rewards, and incentives. By gamifying marketing campaigns, loyalty programs, or customer feedback systems, organizations can create memorable experiences that inspire customer participation and loyalty.
- **Healthcare and Wellness:** In healthcare and wellness programs, gamification platforms promote behavior change, adherence to treatment plans, and healthy lifestyle choices. By gamifying fitness challenges, wellness programs, or patient education initiatives, healthcare providers can motivate individuals to adopt healthier habits, manage chronic conditions, and achieve positive health outcomes.

Benefits of Gamification Platforms

- **Increased Engagement and Motivation:** Gamification platforms leverage game design principles to captivate users' interest, sustain their attention, and motivate them to participate actively in activities or tasks. By introducing elements of challenge, competition, and reward, gamification platforms enhance engagement and foster intrinsic motivation, leading to higher levels of involvement and commitment.
- **Improved Performance and Learning Outcomes:** Gamification platforms facilitate skill acquisition, knowledge retention, and performance improvement by providing interactive, immersive, and goal-oriented experiences. By offering feedback, rewards, and progression pathways, gamification platforms motivate users to master skills, overcome challenges, and achieve their objectives effectively.
- **Enhanced Data Collection and Analysis:** Gamification platforms generate valuable data insights into user behavior, preferences, and performance through analytics dashboards and reporting tools. By tracking user engagement metrics, completion rates, and performance indicators, gamification platforms provide actionable data that can inform decision-making, optimize user experiences, and drive continuous improvement.

Considerations for Effective Implementation

- **Alignment with Objectives and Audience:** Effective implementation of gamification platforms requires alignment with organizational goals, user needs, and contextual factors. Gamification strategies should be tailored to the specific objectives, target audience, and desired outcomes to maximize effectiveness and user engagement.
- **Designing Engaging and Meaningful Experiences:** Gamification platforms should offer engaging and meaningful experiences that resonate with users' interests, preferences, and motivations. Designing compelling narratives, well-designed challenges, and rewarding experiences is essential for capturing users' attention and sustaining their engagement over time.
- **Providing Clear Goals and Feedback:** Clear goals, instructions, and feedback mechanisms are critical for guiding users' actions, progress, and performance within gamification platforms. Providing users with clear objectives, real-time feedback, and progress tracking tools helps them understand expectations, stay motivated, and monitor their progress towards achieving their goals.
- **Fostering Community and Collaboration:** Gamification platforms should foster a sense of community, collaboration, and social interaction among users to enhance engagement and participation. Incorporating social features, multiplayer challenges, and collaborative activities encourages peer support, interaction, and shared experiences, enriching the overall user experience.

3.3 THE IMPACT OF TECHNOLOGY ON EDUCATION

Technology is changing the way we learn. From zero to hero, technology has gone leaps and bounds. Gone are those days when we used to memorize things and regurgitate them at exam. The education sector has undergone a sea change and completely transformed with the introduction of new technology and gadgets. There is no longer time for theory and rote learning, as more emphasis is laid on skill development and on problem-solving abilities.

3.3.1 Advantages of Technology in Education

There are lots of benefits that comes out of using technology in education sector. Technology has changed the way of learning.

It has made our life more colourful and make studies interesting through the gadgets like smartphones, laptops, tablets etc. The use of technology in education is beneficial in many ways like:

- **Teacher Productivity and Efficiency have Increased:** Teachers and trainers use technology to boost their productivity, incorporate valuable digital tools to enhance their students' learning options, and boost student support and participation. Technology enables teachers to improve their teaching methods and tailor learning for their students. Schools profit from technology by lowering the cost of physical teaching materials, increasing the efficiency of educational programs, and maximizing teacher time. Access to an infinite amount of current data and information from a number of sources.
- **Automation:** For teachers, automation is a big benefit of educational technology. You can upload lessons to a learning management system (LMS) for students to access at their leisure. Grading is simplified using online tests, and parents can be notified instantly when their children earn a failing mark. Teachers are always seeking for methods to make extra time in their days, and technology may help them tremendously.
- **Reduces the Cost of Schooling:** Resources have become more available as a result of the introduction of technology in education, resulting in lower tuition costs, a decrease in the demand for books and their price, and a decrease in the need for school supplies. The arrival of e-books has simplified things for low-income families and allowed pupils to approach learning on an equal footing with their peers, without parental pressure for good performance resulting from big investments in their children's education. In addition, employing e-books in education has the positive side effect of indirectly contributing to the reduction of deforestation.
- **It Encourages More Communication between Teachers and Parents:** Utilization of education apps also helps in the exchange of information between parents and teachers.
- **Encourages Collaboration in Classrooms:** Technology in classrooms encourages collaboration by breaking down barriers that are prevalent in the real world. Instead of relying on limited face-to-face social interaction, online spaces allow collaboration to occur more naturally.
- **Technology Aids in the Preparation of Pupils for their Future Lives:** It helps children to become more creative, inventive and flexible. It is an effective way to use technology in education because there are many programs that may help you to learn the skills necessary for the future. Technological skills are needed for the future generation. Every program has its benefit, which may be suited to your learning style or personal preferences.

- **Technology has Played a Significant Role in Education since the Beginning of Recorded History:** However, technology has also had an impact on education beyond just facilitating communication and information exchange among learners and instructors.
- **Plays a Vital Role in Teaching and Learning Process:** Educational apps make it possible for students to access virtual classrooms from home, school or anywhere else they have access to the internet. These can include things like reducing costs, increasing productivity and improving communication.

3.3.2 Disadvantages of Technology in Education

As more and more technology is being introduced into the classroom today, there are still many concerns about the consequences of rapidly integrating new technologies.

A lot of these concerns are valid because most teachers are not equipped to integrate technology properly with their teaching methods. Here are some disadvantages of using technology in education sector.

- **Higher Management and Training:** Due to the rise of technology, being effective in the classroom now necessitates teachers' ability to be effective on a screen and on a technology platforms. Research has been done that shows three-quarters of teachers feel the internet and other digital tools have increased their workload and drastically increased the range of topics and abilities about which they must be educated. This is whereby IT specialists are needed to help set up, manage, and support teachers and students using new technology in the classroom.
- **Expensive:** Technology required in the education includes internet services, computer hardware, printers, Internet browsers etc. Acquiring all of these needs a lot of moncy to invest in technology at your school.
- **Distraction:** With social media sites like Facebook, Twitter, YouTube are becoming very popular among the youth. They are spending most of their time on these sites, which is having bad effect on their studies. Cell phones have become a great source of distraction in the classroom. Students use cell phones in their free time in school too, especially in breaks.
- **Makes Students to Cheat:** When phones couldn't be used to access the internet during tests, cheating was far more difficult. To outsmart the system, students have taken use of new technology to cheat in their exams and Continuous Assessment Tests (CATs). As a result, a

significant proportion of students get away with it and earn their degrees. They go on to become true professionals in their fields while not being academically qualified for them.

- **Students Acquiring Wrong Information:** Many websites and other online platforms are providing wrong information that users require. Many websites post deceptive material online in order to increase traffic, even if the information is inaccurate. As a student, you are sure to come across some of these sites that contain inaccurate information or incorrect details. Other websites replicate stuff from other websites without verifying its authenticity. Readers are misled in any case, which is bad for learners.

PART-II

GAMIFICATION IN EDUCATION

CHAPTER 4

GAMIFICATION PRINCIPLES AND STRATEGIES

4.1 CORE PRINCIPLES OF GAMIFICATION

Gamification, the application of game elements and mechanics to non-game contexts, is grounded in several core principles that underpin its effectiveness in motivating, engaging, and rewarding users. The core principles of gamification—autonomy, mastery, purpose, progression, social interaction, and feedback—form the foundation of effective gamification design. By understanding and applying these principles, designers can create engaging, motivating, and rewarding gamified experiences that inspire action, drive behavior change, and achieve meaningful outcomes. Whether in education, marketing, workplace productivity, or healthcare, gamification principles offer powerful tools for enhancing engagement, motivation, and success in diverse contexts.

4.1.1 Definition and Purpose

Gamification involves incorporating elements such as points, badges, leaderboards, challenges, and rewards into activities or processes to motivate and engage users. The core purpose of gamification is to tap into intrinsic motivations, such as autonomy, mastery, and purpose, to drive desired behaviors, outcomes, or learning objectives.

4.1.2 Autonomy

Empowering User Choice

Autonomy refers to the sense of control, freedom, and choice that users experience within gamified experiences. By offering users meaningful choices, autonomy empowers them to pursue their goals, preferences, and interests autonomously, enhancing their sense of ownership and motivation.

Example: Customization Options

Gamification platforms often provide users with customization options, allowing them to personalize their profiles, avatars, or preferences. By enabling users to tailor their experiences to their preferences, gamification platforms enhance autonomy and create a sense of ownership over their journey.

4.1.3 Mastery

Fostering Skill Development and Progression

Mastery involves the pursuit of continuous improvement, skill development, and progress towards mastery within gamified experiences. By offering challenges, feedback, and opportunities for skill development, gamification fosters a sense of competence and achievement, motivating users to strive for mastery.

Example: Leveling Systems

Gamification platforms often incorporate leveling systems that reward users with experience points or levels as they progress through challenges or activities. By providing tangible markers of progress and achievement, leveling systems reinforce mastery and encourage users to continue advancing.

4.1.4 Purpose

Connecting Activities to Meaningful Goals

Purpose involves aligning users' activities with meaningful goals, objectives, or values within gamified experiences. By establishing clear goals, objectives, or missions, gamification platforms provide users with a sense of purpose and direction, motivating them to engage in activities that align with their interests and values.

Example: Quests and Missions

Gamification platforms often feature quests, missions, or challenges that provide users with specific goals to accomplish. By framing activities as quests or missions with clear objectives and rewards, gamification platforms imbue users' actions with purpose and meaning, enhancing motivation and engagement.

4.1.5 Progression

Facilitating Continuous Growth and Advancement

Progression involves facilitating users' continuous growth, advancement, and achievement of milestones within gamified experiences. By offering progression pathways, rewards, and feedback mechanisms, gamification platforms motivate users to set goals, overcome challenges, and track their progress towards success.

Example: Unlockable Content

Gamification platforms may include unlockable content, such as badges, rewards, or features, that users can access as they progress through challenges or levels. By providing tangible rewards for progress and achievement, unlockable content reinforces progression and incentivizes users to continue their journey.

4.1.6 Social Interaction

Fostering Collaboration and Community

Social interaction involves facilitating communication, collaboration, and community-building among users within gamified experiences. By incorporating social features, multiplayer challenges, or collaborative activities, gamification platforms foster peer support, interaction, and shared experiences, enriching the overall user experience.

Example: Leaderboards and Challenges

Gamification platforms often include leaderboards or challenges that allow users to compare their performance or achievements with others. By fostering competition, recognition, and social comparison, leaderboards and challenges encourage social interaction and engagement among users.

4.1.7 Feedback

Providing Timely and Informative Feedback

Feedback involves providing users with timely, informative, and actionable feedback on their actions, progress, or performance within gamified experiences. By offering feedback mechanisms, progress tracking tools, and performance metrics, gamification platforms help users understand their strengths, areas for improvement, and progress towards goals.

Example: Progress Bars and Performance Metrics

Gamification platforms may feature progress bars, performance metrics, or visual indicators that provide users with real-time feedback on their progress or completion status. By visualizing goals, milestones, or task completion, progress bars enhance motivation, clarify expectations, and promote a sense of accomplishment.

4.2 GAME ELEMENTS IN EDUCATION

Integrating game elements into educational contexts has gained traction as a means to enhance student engagement, motivation, and learning outcomes. Integrating game elements into education offers exciting opportunities to transform teaching and learning experiences.

By leveraging principles from game design, educators can create engaging, interactive, and immersive learning environments that motivate students, foster collaboration, and promote deep learning. While challenges and considerations exist, the benefits of gamification in education are vast, paving the way for innovative approaches to education that inspire curiosity, creativity, and lifelong learning.

4.2.1 Introduction to Game Elements in Education

Incorporating game elements, such as points, badges, levels, quests, and leaderboards, into educational settings aims to make learning more interactive, immersive, and enjoyable. By leveraging principles from game design, educators seek to create engaging learning experiences that captivate students' interest, foster collaboration, and promote deep learning.

4.2.2 Points and Rewards

- **Motivating Progress and Achievement:** Points and rewards systems provide tangible incentives for students to engage in learning activities, complete assignments, and achieve learning objectives. By earning points for participation, effort, or mastery, students are motivated to strive for progress and excellence, fostering a sense of achievement and accomplishment.
- **Example:** Gamified Assignments: In a gamified classroom, assignments may be structured as quests or challenges, with students earning points or rewards for completing tasks, demonstrating understanding, or achieving mastery. By incorporating elements of challenge, competition, and reward, gamified assignments motivate students to actively participate and invest effort in their learning.

4.2.3 Badges and Achievements

- **Recognizing Skills and Milestones:** Badges and achievements serve as digital representations of students' accomplishments, skills, and milestones within the learning environment. By earning badges for specific achievements, such as mastering a concept, completing a project, or demonstrating a skill, students receive recognition and validation for their efforts, boosting their self-esteem and motivation.
- **Example:** Mastery Badges: In a gamified curriculum, students may earn mastery badges for demonstrating proficiency in specific subject areas, topics, or skills. By offering badges as visual symbols of achievement, educators reinforce students' progress and provide incentives for continued learning and skill development.

4.2.4 Levels and Progression

- **Fostering Continuous Growth:** Levels and progression systems provide students with clear pathways for advancing through learning objectives, mastering content, and achieving higher levels of proficiency. By offering progressively challenging tasks, feedback, and opportunities for advancement, gamified learning environments encourage students to set goals, overcome obstacles, and track their progress over time.

- **Example:** Leveling Up: In a gamified course, students may progress through levels or tiers of mastery as they demonstrate proficiency in learning objectives or complete assignments. By leveling up, students unlock new challenges, content, or privileges, motivating them to continue their learning journey and strive for higher levels of achievement.

4.2.5 Quests and Challenges

- **Engaging Students in Active Learning:** Quests and challenges present students with meaningful, goal-oriented tasks or missions to complete within the learning environment. By framing learning activities as quests or challenges with clear objectives, rewards, and deadlines, educators create opportunities for students to apply their knowledge, solve problems, and collaborate with peers in authentic contexts.
- **Example:** Learning Quests: In a gamified curriculum, students may embark on learning quests that involve researching a topic, solving real-world problems, or completing project-based assignments. By structuring learning activities as quests with narrative elements, educators engage students in active learning experiences that promote critical thinking, creativity, and collaboration.

4.2.6 Leaderboards and Competition

- **Fostering Healthy Competition and Collaboration:** Leaderboards and competition elements introduce elements of social comparison and friendly rivalry among students, motivating them to excel and outperform their peers. By displaying rankings or standings based on performance, leaderboards create a sense of competition, recognition, and accountability that drives student engagement and effort.
- **Example:** Class Leaderboards: In a gamified classroom, educators may implement class leaderboards that display students' scores, achievements, or progress in real-time. By showcasing students' performance relative to their peers, leaderboards foster a sense of competition and camaraderie, motivating students to strive for excellence and celebrate each other's successes.

4.2.7 Challenges and Considerations

- **Balancing Competition and Collaboration:** While competition can be a powerful motivator, educators must ensure that gamified learning environments promote collaboration, teamwork, and inclusivity. Balancing competition with cooperative learning activities and fostering a supportive classroom culture is essential for creating an inclusive and equitable learning environment for all students.

- **Avoiding Extrinsic Motivation:** Gamification should aim to cultivate intrinsic motivation—the drive to engage in learning for its own sake—rather than relying solely on extrinsic rewards or incentives. Educators should design gamified experiences that promote autonomy, mastery, and purpose, fostering students' intrinsic motivation to learn and achieve success.

4.3 DESIGNING EFFECTIVE GAMIFIED EXPERIENCES

Gamification has become increasingly prevalent in various fields, from education to marketing, as a means to engage users and drive desired behaviors. Designing effective gamified experiences requires a deep understanding of human psychology, game mechanics, and user experience principles. Designing effective gamified experiences requires a multidisciplinary approach that integrates game design principles, user experience strategies, and behavioral psychology insights. By understanding the needs and motivations of the target audience, leveraging engaging game mechanics, and fostering social interaction and progression, designers can create compelling experiences that captivate and motivate users. Through continuous testing and iteration, gamified experiences can evolve to meet the evolving needs and preferences of users, driving sustained engagement and delivering tangible results.

Gamification is the integration of game elements and principles into non-game contexts to enhance user engagement and motivation. At its core, gamification leverages intrinsic and extrinsic motivators to encourage specific actions or behaviors. By tapping into people's natural inclination towards play and competition, gamified experiences can foster a sense of accomplishment and enjoyment, driving desired outcomes.

4.3.1 Identifying Goals and Objectives

Before embarking on the design process, it is crucial to define clear goals and objectives for the gamified experience. Whether it's increasing user retention, promoting learning, or driving sales, understanding the desired outcomes will inform the design decisions and mechanics implemented. Setting measurable metrics allows for the evaluation of the gamified experience's effectiveness and iteration based on user feedback and data analysis.

4.3.2 Understanding the Target Audience

A successful gamified experience resonates with its target audience. Conducting thorough research to understand the demographics, preferences, and motivations of the intended users is paramount. By gaining insights into user behavior and preferences, designers can tailor the gamified experience to align with user expectations and interests, increasing its relevance and appeal.

4.3.3 Leveraging Game Mechanics

Game mechanics serve as the building blocks of gamified experiences, influencing user behavior and engagement. From points and badges to leaderboards and progression systems, each mechanic contributes to shaping the user experience. However, it is essential to strike a balance between providing meaningful rewards and avoiding extrinsic motivators that may undermine intrinsic motivation over time.

4.3.4 Creating Immersive Narratives

Narratives add depth and context to gamified experiences, immersing users in compelling storylines and scenarios. By weaving narratives into the gameplay, designers can evoke emotions, spark curiosity, and enhance user engagement. Whether it's guiding users on a quest or unfolding a mystery, narratives provide a cohesive framework that drives user interaction and investment in the experience.

4.3.5 Promoting Social Interaction

Social interaction is a fundamental aspect of gamified experiences, fostering collaboration, competition, and community building. Integrating social features such as multiplayer modes, leaderboards, and social sharing functionalities enables users to connect with peers, compare achievements, and engage in friendly competition. The sense of belonging and camaraderie enhances user retention and amplifies the overall enjoyment of the experience.

4.3.6 Designing for Progression and Mastery

Progression and mastery are powerful motivators that keep users engaged and invested in the long term. Designing a well-paced progression system that offers a sense of achievement and continuous growth is essential. Introducing challenges of increasing difficulty, unlocking new abilities or content, and providing feedback on user performance fosters a sense of mastery and competence, driving sustained engagement.

4.3.7 Incorporating Feedback Loops

Feedback loops play a crucial role in shaping user behavior and learning within gamified experiences. Providing timely feedback on user actions, progress, and achievements reinforces desired behaviors and guides users towards their goals. Whether it's visual cues, notifications, or personalized feedback messages, incorporating feedback loops enhances user engagement and motivation by maintaining a sense of progress and accomplishment.

4.3.8 Balancing Challenge and Skill

Achieving the right balance between challenge and skill is essential for maintaining user engagement and preventing boredom or frustration. Designers must calibrate the difficulty level of tasks and challenges to match the user's skill level and learning curve. Incorporating adaptive difficulty algorithms or allowing users to customize their experience ensures that each player is appropriately challenged, maximizing enjoyment and motivation.

4.3.9 Ensuring Accessibility and Inclusivity

Designing inclusive gamified experiences involves considering the diverse needs and abilities of users. Accessibility features such as customizable controls, text-to-speech options, and color-blind-friendly designs ensure that all users can participate and enjoy the experience. By prioritizing inclusivity, designers can create gamified experiences that are welcoming and accommodating to a broad audience, enriching the overall user experience.

4.3.10 Testing and Iteration

Continuous testing and iteration are essential components of the design process, allowing designers to refine and optimize the gamified experience based on user feedback and data insights. Conducting usability tests, analyzing user behavior metrics, and soliciting feedback through surveys or focus groups enables designers to identify areas for improvement and implement changes iteratively. By embracing a user-centric approach, designers can create gamified experiences that resonate with their audience and deliver meaningful outcomes.

CHAPTER 5

GAMIFICATION IN DIFFERENT EDUCATIONAL SETTINGS

5.1 GAMEFICATION IN K-12 EDUCATION

In recent years, gamification has emerged as a powerful tool to enhance engagement and learning outcomes in K-12 education. By integrating game elements and mechanics into the classroom environment, educators can create dynamic and interactive experiences that motivate students and foster deeper learning.

Gamification has the potential to revolutionize K-12 education by enhancing engagement, motivation, and learning outcomes for students. By leveraging game elements and mechanics, educators can create dynamic and interactive learning experiences that captivate students' interest and foster deeper understanding and mastery of academic concepts. Despite challenges such as integration with curriculum standards, accessibility, and resistance to change, gamification offers tremendous opportunities to transform traditional educational practices and cultivate a new generation of empowered, self-directed learners. Through thoughtful design, implementation, and ongoing iteration, gamified experiences can become integral components of the modern K-12 classroom, enriching the educational journey and preparing students for success in an ever-evolving world.

5.1.1 Understanding K-12 Education

K–12, from kindergarten to 12th grade, is an English language expression that indicates the range of years of publicly supported primary and secondary education found in the United States and Canada, which is similar to publicly supported school grades before tertiary education in several other countries, such as Afghanistan, Australia, Canada, China, Ecuador, Egypt, India, Iran, the Philippines, South Korea, and Turkey. K–12 refers to the American system which affords authority to local intersectional "districts" which may be specific to a municipality, county, or several regions, depending on population and proximity.

History

U.S. public education was conceived of in the late 18th century. In 1790, Pennsylvania became the first state to require some form of free education for everyone regardless of whether they could afford it. New York passed similar legislation in 1805. In 1820, Massachusetts became the first state to create a tuition-free high school, Boston English. The first K–12 public school systems appeared in the early 19th century. In the 1830s and 1840s, Ohioans were taking a significant interest in the idea of public education. At that point in time, schools were commonly operated independently of each other, with little attempt at uniformity. The Akron School Law of 1847 changed this. The city of Akron unified the operations, curriculum and funding of local schools into a single public school district:

- "Under the Akron School Law, there was to be one school district encompassing the entire city. Within that district would be a number of elementary schools, with students divided into separate "grades" based on achievement. When enough demand existed, the school board would establish a high school as well. Property taxes would pay for the new school system. A school board, elected by the community, would make decisions about the system's management and hire the necessary professionals to run each school. Illustrating the racism that existed in Ohio during this era, the Akron School Law excluded African-American children from the public school system."

In 1849, the state of Ohio enacted a law modeled after the Akron law which extended the idea of school districts to cover the rest of the state.

By 1930, all 48 states had passed laws making education compulsory, and in 1965, President Lyndon B. Johnson signed the Elementary and Secondary Education Act (ESEA), which committed the federal government to significant ongoing expenditures to each state for the purpose of sustaining local K–12 school systems. The ESEA essentially made K–12 education the law of the land.

Since its inception, public K–12 has been debated and subject to several waves of reform throughout the 20th and 21st centuries. In the 1980s, Reagan's 'A Nation at Risk' initiative included provisions requiring public education to be evaluated based on standards, and teacher pay to be based on evaluations. In the 1990s, the Goals 2000 Act and the "Improving America's Schools" act provided additional federal funding to states to bolster local K–12 systems. This was followed in the 2000s by a rigorous uptick in standards-based evaluations with the No Child Left Behind Act, and the Race to the Top Act. In 2015, President Barack Obama signed the Every Student Succeeds Act (ESSA), which returned some power to state governments with respect to evaluations and standards.

Usage

The term is often used as a kind of shorthand to collectively refer to the entirety of primary and secondary education, as it is much easier than having to say one is referring in the aggregate to elementary, middle, and high school education. However, it is rare for a school district to actually teach all K–12 grades at one unified school campus. Even the smallest school districts try to maintain, at a minimum, a two-tier distinction between an elementary school (K–8) and a high school (9–12). Unified K–12 schools are common, however, in rural and remote areas throughout Canada. The term is often used in school website URLs, generally appearing before the country code top-level domain (or in the United States, the state top-level domain). The terms "PK–12", "PreK–12", or "Pre-K–12" are sometimes used to add pre-kindergarten. It is also used by American multinationals selling into the educational sector, such as Dell where UK customers are presented with this as a market segment choice.

P–12

In Australia, P–12 is sometimes used in place of K–12, particularly in Queensland, where it is used as an official term in the curriculum framework. P–12 schools serve children for the thirteen years from prep until Year 12, without including the separate kindergarten component. In Canada (Nova Scotia) P–12 is used commonly in place of K–12 and serves students from grade Primary through 12.

K–14, K–16, K–18 and K–20

K–14 education also includes community colleges (the first two years of university). K–16 education adds a four-year undergraduate university degree. For simplicity purposes education shorthand was created to denote specific education levels of achievement. This shorthand is commonly used in articles, publications and educational legislation. The following list contains the most commonly found shorthand descriptors:

- **P–14:** Pre-school to associate degree
- **P–16:** Pre-school to bachelor's degree
- **P–18:** Pre-school to master's degree
- **P–20:** Pre-school to graduate degree
- **K–14:** Kindergarten to associate degree
- **K–16:** Kindergarten to bachelor's degree
- **K–18:** Kindergarten to master's degree
- **K–20:** Kindergarten to graduate degree

The Career Technical Education (CTE) Unit of the California Community College Economic Development and Workforce Preparation Division focuses on program coordination and advocacy, policy development and coordination with K–18 workforce preparation and career and technical education systems.

The ASCCC Chancellor's Office Career Technical Education (CTE) Unit of the Economic Development and Workforce Preparation Division focuses on program coordination and advocacy, policy development and coordination with K–18 workforce preparation and career and technical education systems. Responsible for the implementation of the Vocational and Technical Education Act (VTEA), managing and coordinating activities that impact other interagency and intra-agency objectives. In addition, the CTE Unit is also responsible for the development, dissemination, and implementation of the California State Plan and the annual performance reports.

Further reference to K–18 education can be found in this publication by Ann Diver-Stamnes and Linda Catelli in chapter 4 "College/University Partnership Projects for Instituting Change and Improvement in K–18 Education".

5.1.2 Gamification in K-12 Education

Gamification in education involves the use of game elements, such as points, badges, leaderboards, and quests, to motivate students and facilitate learning. By tapping into students' intrinsic motivation to play and compete, gamified experiences can increase engagement, encourage active participation, and promote mastery of academic concepts. Moreover, gamification provides opportunities for personalized learning experiences tailored to individual student needs and preferences.

5.1.3 Benefits of Gamification in K-12 Education

- **Increased Engagement:** Gamified experiences capture students' interest and attention, making learning more enjoyable and stimulating. By incorporating elements of challenge, competition, and reward, educators can create an immersive learning environment that motivates students to actively participate and persevere through academic tasks.
- **Improved Learning Outcomes:** Gamification encourages active learning and problem-solving, leading to deeper understanding and retention of academic content. By presenting concepts in a contextualized and interactive manner, students are better able to apply their knowledge and skills to real-world situations, enhancing their overall academic performance.
- **Personalized Learning Experiences:** Gamification allows for customization and adaptation to meet the diverse needs and learning styles of individual students. By offering branching pathways, adaptive challenges, and differentiated feedback, educators can provide tailored learning experiences that address students' strengths, weaknesses, and interests.
- **Fostering Collaboration and Social Interaction:** Gamified experiences promote collaboration and teamwork among students, fostering a sense

of community and peer support. By incorporating cooperative tasks, multiplayer games, and interactive challenges, educators can create opportunities for students to collaborate, communicate, and problem-solve together, enhancing social skills and interpersonal relationships.

- **Encouraging Growth Mindset and Resilience:** Gamification encourages a growth mindset by framing challenges as opportunities for learning and improvement. By rewarding effort, persistence, and incremental progress, educators can instill resilience and self-efficacy in students, empowering them to overcome obstacles and persevere through academic challenges.

5.1.4 Challenges of Implementing Gamification in K-12 Education

- **Integration with Curriculum:** One of the challenges of implementing gamification in K-12 education is ensuring alignment with curriculum standards and learning objectives. Educators must carefully design gamified experiences that complement existing instructional materials and support academic goals, rather than detracting from core content areas.
- **Resistance to Change:** Implementing gamification in K-12 education may face resistance from stakeholders, including administrators, parents, and traditional educators. Educators must effectively communicate the benefits of gamification and address concerns about its perceived novelty or lack of rigor, demonstrating how gamified experiences can enhance engagement, motivation, and learning outcomes for students.

5.1.5 Best Practices for Implementing Gamification in K-12 Education

- **Collaborate with Stakeholders:** Engage administrators, parents, and fellow educators in the design and implementation of gamified experiences, fostering buy-in and support for innovative teaching practices.

5.2 GAMIFICATION IN HIGHER EDUCATION

Gamification has emerged as a promising approach to enhance engagement and learning outcomes in higher education. By integrating game elements and mechanics into the learning environment, educators can create dynamic and interactive experiences that motivate students and promote deeper understanding and mastery of academic concepts.

Gamification holds tremendous potential to transform higher education by enhancing engagement, motivation, and learning outcomes for students. By leveraging game elements and mechanics, educators can create dynamic and interactive learning experiences that captivate students' interest and foster deeper understanding and mastery of academic concepts. Despite challenges such as integration with curriculum standards, accessibility, and resistance to change, gamification offers a compelling approach to address the evolving needs and preferences of today's learners. Through thoughtful design, implementation, and ongoing iteration, gamified experiences can become integral components of the modern higher education landscape, empowering students to become lifelong learners and successful contributors to society.

5.2.1 Understanding Higher Education

Higher education is tertiary education leading to the award of an academic degree. Higher education, which makes up a component of post-secondary, third-level, or tertiary education, is an optional final stage of formal learning that occurs after completion of secondary education. It represents levels 5, 6, 7, and 8 of the 2011 version of the International Standard Classification of Education structure. Tertiary education at a nondegree level is sometimes referred to as further education or continuing education as distinct from higher education.

The Right of Access to Higher Education

The right of access to higher education is mentioned in a number of international human rights instruments. The UN International Covenant on Economic, Social and Cultural Rights of 1966 declares, in Article 13, that "higher education shall be made equally accessible to all, on the basis of capacity, by every appropriate means, and in particular by the progressive introduction of free education". In Europe, Article 2 of the First Protocol to the European Convention on Human Rights, adopted in 1950, obliges all signatory parties to guarantee the right to education.

Definition

Higher education, also called post-secondary education, third-level or tertiary education, is an optional final stage of formal learning that occurs after completion of secondary education. This consists of universities, colleges and polytechnics that offer formal degrees beyond high school or secondary school education.

The International Standard Classification of Education in 1997 initially classified all tertiary education together in the 1997 version of its schema. They were referred to as level 5 and doctoral studies at level 6. In 2011, this was refined and expanded in the 2011 version of the structure. Higher education at undergraduate level, masters and doctoral level became levels 6, 7, and 8. Nondegree level tertiary education, sometimes referred to as further education or continuing education was reordered as level 4, with level 5 for some higher courses.

In the days when few pupils progressed beyond primary education or basic education, the term "higher education" was often used to refer to secondary education, which can create some confusion. This is the origin of the term *high school* for various schools for children between the ages of 14 and 18 (United States) or 11 and 18 (United Kingdom and Australia).

Providers

In the U.S., higher education is provided by universities, academies, colleges, seminaries, conservatories, and institutes of technology, and certain college-level institutions, including vocational schools, universities of applied sciences, trade schools, and other career-based colleges that award degrees. Tertiary education at a nondegree level is sometimes referred to as further education or continuing education as distinct from higher education.

Higher education includes teaching, research, exacting applied work, as exists in medical schools and dental schools, and social services activities of universities.

Within the realm of teaching, it includes both the *undergraduate* level, and beyond that, *graduate-level* (or *postgraduate* level). The latter level of education is often referred to as graduate school, especially in North America. In addition to the skills that are specific to any particular degree, potential employers in any profession are looking for evidence of critical thinking and analytical reasoning skills, teamworking skills, information literacy, ethical judgment, decision-making skills, fluency in speaking and writing, problem solving skills, and a wide knowledge of liberal arts and sciences.

History

The oldest known institutions of higher education are credited to Dynastic Egypt, with Pr-Anx (houses of life) built as libraries and scriptoriums, containing works on law, architecture, mathematics, and medicine, and involved in the training of "swnw" and "swnwt" (male and female doctors); extant Egyptian papyri from the 3rd millennia BC are in several collections.

In the Greek world, Plato's Academy (c.387 - 86 BC), Aristotle's Lyceum (c.334 - 86 BC) and other philosophical-mathematical schools became models for other establishments, particularly in Alexandria of Egypt, under the Ptolemies.

In South Asia, the city of Taxila, later the great Buddhist monastery of Nalanda (c.427 - 1197 CE), attracted students and professors even from distant regions.

In China, the Han dynasty established chairs to teach the Five Confucean Classics, in the Grand School, Taixue (c.3 - 1905 CE), to train cadres for the imperial administration. All these higher-learning institutions became models for other schools within their sphere of cultural influence.

In 425 CE, the Byzantine emperor Theodosius II innovated as he established the Pandidakterion, with a faculty of 31 professors, to train public servants. In the 7th and 8th centuries, "cathedral schools" were created in Western Europe.

Meanwhile, the first Medresahs were founded in the Moslem empire – initially mere primary schools in the premises of major mosques, which gradually evolved toward secondary, later higher education. However high the intellectual level of these schools could be, it would be anachronistic to call them "universities". Their organization and purposes were markedly different from the corporations of students and teachers, independent from both the Church and the State, which established themselves from the 12th century in Western Europe as *Universitas Studiorum*.

According to UNESCO and *Guinness World Records*, the University of al-Qarawiyyin in Fez, Morocco is the oldest existing continually operating higher educational institution in the world. and is occasionally referred to as the oldest university by scholars. Undoubtedly, there are older institutions of higher education, for example, the University of Ez-Zitouna in Montfleury, Tunis, was first established in 737.

The University of Bologna, Italy, founded in 1088, is the world's oldest university in continuous operation, and the first university in the sense of a higher-learning and degree-awarding institute, as the word *universitas* was coined at its foundation.

20th Century

Since World War II, developed and many developing countries have increased the participation of the age group who mostly studies higher education from the elite rate, of up to 15 per cent, to the mass rate of 16 to 50 per cent. In many developed countries, participation in higher education has continued to increase towards universal or, what Trow later called, open access, where over half of the relevant age group participate in higher education.

Higher education is important to national economies, both as an industry, in its own right, and as a source of trained and educated personnel for the rest of the economy. College educated workers have commanded a measurable wage premium and are much less likely to become unemployed than less educated workers.

21st Century

In recent years, universities have been criticized for permitting or actively encouraging grade inflation. Also, the supply of graduates in many fields of study is exceeding the demand for their skills, aggravating graduate unemployment, underemployment, overqualification and educational inflation.

Some commentators have suggested that the impact of the COVID-19 pandemic on education is rapidly making certain aspects of the traditional higher education system obsolete. The involvement and funding by foreign regimes in higher education in the US and Europe raised concerns regarding the erosion of democratic norms and hate speech on campuses.

Statistics

A 2014 report by the Organisation for Economic Co-operation and Development states that by 2014, 84 percent of young people were completing upper secondary education over their lifetimes, in high-income countries. Tertiary-educated individuals were earning twice as much as median workers. In contrast to historical trends in education, young women were more likely to complete upper secondary education than young men. Additionally, access to education was expanding and growth in the number of people receiving university education was rising sharply. By 2014, close to 40 percent of people aged 25–34 (and around 25 percent of those aged 55–64), were being educated at university.

5.2.2 Gamification in Higher Education

Gamification in higher education involves the use of game elements, such as points, badges, leaderboards, and quests, to motivate students and facilitate learning. By tapping into students' intrinsic motivation to play and compete, gamified experiences can increase engagement, encourage active participation, and foster a sense of achievement and progress. Moreover, gamification provides opportunities for personalized learning experiences tailored to individual student needs and preferences, promoting autonomy and self-directed learning.

5.2.3 Benefits of Gamification in Higher Education

- **Increased Engagement:** Gamified experiences capture students' interest and attention, making learning more enjoyable and stimulating. By incorporating elements of challenge, competition, and reward, educators can create an immersive learning environment that motivates students to actively participate and invest in their academic pursuits.
- **Enhanced Learning Outcomes:** Gamification encourages active learning and problem-solving, leading to deeper understanding and retention of academic content. By presenting concepts in a contextualized and interactive manner, students are better able to apply their knowledge and skills to real-world situations, preparing them for success in their future careers.
- **Personalized Learning Experiences:** Gamification allows for customization and adaptation to meet the diverse needs and learning styles of individual students. By offering branching pathways, adaptive challenges, and differentiated feedback, educators can provide tailored learning experiences that address students' strengths, weaknesses, and interests, fostering autonomy and self-directed learning.

- **Promotion of Collaboration and Social Interaction:** Gamified experiences promote collaboration and teamwork among students, fostering a sense of community and peer support. By incorporating cooperative tasks, multiplayer games, and interactive challenges, educators can create opportunities for students to collaborate, communicate, and problem-solve together, enhancing social skills and interpersonal relationships.
- **Development of Critical Thinking and Problem-Solving Skills:** Gamification encourages students to think critically and analytically, as they strategize and navigate through challenges and obstacles. By presenting complex problems and scenarios within a game-based context, students develop problem-solving skills, creativity, and resilience, preparing them to tackle real-world challenges in their academic and professional lives.

5.2.4 Challenges of Implementing Gamification in Higher Education

- **Integration with Curriculum:** One of the challenges of implementing gamification in higher education is ensuring alignment with curriculum standards and learning objectives. Educators must carefully design gamified experiences that complement existing instructional materials and support academic goals, rather than detracting from core content areas.
- **Accessibility and Equity:** Ensuring equitable access to gamified experiences can be challenging, particularly for students with limited access to technology or internet connectivity. Educators must consider the diverse needs and backgrounds of students, providing alternative options and accommodations to ensure that all students can participate and benefit from gamified learning activities.
- **Sustainability and Maintenance:** Developing and maintaining gamified experiences requires ongoing investment of time, resources, and expertise. Educators must be prepared to continually update and iterate on gamified elements based on student feedback and performance data, ensuring that the experience remains engaging and effective over time.
- **Assessment and Accountability:** Assessing student learning and performance within gamified environments presents unique challenges. Educators must devise appropriate methods for evaluating student progress and mastery of academic concepts, balancing formative and summative assessment strategies to provide meaningful feedback and measure learning outcomes accurately.

- **Resistance to Change:** Implementing gamification in higher education may face resistance from stakeholders, including administrators, faculty members, and students. Educators must effectively communicate the benefits of gamification and address concerns about its perceived novelty or lack of rigor, demonstrating how gamified experiences can enhance engagement, motivation, and learning outcomes for students.

5.2.5 Best Practices for Implementing Gamification in Higher Education

- **Set Clear Learning Objectives:** Define clear learning objectives and align gamified experiences with curriculum standards and academic goals to ensure relevance and effectiveness.
- **Design Engaging Game Mechanics:** Incorporate a variety of game mechanics, such as points, badges, quests, and leaderboards, to create a dynamic and immersive learning environment that motivates students and fosters active participation.
- **Provide Feedback and Progress Tracking:** Implement feedback loops and progress tracking mechanisms to provide students with timely feedback on their performance and progress, reinforcing desired behaviors and guiding their learning journey.
- **Promote Collaboration and Social Interaction:** Integrate cooperative tasks, multiplayer games, and interactive challenges to promote collaboration, teamwork, and peer support among students, fostering a sense of community and belonging.
- **Offer Choice and Autonomy:** Provide students with opportunities for choice and autonomy within gamified experiences, allowing them to personalize their learning journey and pursue areas of interest or challenge at their own pace.
- **Incorporate Real-World Relevance:** Contextualize academic concepts within real-world scenarios and applications to increase student engagement and demonstrate the practical relevance of their learning.
- **Foster Reflection and Metacognition:** Encourage students to reflect on their learning experiences and metacognitive processes, helping them develop self-awareness, self-regulation, and a growth mindset towards learning.
- **Collaborate with Stakeholders:** Engage administrators, faculty members, and students in the design and implementation of gamified experiences, fostering buy-in and support for innovative teaching practices.

5.3 CORPORATE TRAINING AND GAMIFIELD LEARNING

In the ever-evolving landscape of corporate training, organizations are constantly seeking innovative approaches to engage employees and enhance learning outcomes. Gamified learning has emerged as a powerful tool to transform traditional training programs into dynamic and interactive experiences. By integrating game elements and mechanics into corporate training, organizations can increase engagement, motivation, and knowledge retention among employees.

Gamified learning offers organizations a compelling approach to transform traditional corporate training programs into dynamic and interactive experiences that engage employees and drive learning outcomes. By leveraging game elements and mechanics, organizations can create immersive learning environments that motivate employees to actively participate and invest in their professional development. Despite challenges such as alignment with training objectives, technology infrastructure, and resistance to change, gamified learning offers tremendous opportunities to enhance employee engagement, promote collaboration, and develop essential skills and competencies. Through thoughtful design, implementation, and ongoing iteration, gamified learning can become an integral component of corporate training initiatives, empowering employees to thrive in an ever-evolving workplace landscape.

5.3.1 Understanding Corporate Training

Training is teaching, or developing in oneself or others, any skills and knowledge or fitness that relate to specific useful competencies. Training has specific goals of improving one's capability, capacity, productivity and performance. It forms the core of apprenticeships and provides the backbone of content at institutes of technology (also known as technical colleges or polytechnics). In addition to the basic training required for a trade, occupation or profession, training may continue beyond initial competence to maintain, upgrade and update skills throughout working life. People within some professions and occupations may refer to this sort of training as professional development. Training also refers to the development of physical fitness related to a specific competence, such as sport, martial arts, military applications and some other occupations.

Corporate Education

Corporate education refers to a system of professional development activities provided to educate employees. It may consist of formal university or college training or informal training provided by non-collegiate institutions. The simplest form of corporate education may be training programs designed "in-house" for an organization that may wish to train their employees on specific aspects of their job processes or responsibilities. More formal relationships may further exist where corporate training is provided to employees through contracts or relationships with educational institutions who may award credit, either at the institution or through a system of CEUs (Continuing Education Units).

Many institutions or trainers offering corporate education will provide certificates or diplomas verifying the attendance of the employee. Some employers use corporate and continuing education as part of a holistic human resources effort to determine the performance of the employee and as part of their review systems.

Increasingly organisations appear to be using corporate education and training as an incentive to retain managers and key employees within their organisation. This win-win arrangement creates better educated managers for the organisation and provides the employees with a more marketable portfolio of skills and, in many cases, recognised qualifications.

The Difference between Corporate Education and Corporate Training

Most organisations tend to think of corporate education as corporate training. Corporate training programs are often competency based and related to the essential training employees need to operate certain equipment or perform certain tasks in a competent, safe and effective manner. The outcome of a corporate training program is a participant who is either able to operate a piece of equipment or perform a specific task in an effective manner according to pre-determined training criteria.

The primary role of corporate training is to ensure an employee has the knowledge and skills to undertake a specific operation to enable an organisation can continue to operate. Fundamentally, corporate training is centred on knowledge transfer, with an instructor teaching or demonstrating a particular function and the student learning and demonstrating they can apply what they have learnt to a particular operation.

Corporate education, however, adds another dimension and depth to training by involving learners as participants in generating new knowledge that assists an organisation to develop and evolve, rather than maintain the status quo. Corporate education focuses on developing the capability of an organisation to be able to do things and, in particular, the right things in order to be a sustainable and successful organisation.

Corporate education involves a facilitator, rather than an instructor or trainer, to engage participants and encourage them to think about the what, how and why of what they are doing and to challenge their current paradigms. Corporate education is centred on introducing learning techniques to stimulate employees to think about what their organisation does, where it is heading, potential new opportunities for the organisation and new and better ways of doing things.

While the role of corporate training is to develop the operational competency of individuals, the purpose of corporate education is to promote the development of capability of both an individual and their organisation.

Increasingly organisations appear to be using corporate education as an incentive to retain managers and key employees within their organisation. This win-win arrangement creates better educated managers and employees for the organisation and gives individual employees a more marketable portfolio of skills and, in many cases, recognised qualifications.

Training and Development

Training and development involve improving the effectiveness of organizations and the individuals and teams within them. Training may be viewed as related to immediate changes in organizational effectiveness via organized instruction, while development is related to the progress of longer-term organizational and employee goals. While training and development technically have differing definitions, the two are oftentimes used interchangeably and/or together. Training and development have historically been topics within adult education and applied psychology but have within the last two decades become closely associated with human resources management, talent management, human resources development, instructional design, human factors, and knowledge management.

History

Aspects of training and development have been linked to ancient civilizations around the globe. Early training-related articles appeared in journals marketed to enslavers in the antebellum south and training approaches and philosophies were discussed extensively by Booker T. Washington. Early academic was publishing related to training included a 1918 article in the Journal of Applied Psychology. This article explored an undergraduate curriculum designed for applied psychologists. Training was also discussed in first handbook on adult education in 1934. World War II influenced the focus of applied psychology research to be on effectiveness of training programs, particularly in military contexts. By the 1960s and 70s, the field began developing theories and conducting theory-based research because up until that point, the field had been rooted in trial-and-error intervention research. This era also brought along the development of new training methods such as the use of computers, television, case studies, and role playing. The scope of training and development also expanded to include cross-cultural training, focus on the development of the individual employee, and the use of new organization development literature to frame training programs. The 1980s marked a shift to focus on how employees were receiving and implementing training programs, and encouraged the collection of data for evaluation purposes, particularly management training programs. The development piece of training and development became increasingly popular in the 1980s and 90s, with employees more frequently being influenced by the concept of "lifelong learning". It was in this decade that research revealing the impact and importance of fostering a training and development-positive culture (including management and co-worker) was first conducted. The turn of the century brought more research in topics such as team-training, for example cross-training. Cross-training emphasizes training in coworkers' responsibilities.

Skills training has taken on varying organizational forms across industrialized economies. Germany has an elaborate vocational training system whereas the United States and the United Kingdom have weak vocational training system.

Training Practice and Methods

Training and development encompasses three main activities: training, education, and development. The "stakeholders" in training and development are categorized into several classes. The sponsors of training and development are senior managers. The clients of training and development are business planners. Line managers are responsible for coaching, resources, and performance. The participants are those who actually undergo the processes. The facilitators are human resource management staff. And the providers are specialists in the field. Each of these groups has its own agenda and motivations, which sometimes conflict with the agendas and motivations of the others.

Especially in the last couple decades, training has become more trainee-focused, which allows those being trained more flexibility and active learning opportunities. For example, these active learning techniques include exploratory/discovery learning, error management training, guided exploration, and mastery training. Typical projects in the field include executive and supervisory/management development, new-employee orientation, professional-skills training, technical/job training, customer-service training, sales-and-marketing training, and health-and-safety training. Training is particularly critical in high-reliability organizations, which rely on high safety standards to prevent catastrophic damage to employees, equipment, or the environment (e.g. nuclear power plants, operating rooms).

It is important to note that all employees require different levels and types of development in order to fulfill their job roles in the organization. All employees need some type(s) of training and development on an ongoing basis to maintain effective performance, adjust to new ways or work, and remain motivated and engaged. The instructional systems design approach (often referred to as ADDIE model) is great for designing effective learning programs and used for instructional design. Instructional design is the process of designing, developing and delivering learning content. There are 5 phases in the ADDIE model: (1) needs assessment, (2) program design, (3) program development, (4) training delivery or implementation, and (5) evaluation of training.

- **Analyze:** Problem identification, (TNA) training needs analysis, target audience determined, stakeholder's needs identified, identify the resources required.
- **Design:** Learning intervention/implementation outline and mapped, mapping evaluation methods.
- **Development:** Determine delivery method, production of learning product that is in line with design, determine instructional strategies/ media/methods, quality evaluation of the learning product, development of communication strategy, development of required technology, development and evaluation of assessments and evaluation tools.
- **Implement:** Participation in side-programs, training delivery, learning participation, implementation of a communication plan, evaluation of business, execution of formal evaluations.
- **Evaluation:** Formal evaluation, continuous learning evaluation, evaluation of business, potential points of improvement.

Many different training methods exist today, including both on and off-the-job methods. On-the-job training methods happen within the organization where employees learn by working alongside co-workers in ways such as coaching, mentorship, internship, apprenticeship, job rotation, job instructional technique (JIT), or by being an understudy. To contrast, off-the-job training methods happen outside the organization where employees attend things such as lectures, seminars, and conferences or they take part in simulation exercises like case studies and role-playing. It could also include vestibule, sensitivity or transactional training activities. Other training methods include:

- **Apprenticeship Training:** System of training in which a worker entering the skilled trades is given thorough instruction and experience, both on and off the job, in the practical and theoretical aspects of the work.
- **Co-operative Programs and Internship Programs:** Training programs that combine practical, on-the-job experience with formal education. Typically these programs are offered at colleges and universities.
- **Classroom Instruction:** Information can be presented in lectures, demonstrations, films, and videotapes or through computer instruction.

(This includes vestibule training where trainees are instructed in the operation of equipment.)

- **Self-Directed Learning:** Individuals work at their own pace during programmed instruction. Including books, manuals, or computers to break down subject-matter content into highly organized, logical sequences that demand a continuous response on the trainee's part.
- **Audiovisual:** Methods used to teach the skills and procedures required for a number of jobs.
- **Simulation:** Used when it is not practical or safe to train people on the actual equipment or within the actual work environment.
- **E-learning:** Training that uses computer and/or online resources. Such as CBT (computer-based training), videotapes, satellites and broadcast interactive TV/DVD/CD-ROM.

The benefits of training employees are increased productivity and performance in the workplace, uniformity of work processes, reduced supervision and reduced wastage, promoting employees from within, improving organizational structure and designs, boosting morale, better knowledge of policies and organization's goals, improved customer valuation and improved/updated technology. There is significant importance in training as it prepares employees for higher job responsibilities, shows employees they are valued, improves IT and computer processes, and tests the efficiency of new performance management systems. However, some believe training wastes time and money because, in certain cases, real life experience may trump education, and organizations want to spend less, not more.

Principles

When a company puts its employees through training programs, it must ensure that they are efficient and relevant to the employees' tasks in the organization as it is estimated that only 20-30% of training given to employees are used in the month later. To help mitigate this issue, some general principles should be followed to increase employees desire to take part in the program. These include:

- **Self-efficacy:** This means increasing the learners belief that they can fully comprehend the teachings.
- **Attitude:** An uncooperative attitude towards learning could hinder the individual's capability to grasp the knowledge being provided.
- **Competence:** This is the skill an individual develops that enables them to make good decisions efficiently.
- **External Motivators:** These are the behaviours individuals present when a reward or extrinsic goal is given to them.

Motivation is an internal process that leads to an employee's behaviour and willingness to achieve organizational goals. Creating a motivational environment within an organization can help ensure employees achieve their highest level of productivity. Motivation can create an engaged workforce that enhances individual and organizational performance. The model for motivation is represented at the most basic level by motivators separated into two different categories:

- **Intrinsic Factors:** These represent the internal factors to an individual, such as the difficulty of the work, achievement recognition, responsibility, opportunity for meaningful work, involvement in decision making, and importance within the organization.
- **Extrinsic Factors:** These are external factors to the individual, such as job security, salary, benefits, work conditions, and vacations.

Both intrinsic and extrinsic motivators link to employee performance in the workplace. A company's techniques to motivate employees are continually changing and evolving. Finding out what motivates employees can help businesses determine why people work in specific ways and perform at varying levels.

There are many basic training and development principles in human resource management. For instance, performance feedback is important as managers can use it to identify the employee's lack of skills in areas of the job and their approach to improving that weakness while maintaining behaviour.

Traditional constructive feedback, also known as weakness-based feedback, can often be viewed as malicious from the employees' perspective. When interpreted negatively, employees lose motivation on the job, affecting their production level. The other kind of feedback that is more effective is known as strengths-based feedback. This feedback is more effective because it is easier to adjust the performance once the individual can separate flaws from strengths. The strengths-based feedback is positive feedback that allows the employees to recognize their strengths and further improve their performance with that knowledge. Using this strategy as a base for constructive feedback shows support and encouragement towards the employee, which boosts their confidence. Confidence in the workplace allows individuals to stay focused and engaged. However, the disadvantage of strengths-based feedback is failing to perform at one's full potential due to overconfidence.

Reinforcement is another critical principle of employee training and development. By positively reinforcing employees with encouragement or reward, managers can establish a desired pattern of behaviour. Studies have shown that reinforcement directly influences employee learning, which is highly correlated with performance after training. Reinforcement based training emphasizes the importance of communication between managers and trainees in the workplace. The more the training environment can be a positive, nurturing experience, the more—and faster—attendees are apt to learn.

Another essential aspect of reinforcement-based training is to discuss what has been taught in a training session and how employees can apply what they have learned to the job. This can be done by conducting pre and post-training brainstorming sessions.

Overall, managers play a significant role in reinforcing learning by systematically looking for ways to notice and thank the employee when they use the skills and knowledge from the training session. By positively reinforcing employees like this, they will become more comfortable in the workplace and more confident in their abilities, which ultimately positively affects their future performance.

Benefits

Training has been used in organizations for the past several decades. Although training and development requires investments of many types, there are cited benefits to integrating training and development into organizations:

- Increased productivity and job performance
- Skills development
- Team development
- Decreasing safety-related accidents

However, if the training and development is not strategic and pointed at specific goals, it can lead to more harm than good. Needs assessments, especially when the training is being conducted on a large-scale, are frequently conducted in order to gauge what needs to be trained, how it should be trained, and how extensively. Needs assessments in the training and development context often reveal employee and management-specific skills to develop (e.g. for new employees), organizational-wide problems to address (e.g. performance issues), adaptations needed to suit changing environments (e.g. new technology), or employee development needs (e.g. career planning). The needs assessment can predict the degree of effectiveness of training and development programs and how closely the needs were met, the execution of the training (i.e. how effective the trainer was), and trainee characteristics (e.g. motivation, cognitive abilities). Effectiveness of training is typically done on an individual or team-level, with few studies investigating the impacts on organizations.

Occupation

The Occupational Information Network (O*NET) cites Training and Development Specialists as having a bright outlook, meaning that the occupation will grow rapidly or have several job openings in the next few years. Related professions include training and development managers, (chief) learning officers, industrial-organizational psychologists, and organization development consultants. Training and development specialists are equipped with the tools to conduct needs analyses, build training programs to suit the organization's needs by using various training techniques, create training materials, and execute and guide training programs.

On-the-Job Training

On-the-job training (widely known as OJT) is an important topic of human resource management. It helps develop the career of the individual and the prosperous growth of the organization. On-the-job training is a form of training provided at the workplace. During the training, employees are familiarized with the working environment they will become part of. Employees also get a hands-on experience using machinery, equipment, tools, materials, etc. Part of on-the-job training is to face the challenges that occur during the performance of the job. An experienced employee or a manager are executing the role of the mentor who through written, or verbal instructions and demonstrations are passing on his/her knowledge and company-specific skills to the new employee. Executing the training on at the job location, rather than the classroom, creates a stress-free environment for the employees. On-the-job training is the most popular method of training not only in the United States but in most of the developed countries, such as the United Kingdom, Canada, Australia, etc. Its effectiveness is based on the use of existing workplace tools, machines, documents and equipment, and the knowledge of specialists who are working in this field. On-the-job training is easy to arrange and manage and it simplifies the process of adapting to the new workplace. On-the-job training is highly used for practical tasks. It is inexpensive, and it doesn't require special equipment that is normally used for a specific job. Upon satisfaction of completion of the training, the employer is expected to retain participants as regular employees.

History

On-the-job training is one of the earliest forms of training in the world, with masters taking on young apprentices and introducing them to their work, educating them on the techniques necessary for them to become masters themselves. The on-the-job training method dates from times as early as 2400 B.C when masons would instruct their apprentices on construction methods since not everyone was literate and it was the most convenient way to understand the requirements needed for the new job, on a one-to-one basis. In antiquity, the work performed by most people did not rely on abstract thinking or academic education. Parents or community members, who knew the skills necessary for survival, passed their knowledge on to the children through direct instruction. This method is still widely used today.

It is a frequently used because it requires only a person who knows how to do the task and use the tools to complete the task. Over the years, as society grew, on-the-job training has become less popular. Many companies have switched to doing simulation training and using training guides. Businesses now prefer to hire employees who are already experienced and have a required skill set. However, there are still many companies who feel that on-the-job training is best for their employees.

While some companies do not see on-the-job training as an essential aspect of the workforce, Gary Becker, an economic scientist during 1962, referred to on-the-job training as an investment similar to conventional schooling. On-the-job training was deemed an investment like school because while they differ in effects on earnings, both improve people's physical and mental abilities and raise real income prospects. Whether that is the ability to gain a job or improve one's skills to become a more vital part of the workforce. Additionally, one of the earlier forms of on-the-job training can be traced back to the middle ages dating as early as the 5th to 15th century. During this time, apprenticeship was a system by which "men and women in pre-industrialized societies acquired skills necessary to become a specialized artisan". Apprenticeship contracts usually lasted six years. Young girls at the age of 12 and young boys at the age of 14 would work, alongside getting the needed training and hands-on experience to become an artisan themselves.

Psychology

The concept of observational learning was introduced by Albert Bandura, whose social cognitive theory Bandura believes that people learn best by observing others. According to his theory, people must pay attention to those around them first, retain what they have observed, and try to reproduce it. Bandura's theory is implemented in the aspect of on-the-job training, where the new employees observe first their trainer completing the tasks, before trying to perform the task themselves. After observing for some time, typically, they will imitate the action they had observed. This is exactly how on-the-job training is expected to occur, if necessary until the new employee is can perform the task on their own.

Albert Bandura's Social Cognitive Theory "is a psychological perspective on human functioning that emphasizes the critical role played by the social environment on motivation, learning, and self-regulation". Bandura's earlier Social Learning Theory placed great emphasis on the importance of observational or vicarious learning. Bandura proposed that for observational learning to occur, individuals must follow a model, retain what the model did, recreate the modelled behaviour, and have the motivation to do so. Motivation is an essential aspect of this theory; Bandura suggested that "motivation comprises internal processes that manifest themselves overtly in goal-directed action". This suggests that for a modelled action to be retained by an individual, there must be some motivation, such as the motivation to complete goals in the workplace.

On-the-Job vs. Off-the-Job Training

There are two methods used for training new employees: on-the-job training and off-the-job training (training simulation). Both methods are effective; however, they are very different and require specific measures. On-the-job training refers to the training provided at the job location by an experienced supervisor or manager who is passionate about their job and will relay the information to the newly hired, whereas the off-the-job method involves giving training to the employees at a place other than the real job location, where simulations, videos, and tests are replacing the human interaction. Off-the-job training is usually executed by an outsourced vendor outside of the company.

On-the-job training is when employees observe the processes and procedures that their employer uses to create an efficient and effective workplace. Whether that is learning how to operate specialized machinery and equipment or observing methods that facilitate the employee to perform specific jobs. Usually, this is done by shadowing an experienced employee who can give hands-on instructions and training, which can help develop the skills and knowledge needed to carry out roles in the company effectively.

On-the-job training is a cheaper option as companies usually do not need to pay for external professional development classes, instead employees gain knowledge from within their workplace. Unlike On-the-job training, Off-the-Job training requires employees to train away from their workplace. Usually, this is in the form of classes, lectures, and sometimes role play. Off-the-job training takes more time and is most often expensive as the company is required to hire external trainers or pay for conferences and classes.

Most companies prefer on-the-job training rather than off-the-job training because it is cheaper, and the company can train their employees based on their requirements. Additionally, companies can train their employees on specific company policies while teaching them hands-on. Companies prefer hands-on learning because it helps individuals retain more information, which, as a result, would cause fewer errors.

Category	On-the-job Training	Off-the-job Training
Location	Imparted at the actual job location	At a place other than the real job location
Approach	Practical	Theoretical
Time Consumption	Less time	More Time

Learning Method	Learning by doing the task	Learning by acquiring knowledge
Effect on Production	No, because trainees produce the products during learning	Yes, because training is provided first, which is followed by a performance
Who Performs the Training	Employees, internal trainers or managers	Experts outside of the company
Cost	Inexpensive	Expensive

On-the-Job Training Plan

On-the-job is a form of investment in human capital. In order to be executed efficiently, it needs a good on-the-job training plan in place. The initial cost for the company is the time spent on training and the resources used, such as trainee time and equipment. When the training plan is well executed, the return on investment for the company is imminent and the result is an increase in productivity. On-the-job training is based on the requirements of the job description and is specific for each company. Every company is unique and requires a unique approach when it comes to creating a training program. Key elements of the training plan are measures, such as working hours, due date and evaluation. Another key element is the choice of a trainer or coach assigned to the project. In order for the plan to be effective, a knowledgeable coach, a co-worker, a training vendor or a manager with excellent leadership skills is needed to conduct the training.

Research shows that companies who invest in teaching their managers how to train new employees are more successful. They can articulate their beliefs to reinforce their ideas with employees.

Having the knowledge and the understanding of companies culture makes them a perfect example of what is required from the new employee. Using managers to train employees is an effective on-the-job training strategy because it allows them to connect the training to the actual operation that employees will conduct in their routine work.

Training employees to train coworkers is another effective strategy since they are familiar with the company's culture, strengths, and weaknesses. As well as making it easier for the new hire to get to know the team. An experienced employee is the ultimate choice for a trainer (business)

Some guidelines for developing and implementing an effective on-the-job training program include and are not limited to:

- Understanding the company's needs.
- Identifying the skills and knowledge required in an employee.
- Inclusiveness when selecting an employee for training.

- **Evaluation:** Evaluating each trainee will determine the effectiveness of the training, resulting in increased performance
- **Follow-up:** Feedback helps determine how much of the training employees are retaining and using.

Advantages

On-the-job training is beneficial for both employers and employees. For the employers, it is beneficial because it narrows down and prepares the skilled employees who are right for the company. By the end of the training process, the company's values, strategy, and goals are introduced and resulting in an employee's loyalty to the business. Employees trained in the job are an important asset for the company because they can cover more areas than just the tasks in their job description. On-the-job training creates a culture which extends past the bare minimum required by the job and allows continuing education as part of the working process. As a result, an uninterrupted production process increases the company's gains when opting out from the need of an initial investment for an off-site training. On-the-job training is cost-effective.

For employees, on-the-job training is beneficial because it allows them to learn a new skill or qualification within their field of work in a timely matter. During on-the-job training, they are engaged in the real production process instead of the simulated learning process. The new teammate is being introduced to the team and the company's values during the first step of the on-the-job training. On-the-job training leads to more opportunities to grow within the organization.

Disadvantages

On-the-job training can be a disadvantage for the company when the new employee doesn't have the required skills. This will result in more time needed for the training to be completed and will cost the company more since it takes the trainer and materials out of production for the duration of the training time. On-the-job training can often cause distraction of the regular working day which can affect productivity. If employees are not introduced to the safety features and safety precautions are not taught prior to entering the job field, there could be injuries since on-the-job training is most often used for practical tasks and working with machinery. Such an issue can cause a company a lawsuit and loss of assets. Finally, oftentimes on-the-job training is rushed and that can cause a negative effect on productivity.

5.3.2 Gamified Learning in Corporate Training

Gamified learning in corporate training involves the use of game elements, such as points, badges, leaderboards, and quests, to engage employees and facilitate learning. By tapping into employees' intrinsic motivation to play and compete, gamified experiences can transform mundane training tasks into exciting and rewarding challenges.

Moreover, gamification provides opportunities for personalized learning experiences tailored to individual employee needs and preferences, fostering autonomy and self-directed learning.

5.3.3 Benefits of Gamified Learning in Corporate Training

- **Increased Engagement:** Gamified learning captures employees' interest and attention, making training more enjoyable and stimulating. By incorporating elements of challenge, competition, and reward, organizations can create an immersive learning environment that motivates employees to actively participate and invest in their professional development.
- **Enhanced Learning Outcomes:** Gamification encourages active learning and problem-solving, leading to deeper understanding and retention of training content. By presenting concepts in a contextualized and interactive manner, employees are better able to apply their knowledge and skills to real-world situations, improving job performance and productivity.
- **Personalized Learning Experiences:** Gamification allows for customization and adaptation to meet the diverse needs and learning styles of individual employees. By offering branching pathways, adaptive challenges, and differentiated feedback, organizations can provide tailored learning experiences that address employees' strengths, weaknesses, and career aspirations, fostering a culture of continuous learning and growth.
- **Promotion of Collaboration and Team Building:** Gamified learning promotes collaboration and teamwork among employees, fostering a sense of camaraderie and peer support. By incorporating cooperative tasks, multiplayer games, and interactive challenges, organizations can create opportunities for employees to collaborate, communicate, and problem-solve together, enhancing team cohesion and morale.
- **Development of Skills and Competencies:** Gamification facilitates the development of critical skills and competencies essential for success in the workplace. By presenting employees with challenges and scenarios relevant to their roles and responsibilities, organizations can help employees develop problem-solving skills, decision-making abilities, and leadership qualities, empowering them to excel in their careers.

5.3.4 Challenges of Implementing Gamified Learning in Corporate Training

- **Integration with Training Objectives:** One of the challenges of implementing gamified learning in corporate training is ensuring alignment with training objectives and organizational goals. Organizations must carefully design gamified experiences that complement existing training programs and address specific learning outcomes, rather than detracting from core competencies or compliance requirements.
- **Technology Infrastructure and Accessibility:** Ensuring equitable access to gamified learning experiences can be challenging, particularly for employees with limited access to technology or internet connectivity. Organizations must consider the diverse needs and preferences of employees, providing alternative options and accommodations to ensure that all employees can participate and benefit from gamified training activities.
- **Sustainability and Maintenance:** Developing and maintaining gamified learning experiences requires ongoing investment of time, resources, and expertise. Organizations must be prepared to continually update and iterate on gamified elements based on employee feedback and performance data, ensuring that the experience remains engaging and effective over time.
- **Assessment and Evaluation:** Assessing employee learning and performance within gamified environments presents unique challenges. Organizations must devise appropriate methods for evaluating employee progress and mastery of training content, balancing formative and summative assessment strategies to provide meaningful feedback and measure learning outcomes accurately.
- **Resistance to Change:** Implementing gamified learning in corporate training may face resistance from stakeholders, including executives, managers, and employees. Organizations must effectively communicate the benefits of gamification and address concerns about its perceived novelty or lack of rigor, demonstrating how gamified experiences can enhance engagement, motivation, and learning outcomes for employees.

5.3.5 Best Practices for Implementing Gamified Learning in Corporate Training

- **Set Clear Training Objectives:** Define clear training objectives and align gamified learning experiences with organizational goals and performance metrics to ensure relevance and effectiveness.

- **Design Engaging Game Mechanics:** Incorporate a variety of game mechanics, such as points, badges, quests, and leaderboards, to create a dynamic and immersive learning environment that motivates employees and fosters active participation.
- **Provide Feedback and Progress Tracking:** Implement feedback loops and progress tracking mechanisms to provide employees with timely feedback on their performance and progress, reinforcing desired behaviors and guiding their learning journey.
- **Promote Collaboration and Team Building:** Integrate cooperative tasks, multiplayer games, and interactive challenges to promote collaboration, teamwork, and peer support among employees, fostering a culture of collaboration and innovation within the organization.
- **Offer Choice and Autonomy:** Provide employees with opportunities for choice and autonomy within gamified learning experiences, allowing them to personalize their learning journey and pursue areas of interest or challenge at their own pace.
- **Incorporate Real-World Relevance:** Contextualize training content within real-world scenarios and applications to increase employee engagement and demonstrate the practical relevance of their learning to their roles and responsibilities.
- **Foster Reflection and Application:** Encourage employees to reflect on their learning experiences and apply their knowledge and skills to real-world situations, helping them develop critical thinking skills, problem-solving abilities, and confidence in their abilities.
- **Collaborate with Stakeholders:** Engage executives, managers, and employees in the design and implementation of gamified learning experiences, fostering buy-in and support for innovative training initiatives that drive employee engagement, motivation, and performance.

CHAPTER 6

ASSESSMENT AND EVALUATION IN GAMEFICATION

6.1 MEASURING LEARNING OUTCOMES IN GAMIFIELD CONTEXTS

In recent years, gamification has emerged as a powerful tool in various fields, including education. By integrating game elements into learning environments, educators aim to enhance engagement, motivation, and ultimately, learning outcomes. However, assessing the effectiveness of gamified learning approaches requires careful consideration and innovative measurement techniques.

Measuring learning outcomes in gamified contexts requires a multifaceted approach that encompasses both quantitative and qualitative methods. By leveraging formative assessments, engagement metrics, learning analytics, and qualitative assessments, educators can gain comprehensive insights into the effectiveness of gamification in promoting learning and skill acquisition. Challenges such as balancing extrinsic and intrinsic motivation, addressing diverse learner needs, and ensuring ethical considerations remain critical considerations in the design and evaluation of gamified learning environments. With continued research and innovation, gamification has the potential to revolutionize education, making learning more engaging, accessible, and impactful for learners worldwide.

Gamification, broadly defined as the application of game design principles and mechanics to non-game contexts, holds immense potential for transforming traditional educational settings.

By leveraging elements such as points, levels, badges, leaderboards, and rewards, educators can create immersive learning experiences that captivate learners' interest and drive participation. The allure of gamification lies in its ability to foster intrinsic motivation, encourage skill development, and promote active learning.

However, assessing the impact of gamification on learning outcomes presents unique challenges. Traditional metrics like test scores or grades may not fully capture the multifaceted nature of learning in gamified environments. Therefore, educators and researchers must explore alternative methods to evaluate the effectiveness of gamification in facilitating learning and skill acquisition. One approach to measuring learning outcomes in gamified contexts involves the use of formative assessments. Unlike summative assessments that occur at the end of a learning period, formative assessments provide ongoing feedback to both learners and instructors, allowing for continuous improvement. In gamified settings, formative assessments can take various forms, such as quizzes, challenges, simulations, or quests embedded within the game framework. These assessments not only gauge learners' understanding and progress but also inform adjustments to the gamified elements to better align with educational objectives.

Another crucial aspect of measuring learning outcomes in gamified contexts is the analysis of engagement metrics. Gamification inherently encourages active participation and interaction, which can be tracked and analyzed to provide insights into learners' behaviors and preferences. Metrics such as time spent playing, frequency of logins, completion rates, and social interactions within the game environment offer valuable indicators of engagement levels. By monitoring these metrics, educators can assess the effectiveness of gamified elements in sustaining learners' interest and motivation over time.

Furthermore, the incorporation of learning analytics tools enables educators to collect and analyze data generated within gamified learning environments. These tools leverage technology to gather real-time information on learners' interactions, progress, and performance, allowing for personalized feedback and adaptive interventions. By harnessing the power of data analytics, educators can gain deeper insights into learners' behaviors and learning patterns, facilitating informed decision-making and targeted instructional strategies.

Beyond quantitative metrics, qualitative assessments play a vital role in evaluating learning outcomes in gamified contexts. Surveys, interviews, focus groups, and reflective journals offer opportunities for learners to articulate their experiences, perceptions, and learning processes. Qualitative data provide valuable context and rich narratives that complement quantitative findings, offering a holistic understanding of the impact of gamification on learners' attitudes and learning outcomes.

However, measuring learning outcomes in gamified contexts is not without its challenges. One significant challenge is the potential for extrinsic motivation to overshadow intrinsic motivation. While gamification can initially motivate learners through external rewards and incentives, sustaining intrinsic motivation for long-term engagement and learning is essential. Educators must strike a balance between extrinsic and intrinsic motivators, designing gamified experiences that foster a sense of autonomy, competence, and relatedness.

Moreover, the design and implementation of gamified learning environments require careful consideration of individual differences and diverse learner needs. Not all learners respond similarly to gamification, and factors such as age, prior experience, cultural background, and learning styles can influence its effectiveness. Therefore, personalized approaches that cater to the unique preferences and abilities of learners are essential for maximizing learning outcomes in gamified contexts.

Ethical considerations also arise in the measurement of learning outcomes in gamified environments, particularly concerning data privacy and learner autonomy. As educators collect and analyze vast amounts of data on learners' interactions and behaviors, ensuring the confidentiality and security of sensitive information is paramount. Additionally, learners should have agency and control over their data, with transparent policies regarding its use and dissemination.

Despite these challenges, advances in technology and pedagogical research offer promising strategies for effectively measuring learning outcomes in gamified contexts. Adaptive learning systems, which adjust content and difficulty levels based on learners' performance and preferences, hold potential for optimizing engagement and learning outcomes. Virtual reality (VR) and augmented reality (AR) technologies provide immersive experiences that enhance learning retention and transfer. Furthermore, interdisciplinary collaborations between educators, game designers, psychologists, and data scientists can yield innovative approaches to evaluating the impact of gamification on learning.

6.2 GAMIFIELD ASSESSMENT STRATEGIES

In the realm of education and professional development, assessment is a vital tool for evaluating progress and understanding. Traditional assessment methods, however, often lack engagement and fail to capture the full potential of learners. Gamification offers a dynamic solution to this challenge, transforming assessment into an interactive and immersive experience.

Gamified assessment strategies offer a powerful approach to enhancing engagement, motivation, and learning outcomes in educational and professional settings. By integrating game elements into assessment processes, educators and trainers can create dynamic and interactive experiences that inspire learners to excel. With careful planning and thoughtful implementation, gamification can revolutionize assessment practices, unlocking the full potential of learners across diverse contexts.

6.2.1 Gamified Assessment

Gamified assessment involves integrating game elements into assessment processes to enhance motivation, engagement, and learning outcomes. By incorporating elements such as points, levels, badges, and challenges, gamification fosters a sense of achievement and progress among participants. Unlike conventional assessments, which may feel daunting or monotonous, gamified assessments encourage active participation and stimulate intrinsic motivation.

6.2.2 Benefits of Gamified Assessment

- **Increased Engagement:** Gamification makes assessments more enjoyable and interactive, motivating participants to actively participate in learning activities.
- **Enhanced Motivation:** By providing clear goals, feedback, and rewards, gamified assessments inspire learners to strive for excellence and persist in their efforts.
- **Personalized Learning:** Gamification allows for adaptive assessment techniques, tailoring challenges and feedback to individual learner preferences and capabilities.
- **Real-time Feedback:** Through instant feedback mechanisms, gamified assessments offer learners immediate insight into their performance, enabling timely adjustments and improvements.
- **Collaborative Learning:** Gamified assessments often incorporate social elements, fostering collaboration and peer interaction, which enhances learning through shared experiences.

6.2.3 Strategies for Implementing Gamified Assessment

- **Define Clear Objectives:** Begin by outlining the learning objectives and desired outcomes of the assessment. Identify key skills and knowledge areas to be assessed, ensuring alignment with instructional goals.
- **Select Appropriate Game Mechanics:** Choose game elements that align with the assessment objectives and target audience preferences. Consider incorporating elements such as points, levels, leaderboards, badges, quests, and challenges.
- **Design Engaging Challenges:** Develop assessment tasks that are challenging yet achievable, providing opportunities for skill development and mastery. Incorporate variety to maintain interest and cater to diverse learning styles.
- **Provide Meaningful Feedback:** Implement feedback mechanisms that offer constructive guidance and reinforcement. Ensure feedback is timely, specific, and actionable, enabling learners to understand their strengths and areas for improvement.
- **Foster Competition and Collaboration:** Introduce competitive elements such as leaderboards or multiplayer challenges to motivate learners and stimulate engagement. Encourage collaboration through team-based activities and cooperative challenges.

- **Monitor Progress and Adjustments:** Continuously monitor learner progress and performance metrics to identify areas of success and areas for improvement. Adapt assessment strategies based on feedback and learner responses to optimize effectiveness.
- **Promote Reflection and Metacognition:** Encourage learners to reflect on their experiences and learning processes, fostering metacognitive awareness and self-regulated learning behaviors. Provide opportunities for self-assessment and goal setting to empower learners in their educational journey.

6.2.4 Case Studies: Successful Applications of Gamified Assessment

Duolingo

Duolingo is an American educational technology company that produces learning apps and provides language certification.

Duolingo offers courses on music, math and over 40 languages, ranging from English, French, and Spanish to less commonly studied languages such as Welsh, Irish, and Swahili. Other services include the Duolingo English Test, an online certification program, and Duolingo ABC, a literacy app for children. The company uses a freemium model, with its optional premium service, Super Duolingo, being ad-free and offering more features.

As of February 2023, Duolingo was the world's most popular language learning app based on monthly downloads, with almost 13.4 million users downloading it that month. A systematic review of research on Duolingo from 2012 to 2020 found comparatively few studies on the platform's efficacy for language learning, but identified several studies that reported relatively high user satisfaction and enjoyment and positive perceptions of the app's effectiveness.

History

The idea for Duolingo was formulated in 2009 by Carnegie Mellon University professor Luis von Ahn and his Swiss-born post-graduate student Severin Hacker. Von Ahn had sold his second company, reCAPTCHA, to Google and, with Hacker, wanted to work on an education-related project.

A driving motivation was Von Ahn's upbringing in Guatemala, where he saw how expensive it was for people in his community to learn English. Hacker (co-founder and current CTO of Duolingo) believed that "free education will really change the world" and wanted to provide an accessible means for doing so. In recognition of his contributions to language-learning and technological development, he was recognized by the National Inventors Hall of Fame. The project was originally financed by Von Ahn's MacArthur fellowship and a National Science Foundation grant. The founders considered creating Duolingo as a nonprofit organization, but Von Ahn judged this model unsustainable. An early revenue stream, a crowdsourced translation service, was replaced by a Duolingo English Test certification program, advertising, and subscription.

In October 2011, Duolingo announced that it had raised $3.3 million from a Series A round of funding, led by Union Square Ventures, with participation from author Tim Ferriss and actor Ashton Kutcher's investing firm A-Grade Investments. Duolingo launched a private beta on November 27, 2011, and accumulated a waiting list of more than 300,000 people. It launched to the general public on June 19, 2012, at which point the waiting list had grown to around 500,000.

In September 2012, Duolingo announced that it had raised a further $15 million from a Series B funding round led by New Enterprise Associates, with participation from Union Square Ventures. In November 2012, Duolingo released an iPhone app, followed by an Android app in May 2013, at which time Duolingo had around 3 million users. By July 2013, it had grown to 5 million users and was rated the No. 1 free education app in the Google Play Store.

In February 2014, Duolingo announced that it had raised $20 million from a Series C funding round led by Kleiner Caufield & Byers, with prior investors also participating. At this time, it had 34 employees, and reported about 25 million registered users and 12.5 million active users; it later reported a figure closer to 60 million users.

In June 2015, it announced that it had raised $45 million from a Series D funding round led by Google Capital, bringing its total funding to $83.3 million. The round valued the company at around $470 million, with 100 million registered users globally. In April 2016, it was reported that Duolingo had more than 18 million monthly users. In July 2017, Duolingo announced that it had raised $25 million in a Series E funding round led by Drive Capital, bringing its total funding to $108.3 million. The round valued Duolingo at $700 million, and the company reported passing 200 million registered users, with 25 million active users. It was reported that Duolingo had 95 employees. Funds from the Series E round would be directed toward creating initiatives such as a related educational flashcard app, TinyCards, and testbeds for initiatives related to reading and listening comprehension. On August 1, 2018, Duolingo surpassed 300 million registered users.

In December 2019, it was announced that Duolingo raised $30 million in a Series F funding round from Alphabet's investment company CapitalG. The round valued Duolingo at $1.5 billion. Duolingo reported 30 million active users at this time. The headcount at the company had increased to 200, and new offices had been opened in Seattle, New York and Beijing.

Duolingo planned to use the funds to develop new products and further expand its team in sectors like engineering, business development, design, curriculum and content creators, community outreach, and marketing.

In October 2013, Duolingo launched a crowdsourced language incubator. In March 2021, it announced that it would be ending its volunteer contributor program and donating money to its volunteer contributors who helped develop it. The company said that from now on, language courses would be maintained and developed by professional linguists aligning with CEFR standards. On June 28, 2021, Duolingo filed for an initial public offering on NASDAQ under the ticker DUOL. From August 2021 to June 2022, the Duolingo language learning app was removed from some app stores in China.

In the early-2020s, Duolingo was noted for its viral videos on the social media platform TikTok.

In August 2022, Duolingo overhauled its interface, changing its course structure from a tree-like design, where users could choose from a range of lessons after completing previous ones, to a linear progression. This was widely criticized by users across a variety of social media outlets, including Reddit and Twitter. CEO Luis von Ahn stated there were no plans to reverse the changes, which were intended to simplify Duolingo for new users, and that maintaining both the old and new versions would be difficult.

In October 2022, Duolingo acquired Detroit-based animation studio Gunner. In October 2023 Duolingo released math and music courses in English and Spanish for iOS users.

In January 2024, after having laid off ten percent of its contractors, Duolingo began using artificial intelligence to replace tasks normally done by its contractors.

Table: Duolingo's Monthly Active Users (2016–2022)

Year	Monthly Active Users (In Millions)
2016	30
2017	28
2018	25
2019	30
2020	42
2021	37
2022	54

Duolingo

Duolingo uses a gamified approach to language learning, with lessons that incorporate translating, interactive exercises, quizzes and stories to make learning more engaging and fun. It also uses a unique algorithm that adapts to each learner's level and learning style, providing personalized feedback and recommendations. For some languages, it offers podcasts for intermediate learners, consisting of stories usually told by native speakers from different parts of the world where the target language is spoken. The programs use simplified grammar and vocabulary and slower intonation, and include occasional assistance with context and explanations of unusual words.

Duolingo has been through many design phases. It originally provided users with different "skills" placed along a "tree", where they could progress by completing every skill above them. At any time, the user could upgrade the skill, with the final goal of turning it "golden" or "legendary". In November 2022, Duolingo switched to an AI-assisted path, where each user's learning is streamlined without requiring as many decisions.

After its switch to this new format, it removed the audio-only lessons it had offered for certain languages. Duolingo also provides a competitive space, such as in Leagues, where people can compete against their friends or see how they compare with randomly selected worldwide-player groupings of up to 30 users. Rankings in leagues are determined by the amount of "XP" (eXperience Points) earned in a week. Badges in Duolingo represent achievements earned from completing specific objectives or challenges. Players have reported that gamification has led to cheating, hacking, and incentivized game strategies that conflict with actual learning.

Duolingo provides features that allow teachers to track their students' progress. Most of Duolingo's language-learning features are free, but it has periodic advertising in both its mobile and web browser applications, which users can remove by paying a subscription fee or promoting referral links. This program, known as Super Duolingo, includes benefits such as unlimited hearts (retries), level-skipping, no ads, and progress quizzes.

Duolingo ABC

Duolingo ABC is a free mobile app designed for young children to learn letters, their sounds, phonics, and other early reading concepts. Released in 2020, it does not contain ads or in-app purchases. iOS and Android versions are available, currently only in English.

Duolingo Math

Duolingo Math is a mobile app for learning elementary mathematics in a form similar to the original app, released in October 2022. It is currently only available on iOS devices.

Duolingo Music

In March 2023, Duolingo was reportedly developing a new music course that would allow users to learn how to read and play music through its signature gamified learning experience. On October 11, 2023, Duolingo formally unveiled Duolingo Music in a YouTube Short, a new platform within the existing app that provides basic music learning through piano, drums, and sheet music lessons.

Duolingo English Test

The Duolingo English Test (DET) is an online English proficiency test that measures proficiency in reading, writing, speaking and listening in English. It is a computer-based test scored on a scale of 10–160, with scores above 120 considered English proficiency. The test is adaptive, with the questions automatically adjusting to the test-taker's ability level.

Business Model

Duolingo had revenue of $1 million in 2016, $13 million in 2017, $36 million in 2018, and $250.77 million in 2021. In May 2022, it was reported that 6.8% of its monthly active users paid for the ad-free version of the app. Duolingo has derived most of its revenue from subscriptions, advertising, and its Duolingo English Test. In April 2020, it passed one million paid subscribers; it reached 2.9 million in March 2022, and 4.8 million at the end of March 2023.

Effectiveness

A 2017 study found no significant difference between elementary students learning Spanish through the "gamification" of Duolingo and those learning in classroom environments, with both groups demonstrating a similar increase in achievements and self-efficacy.

A 2022 study on adults using Duolingo as their only language learning tool, published in the journal Foreign Language Annals, found that the participants that completed a course had similar reading and listening proficiency to university students after four semesters of study, concluding that Duolingo could be an effective tool for language learning. Another 2022 study of Malaysian students learning French, published by the National University of Malaysia Press, found that it facilitated the acquisition of vocabulary, and concluded it was well suited for beginners in this regard.

Some language professionals have criticized the app for its limitations and its gamified design. Elizabeth Bernhardt-Kamil, director of the Language Center at Stanford University, said: "Everybody is focused on the shortcut to everything, and real language learning can't be done in a shortcut." Others have pointed out that Duolingo and similar apps can be a starting point but lack the human interaction required to be fluent in a language.

Awards

In 2013, Apple chose Duolingo as its iPhone App of the Year, a first for an educational application. That year, Duolingo ranked No. 7 on *Fast Company*'s "The World's Most Innovative Companies: Education Honorees" list "for crowdsourcing web translation by turning it into a free language-learning program". Duolingo won Best Education Startup at the 2014 Crunchies, and was the most downloaded education app in Google Play in 2013 and 2014. In July 2020, *PCMag* named it "The Best Free Language Learning App".

As a company, Duolingo has likewise won several awards and recognitions. In 2015, it was announced as that year's Index Award winner in the Play & Learning category by The Index Project. It won *Inc.* magazine's Best Workplaces 2018, made *Entrepreneur* magazine's Top Company Culture List 2018, was among CNBC's "Disruptor 50" lists for 2018 and 2019, and was ranked as one of *TIME* magazine's 50 Genius Companies. Duolingo was named one of *Forbes*' "Next Billion-Dollar Startups 2019".

Kahoot!

Kahoot! is a Norwegian online game-based learning platform. It has learning games, also known as "kahoots", which are user-generated multiple-choice quizzes that can be accessed via a web browser or the Kahoot! app.

In July 2023, Kahoot agreed to be acquired by Goldman Sachs Asset Management alongside General Atlantic, Glitrafjord, and others in a $1.72 billion all-cash deal.

History and Development

Kahoot! was founded in 2012 by Morten Versvik, as well as a team of co-founders such as Johan Brand, Jamie Brooker and Asmund Furuseth in a joint project with the Norwegian University of Science and Technology, collaborating with professor Alfe Inge Wang to develop the website. Kahoot! was launched in a private beta at SXSWedu in March 2013, and the beta was released to the public in September 2013.

In 2017, Kahoot! had raised $26.5 million in funding from Northzone, Creandum and Microsoft Ventures. In October 11, 2018, Kahoot! was valued at $300 million. As of 11 June 2020, Kahoot! was valued at $1.5 billion and raised further capital from Northzone. In 2019, Kahoot! acquired the Scandinavian education company Poio. It also acquired DragonBox, an educational games developer, for $18 million. Kahoot! raised $28 million in venture capital investments the following June. Kahoot! raised an additional $215 million in venture capital funding from SoftBank in October 2020.

Afterwards, Kahoot! made a series of acquisitions. It acquired Drops, which was focused on teaching languages, for about $50 million. This was followed by

Whiteboard.fi, which develops software for digital, online whiteboards. Kahoot! also acquired the Danish startup Actimo for approximately $33 million. Actimo developed software for training and engaging with employees. It was acquired to expand Kahoot's features for business users. In March 2021, the company went public on the Oslo stock exchange. In April 2021, Kahoot! acquired Motimate, a corporate learning company based in Norway, for about $25 million. In 2021, Kahoot! announced that it would acquire SSO digital learning platform Clever, Inc. for $500 million to expand Clever Inc.'s reach globally. Kahoot's user base grew more than 40 percent from 2020 to 2021.

Software and Services

Kahoot! users gather around a common screen such as an interactive whiteboard, projector, or a computer monitor. The site can also be used through screen-sharing tools, like Zoom or Google Hangouts. The game design is such that the players are required to frequently look up from their devices. All players connect using a generated game PIN shown on the common screen, and use a device to answer questions.

In March 2017, Kahoot! reached one billion cumulative participating players. In September 2017, Kahoot! launched a mobile application for homework.

Research and Prototypes

The game concept used in Kahoot! started out as an idea of Professor Alf Inge Wang, at the Department for Computer Science at the Norwegian University of Science and Technology in 2006. He developed multiple prototypes that were developed and tested in experiments conducted in collaboration with master students. The idea was to transform the classroom, where the teacher acted as the game show host, and the students were contenders, using their own mobile devices. The initial prototype was named Lecture Quiz.

Lecture Quiz 1.0 was developed in 2006, before modern smartphones were available (the first generation iPhone was released June 29, 2007). The server was implemented in Java and MySQL, integrated with an Apache Web server. The teacher client was implemented as a Java application, in combination with OpenGL for graphics, while the student clients were implemented on Java 2 Micro Edition. This made it possible to run the client on both mobile phones and laptops. The students who played the game using their own laptops could use the Wi-Fi available at the university, while those playing using mobile phones had to use 3G over the cellular network. The latter was a disadvantage, as the students had to pay out of their own pocket to play Lecture Quiz, as the telecom providers at that time charged per megabyte transferred. The first experiment with Lecture Quiz was carried out in a classroom with twenty students at the Norwegian University of Science and Technology, where the focus was on efficiency and usefulness. The results from the experiment showed that Lecture Quiz was relatively easy to use, and contributed to increased learning. They also found that it was entertaining for both the teacher and students, and increased the motivation for attending more lectures. From 2006 to 2011, four versions of Lecture Quiz were developed, where the main changes were related to improved usability, thus making it easier to create quizzes, and using newer technology for implementation.

Lecture Quiz 2.0 was the first prototype where both teacher and student clients had web-interfaces. An experiment testing the 2.0 prototype showed that the usability had been improved both for the teacher and the student clients, and that the concept increased students' motivation, engagement, concentration, and perceived learning. The last version of Lecture Quiz was version 3.0, with significantly improved user-interface implemented using HTML 5 and CSS3, avatars, and multiple game/team modes. Lecture Quiz 3.0 was tested internally at the NTNU, as well as externally at various schools such as at Skaun Ungdomsskole, where the students rejoiced over having a test in social science.

Since Kahoot! was launched in 2013, the research community has conducted many experiments related to the effects of using the game-based learning platform in classrooms. A quasi-experiment conducted at the Norwegian University of Science and Technology with 252 students participating investigated the wear-out effect of Kahoot!, by comparing students' perception of the system after playing once, vs. playing frequently over five months. The results did not show any statistically significant reductions in students' engagement, motivation, concentration, or perceived learning over time, but there was a significant change in classroom dynamics (less communication among players after five months). The conclusion was that Kahoot! managed to boost students' engagement, motivation, concentration, and learning after using it repeatedly for five months. The core factor to keep students' attention after heavy repeated usage was found to be the competitive nature of Kahoot!.

There is also research that investigates how Kahoot! performs compared to other tools and platforms. In a quasi-experiment with 384 students at the Norwegian University of Science and Technology, Kahoot! was compared to using a paper quiz and a simple polling system called Clicker. The results show statistically significant improvement in motivation, engagement, enjoyment, and concentration for the gamified approach (Kahoot!) compared to the two others. However, the results did not show any significant differences in learning outcomes.

Another quasi-experiment at the Norwegian University of Science and Technology, in which 593 students participated, investigated how the use of points and audio in Kahoot! affects concentration, engagement, enjoyment, learning, motivation, and classroom dynamics. The results reveal that there are some significant differences whether audio and points are used in the areas of concentration, engagement, enjoyment, and motivation. The worst result was for the case where both audio and points were turned off. The most surprising finding was how classroom dynamics was positively affected by the use of audio.

According to research by two students at the Norwegian University of Science and Technology, the network latency in accessing the website greatly influences the quality of experience of the platform, in both longitudinal and cross-sectional studies, with a sample size N=21. It was found that about 70% of the sample size regard Kahoot! as having positive results on all delay levels, while a varying number of students (between 10-20%) report that the platform is too time-consuming, forming a direct relationship with the duration of the delay.

A literature review containing 93 studies on the effect of using Kahoot! for learning was published in the journal *Computers & Education* in 2020. This is the first literature review that investigates most published studies (experiments, case studies, surveys, etc.) on how using Kahoot! affects learning in the classroom. The focus of the review is on learning performance, classroom dynamics, students' and teachers' attitudes and perceptions, and student anxiety. The main conclusion is that Kahoot! has a positive effect on learning performance, classroom dynamics, attitudes, and anxiety, and the main challenges include "technical problems", "seeing questions and answers", "time stress", "fear of losing", and "it being hard to catch up". Studies included in this review use a mixture of quantitative and qualitative research methods, that reveal, among other things, that Kahoot! creates statistically significant improvement in learning performance compared to traditional teaching and other tools, on students' and teachers' perception of lectures, in classroom dynamics, and that Kahoot! can reduce students' anxiety compared to traditional teaching and other tools.

In 2016, Kahoot!'s pedagogical quality was evaluated and certified by Education Alliance Finland (formerly Kokoa Standard). The quality certification is based on a qualitative assessment of the product's design. The assessment was done and developed by Education Alliance Finland in collaboration with Lauri Hietajärvi and Erika Maksniemi, researchers from the University of Helsinki. The evaluation suggests that Kahoot!'s educational value is highest when students are creating quizzes of relevant topics themselves, because it uses creativity, and practices 21st-century skills.

CodeCombat

CodeCombat is an educational video game for learning software programming concepts and languages. This game is recommended for students ages 9–16. Students learn to type coding languages like JavaScript, Python, HTML and CoffeeScript, as well as learning the fundamentals of computer science. *CodeCombat* has 11 units - three game development units, two web development units, and six computer science units.

The first unit, Computer Science 1, is free to all students and teachers. In 2019, *CodeCombat* was recognized by the College Board as an endorsed provider of curriculum and professional development for AP Computer Science Principles (AP CSP).

CodeCombat works directly with schools and districts, as well as offering self-paced learners a monthly paid subscription that gives access to additional game content. In order to advance through the game's levels, players must prove their knowledge by writing code. It includes both single-player and multi-player components, and is ideally suited for 4th-12th graders. The game was positively reviewed by PC Magazine, won the 2017 SIIA CODiE award for Best Creativity Tool for Students, and has been named a top pick for learning by Common Sense Education.

In January 2014, *CodeCombat* made their software open-source, and released a level editor so that users could create their own game content. In August 2019, *CodeCombat* released its newest game, *Ozaria*.

6.3 GAMIFICATION ANALYTICS

In the digital age, gamification has emerged as a potent tool for enhancing engagement, motivation, and learning outcomes across various domains. As organizations harness the power of gamified experiences, the need for effective evaluation and optimization becomes paramount. Gamification analytics serves as a valuable resource, offering insights into user behavior, performance trends, and the impact of gamified interventions.

Gamification analytics holds immense potential for unlocking actionable insights and optimizing the effectiveness of gamified experiences across diverse domains. By leveraging data-driven approaches, organizations can enhance user engagement, drive performance improvements, and achieve their strategic objectives. As gamification continues to evolve, the integration of robust analytics capabilities will be essential for informing evidence-based decision-making and delivering meaningful outcomes for users and stakeholders alike.

Gamification analytics involves the systematic collection, analysis, and interpretation of data generated by gamified experiences. It encompasses a range of metrics and indicators that provide valuable insights into user engagement, performance, and satisfaction. By leveraging data-driven approaches, organizations can optimize gamification strategies, refine user experiences, and achieve desired outcomes.

6.3.1 Key Metrics in Gamification Analytics

Engagement Metrics

Engagement metrics play a crucial role in gamification analytics, providing valuable insights into how users interact with gamified experiences. By measuring various aspects of user participation and involvement, organizations can assess the effectiveness of their gamification strategies and identify opportunities for improvement.

Engagement metrics serve as vital indicators of user participation, interaction, and satisfaction within gamified environments. By analyzing these metrics, organizations can gain valuable insights into user behavior, preferences, and performance trends. Leveraging engagement metrics allows for data-driven decision-making, iterative refinement, and optimization of gamification strategies to enhance user engagement and achieve desired outcomes.

- **Time Spent:** Time spent refers to the duration that users engage with a gamified experience. This metric provides insights into user immersion and interest levels. Longer durations typically indicate higher engagement, while shorter durations may suggest potential areas for enhancement or boredom.
- **Frequency of Visits:** Frequency of visits measures how often users return to the gamified platform or application. Higher frequencies indicate sustained interest and ongoing engagement, while infrequent visits may signal a lack of interest or relevance. Analyzing visit patterns can help identify factors that influence user retention and loyalty.
- **Active User Counts:** Active user counts quantify the number of users who actively participate in gamified activities within a specific time period. This metric provides a snapshot of user engagement and can help assess the reach and impact of gamification initiatives. Monitoring changes in active user counts over time can reveal trends and seasonality in user behavior.
- **Interaction Metrics:** Interaction metrics track user interactions within the gamified environment, such as clicks, taps, swipes, and gestures. These metrics measure the depth and breadth of user engagement with gamification elements, such as challenges, rewards, and progress indicators. Analyzing interaction patterns can inform the design and optimization of user interfaces and gameplay mechanics.
- **Completion Rates:** Completion rates measure the percentage of users who successfully complete gamified tasks, levels, or challenges. High completion rates indicate effective task design and user engagement,

while low completion rates may indicate obstacles or barriers that hinder user progress. Analyzing completion rates can help identify areas for refinement and optimization within gamified experiences.

- **Achievement Unlocks:** Achievement unlocks represent milestones or accomplishments attained by users within the gamified environment. These may include earning badges, leveling up, or reaching specific performance thresholds. Tracking achievement unlocks provides insights into user motivation, progress, and skill mastery. Celebrating achievements can reinforce positive behavior and encourage continued engagement.
- **Social Interactions:** Social interactions metrics quantify user engagement with social features within gamified experiences, such as likes, comments, shares, and collaborations. These metrics assess the level of community engagement, collaboration, and peer interaction facilitated by gamification. Leveraging social interactions can enhance user satisfaction, foster a sense of belonging, and amplify the reach of gamified initiatives.
- **Feedback and Surveys:** Feedback and survey metrics capture user sentiment, satisfaction, and preferences through qualitative assessments. Gathering user feedback allows organizations to gain deeper insights into user perceptions, preferences, and pain points. Analyzing feedback data can inform iterative improvements and optimization strategies for gamified experiences.

Progression Metrics

In the realm of gamification, progression metrics play a crucial role in assessing users' advancement and development within gamified experiences. These metrics provide valuable insights into how users navigate through levels, challenges, or milestones, offering a deeper understanding of their progression journey and engagement levels. By tracking progression metrics, organizations can refine gamification strategies, optimize learning pathways, and enhance user satisfaction.

Progression metrics in gamification analytics provide valuable insights into users' advancement, engagement, and learning trajectories within gamified experiences.

By tracking these metrics, organizations can optimize instructional design, tailor learning pathways, and enhance user satisfaction. As gamification continues to evolve, the integration of robust analytics capabilities will be essential for informed decision-making and the delivery of impactful user experiences.

Level Completion Rate

- **Definition:** The percentage of users who successfully complete a particular level or stage within a gamified experience.
- **Importance:** Level completion rate indicates users' ability to overcome challenges and advance through the gamified journey. It reflects the difficulty level of the tasks and the effectiveness of instructional design.
- **Analysis:** Analyzing level completion rates helps identify bottlenecks, areas of difficulty, or points of attrition within the gamified experience. Discrepancies in completion rates between different levels can inform adjustments to the learning curve or content complexity.

Progression Velocity

- **Definition:** The speed at which users progress through successive levels or stages within a gamified environment.
- **Importance:** Progression velocity provides insights into users' pace of learning and adaptation. It indicates the efficiency of instructional design, the effectiveness of feedback mechanisms, and users' motivation levels.
- **Analysis:** Monitoring progression velocity over time enables organizations to identify trends and patterns in user behavior. Sudden fluctuations or deviations from the expected progression rate may signal changes in user engagement or challenges within the gamified experience.

Time-to-Completion

- **Definition:** The amount of time users take to complete specific levels, challenges, or tasks within a gamified environment.
- **Importance:** Time-to-completion metrics reveal users' efficiency and proficiency in completing gamified activities. They provide insights into the complexity of tasks, user skill levels, and potential areas for optimization.
- **Analysis:** Analyzing time-to-completion metrics helps identify outliers, outliers, and outliers, outliers, outliers, and identify outliers., bottlenecks, or usability issues within the gamified experience. Discrepancies in completion times between different user groups or demographics may indicate the need for personalized learning pathways or additional support resources.

Achievement Unlocks

- **Definition:** The attainment of specific achievements, badges, or rewards within the gamified environment.

- **Importance:** Achievement unlocks signify users' mastery of skills, knowledge acquisition, and progress within the gamified journey. They serve as tangible milestones and incentives for continued engagement.
- **Analysis:** Tracking achievement unlocks allows organizations to assess the effectiveness of reward systems, incentive structures, and feedback mechanisms. Analyzing the distribution of achievements across user segments can reveal patterns of engagement and motivation.

Path Divergence and Convergence

- **Definition:** The branching paths or convergence points within the gamified experience, where users make choices or encounter decision points.
- **Importance:** Path divergence and convergence metrics reflect users' autonomy, decision-making processes, and exploration behaviors within the gamified environment. They highlight the diversity of user experiences and learning pathways.
- **Analysis:** Analyzing path divergence and convergence helps identify popular routes, alternative strategies, or areas of interest within the gamified experience. It informs the design of adaptive learning systems and personalized content recommendations.

Mastery Levels and Skill Proficiency

- **Definition:** Users' proficiency levels and mastery of specific skills or competencies within the gamified context.
- **Importance:** Mastery levels and skill proficiency metrics indicate users' depth of understanding, application, and retention of knowledge and skills. They reflect the effectiveness of instructional methods and the alignment with learning objectives.
- **Analysis:** Tracking mastery levels and skill proficiency allows organizations to assess the impact of gamified interventions on learning outcomes. Analyzing proficiency gaps or competency clusters informs targeted interventions and personalized learning pathways.

Performance Metrics

Performance metrics in gamification analytics are essential for evaluating users' proficiency, skill development, and task completion within gamified experiences. These metrics provide valuable insights into users' abilities, competencies, and effectiveness in achieving desired outcomes. By tracking performance metrics, organizations can identify strengths, areas for improvement, and opportunities for optimization.

Performance metrics in gamification analytics offer valuable insights into users' proficiency, skill development, and task completion within gamified experiences. By tracking these metrics, organizations can assess learning progress, identify areas for improvement, and optimize instructional design. As gamification continues to evolve, the integration of robust analytics capabilities will be essential for informed decision-making and the delivery of impactful user experiences.

Score or Point Accumulation

- **Definition:** The accumulation of points or scores based on users' performance in completing tasks, challenges, or activities within the gamified environment.
- **Importance:** Score accumulation serves as a tangible measure of users' progress, achievement, and mastery within the gamified experience. It provides immediate feedback and incentivizes continued engagement.
- **Analysis:** Analyzing score accumulation trends over time helps assess users' learning trajectory, motivation levels, and responsiveness to gamification elements. Discrepancies in scores between user segments or demographics may indicate varying levels of engagement or effectiveness of instructional design.

Accuracy Rate

- **Definition:** The percentage of correctly completed tasks or responses compared to the total number of attempts within the gamified environment.
- **Importance:** Accuracy rate reflects users' precision, proficiency, and understanding of the content or skills being assessed. It indicates the effectiveness of learning materials, feedback mechanisms, and instructional strategies.
- **Analysis:** Monitoring accuracy rates enables organizations to identify areas of difficulty, misconceptions, or knowledge gaps among users. Analyzing trends in accuracy rates across different tasks or challenges informs targeted interventions and content refinement efforts.

Completion Time

- **Definition:** The amount of time users take to complete specific tasks, challenges, or activities within the gamified environment.
- **Importance:** Completion time metrics assess users' efficiency, time management skills, and task complexity perception within the gamified experience. They provide insights into usability issues, cognitive load, and learning pacing.

- **Analysis:** Analyzing completion time distributions helps identify outliers, bottlenecks, or areas of frustration within the gamified environment. Discrepancies in completion times between user segments may indicate the need for personalized learning pathways or adaptive interventions.

Task Completion Rate

- **Definition:** The percentage of users who successfully complete specific tasks or challenges within the gamified environment.
- **Importance:** Task completion rate measures users' ability to overcome obstacles, solve problems, and achieve predefined objectives within the gamified experience. It reflects the clarity of instructions, task difficulty, and user engagement levels.
- **Analysis:** Monitoring task completion rates allows organizations to identify barriers to completion, usability issues, or gaps in instructional design. Analyzing completion rates by task type or complexity informs the refinement of learning objectives and the adjustment of difficulty levels.

Skill Proficiency Levels

- **Definition:** Users' proficiency levels in specific skills or competencies assessed within the gamified context.
- **Importance:** Skill proficiency levels indicate users' depth of understanding, application, and mastery of essential knowledge or abilities. They serve as benchmarks for learning progress and performance improvement.
- **Analysis:** Tracking skill proficiency levels over time helps assess the effectiveness of instructional methods, feedback mechanisms, and reinforcement strategies. Identifying proficiency gaps or skill clusters informs personalized learning pathways and targeted interventions.

Error Rate

- **Definition:** The frequency or percentage of errors, mistakes, or incorrect responses made by users within the gamified environment.
- **Importance:** Error rate metrics highlight users' misconceptions, knowledge gaps, or areas of difficulty within the gamified experience. They indicate the effectiveness of feedback mechanisms and the need for additional support or clarification.

- **Analysis:** Analyzing error rates allows organizations to identify common misconceptions, recurring errors, or patterns of misunderstanding among users. Targeted interventions, remedial activities, or adaptive feedback can address identified error sources and enhance learning outcomes.

Retention Metrics

Retention metrics are pivotal in evaluating the long-term engagement and sustainability of gamified experiences. They provide insights into users' continued participation, loyalty, and retention over time. By tracking retention metrics, organizations can assess the effectiveness of gamification strategies, identify factors influencing user retention, and implement targeted interventions to enhance user engagement.

Retention metrics in gamification analytics provide essential insights into users' continued engagement, loyalty, and satisfaction within gamified experiences. By tracking these metrics, organizations can identify retention drivers, mitigate churn, and foster long-term user relationships. As gamification continues to evolve, the integration of robust analytics capabilities will be essential for maximizing user retention and delivering sustained value for users and stakeholders alike.

User Retention Rate

- **Definition:** The percentage of users who continue to engage with the gamified experience over a specified period, such as days, weeks, or months.
- **Importance:** User retention rate reflects the ability of the gamified experience to maintain user interest and commitment over time. It indicates the sustainability of engagement and the effectiveness of retention strategies.
- **Analysis:** Monitoring user retention rate allows organizations to identify trends, seasonal variations, or fluctuations in user engagement. Analyzing retention cohorts based on user demographics or behavior patterns provides insights into retention drivers and informs targeted interventions.

Churn Rate

- **Definition:** The rate at which users disengage or stop participating in the gamified experience over a specific period.
- **Importance:** Churn rate measures the attrition or loss of users within the gamified environment. It highlights areas of dissatisfaction, points of friction, or factors contributing to user disengagement.

- **Analysis:** Analyzing churn rate helps identify high-churn segments, common churn triggers, or usability issues within the gamified experience. Proactive measures such as targeted re-engagement campaigns or user feedback mechanisms can mitigate churn and improve retention.

Session Frequency

- **Definition:** The average number of sessions or interactions per user within a defined time frame, such as daily, weekly, or monthly.
- **Importance:** Session frequency reflects users' active engagement and habitual usage patterns within the gamified environment. It indicates the stickiness of the experience and the frequency of return visits.
- **Analysis:** Monitoring session frequency allows organizations to assess user engagement trends and identify opportunities to increase interaction frequency. Analyzing session duration, session depth, or session-to-session transitions provides insights into user behaviors and preferences.

Time Between Sessions

- **Definition:** The average duration of time elapsed between consecutive user sessions or interactions within the gamified environment.
- **Importance:** Time between sessions measures users' re-engagement intervals and retention intervals. It indicates the frequency of return visits and the persistence of user interest over time.
- **Analysis:** Analyzing time between sessions helps identify user retention patterns, seasonal variations, or changes in engagement dynamics. Shortening re-engagement intervals through targeted notifications, reminders, or personalized content recommendations can improve user retention.

Lifetime Value (LTV)

- **Definition:** The total value or contribution of a user to the gamified experience over their entire lifecycle.
- **Importance:** Lifetime value quantifies the economic or strategic significance of individual users in terms of their engagement, retention, and contribution to organizational goals.
- **Analysis:** Calculating lifetime value enables organizations to prioritize retention efforts, segment users based on value tiers, and allocate resources effectively. Enhancing user engagement, satisfaction, and

loyalty through personalized experiences and incentives can maximize lifetime value.

Return on Retention (RoR)

- **Definition:** The ratio of the revenue or value generated from retained users to the cost of retaining those users.
- **Importance:** Return on retention measures the efficiency and effectiveness of retention strategies in generating tangible outcomes or returns on investment.
- **Analysis:** Calculating return on retention allows organizations to evaluate the impact of retention initiatives on revenue growth, customer lifetime value, and overall business performance. Optimizing retention tactics based on RoR insights ensures a sustainable and profitable gamified ecosystem.

Social Metrics

Social metrics in gamification analytics focus on evaluating the social interactions and dynamics within gamified experiences. These metrics provide insights into how users engage with each other, collaborate, compete, and form communities within the gamified environment. By tracking social metrics, organizations can assess the effectiveness of social features, foster community participation, and enhance user engagement.

Social metrics in gamification analytics provide valuable insights into the social interactions, collaboration dynamics, and community engagement within gamified experiences. By tracking these metrics, organizations can foster a sense of community, stimulate user engagement, and amplify the impact of gamified interventions. As gamification continues to evolve, leveraging social analytics capabilities will be essential for building thriving communities and delivering meaningful user experiences.

Social Interactions

- **Definition:** The frequency and types of interactions users have with each other within the gamified environment, such as messages, comments, likes, and shares.
- **Importance:** Social interactions reflect users' engagement with community members, content, and activities. They foster a sense of belonging, social presence, and camaraderie within the gamified experience.
- **Analysis:** Analyzing social interaction metrics helps identify popular communication channels, influential users, and topics of interest. It

allows organizations to gauge the vibrancy of the community and the effectiveness of social features in facilitating user engagement.

Collaboration Rates

- **Definition:** The extent to which users collaborate, cooperate, or work together to achieve shared goals or complete tasks within the gamified environment.
- **Importance:** Collaboration rates indicate the level of teamwork, coordination, and mutual support among users. They promote collective problem-solving, knowledge sharing, and skill development.
- **Analysis:** Tracking collaboration rates enables organizations to identify collaborative patterns, team dynamics, and areas of synergy within the gamified community. Analyzing collaborative behaviors helps optimize group-based activities and foster a culture of teamwork.

Competition Dynamics

- **Definition:** The nature and intensity of competitive interactions among users, such as leaderboard rankings, challenges, and tournaments.
- **Importance:** Competition dynamics stimulate user motivation, engagement, and performance improvement within the gamified environment. They drive goal-setting, skill development, and achievement striving.
- **Analysis:** Analyzing competition dynamics allows organizations to assess the impact of competitive elements on user behavior and performance. It helps identify high-performing users, competitive strategies, and opportunities for gamification refinement.

Community Engagement

- **Definition:** The degree of user participation, contribution, and involvement in community activities, discussions, and events within the gamified environment.
- **Importance:** Community engagement fosters a sense of belonging, identity, and loyalty among users. It promotes knowledge sharing, peer support, and social cohesion within the gamified community.
- **Analysis:** Tracking community engagement metrics helps measure the health and vibrancy of the community. It enables organizations to identify influential community members, emerging trends, and topics of interest for targeted engagement strategies.

Social Influence and Virality

- **Definition:** The extent to which users influence each other's behaviors, attitudes, and participation within the gamified environment, as well as the spread of gamified content through social networks.
- **Importance:** Social influence and virality metrics highlight the impact of user-generated content, referrals, and recommendations on community growth and engagement. They amplify the reach and impact of gamified experiences.
- **Analysis:** Analyzing social influence and virality metrics helps identify key influencers, viral loops, and amplification mechanisms within the gamified community. It informs strategies for incentivizing user-generated content, fostering word-of-mouth marketing, and expanding community reach.

Feedback Metrics

Feedback metrics in gamification analytics focus on evaluating the quality, quantity, and sentiment of user-generated feedback within gamified experiences. These metrics provide valuable insights into users' perceptions, satisfaction levels, and areas for improvement, helping organizations refine gamification strategies and enhance user engagement. By tracking feedback metrics, organizations can gather actionable insights, foster continuous improvement, and cultivate a user-centered approach to gamification.

Feedback metrics in gamification analytics offer valuable insights into users' perceptions, satisfaction levels, and engagement within gamified experiences. By tracking these metrics, organizations can gather actionable feedback, prioritize improvement efforts, and enhance the overall user experience. As gamification continues to evolve, leveraging feedback analytics capabilities will be essential for cultivating user-centered design practices and delivering meaningful, user-driven gamified experiences.

Quantity of Feedback

- **Definition:** The volume or frequency of user-generated feedback, including comments, suggestions, bug reports, and feature requests, submitted within the gamified environment.
- **Importance:** Quantity of feedback metrics indicate users' willingness to engage with the gamified experience and provide input. They reflect the level of user involvement and investment in shaping the gamification design and features.

- **Analysis:** Analyzing the quantity of feedback helps identify trends, spikes, or patterns in user engagement and interaction. It enables organizations to prioritize feedback collection efforts and allocate resources effectively.

Feedback Sentiment

- **Definition:** The emotional tone or sentiment conveyed in user-generated feedback, such as positive, neutral, or negative sentiments, expressed through text or sentiment analysis algorithms.
- **Importance:** Feedback sentiment metrics offer insights into users' attitudes, perceptions, and satisfaction levels regarding the gamified experience. They highlight areas of strength and potential pain points that require attention.
- **Analysis:** Analyzing feedback sentiment allows organizations to gauge user satisfaction, identify areas for improvement, and prioritize enhancement efforts. It facilitates sentiment trend analysis over time to track changes in user sentiment and assess the impact of gamification interventions.

Feedback Topics and Themes

- **Definition:** The recurring themes, topics, or categories addressed in user-generated feedback, such as usability issues, feature requests, gameplay mechanics, or content-related feedback.
- **Importance:** Feedback topics and themes provide insights into users' concerns, preferences, and priorities within the gamified environment. They highlight areas of consensus or contention among users.
- **Analysis:** Analyzing feedback topics and themes helps categorize and prioritize user feedback for action. It informs decision-making regarding gamification design, content development, and feature enhancements based on user needs and preferences.

Responsiveness and Resolution Time

- **Definition:** The time it takes for organizations to acknowledge, respond to, and resolve user-generated feedback or inquiries within the gamified environment.
- **Importance:** Responsiveness and resolution time metrics reflect organizations' commitment to addressing user concerns, fostering trust, and maintaining user satisfaction. They impact user perception of customer support quality and service reliability.

- **Analysis:** Analyzing responsiveness and resolution time enables organizations to assess their effectiveness in handling user feedback and support requests. It helps identify bottlenecks, optimize response workflows, and improve communication processes with users.

User Engagement Impact

- **Definition:** The influence of user-generated feedback on user engagement metrics, such as retention rates, session durations, and interaction frequencies within the gamified environment.
- **Importance:** User engagement impact metrics quantify the effect of feedback-driven improvements or changes on user behavior and participation. They provide evidence of the effectiveness of feedback-driven iterations.
- **Analysis:** Analyzing user engagement impact helps evaluate the ROI of feedback-driven initiatives and optimization efforts. It informs decisions regarding future enhancements and prioritization of feedback implementation based on their potential impact on user engagement metrics.

6.3.2 Methodologies for Gamification Analytics

Data Collection

Data collection for gamification analytics involves gathering relevant data points from various sources within the gamified environment. These data sources provide insights into user behavior, engagement patterns, performance metrics, and other key indicators necessary for assessing the effectiveness of gamification strategies. Effective data collection ensures that organizations have access to comprehensive and accurate information for analysis and decision-making.

Effective data collection is essential for obtaining actionable insights and driving informed decision-making in gamification analytics. By leveraging diverse data sources and adhering to best practices, organizations can gain a comprehensive understanding of user behavior, engagement patterns, and performance metrics within gamified environments.

User Interactions

- **Description:** User interactions encompass the actions, behaviors, and activities performed by users within the gamified environment. This includes interactions with game elements, challenges, levels, rewards, and social features.
- **Data Points:** Data points may include user clicks, navigation paths, time spent on specific activities, completion of tasks or challenges,

participation in multiplayer interactions, and engagement with gamification elements such as badges or leaderboards.

System Logs

- **Description:** System logs record various system-level events, transactions, and activities occurring within the gamified platform or application. This includes user logins, sessions, transactions, API calls, and error logs.
- **Data Points:** Data points logged in system logs may include timestamps, user identifiers, session durations, transaction details, error codes, and system performance metrics such as response times or latency.

Performance Metrics

- **Description:** Performance metrics capture users' performance and achievements within the gamified environment. This includes scores, completion rates, proficiency levels, mastery levels, and skill assessments.
- **Data Points:** Data points for performance metrics may include user scores, level completion statuses, progress towards goals or milestones, skill assessments, and proficiency levels achieved in specific tasks or challenges.

Feedback Mechanisms

- **Description:** Feedback mechanisms enable users to provide input, suggestions, comments, or ratings regarding their experiences within the gamified environment. This includes feedback forms, surveys, rating systems, and user reviews.
- **Data Points:** Data points collected from feedback mechanisms may include textual feedback, ratings, sentiment analysis scores, user identifiers, timestamps, and metadata related to the feedback source or context.

Social Interactions

- **Description:** Social interactions capture users' engagement with social features, collaboration with other users, and participation in community activities within the gamified environment. This includes likes, shares, comments, messages, and participation in multiplayer challenges or competitions.
- **Data Points:** Data points for social interactions may include user interactions, content shared, comments posted, messages exchanged, social network connections, and engagement levels with social features.

User Profiles and Demographics

- **Description:** User profiles and demographics provide information about users' characteristics, preferences, and demographics within the gamified environment. This includes user profiles, registration data, preferences, and demographic information.
- **Data Points:** Data points for user profiles and demographics may include user identifiers, demographic attributes (such as age, gender, location), preferences, interests, past behavior, and user-generated content.

External Data Sources

- **Description:** External data sources may include data from third-party APIs, integration with other systems or platforms, and external databases or repositories. This data can enrich gamification analytics with additional context or complementary information.
- **Data Points:** Data points from external sources may vary depending on the integration and data sharing agreements but may include user activity from external platforms, transaction data, social media interactions, or user-generated content from other sources.

Data Collection Best Practices

- **Ensure Data Privacy and Security:** Implement measures to protect user privacy and comply with data protection regulations when collecting and handling user data.
- **Use Tracking Tools:** Employ tracking tools or analytics platforms specifically designed for gamification environments to streamline data collection and analysis.
- **Aggregate and Anonymize Data:** Aggregate data to protect individual user identities and anonymize sensitive information where necessary to ensure privacy and confidentiality.
- **Regularly Audit Data Sources:** Conduct regular audits of data sources to ensure data accuracy, consistency, and relevance for analytics purposes.
- **Optimize Data Collection Processes:** Continuously refine data collection processes to minimize data latency, improve data quality, and optimize resource utilization.

Data Processing

Data processing for gamification analytics involves transforming raw data collected from various sources within the gamified environment into a structured format suitable for analysis. This process includes cleaning, preprocessing, aggregating, and organizing data to extract meaningful insights and derive actionable conclusions. Data processing is a critical step in gamification analytics, transforming raw data into actionable insights that drive informed decision-making. By cleaning, integrating, transforming, aggregating, enriching, sampling, storing, and quality-assuring the data, organizations can derive valuable insights and optimize gamification strategies for enhanced user engagement and satisfaction.

Data Cleaning

- **Description:** Data cleaning involves identifying and correcting errors, inconsistencies, missing values, and outliers in the raw data collected from different sources. This ensures data accuracy and reliability for subsequent analysis.
- **Methods:** Use techniques such as data validation, outlier detection, and imputation to clean the data. Remove duplicate records, standardize data formats, and resolve discrepancies to prepare the data for further processing.

Data Integration

- **Description:** Data integration combines data from multiple sources, such as user interactions, system logs, performance metrics, feedback mechanisms, and social interactions, into a unified dataset. This enables comprehensive analysis and correlation of data across different dimensions.
- **Methods:** Use data integration techniques such as data merging, joining, or linking to combine datasets from disparate sources. Ensure consistency in data formats, keys, and identifiers to facilitate seamless integration.

Data Transformation

- **Description:** Data transformation involves converting raw data into a structured format suitable for analysis. This may include feature engineering, normalization, scaling, and transformation of variables to extract meaningful insights and patterns.
- **Methods:** Apply transformation techniques such as feature extraction, dimensionality reduction, and data normalization to preprocess the data. Convert categorical variables into numerical representations and scale numerical variables to a common range for consistency.

Data Aggregation

- **Description:** Data aggregation combines individual data points into summary statistics or aggregated metrics to analyze trends, patterns, and behavior at higher levels of granularity. This allows for the analysis of data over time, across user segments, or within specific contexts.

- **Methods:** Aggregate data using statistical functions such as sum, average, count, or percentile to derive key performance indicators (KPIs) and summary metrics. Aggregate data at different levels of granularity, such as daily, weekly, or monthly, to capture trends and patterns effectively.

Data Enrichment

- **Description:** Data enrichment enhances the raw data with additional context, metadata, or external information to enrich the analysis and provide deeper insights. This may involve supplementing gamification data with demographic data, user profiles, or external datasets.
- **Methods:** Integrate external data sources or APIs to enrich gamification data with additional context or complementary information. Use data enrichment techniques such as geocoding, sentiment analysis, or social network analysis to add value to the dataset.

Data Sampling

- **Description:** Data sampling involves selecting a representative subset of data from the larger dataset for analysis, especially in cases of large volumes of data or resource constraints. This helps reduce computational complexity and improve analysis efficiency.
- **Methods:** Use random sampling, stratified sampling, or other sampling techniques to select a subset of data that accurately represents the larger population. Ensure that the sampled data retains the characteristics and distribution of the original dataset.

Data Storage and Management

- **Description:** Data storage and management involve storing processed data in a secure and accessible repository for analysis, visualization, and reporting. This may include data warehouses, databases, or cloud storage solutions.
- **Methods:** Choose appropriate data storage solutions based on scalability, performance, and security requirements. Implement data governance policies, access controls, and backup procedures to ensure data integrity and availability.

Data Quality Assurance

- **Description:** Data quality assurance involves validating the accuracy, completeness, and consistency of processed data to ensure its reliability for analysis and decision-making. This includes data validation, quality checks, and validation against predefined criteria.

- **Methods:** Perform data quality checks, validation tests, and data profiling to identify and rectify any discrepancies or anomalies in the processed data. Implement data validation rules, data lineage tracking, and error detection mechanisms to maintain data quality.

Descriptive Analytics

Descriptive analytics for gamification involves summarizing and interpreting key metrics and trends within gamified experiences to gain insights into user behavior, engagement patterns, and performance metrics. This analytical approach focuses on understanding what has happened within the gamified environment, identifying patterns, and highlighting areas of interest or concern. Descriptive analytics forms the foundation for further analysis and decision-making in gamification strategies.

Descriptive analytics provides valuable insights into user behavior, engagement patterns, and performance metrics within gamified experiences. By summarizing key metrics, visualizing data, analyzing trends, conducting cohort analysis, benchmarking performance, and segmenting users, organizations can gain a comprehensive understanding of gamification effectiveness and identify areas for optimization. Descriptive analytics serves as the basis for further analysis and decision-making in gamification strategies, driving continuous improvement and enhancing user engagement and satisfaction.

Summary Statistics

- **Description:** Summary statistics provide an overview of key metrics and indicators within the gamified environment. This includes measures such as mean, median, mode, range, standard deviation, and percentiles.
- **Application:** Calculate summary statistics for performance metrics (e.g., scores, completion rates), engagement metrics (e.g., time spent, frequency of visits), social metrics (e.g., interactions, collaboration rates), and feedback metrics (e.g., sentiment scores, quantity of feedback) to understand their central tendency, variability, and distribution.

Data Visualization

- **Description:** Data visualization techniques represent gamification data visually using charts, graphs, and dashboards. This helps identify trends, patterns, and outliers more intuitively and facilitates communication of insights to stakeholders.
- **Application:** Create visualizations such as line charts, bar charts, pie charts, histograms, scatter plots, heatmaps, and network graphs to

depict user engagement over time, distribution of performance scores, correlation between variables, and sentiment analysis results.

Trend Analysis

- **Description:** Trend analysis examines historical data to identify patterns, trends, and recurring themes within the gamified environment. This helps identify changes or developments over time and anticipate future behavior.
- **Application:** Analyze trends in user engagement metrics (e.g., active users, session durations), performance metrics (e.g., completion rates, progression velocity), social metrics (e.g., collaboration rates, community engagement), and feedback metrics (e.g., sentiment trends, feedback volumes) to identify shifts in user behavior or sentiment.

Cohort Analysis

- **Description:** Cohort analysis groups users into segments based on shared characteristics or behaviors and compares their performance or engagement metrics over time. This helps identify differences and similarities between user groups and assess the impact of gamification interventions.
- **Application:** Segment users based on demographic attributes (e.g., age, gender), user behavior (e.g., frequency of engagement, skill proficiency), or other relevant factors. Compare cohort performance metrics (e.g., retention rates, completion rates) to evaluate the effectiveness of gamification strategies for different user segments.

Benchmarking

- **Description:** Benchmarking compares gamification metrics against industry standards, best practices, or internal benchmarks to assess performance relative to peers or targets. This helps identify areas of strength, areas for improvement, and opportunities for optimization.
- **Application:** Benchmark gamification metrics such as engagement rates, completion rates, and feedback sentiment scores against industry benchmarks or historical performance data. Identify performance gaps and prioritize initiatives to achieve desired outcomes.

Segmentation Analysis

- **Description:** Segmentation analysis divides users into distinct groups based on shared characteristics, behaviors, or preferences and analyzes their performance or engagement metrics separately. This helps tailor gamification strategies to different user segments and personalize the user experience.

- **Application:** Segment users based on factors such as user demographics, behavior patterns, skill levels, or interaction preferences. Analyze performance and engagement metrics within each segment to identify unique needs, preferences, and opportunities for customization.

Predictive Analytics

Predictive analytics in gamification involves leveraging historical data and statistical modeling techniques to forecast future user behavior, performance outcomes, or trends within gamified experiences. By analyzing patterns, identifying correlations, and building predictive models, organizations can anticipate user actions, optimize engagement strategies, and tailor gamification interventions to individual user preferences.

Predictive analytics empowers organizations to proactively identify opportunities, mitigate risks, and optimize gamification strategies to drive user engagement, satisfaction, and performance outcomes. By leveraging advanced analytical techniques and predictive modeling, organizations can unlock the full potential of gamified experiences and deliver personalized, impactful user experiences.

Data Preparation and Exploration

- **Data Cleaning and Integration:** Cleanse and integrate raw data from various sources, including user interactions, performance metrics, and feedback mechanisms, to create a unified dataset suitable for analysis.
- **Feature Engineering:** Extract relevant features from the dataset, such as user demographics, engagement metrics, and historical behavior, to serve as inputs for predictive modeling.
- **Exploratory Data Analysis (EDA):** Conduct exploratory data analysis to identify patterns, correlations, and trends in the data, gaining insights into user behavior and performance metrics.

Model Selection and Training

- **Algorithm Selection:** Choose appropriate machine learning algorithms based on the nature of the prediction task and characteristics of the dataset. Common algorithms for predictive analytics in gamification include regression models, classification algorithms, and clustering techniques.
- **Model Training:** Train predictive models using historical data, splitting the dataset into training and validation sets to evaluate model

performance. Tune model hyperparameters and assess model accuracy, precision, recall, and other performance metrics.

Feature Selection and Engineering

- **Feature Selection:** Identify relevant predictors or features from the dataset that contribute most significantly to the prediction task. Use techniques such as feature importance analysis, correlation analysis, and dimensionality reduction to select informative features.
- **Feature Engineering:** Transform and preprocess features to enhance model performance and interpretability. This may include encoding categorical variables, scaling numerical features, and creating new derived features.

Model Evaluation and Validation

- **Cross-Validation:** Validate predictive models using techniques such as k-fold cross-validation to assess generalization performance and robustness across different subsets of the data.
- **Evaluation Metrics:** Measure model performance using appropriate evaluation metrics, such as accuracy, precision, recall, F1-score, area under the ROC curve (AUC-ROC), or mean squared error (MSE), depending on the prediction task.

Deployment and Implementation

- **Model Deployment:** Deploy trained predictive models into production environments, integrating them into gamified platforms or applications to generate real-time predictions.
- **Monitoring and Maintenance:** Continuously monitor model performance and recalibrate models as needed to adapt to changing user behavior, evolving trends, and new data inputs.

Use Cases of Predictive Analytics in Gamification

- **User Churn Prediction:** Forecast user churn or attrition within gamified environments by analyzing historical engagement patterns, feedback sentiments, and user interactions to identify at-risk users and implement targeted retention strategies.
- **Performance Improvement Prediction:** Predict user performance improvement trajectories based on historical performance metrics, skill assessments, and learning behaviors, enabling personalized interventions and adaptive learning pathways.

- **Content Recommendation:** Anticipate user preferences and interests to deliver personalized content recommendations, challenges, or rewards tailored to individual user profiles and engagement histories.
- **Dynamic Difficulty Adjustment:** Dynamically adjust the difficulty level of gamified challenges, tasks, or levels based on predictive models that anticipate user skill levels, learning progress, and performance capabilities.
- **Gamification Effectiveness Prediction:** Forecast the effectiveness of gamification interventions, feature enhancements, or engagement strategies by analyzing historical data and user feedback to optimize future gamification initiatives.

Prescriptive Analytics

Prescriptive analytics in gamification involves using insights from descriptive and predictive analytics to recommend actionable strategies and interventions aimed at optimizing user engagement, satisfaction, and performance outcomes within gamified experiences. By leveraging data-driven approaches and optimization algorithms, organizations can proactively prescribe personalized interventions, adaptive learning pathways, and targeted gamification strategies to drive desired user behaviors and outcomes.

Prescriptive analytics empowers organizations to go beyond descriptive and predictive insights to proactively recommend actionable strategies and interventions aimed at optimizing user engagement, satisfaction, and performance outcomes within gamified experiences. By leveraging advanced analytical techniques, optimization algorithms, and decision models, organizations can unlock the full potential of gamification and deliver personalized, impactful user experiences.

Data Preparation and Analysis

- **Data Cleaning and Integration:** Cleanse and integrate raw data from various sources, including user interactions, performance metrics, feedback mechanisms, and predictive modeling outputs, to create a unified dataset for analysis.
- **Descriptive Analysis:** Conduct descriptive analytics to explore historical trends, patterns, and correlations in user behavior, performance metrics, and gamification features, gaining insights into key drivers of user engagement and satisfaction.

Predictive Modeling and Insights

- **Predictive Modeling:** Train machine learning models to forecast future user behavior, performance outcomes, and trends within gamified experiences based on historical data and feature inputs.

- **Insights Generation:** Analyze predictive modeling outputs to identify opportunities, risks, and areas for improvement in user engagement, satisfaction, and performance outcomes. Extract actionable insights from predictive analytics outputs to inform prescriptive recommendations.

Optimization Algorithms and Decision Models

- **Optimization Techniques:** Employ optimization algorithms, decision models, and simulation methods to generate prescriptive recommendations and intervention strategies aimed at maximizing desired user behaviors and outcomes.
- **Multi-Criteria Decision Analysis:** Use multi-criteria decision analysis (MCDA) techniques to evaluate alternative intervention strategies, considering multiple objectives, constraints, and stakeholder preferences.

Prescriptive Recommendations

- **Personalized Interventions:** Prescribe personalized interventions, adaptive learning pathways, and gamification strategies tailored to individual user profiles, preferences, and engagement histories.
- **Dynamic Adjustments:** Recommend dynamic adjustments to gamification features, challenges, and rewards based on real-time user interactions, feedback sentiments, and predictive modeling insights.

Implementation and Evaluation

- **Implementation Framework:** Develop an implementation framework to deploy and operationalize prescriptive recommendations within gamified platforms or applications. Integrate prescriptive analytics solutions into existing gamification workflows and user engagement mechanisms.
- **Performance Monitoring:** Continuously monitor the effectiveness and impact of prescriptive recommendations on user engagement, satisfaction, and performance outcomes. Evaluate the success of implemented interventions through key performance indicators (KPIs) and feedback mechanisms.

Use Cases of Prescriptive Analytics in Gamification

- **Adaptive Learning Paths:** Prescribe adaptive learning paths and personalized content recommendations based on user skill levels, learning preferences, and performance trajectories to optimize learning outcomes.

- **Gamification Feature Optimization:** Recommend adjustments to gamification features, challenges, and rewards to enhance user engagement, motivation, and retention over time.
- **Retention Strategies:** Prescribe targeted retention strategies and interventions to mitigate user churn, enhance user loyalty, and foster long-term engagement within gamified environments.
- **Performance Improvement Tactics:** Recommend personalized performance improvement tactics, skill-building exercises, and challenges tailored to individual user needs and learning objectives.
- **Social Influence Strategies:** Prescribe social influence strategies, collaborative activities, and community-building initiatives to amplify user engagement, encourage peer interaction, and foster a sense of belonging within the gamified community.

Continuous Monitoring

Continuous monitoring for gamification analytics involves the ongoing assessment and tracking of key metrics, user behaviors, and performance outcomes within gamified experiences. By continuously monitoring user engagement, satisfaction levels, and performance metrics, organizations can identify trends, detect anomalies, and adapt gamification strategies in real-time to optimize user experiences and achieve desired outcomes.

Continuous monitoring for gamification analytics enables organizations to stay agile, responsive, and adaptive in optimizing user experiences and achieving desired outcomes within gamified environments. By leveraging real-time data insights, anomaly detection techniques, and iterative refinement processes, organizations can maintain high levels of user engagement, satisfaction, and performance over time.

Real-Time Data Collection

- Implement mechanisms to collect and ingest data from various sources within the gamified environment in real-time. This includes user interactions, system logs, performance metrics, feedback mechanisms, and social interactions.
- Utilize tracking tools, event listeners, and API integrations to capture and stream real-time data inputs into analytics platforms or dashboards for immediate analysis.

Key Performance Indicators (KPIs)

- Define a set of key performance indicators (KPIs) aligned with gamification objectives, user engagement goals, and performance outcomes. These KPIs serve as benchmarks for evaluating the effectiveness of gamification strategies.

- Identify leading indicators that provide early warning signs of potential issues or opportunities for improvement within the gamified environment.

Real-Time Analytics and Visualization

- Leverage analytics platforms and visualization tools to analyze real-time data streams and generate actionable insights. Implement dashboards, charts, and reports to visualize KPIs, trends, and user behaviors in real-time.
- Use interactive visualization techniques to drill down into specific user segments, time periods, or gamification features for deeper analysis and exploration.

Anomaly Detection and Alerting

- Deploy anomaly detection algorithms and statistical techniques to identify deviations from expected patterns or thresholds in real-time data streams. This includes detecting sudden changes in user engagement levels, performance metrics, or system behavior.
- Configure alerting mechanisms and notification systems to trigger alerts or notifications when anomalies are detected, enabling timely intervention and response by stakeholders.

A/B Testing and Experimentation

- Conduct A/B testing and experimentation to evaluate the impact of gamification interventions, feature enhancements, or user experience modifications in real-time. Implement randomized control trials and split-testing methodologies to compare alternative strategies and measure their effectiveness.
- Monitor user responses, engagement metrics, and performance outcomes in real-time to assess the success of A/B tests and experiments and make data-driven decisions accordingly.

User Feedback and Sentiment Analysis

- Continuously collect and analyze user feedback, comments, and sentiments expressed within the gamified environment in real-time. Use natural language processing (NLP) techniques and sentiment analysis algorithms to extract insights from textual data.

- Monitor user sentiment trends, identify emerging issues, and address user concerns promptly to maintain high levels of user satisfaction and engagement.

Iterative Refinement and Adaptation

- Continuously iterate and refine gamification strategies, features, and interventions based on insights gathered from real-time monitoring and analysis. Implement agile development methodologies to adapt to changing user needs, preferences, and trends.
- Collaborate cross-functionally with stakeholders, gamification experts, and data analysts to prioritize optimization efforts and implement iterative improvements to the gamified experience.

Performance Review and Reporting

- Regularly review performance metrics, KPIs, and trends observed through continuous monitoring efforts. Generate periodic reports, performance summaries, and executive dashboards to communicate insights and progress to stakeholders.
- Conduct post-mortem analyses to evaluate the effectiveness of interventions, initiatives, or changes implemented based on real-time monitoring data. Identify lessons learned and best practices for future gamification endeavors.

6.3.3 Practical Applications of Gamification Analytics

Employee Training and Development

In today's dynamic work environment, employee training and development have become crucial for organizational success. Companies are constantly seeking innovative methods to enhance the effectiveness of their training programs. One such method gaining traction is gamification, which incorporates game elements into non-game contexts to engage and motivate employees. Gamification analytics further refine this approach by providing valuable insights into employee behavior and performance. This article explores the practical applications of gamification analytics in employee training and development.

Gamification analytics offer a transformative approach to employee training and development, leveraging game mechanics and data insights to enhance engagement, performance, and learning outcomes. By incorporating gamification into various aspects of training, organizations can create immersive, personalized experiences that motivate employees and drive continuous improvement. However, successful implementation requires careful planning, meaningful design, and ongoing evaluation to ensure alignment with organizational goals and employee needs. As technology continues to advance, gamification analytics will likely play an increasingly prominent role in shaping the future of workplace learning and development.

Gamification is the integration of game mechanics and design techniques into non-game activities to increase participation and engagement. By applying elements such as points, badges, leaderboards, and challenges, organizations can make learning more enjoyable and motivating for employees. Unlike traditional training methods, gamification leverages intrinsic motivators, such as competition and achievement, to drive desired behaviors and outcomes.

The Role of Analytics in Gamification

Analytics play a vital role in gamification by enabling organizations to measure, analyze, and interpret data related to employee participation and performance. Gamification analytics provide insights into various metrics, including engagement levels, completion rates, knowledge retention, and skill acquisition. By tracking these metrics, organizations can evaluate the effectiveness of their training initiatives and make data-driven decisions to optimize learning experiences.

Components of Gamification Analytics

- **Engagement Metrics:** Gamification analytics measure the level of engagement among employees participating in training activities. Metrics such as time spent, frequency of interactions, and participation rates help gauge the effectiveness of gamified elements in capturing employees' interest and attention.
- **Performance Indicators:** Analyzing performance indicators such as quiz scores, skill assessments, and task completion rates allows organizations to assess the impact of gamification on learning outcomes. By correlating performance data with gamified interventions, organizations can identify areas of improvement and tailor training content accordingly.
- **Behavioral Patterns:** Gamification analytics track employees' behavioral patterns within gamified systems, including their preferences, tendencies, and progression paths. Understanding these patterns enables organizations to personalize training experiences, adapt gamified elements to individual needs, and intervene proactively to address challenges.
- **Social Dynamics:** Social interactions play a significant role in gamification, with features like leaderboards, team challenges, and peer-to-peer recognition fostering collaboration and healthy competition. Analytics help monitor social dynamics within gamified environments, revealing influencers, collaboration patterns, and the impact of social reinforcement on learning outcomes.

Practical Applications of Gamification Analytics

- **Onboarding and Orientation:** Gamification analytics can enhance the onboarding process by providing real-time feedback on new hires' progress and proficiency levels. By gamifying orientation activities, organizations can accelerate learning curves, improve retention of critical information, and foster a sense of belonging among employees.
- **Skills Development:** Gamification analytics enable organizations to track employees' skill development journeys and identify areas where additional support or resources may be needed. By gamifying skill-building exercises and training modules, organizations can create immersive learning experiences that encourage continuous improvement and mastery.
- **Compliance Training:** Compliance training often suffers from low engagement and retention rates due to its repetitive and dry nature. Gamification analytics offer a solution by transforming compliance modules into interactive experiences that motivate employees to comply with regulations while tracking their adherence and comprehension levels.
- **Sales Training and Incentives:** In sales environments, gamification analytics can optimize training programs by incentivizing desired behaviors, such as product knowledge acquisition, sales performance, and customer engagement. By gamifying sales training and offering rewards tied to specific metrics, organizations can drive sales effectiveness and enhance revenue generation.
- **Professional Development:** Gamification analytics support professional development initiatives by providing insights into employees' learning preferences, career aspirations, and areas of interest. By gamifying learning pathways and offering personalized development plans, organizations can empower employees to take ownership of their growth while tracking their progress and achievements.

Challenges and Considerations

Despite its potential benefits, implementing gamification analytics in employee training and development is not without challenges. Organizations must address the following considerations:

- **Designing Meaningful Gamified Experiences:** Effective gamification requires thoughtful design that aligns with learning objectives and engages employees authentically. Organizations must carefully select game mechanics and elements that resonate with their workforce and contribute to desired learning outcomes.

- **Data Privacy and Security:** Collecting and analyzing employee data for gamification purposes raises concerns about privacy and security. Organizations must adhere to strict data protection regulations and ensure transparency and consent regarding the use of personal information for analytics purposes.
- **Balancing Competition and Collaboration:** While competition can be a powerful motivator in gamification, it should not overshadow the importance of collaboration and teamwork. Organizations must strike a balance between individual achievement and collective goals to foster a supportive and inclusive learning environment.
- **Continuous Evaluation and Iteration:** Gamification analytics require ongoing evaluation and iteration to remain effective. Organizations must monitor key metrics, gather feedback from participants, and iterate on gamified elements to address evolving needs and preferences.

Health and Wellness

In recent years, the integration of technology into health and wellness initiatives has revolutionized how individuals engage with their personal health journeys. One such innovation is the application of gamification and analytics to promote healthier lifestyles. Gamification, the use of game elements in non-game contexts, combined with analytics, provides valuable insights into user behavior and performance.

Gamification analytics hold immense potential for promoting health and wellness by leveraging game mechanics and data insights to motivate behavior change, foster engagement, and drive positive outcomes. From physical activity tracking to stress reduction and chronic disease management, gamification offers a versatile toolkit to support various aspects of well-being. However, successful implementation requires careful consideration of privacy, sustainability, personalization, and ethics to ensure that gamified interventions effectively empower individuals to lead healthier lives. As technology continues to evolve, gamification analytics will likely play an increasingly integral role in shaping the future of digital health and wellness promotion.

Gamification in health and wellness involves applying game mechanics, such as points, badges, challenges, and rewards, to encourage individuals to adopt and maintain healthy behaviors. By making health-related activities more engaging and enjoyable, gamification motivates users to stay committed to their wellness goals. Whether it's tracking physical activity, monitoring nutrition, managing stress, or promoting mindfulness, gamification offers a gamut of applications to support various aspects of well-being.

The Role of Analytics in Gamification for Health and Wellness

Analytics play a crucial role in gamification for health and wellness by providing insights into user engagement, behavior patterns, and progress towards health goals. Gamification analytics allow organizations and individuals to track key metrics, identify trends, and tailor interventions to optimize outcomes. By leveraging data-driven insights, gamification initiatives can adapt to individual preferences, address barriers to behavior change, and enhance overall effectiveness.

Components of Gamification Analytics in Health and Wellness

- **Engagement Metrics:** Gamification analytics measure user engagement by tracking metrics such as active participation, frequency of interactions, and time spent on health-related activities. These metrics provide valuable feedback on the effectiveness of gamified interventions in capturing users' interest and sustaining their motivation over time.
- **Behavioral Patterns:** Analyzing user behavior within gamified health and wellness platforms reveals insights into patterns, preferences, and challenges. By understanding how users interact with gamified elements, organizations can personalize experiences, optimize usability, and design targeted interventions to address specific needs.
- **Goal Progression:** Gamification analytics track users' progress towards predefined health goals, such as achieving a target weight, increasing physical activity, or improving dietary habits. Monitoring goal progression allows individuals to celebrate milestones, adjust strategies, and stay motivated on their wellness journey.
- **Social Dynamics:** Social interactions play a significant role in gamification for health and wellness, with features like social sharing, peer support, and virtual communities fostering collaboration and accountability. Gamification analytics capture social dynamics within digital health platforms, highlighting influential users, community engagement levels, and the impact of social reinforcement on behavior change.

Practical Applications of Gamification Analytics in Health and Wellness

- **Physical Activity Tracking:** Gamification analytics enhance physical activity tracking by gamifying exercise routines, setting challenges, and rewarding milestones. By incorporating features such as step counts, workout streaks, and virtual badges, fitness apps motivate users to stay active while providing insights into their activity levels and progress.
- **Nutrition and Diet Management:** Gamification analytics support nutrition and diet management by gamifying food logging, meal

planning, and nutritional tracking. By awarding points for healthy food choices, offering personalized recommendations, and visualizing nutritional data, diet apps empower users to make informed decisions and cultivate healthier eating habits.

- **Stress Reduction and Mental Well-being:** Gamification analytics promote stress reduction and mental well-being by gamifying mindfulness practices, relaxation techniques, and stress management strategies. Through interactive games, guided meditations, and mood tracking features, mental health apps help users build resilience, cope with stressors, and improve overall emotional well-being.
- **Chronic Disease Management:** Gamification analytics facilitate chronic disease management by gamifying medication adherence, symptom tracking, and disease self-management tasks. By incorporating reminders, progress trackers, and educational content, health management apps empower individuals with chronic conditions to take control of their health, monitor their progress, and adhere to treatment plans.
- **Employee Wellness Programs:** Gamification analytics are increasingly being used in corporate wellness programs to promote employee health and productivity. By gamifying wellness challenges, incentivizing healthy behaviors, and fostering social support networks, employers can create a culture of well-being while improving employee engagement, satisfaction, and retention.

Challenges and Considerations

While gamification analytics offer promising opportunities for promoting health and wellness, several challenges and considerations must be addressed:

- **Data Privacy and Security:** Collecting and analyzing sensitive health data for gamification purposes raises concerns about privacy and security. Organizations must comply with data protection regulations, implement robust security measures, and prioritize user consent and transparency regarding data usage.
- **Behavioral Sustainability:** Gamification interventions must focus on promoting sustainable behavior change rather than short-term rewards. Organizations should design gamified experiences that foster intrinsic motivation, provide meaningful feedback, and empower users to develop long-lasting habits.
- **Personalization and Adaptation:** Effective gamification requires personalized experiences that cater to individual preferences, needs, and circumstances. Organizations must leverage analytics to customize

interventions, adapt content in real-time, and provide relevant feedback and support to maximize user engagement and outcomes.

- **Ethical Considerations:** Gamification initiatives must adhere to ethical principles, ensuring that incentives and rewards do not promote unhealthy behaviors or reinforce stereotypes. Organizations should prioritize user well-being, promote autonomy, and avoid coercion or manipulation in their gamification strategies.

Marketing and Customer Engagement

In today's competitive business landscape, marketers are constantly seeking innovative ways to capture consumers' attention, drive engagement, and foster brand loyalty. Gamification, the integration of game elements into non-game contexts, has emerged as a powerful tool for enhancing marketing strategies and boosting customer engagement. When combined with analytics, gamification provides valuable insights into consumer behavior, preferences, and motivations.

Gamification analytics offer a dynamic approach to marketing and customer engagement, leveraging game mechanics and data insights to captivate audiences, drive interactions, and foster brand loyalty. From product discovery and loyalty programs to content engagement and event promotion, gamification offers a versatile toolkit to enhance various aspects of marketing strategies. However, successful implementation requires careful consideration of design, data privacy, authenticity, and measurement to ensure that gamification initiatives effectively resonate with consumers and drive meaningful results. As technology continues to evolve, gamification analytics will likely play an increasingly integral role in shaping the future of marketing and customer engagement strategies.

Gamification in marketing involves leveraging game mechanics, such as points, badges, challenges, and rewards, to engage consumers and incentivize desired behaviors. Whether it's encouraging product exploration, promoting brand advocacy, or driving conversions, gamification offers a dynamic approach to captivate audiences and enhance their interaction with marketing campaigns. By tapping into consumers' intrinsic motivations, such as competition, achievement, and social interaction, gamification creates immersive brand experiences that resonate with target audiences.

Role of Analytics in Gamification for Marketing

Analytics play a critical role in gamification for marketing by providing insights into consumer engagement, behavior patterns, and campaign performance. Gamification analytics enable marketers to track key metrics, measure the effectiveness of gamified elements, and optimize marketing initiatives based on data-driven insights. By understanding how consumers interact with gamified experiences, marketers can tailor their strategies, refine their messaging, and maximize the impact of their marketing efforts.

Components of Gamification Analytics in Marketing

- **Engagement Metrics:** Gamification analytics measure consumer engagement by tracking metrics such as participation rates, time spent, and interactions with gamified content. These metrics provide valuable feedback on the effectiveness of gamification in capturing consumers' attention and sustaining their interest throughout the marketing journey.
- **Behavioral Patterns:** Analyzing consumer behavior within gamified marketing campaigns reveals insights into preferences, tendencies, and decision-making processes. By understanding how consumers navigate gamified experiences, marketers can optimize user flows, refine calls-to-action, and design personalized experiences that resonate with individual interests and motivations.
- **Conversion Rates:** Gamification analytics track conversion rates and other key performance indicators (KPIs) to assess the impact of gamified elements on marketing outcomes. Whether it's driving sales, generating leads, or increasing brand engagement, marketers can measure the effectiveness of gamification in achieving desired goals and driving tangible results.
- **Social Sharing and Advocacy:** Social dynamics play a significant role in gamification for marketing, with features like social sharing, peer-to-peer challenges, and user-generated content fostering community engagement and brand advocacy. Gamification analytics capture social interactions within gamified campaigns, highlighting influencers, amplifying brand reach, and identifying opportunities for viral growth.

Practical Applications of Gamification Analytics in Marketing

- **Product Discovery and Exploration:** Gamification analytics enhance product discovery and exploration by gamifying the browsing experience, offering interactive product tours, and rewarding consumers for engaging with product content. By incorporating elements such as quizzes, scavenger hunts, and virtual rewards, marketers can captivate audiences, educate them about product features, and encourage deeper exploration of offerings.
- **Customer Loyalty and Retention:** Gamification analytics support customer loyalty and retention efforts by gamifying loyalty programs, rewarding repeat purchases, and incentivizing customer referrals. By

implementing features such as loyalty points, VIP tiers, and exclusive perks, marketers can strengthen relationships with existing customers, increase brand loyalty, and reduce churn rates.

- **Content Engagement and Interaction:** Gamification analytics drive content engagement and interaction by gamifying marketing campaigns, quizzes, polls, and interactive experiences. By creating gamified challenges, trivia contests, and interactive quizzes, marketers can capture consumers' attention, educate them about brand offerings, and encourage active participation in marketing initiatives.
- **Brand Awareness and Advocacy:** Gamification analytics promote brand awareness and advocacy by gamifying brand experiences, social sharing, and user-generated content. By incentivizing consumers to share branded content, participate in challenges, and create user-generated content, marketers can amplify brand reach, spark conversations, and cultivate brand advocates who champion their brand across digital channels.
- **Event Promotion and Engagement:** Gamification analytics enhance event promotion and engagement by gamifying event experiences, offering virtual badges, and rewarding attendees for participation. By incorporating elements such as scavenger hunts, photo challenges, and live polls, marketers can create immersive event experiences, drive attendee engagement, and increase event attendance and participation.

Challenges and Considerations

While gamification analytics offer promising opportunities for marketing and customer engagement, several challenges and considerations must be addressed:

- **Designing Meaningful Experiences:** Effective gamification requires thoughtful design that aligns with marketing objectives and resonates with target audiences. Marketers must carefully select game mechanics and elements that enhance brand experiences, drive desired behaviors, and provide value to consumers.
- **Data Privacy and Security:** Collecting and analyzing consumer data for gamification purposes raises concerns about privacy and security. Marketers must comply with data protection regulations, obtain consent for data usage, and ensure transparency regarding data collection and processing practices.
- **Balancing Engagement and Authenticity:** Gamification should enhance, not overshadow, the authenticity of brand experiences. Marketers must strike a balance between gamified elements and brand

messaging, ensuring that gamification enhances consumer engagement while maintaining brand integrity and authenticity.

- **Measuring ROI and Effectiveness:** Marketers must establish clear metrics and KPIs to measure the ROI and effectiveness of gamification initiatives. By tracking conversion rates, engagement metrics, and other key indicators, marketers can assess the impact of gamified campaigns and justify investments in gamification.

Education and Learning

In the realm of education and learning, engaging students and facilitating effective learning experiences are perennial challenges. Traditional methods often struggle to maintain student interest and motivation. However, the integration of gamification, coupled with analytics, has emerged as a promising solution to enhance educational outcomes. By applying game elements to learning environments and leveraging analytics to track student progress, educators can create immersive and personalized learning experiences.

Gamification analytics offer a dynamic approach to education and learning, leveraging game elements and data insights to engage students, promote active learning, and optimize learning outcomes. From content delivery and skill development to formative assessment and personalized learning paths, gamification offers a versatile toolkit to enhance various aspects of educational experiences. However, successful implementation requires careful consideration of design, data privacy, accessibility, and inclusivity to ensure that gamified initiatives effectively support student learning and foster a culture of lifelong learning. As technology continues to evolve, gamification analytics will likely play an increasingly integral role in shaping the future of education and learning.

Gamification in education involves incorporating game elements, such as points, badges, leaderboards, and challenges, into educational activities to motivate students and enhance their learning experiences. By transforming learning tasks into interactive and engaging experiences, gamification fosters intrinsic motivation and promotes active participation among students. Whether it's reinforcing concepts, encouraging practice, or facilitating collaboration, gamification offers a versatile approach to cater to diverse learning styles and preferences.

Role of Analytics in Gamification for Education

Analytics play a crucial role in gamification for education by providing insights into student engagement, learning progress, and areas of improvement. Gamification analytics enable educators to track key metrics, such as participation rates, quiz scores, and skill mastery levels, to assess the effectiveness of gamified interventions. By analyzing student data, educators can identify learning trends, adapt instructional strategies, and provide targeted support to maximize student learning outcomes.

Components of Gamification Analytics in Education

- **Engagement Metrics:** Gamification analytics measure student engagement by tracking metrics such as time spent on task, completion rates, and frequency of interactions with gamified content. These metrics offer valuable insights into students' level of interest and involvement in learning activities, helping educators tailor instructional approaches to better engage learners.
- **Progress Tracking:** Analyzing student progress within gamified learning environments allows educators to monitor learning trajectories, identify areas of strength and weakness, and provide timely feedback. Gamification analytics enable educators to track students' mastery of learning objectives, identify potential learning gaps, and intervene proactively to address individual needs.
- **Performance Assessment:** Gamification analytics facilitate performance assessment by tracking student performance on quizzes, assessments, and assignments embedded within gamified activities. By analyzing performance data, educators can evaluate students' understanding of key concepts, identify misconceptions, and adjust instructional content to scaffold learning effectively.
- **Collaborative Learning:** Gamification analytics support collaborative learning by tracking students' participation in group activities, teamwork, and peer interactions within gamified environments. By monitoring collaboration metrics, educators can assess the effectiveness of group work, identify collaborative dynamics, and promote communication and teamwork skills among students.

Practical Applications of Gamification Analytics in Education

- **Content Delivery and Reinforcement:** Gamification analytics enhance content delivery and reinforcement by gamifying educational content, quizzes, and interactive exercises. By incorporating elements such as badges, rewards, and progress trackers, educators can make learning materials more engaging and interactive, reinforcing key concepts and promoting active learning.
- **Skill Development and Practice:** Gamification analytics support skill development and practice by gamifying skill-building exercises, simulations, and problem-solving activities. By offering challenges, quests, and virtual rewards tied to skill mastery, educators can motivate

students to practice and apply their knowledge in real-world contexts, fostering skill acquisition and competence development.

- **Formative Assessment and Feedback:** Gamification analytics facilitate formative assessment and feedback by tracking students' progress in real-time and providing immediate feedback on their performance. By embedding quizzes, polls, and interactive assessments within gamified activities, educators can gauge student understanding, diagnose misconceptions, and offer personalized feedback to guide learning.
- **Motivation and Engagement:** Gamification analytics promote motivation and engagement by gamifying learning experiences, setting goals, and offering rewards for achievement. By incorporating elements such as leaderboards, competitions, and virtual incentives, educators can harness students' intrinsic motivations, foster a sense of accomplishment, and sustain their engagement throughout the learning process.
- **Personalized Learning Paths:** Gamification analytics enable personalized learning paths by tracking students' progress, preferences, and learning styles within gamified environments. By analyzing student data, educators can tailor learning experiences, adapt instructional content, and provide targeted interventions to meet individual needs and maximize learning outcomes.

Challenges and Considerations

While gamification analytics offer promising opportunities for enhancing education and learning, several challenges and considerations must be addressed:

- **Designing Meaningful Experiences:** Effective gamification requires thoughtful design that aligns with educational objectives and promotes deep learning. Educators must carefully select game mechanics and elements that enhance learning outcomes, foster critical thinking, and encourage intrinsic motivation.
- **Data Privacy and Security:** Collecting and analyzing student data for gamification purposes raises concerns about privacy and security. Educators must adhere to data protection regulations, obtain consent for data usage, and ensure that student data is securely stored and managed.
- **Balancing Competition and Collaboration:** While competition can be a powerful motivator in gamification, educators must also promote collaboration and teamwork to create a supportive learning environment. Balancing competition and collaboration ensures that

gamified activities foster healthy competition while encouraging cooperation and mutual support among students.

- **Accessibility and Inclusivity:** Gamification initiatives should be accessible and inclusive to all students, regardless of their abilities or backgrounds. Educators must consider diverse learning needs and preferences when designing gamified experiences, ensuring that they are inclusive, equitable, and accessible to all students.

Product Design and User Experience

In the realm of product design and user experience (UX), companies are constantly striving to create engaging and intuitive products that resonate with their target audience. One innovative approach gaining traction in this field is the integration of gamification and analytics. Gamification, the incorporation of game elements into non-game contexts, coupled with analytics, offers valuable insights into user behavior, preferences, and interactions with products.

Gamification analytics offer powerful tools for enhancing product design and user experience, leveraging game mechanics and data insights to drive user engagement, satisfaction, and retention. From onboarding and feature adoption to user engagement and customization, gamification offers a versatile toolkit to create compelling and intuitive products that resonate with users. However, successful implementation requires careful consideration of usability, data privacy, ethics, and accessibility to ensure that gamified experiences effectively enhance user experiences and foster long-term user loyalty. As technology continues to evolve, gamification analytics will likely play an increasingly integral role in shaping the future of product design and user experience strategies.

Gamification in product design and UX involves the strategic integration of game mechanics, such as points, badges, challenges, and rewards, to enhance user engagement and interaction with products. By tapping into users' intrinsic motivations, such as achievement, progression, and social interaction, gamification creates immersive experiences that captivate and retain users' attention. Whether it's a mobile app, website, or physical product, gamification can be leveraged to guide user behavior, drive desired actions, and foster a sense of enjoyment and accomplishment.

Role of Analytics in Gamification for Product Design and UX

Analytics play a crucial role in gamification for product design and UX by providing insights into user engagement, behavior patterns, and satisfaction levels. Gamification analytics enable designers and product managers to track key metrics, identify usability issues, and optimize product experiences based on data-driven insights. By understanding how users interact with gamified elements, companies can refine their designs, tailor their features, and create more compelling and intuitive products.

Components of Gamification Analytics in Product Design and UX

- **Engagement Metrics:** Gamification analytics measure user engagement by tracking metrics such as time spent, interactions, and completion rates within gamified experiences. These metrics provide valuable feedback on the effectiveness of gamification in capturing users' attention and sustaining their interest over time.
- **Behavioral Patterns:** Analyzing user behavior within gamified products reveals insights into usage patterns, navigation flows, and feature preferences. By understanding how users interact with gamified elements, designers can identify friction points, optimize user journeys, and enhance overall usability and satisfaction.
- **Feedback and Iteration:** Gamification analytics facilitate iterative design processes by providing real-time feedback on user interactions and experiences. Designers can use analytics data to identify areas for improvement, test new features or game mechanics, and iterate on designs to address user needs and preferences effectively.
- **User Satisfaction and Retention:** Gamification analytics measure user satisfaction and retention by tracking metrics such as user feedback, ratings, and retention rates. By monitoring user sentiment and engagement levels, companies can gauge the effectiveness of gamified experiences in fostering positive user experiences and retaining users over the long term.

Practical Applications of Gamification Analytics in Product Design and UX

- **Onboarding and User Training:** Gamification analytics enhance user onboarding and training processes by gamifying tutorials, walkthroughs, and product introductions. By incorporating interactive elements, progress trackers, and rewards, companies can accelerate user learning curves, reduce abandonment rates, and increase user confidence and proficiency in using their products.
- **Feature Adoption and Exploration:** Gamification analytics drive feature adoption and exploration by gamifying feature discovery, usage, and mastery. By incentivizing users to explore different features, complete tasks, and unlock rewards, companies can increase feature engagement, promote product stickiness, and encourage users to discover the full potential of their products.

- **User Engagement and Retention:** Gamification analytics foster user engagement and retention by gamifying user interactions, social sharing, and community participation. By incorporating features such as challenges, leaderboards, and social rewards, companies can create a sense of belonging, foster community engagement, and cultivate loyal user communities around their products.
- **User Feedback and Co-creation:** Gamification analytics facilitate user feedback and co-creation processes by gamifying user feedback collection, ideation sessions, and beta testing programs. By incentivizing users to provide feedback, participate in brainstorming sessions, and contribute ideas, companies can gather valuable insights, prioritize feature development, and involve users in shaping the future direction of their products.
- **Customization and Personalization:** Gamification analytics enable customization and personalization by gamifying user preferences, profiles, and recommendations. By leveraging user data and behavioral insights, companies can offer personalized experiences, recommend relevant content or features, and tailor product experiences to individual user needs and preferences.

Tests and Thoughts

While gamification analytics offer significant opportunities for product design and UX, several challenges and considerations must be addressed:

- **Balancing Gamification and Usability:** Gamification should enhance, not detract from, the usability and intuitiveness of products. Designers must strike a balance between gamified elements and core functionality, ensuring that gamification enhances user experiences without compromising usability or creating unnecessary complexity.
- **Data Privacy and Security:** Collecting and analyzing user data for gamification purposes raises concerns about privacy and security. Companies must adhere to data protection regulations, obtain user consent for data usage, and implement robust security measures to safeguard user information and maintain trust.
- **Ethical Design Practices:** Gamification initiatives must adhere to ethical design principles, ensuring that incentives and rewards align with user well-being and values. Designers should prioritize transparency, fairness, and user autonomy, avoiding manipulative tactics or coercive techniques in their gamified experiences.

- **Accessibility and Inclusivity:** Gamification should be accessible and inclusive to users of all backgrounds, abilities, and preferences. Designers must consider accessibility requirements, accommodate diverse user needs, and ensure that gamified experiences are inclusive and equitable for all users.

6.3.4 Challenges and Considerations

Data Privacy and Security

Gamification, the integration of game elements into non-game contexts, has gained significant traction in various industries, including education, healthcare, and business. As organizations harness the power of gamification to enhance user engagement and motivation, they also encounter challenges related to data privacy and security. Data privacy and security are paramount considerations in the realm of gamification analytics, where the collection and analysis of user data are central to driving engagement and performance. Organizations must navigate various challenges, including consent management, data minimization, and third-party integration, while upholding robust security measures and complying with regulatory requirements. By adopting a privacy-by-design approach, adhering to ethical principles, and leveraging emerging technologies responsibly, organizations can maximize the benefits of gamification while safeguarding user privacy and security.

Gamification analytics involves the collection, analysis, and interpretation of data generated through gamified experiences. These data encompass a wide range of information, including user interactions, performance metrics, and behavioral patterns. By leveraging analytics, organizations can gain insights into user engagement levels, identify areas for improvement, and optimize gamified systems for better outcomes.

Role of Data Privacy in Gamification Analytics

Data privacy is a paramount concern in gamification analytics, as it involves the collection and processing of sensitive user information. Players may provide personal details, such as their names, ages, and contact information, as part of the registration process. Additionally, gameplay data, such as progress, achievements, and preferences, are continuously gathered during interactions with gamified platforms. Ensuring the privacy and confidentiality of this data is essential to maintain user trust and compliance with regulatory requirements.

Challenges in Data Privacy

Several challenges arise concerning data privacy in gamification analytics:

- **Consent Management:** Obtaining explicit consent from users for data collection and processing can be challenging, especially in dynamic gaming environments where interactions occur rapidly.

- **Data Minimization:** Balancing the collection of relevant gameplay data with the principle of data minimization presents a significant challenge. Collecting excessive information increases privacy risks and regulatory compliance burdens.
- **Third-party Integration:** Many gamified platforms incorporate third-party services for analytics and functionality, raising concerns about data sharing and security across multiple entities.
- **Cross-border Data Transfers:** Gamification analytics often involve the transfer of data across international borders, necessitating compliance with diverse privacy regulations and standards.
- **User Anonymity:** While anonymizing user data can mitigate privacy risks, it may compromise the quality and utility of analytics insights, particularly concerning individualized feedback and personalization.

Considerations for Data Security

In addition to privacy concerns, ensuring robust data security is imperative in gamification analytics. Security breaches can result in unauthorized access to sensitive information, leading to reputational damage, financial losses, and legal ramifications.

- **Encryption:** Implementing encryption mechanisms to safeguard data both in transit and at rest is crucial for preventing unauthorized access and data breaches.
- **Access Controls:** Restricting access to sensitive data through role-based permissions and authentication mechanisms helps mitigate insider threats and unauthorized disclosures.
- **Secure Development Practices:** Adhering to secure coding practices and conducting regular security assessments can help identify and mitigate vulnerabilities in gamified systems.
- **Incident Response Planning:** Developing comprehensive incident response plans enables organizations to respond effectively to security incidents, minimize their impact, and facilitate timely recovery.
- **Compliance with Regulations:** Compliance with relevant privacy and security regulations, such as the General Data Protection Regulation (GDPR) and the California Consumer Privacy Act (CCPA), is essential to avoid penalties and legal consequences.

Balancing Innovation with Compliance

Achieving a balance between innovation and compliance is critical in the realm of gamification analytics. While organizations strive to harness the full potential of gamified experiences to drive engagement and performance, they must also uphold stringent privacy and security standards. Adopting a privacy-by-design approach, integrating privacy and security considerations into the design and development of gamified systems from the outset, can help mitigate risks and ensure regulatory compliance.

Ethical Considerations

In addition to legal and regulatory requirements, organizations must also consider the ethical implications of gamification analytics. Ethical principles, such as transparency, fairness, and accountability, should guide the collection, use, and analysis of user data. Transparency in data practices, ensuring informed consent, and providing users with control over their data are essential for fostering trust and ethical engagement.

Emerging Technologies and Trends

Advancements in technologies such as artificial intelligence (AI), machine learning, and blockchain offer new opportunities and challenges in gamification analytics. AI-powered algorithms can analyze vast amounts of gameplay data to uncover insights and personalize experiences, but they also raise concerns about algorithmic bias and privacy risks. Blockchain technology holds promise for enhancing data security and transparency in gamified systems through decentralized and immutable ledgers.

Algorithmic Bias

As gamification becomes increasingly prevalent across various domains, including education, healthcare, and business, the use of analytics to drive engagement and optimize experiences has gained momentum. However, the reliance on algorithms to analyze gameplay data raises concerns about algorithmic bias.

Algorithmic bias poses significant challenges and considerations in the realm of gamification analytics, where algorithms play a central role in driving engagement and optimizing experiences. By understanding the types and sources of bias, addressing challenges in bias detection and mitigation, and upholding ethical principles and user-centric values, organizations can promote fairness, transparency, and inclusivity in gamified systems. Through collective efforts and continued innovation, we can harness the power of gamification analytics to create more equitable and engaging experiences for all users.

Algorithmic bias refers to systematic errors or inaccuracies in algorithms that result in unfair or discriminatory outcomes, often perpetuating existing biases present in the data used for training. In the realm of gamification analytics, algorithmic bias can manifest in various ways, impacting user experiences, recommendations, and decision-making processes. Common sources of bias include biased training data, flawed algorithm design, and inadequate mitigation strategies.

Types of Bias in Gamification Analytics

Several types of bias can affect gamification analytics:

- **Demographic Bias:** Algorithms may exhibit bias based on demographic factors such as age, gender, race, or socioeconomic status, leading to differential treatment or opportunities for certain user groups.
- **Performance Bias:** Algorithms may disproportionately favor certain gameplay styles, preferences, or skill levels, resulting in unequal rewards, feedback, or progression pathways for users.
- **Content Bias:** Biases inherent in the content or design of gamified experiences, such as stereotypes or cultural norms, can influence user engagement and perceptions.
- **Feedback Loop Bias:** Algorithms that rely on user feedback to make recommendations or adaptations may inadvertently reinforce existing biases, creating feedback loops that perpetuate discrimination or inequality.

Challenges in Addressing Algorithmic Bias

Addressing algorithmic bias in gamification analytics poses several challenges:

- **Data Quality:** Ensuring the quality, accuracy, and representativeness of training data is essential for mitigating bias. However, biases inherent in historical data or data collection processes can persist and influence algorithmic outcomes.
- **Interpretability:** The complexity of algorithms used in gamification analytics, such as machine learning models, can make it challenging to understand how biases manifest and to identify appropriate mitigation strategies.
- **Trade-offs:** Balancing the need for algorithmic fairness with other objectives, such as performance optimization or user engagement, may require making trade-offs that impact overall system behavior.
- **Dynamic Environments:** Gamified systems are dynamic and evolving, posing challenges for detecting and addressing bias in real-time as user interactions occur.

Considerations for Mitigating Bias

Several considerations can help mitigate algorithmic bias in gamification analytics:

- **Diversity and Inclusion:** Promoting diversity and inclusion in both the design and evaluation of gamified experiences can help mitigate biases and ensure equitable outcomes for all user groups.
- **Bias Detection and Monitoring:** Implementing robust mechanisms for detecting and monitoring bias in algorithmic decision-making processes enables organizations to identify and address bias proactively.
- **Transparency and Explainability:** Providing transparency into algorithmic processes and decision-making criteria fosters trust and enables users to understand how algorithms may impact their experiences.
- **Fairness-aware Algorithms:** Developing algorithms that explicitly incorporate fairness constraints and considerations can help mitigate bias and promote equitable outcomes.
- **User Empowerment:** Empowering users with control over their data, preferences, and interactions can mitigate the impact of algorithmic bias by allowing users to influence their experiences directly.

Ethical Considerations

Addressing algorithmic bias in gamification analytics raises important ethical considerations. Organizations must prioritize fairness, transparency, and accountability in their algorithmic decision-making processes to uphold ethical standards and prevent harm to users. Ethical guidelines and frameworks, such as the IEEE Global Initiative on Ethics of Autonomous and Intelligent Systems, provide valuable guidance for navigating these complex ethical challenges.

Implications for User Engagement and Satisfaction

Algorithmic bias can significantly impact user engagement and satisfaction in gamified experiences. Biased algorithms may result in unfair treatment, unequal opportunities, or limited representation for certain user groups, leading to dissatisfaction, disengagement, or even harm. Conversely, mitigating bias and promoting fairness can enhance user trust, satisfaction, and long-term engagement with gamified systems.

Future Directions and Opportunities

Addressing algorithmic bias in gamification analytics requires a multifaceted approach that encompasses technical, ethical, and regulatory considerations. Future research and innovation should focus on developing more robust bias detection and mitigation techniques, enhancing algorithmic transparency and explainability, and promoting diversity and inclusion in gamified experiences. Collaboration between researchers, practitioners, policymakers, and other stakeholders is essential to drive progress in this critical area.

Interdisciplinary Collaboration

In the realm of gamification analytics, interdisciplinary collaboration plays a crucial role in driving innovation, enhancing user experiences, and addressing complex challenges. By integrating expertise from diverse fields such as psychology, computer science, data analytics, and game design, organizations can leverage the full potential of gamified systems. However, interdisciplinary collaboration also presents unique challenges and considerations that must be navigated effectively.

Interdisciplinary collaboration is essential for unlocking the full potential of gamification analytics, enabling organizations to create more engaging, effective, and ethical gamified experiences. By overcoming communication barriers, cultivating mutual respect, and embracing diversity and inclusion, interdisciplinary teams can address complex challenges and drive innovation in gamification analytics. Through collective efforts and collaboration across disciplines, we can harness the power of gamified systems to enhance user experiences, promote behavior change, and achieve meaningful outcomes.

Understanding Interdisciplinary Collaboration

Interdisciplinary collaboration involves the integration of knowledge, methods, and perspectives from multiple disciplines to address complex problems and achieve innovative solutions. In the context of gamification analytics, interdisciplinary collaboration brings together experts with diverse backgrounds and skill sets, including:

- **Psychology:** Experts in psychology contribute insights into human behavior, motivation, and engagement, informing the design and optimization of gamified experiences.
- **Computer Science:** Computer scientists develop algorithms, models, and technologies for data collection, analysis, and visualization in gamification analytics.
- **Data Analytics:** Data analysts and statisticians utilize analytical techniques to extract insights from gameplay data, identify patterns, and optimize gamified systems.
- **Game Design:** Game designers focus on creating immersive, engaging, and rewarding gameplay experiences that motivate and captivate users.

Challenges in Interdisciplinary Collaboration

Despite its potential benefits, interdisciplinary collaboration in gamification analytics presents several challenges:

- **Communication Barriers:** Differences in terminology, methodologies, and perspectives across disciplines can hinder effective communication and collaboration, leading to misunderstandings and inefficiencies.

- **Siloed Expertise:** Siloed expertise within disciplinary boundaries may limit cross-disciplinary learning and collaboration, preventing the integration of diverse insights and approaches.
- **Power Dynamics:** Power differentials between disciplines, such as perceived hierarchies or dominance of certain fields, can impede collaboration and inhibit the exchange of ideas and contributions.
- **Coordination and Leadership:** Effective coordination and leadership are essential for fostering collaboration, aligning goals and priorities, and managing interdisciplinary teams effectively.

Considerations for Successful Collaboration

Several considerations can facilitate successful interdisciplinary collaboration in gamification analytics:

- **Establishing Shared Goals:** Aligning stakeholders around common goals and objectives fosters a sense of purpose and collective ownership, driving collaboration and innovation.
- **Cultivating Mutual Respect:** Promoting mutual respect, appreciation, and recognition for diverse expertise and perspectives encourages open communication and collaboration.
- **Facilitating Interdisciplinary Learning:** Creating opportunities for interdisciplinary learning, training, and knowledge exchange enhances understanding and appreciation of different disciplines' contributions.
- **Fostering Trust and Psychological Safety:** Creating an environment of trust and psychological safety enables team members to express ideas, ask questions, and take risks without fear of judgment or reprisal.
- **Embracing Diversity and Inclusion:** Embracing diversity and inclusion in interdisciplinary teams enhances creativity, problem-solving, and innovation by incorporating a wide range of perspectives and experiences.

Ethical Considerations

Interdisciplinary collaboration in gamification analytics raises important ethical considerations related to data privacy, algorithmic bias, and user well-being. Collaborators must prioritize ethical principles such as transparency, fairness, and user autonomy to ensure responsible and ethical use of gamified systems. Ethical guidelines and frameworks, such as the ACM Code of Ethics and Professional Conduct, provide valuable guidance for navigating these complex ethical challenges.

Implications for Gamification Analytics

Effective interdisciplinary collaboration has significant implications for the design, implementation, and evaluation of gamification analytics:

- **Enhanced User Experiences:** By integrating insights from psychology, game design, and data analytics, interdisciplinary teams can create more engaging, immersive, and personalized gamified experiences that motivate and delight users.
- **Improved Data Analysis:** Leveraging expertise from computer science and data analytics enables organizations to develop more robust algorithms, models, and techniques for analyzing gameplay data and extracting actionable insights.
- **Ethical Design and Implementation:** Interdisciplinary collaboration facilitates the integration of ethical considerations into the design and implementation of gamified systems, promoting user privacy, fairness, and well-being.
- **Innovation and Creativity:** By fostering collaboration and cross-disciplinary learning, interdisciplinary teams drive innovation and creativity in gamification analytics, pushing the boundaries of what is possible and exploring new avenues for research and development.

User-Centered Design

User-centered design (UCD) is a fundamental approach in creating effective and engaging gamified experiences. It emphasizes understanding users' needs, preferences, and behaviors to design systems that are intuitive, enjoyable, and impactful. In the context of gamification analytics, UCD plays a crucial role in optimizing user experiences, driving engagement, and achieving desired outcomes. However, implementing UCD in gamification analytics presents unique challenges and considerations that must be addressed to create successful gamified systems.

User-centered design is essential for creating effective, engaging, and ethical gamified experiences that meet users' needs, preferences, and goals. By overcoming challenges and considerations related to understanding user motivations, balancing engagement and effectiveness, and addressing ethical concerns, organizations can design gamified systems that drive engagement, foster behavior change, and achieve meaningful outcomes. Through a user-centric approach and continuous iteration, we can harness the power of gamification analytics to create positive impacts on individuals and communities.

Understanding User-Centered Design

User-centered design (UCD) or user-driven development (UDD) is a framework of process (not restricted to interfaces or technologies) in which usability goals, user characteristics, environment, tasks and workflow of a product, service or process are given extensive attention at each stage of the design process. These tests are conducted with/without actual users during each stage of the process from requirements, pre-production models and post production, completing a circle of proof back to and ensuring that "development proceeds with the user as the center of focus." Such testing is necessary as it is often very difficult for the designers of a product to understand intuitively the first-time users of their design experiences, and what each user's learning curve may look like. User-centered design is based on the understanding of a user, their demands, priorities and experiences and when used, is known to lead to an increased product usefulness and usability as it delivers satisfaction to the user.

The chief difference from other product design philosophies is that user-centered design tries to optimize the product around how users can, want, or need to use it so that users are not forced to change their behavior and expectations to accommodate the product. The users thus stand in the center of two concentric circles. The inner circle includes the context of the product, the objectives of developing it, and the environment it would run in. The outer circle involves more granular details of task detail, task organization, and task flow.

The term "User-Centered Design" was coined by Rob Kling in 1977 and later adopted in Donald A. Norman's research laboratory at the University of California, San Diego. The concept became widely popular as a result of the publication of the book User-Centered System Design: New Perspectives on Human-Computer Interaction in 1986. The concept gained further attention and acceptance in Norman's seminal book The Design of Everyday Things (originally called The Psychology of Everyday Things). In this book, Norman describes the psychology behind what he deems 'good' and 'bad' design through examples. He exalts the importance of design in our everyday lives and the consequences of errors caused by bad designs.

The two books include principles for building well-designed products. His recommendations are based on the user's needs, leaving aside what he considers secondary issues like aesthetics. The main highlights of these are:

- Simplifying the structure of the tasks such that the possible actions at any moment are intuitive.
- Make things visible, including the conceptual model of the system, actions, results of actions and feedback.
- Getting the mappings right between intended results and required actions.
- Embracing and exploiting the constraints of systems.

In a later book, Emotional Design, Norman returns to some of his earlier ideas to elaborate what he had come to find as overly reductive.

For example, the User-Centered Design process can help software designers fulfill the goal of a product engineered for their users. User requirements are considered right from the beginning and included in the whole product cycle. These requirements are noted and refined through investigative methods including: ethnographic study, contextual inquiry, prototype testing, usability testing and other methods. Generative methods may also be used including: card sorting, affinity diagramming and participatory design sessions. In addition, user requirements can be inferred by careful analysis of usable products similar to the product being designed. User-Centered Design takes inspiration from the following models:

- **Cooperative Design:** Involving designers and users on an equal footing. This is the Scandinavian tradition of design of IT artifacts and it has been evolving since 1970. This is also called Co-design.
- **Participatory Design (PD):** A North American term for the same concept, inspired by Cooperative Design, focuses on the participation of users. Since 1990, there has been a bi-annual Participatory Design Conference.
- **Contextual Design:** "Customer-centered design" in the actual context, including some ideas from Participatory design

Here are the principles that help in ensuring a design is user-centered:

- Design is based upon an explicit understanding of users, tasks and environments.
- Users are involved throughout design and development.
- Design is driven and refined by user-centered evaluation.
- Process is iterative.
- Design addresses the whole user experience.
- Design team includes multidisciplinary skills and perspectives.

The goal of user-centered design is to make products that have very high usability. This includes how convenient the product is its usage, manageability, effectiveness, and how well the product is mapped to the user requirements. The general phases of User-Centered Design process:

- **Specify Context of Use:** Identify who the primary users of the product are, why they will use the product, what are their requirements and under what environment they will use it.

- **Specify Requirements:** Once the context is specified, it is time to identify the granular requirements of the product. This is an important phase which can further facilitate the designers to create storyboards, and set important goals to make the product successful.
- **Create Design Solutions and Development:** Based on product goals and requirements, start an iterative process of product design and development.
- **Evaluate Product:** Product designers do usability testing to get users' feedback for the product at every stage of User-Centered Design.

The above procedure is repeated in the next steps to finish the product further. These phases are general approaches and factors like design goals, team and their timeline, and environment in which the product is developed, determine the appropriate phases for a project and their order. You can either follow a waterfall model, agile model or any other software engineering practice.

UCD asks questions about users and their tasks and goals, then uses the findings to make decisions about development and design. The UCD of a web site, for instance, seeks to answer the following questions:

- Who are the users of the website?
- What are the users' tasks and goals?
- What are the users' experience levels with the website, and the similar websites?
- What functions do the users need from the website?
- What information might the users need, and in what form do they need it?
- How do users think the website should work?
- What are the extreme environments in which website can be accessed in?
- Is the user multitasking?
- Does the interface utilize different input modes, such as touch, speech, gestures or orientation?

As an example of UCD viewpoints, the essential elements of UCD of a website usually are the considerations of visibility, accessibility, legibility and language.

Visibility helps the user construct a mental model of the document. Models help the user predict the effect(s) of their actions while using the document. Important elements (such as those that aid navigation) should be emphatic. Users should be able to tell from a glance what they can and cannot do with the document.

Users should be able to find information quickly and easily throughout the document, regardless of its length. Users should be offered various ways to find information (such as navigational elements, search functions, table of contents, clearly labeled sections, page numbers, color-coding, etc.). Navigational elements should be consistent with the genre of the document. 'Chunking' is a useful strategy that involves breaking information into small pieces that can be organized into some meaningful order or hierarchy. The ability to skim the document allows users to find their piece of information by scanning rather than reading. Bold and italic words are often used to this end.

Text should be easy to read: Through analysis of the rhetorical situation, the designer should be able to determine a useful font-family and font style. Ornamental fonts, text in all capital letters, large or small body text can be hard to read and should be avoided. Text-colouring and bolding can be helpful when used in text-heavy scenarios. High figure-ground contrast between text and background increases legibility. Dark text against a light background is most legible.

Certain types of languages are needed depending on the rhetorical situation. Short sentences are helpful, as are well-written texts used in explanations and similar bulk-text situations. Unless the situation calls for it, jargon or heavily technical terms should not be used. Many writers will choose to use the active voice, verbs (instead of noun strings or nominals), and a simple sentence structure.

There are a number of tools that are used in the analysis of User-Centered Design, mainly: personas, scenarios, and essential use cases.

During the UCD process, a Persona representing the user may be created. A persona is a user archetype used to help guide decisions about product features, navigation, interactions, and even visual design. In most cases, personas are synthesized from a series of ethnographic interviews with real people, then captured in 1-2 page descriptions that include behavior patterns, goals, skills, attitudes, and environment, with a few fictional personal details to bring the persona to life.

For each product, or sometimes for each set of tools within a product, there is a small set of personas, one of whom is the primary focus for the design. There is also what is called a secondary persona, where the character is not the main target of the design, but their needs should be met and problems solved if possible. They exist to help account for further possible problems and difficulties that may occur even though the primary persona is satisfied with their solution. There is also an anti-persona, which is the character for which the design is specifically not made.

Personas are useful because they create a common shared understanding of the user group that the design process is built around. Also, they help prioritize the design considerations by providing a context of what the user needs and what functions are nice to add and have. They can also provide a human face and existence to a diversified and scattered user group and help create empathy and add emotions when referring to the users. However, since personas are a generalized perception of the primary stakeholder group from collected data, the characteristics may be too broad and typical or too much of an "average Joe". Sometimes, personas can have stereotypical properties, which may hurt the entire design process. Overall, personas can be a useful tool to be used by designers to make informed design decisions, as opposed to referring to a set of data or a wide range of individuals.

Personas can also be modified all through the UCD of a product, based on user testing and changing environment. This is not an ideal way to use Personas but should not be a taboo either, particularly when it becomes apparent that variables surrounding a product's development have changed since the design started and current persona/s may not cater well to the changed conditions.

A scenario created in the UCD process is a fictional story about the "daily life of" or a sequence of events with the primary stakeholder group as the main character. Typically, a persona created earlier is used as the main character of this story. The story should be specific to the events that relate to the problems of the primary stakeholder group, and, normally the main research questions the design process is built upon. These may turn out to be a simple story about an individual's daily life. Still, small details from the events should imply details about the users, and may include emotional or physical characteristics. There can be the best-case scenario, where everything works out best for the main character, the worst-case scenario, where the main character experiences everything going wrong around him or her, and an average-case scenario, which is the typical life of the individual, where nothing really special or depressing occurs, and the day moves on.

Scenarios create a social context in which the personas exist and create an actual physical world, instead of imagining a character with internal characteristics from gathered data and nothing else, there is more action involved in the persona's existence. A scenario is also more easily understood by people since it is a story and is easier to follow. Yet, like the personas, these scenarios are assumptions made by the researcher and designer and is also created from a set of organized data. It is important to ensure that scenarios are created as close as possible to real world scenarios. Nevertheless, it can sometimes be difficult to explain and inform how low level tasks occur, for ex- the thought process of a persona before acting.

Challenges in Implementing User-Centered Design

Implementing user-centered design in gamification analytics presents several challenges:

- **Understanding User Motivations:** Identifying and understanding users' motivations for engaging with gamified systems can be challenging, as motivations may vary widely among different user groups and contexts.

- **Balancing Engagement and Effectiveness:** Balancing the need for engagement and enjoyment with the effectiveness of gamified interventions in achieving desired outcomes requires careful consideration and iterative refinement.
- **Personalization and Customization:** Designing gamified systems that offer personalized and customizable experiences to accommodate diverse user preferences and goals can be complex, requiring robust data analytics and adaptive algorithms.
- **Feedback and Progression:** Providing meaningful feedback and progression pathways that motivate users to achieve their goals while maintaining their interest and engagement presents a significant challenge in gamification analytics.

Considerations for Successful User-Centered Design

Several considerations can help overcome challenges and facilitate successful user-centered design in gamification analytics:

- **User Research and Empathy:** Conducting thorough user research and developing empathy for users' needs, preferences, and behaviors are essential for informing design decisions and creating user-centric experiences.
- **Iterative Design and Evaluation:** Adopting an iterative design process that involves prototyping, testing, and refining gamified systems based on user feedback enables continuous improvement and optimization.
- **Co-Creation and Stakeholder Engagement:** Involving users and stakeholders in the design process through co-creation workshops, usability testing, and participatory design activities fosters collaboration, ownership, and alignment with users' needs.
- **Accessibility and Inclusivity:** Ensuring that gamified systems are accessible and inclusive to users with diverse abilities, backgrounds, and preferences is essential for promoting equity and diversity in user experiences.

Ethical Considerations

User-centered design in gamification analytics raises important ethical considerations related to user privacy, autonomy, and well-being. Designers must prioritize ethical principles such as transparency, consent, and user control to ensure that gamified systems respect users' rights and interests. Ethical guidelines and frameworks, such as the UXPA Code of Conduct and the Design Justice Principles, provide valuable guidance for navigating these complex ethical challenges.

Implications for Gamification Analytics

User-centered design has significant implications for the design, implementation, and evaluation of gamification analytics:

- **Enhanced User Engagement:** By prioritizing users' needs, preferences, and motivations, user-centered design fosters engagement and enjoyment in gamified experiences, driving sustained participation and behavior change.
- **Improved Effectiveness:** Designing gamified systems with a focus on user-centered principles increases the likelihood of achieving desired outcomes, such as learning, skill development, or behavior modification, effectively.
- **Ethical Design and User Trust:** Incorporating ethical considerations into the design and implementation of gamification analytics promotes user trust, satisfaction, and long-term engagement by respecting users' rights and interests.
- **Innovation and Creativity:** By embracing user-centered design principles and methodologies, organizations can innovate and differentiate their gamified offerings, creating unique and compelling experiences that resonate with users.

PART-III

GAME-BASED LEARNING APPROACHES

CHAPTER 7

DESIGNING EDUCATIONAL GAMES

7.1 PRINCIPLES OF EDUCATIONAL GAMES DESIGN

Educational games have emerged as powerful tools for enhancing learning experiences across various educational settings. Combining entertainment with educational content, these games engage learners in dynamic ways, fostering deeper understanding and retention of concepts. However, designing effective educational games requires careful consideration of various principles to ensure they are both engaging and pedagogically sound.

Educational games design is a multifaceted endeavor that requires careful consideration of various principles to create engaging, effective, and pedagogically sound experiences. By aligning gameplay with learning objectives, fostering immersion, providing appropriate challenges, delivering constructive feedback, integrating pedagogical strategies, promoting accessibility and inclusivity, encouraging collaboration, prioritizing ethical considerations, and embracing continuous evaluation and improvement, developers can harness the transformative potential of games to enhance learning outcomes. Through innovative design approaches and a commitment to educational excellence, educational games continue to shape the future of learning in diverse educational contexts.

7.1.1 Understanding Learning Objectives

A Student Learning Objectives (SLO) is an assessment tool that allows a teacher to quantify their impact on student achievement as measured within the parameters of a particular academic or elective standard.

Characteristics

In many cases, the standards that will be addressed will be drawn from the Common Core State Standards. Typically the SLO is developed between the teacher and their direct supervisor or principal.

A SLO is an assessment tool that allows a teacher to quantify their impact on student achievement as measured within the parameters of a particular academic or elective standard. In many cases, the standards that will be addressed will be drawn from the Common Core State Standards. Typically the SLO is developed between the teacher and their direct supervisor or principal. As the school year or pre-selected term of the SLO administration proceeds, the teacher will make frequent checks for understanding through various formative assessments. This will allow the teacher to determine the progression of learning for the student research group. At the conclusion of the school year, the teacher will collect the results and meet with their direct supervisor to discuss the data as it applies to the original goal statement. It is important to remember that SLOs have to be content and course specific with outcomes that can be measured. One of the main benefits of developing and implementing strong SLOs is the ability to increase student achievement at the classroom level. SLOs are being used as a percentage in the overall teacher evaluation system because it can quantify the pedagogical impact a teacher has on a specific set of students.

An objective is a small goal that needs to be met on the way to fulfilling the larger course outcome or goal. A typical course will have four to five objectives that focus the various learning activities.

Elements

- **Data-driven Instruction & Assessment:** The local education agency (LEA) should review past data gathering systems to determine an overarching goal for individual teacher SLO development. It is important to include all educational stakeholders in this process. One was that this could be accomplished is to discuss the SLO with parents on "Meet the Teacher" night. The feedback from the parents would help to validate the importance of the SLO in the lives of students and their parents. Another way to include parents in the discussion would be to sponsor a Google Document that encourages collaboration on the actual SLO document itself.
- **Standards-alignment:** The development of an effective SLO starts with locating an academic standard that promotes rigorous student learning that results in a measurable student product or outcome. One way to motivate reluctant learners to engage in rigorous academic achievement is to add relevance to their instruction and assessments. For example, when working with a literacy standard dealing with non-fiction reading comprehension it would be beneficial to use real-world documents like an electric bill or an over-the-counter children's pain relief label. The students apply their reading comprehension strategies to documents that they are likely to encounter in the future.
- **Instructional Timeframe:** A SLO can occur within any given timeframe between pre-assessment and post-assessment, but the recommended time period is one academic year.

Parts

- **Learning Goals:** A teacher-developed description of what the student will know and be able to do at the end of a course based upon an overarching idea for the academic or elective discipline. A teacher will know that they have an effective learning goal when the knowledge or skill can be applied to life outside the classroom. Learning goals provide a common thread that link all units and learning situations within a course. It often answers the question, "What is the BIG idea?"
- **Assessments:** Valid assessments should support the student progress toward meeting an enduring understanding within the learning goal. The assessments should be based upon standards-aligned to the learning goal. Formative assessment should be collected at multiple points in the semester to determine if the students are on pace to meet the learning goal in the final summative assessment.
- **Targets:** Using baseline data gleaned from past performance or collected with a pre-assessment, the teacher will contextualize the SLO by establishing class-specific targets for performance levels. It is important to be ambitious and also realistic about expectations of student performance.

7.1.2 Engagement through Immersive Experiences

One of the key principles of educational games design is creating immersive experiences that captivate learners' attention. Immersion goes beyond mere entertainment; it involves designing a virtual environment that transports players into the learning context. Whether exploring historical civilizations or solving complex mathematical problems, immersion fosters deep engagement by making learning feel like an adventure rather than a chore. By leveraging elements such as narrative, visuals, and sound, developers can craft compelling experiences that keep players invested in the learning process.

7.1.3 Balancing Challenge and Skill Level

Effective educational games strike a delicate balance between challenge and skill level to ensure optimal learning outcomes. Games that are too easy fail to stimulate learners' cognitive abilities, leading to boredom and disengagement. Conversely, overly difficult games can frustrate players, hindering learning progress. The principle of maintaining an appropriate challenge level involves gradually increasing complexity as players advance, providing opportunities for mastery while avoiding overwhelming them. Adaptive difficulty systems, where the game adjusts the challenge based on players' performance, are particularly effective in catering to individual learning needs.

7.1.4 Feedback as a Learning Mechanism

Feedback plays a pivotal role in educational games, serving as a mechanism for learning reinforcement and improvement. Timely and informative feedback informs players of their progress, highlighting areas of strength and areas needing improvement. Whether through immediate responses to in-game actions or comprehensive performance reports, effective feedback mechanisms empower learners to reflect on their performance and adjust their strategies accordingly. Furthermore, feedback should be constructive and motivational, encouraging players to persevere through challenges and strive for mastery.

7.1.5 Integration of Pedagogical Strategies

Educational games design draws upon a diverse range of pedagogical strategies to facilitate learning. From problem-based learning to inquiry-based approaches, developers incorporate proven instructional methods into game mechanics to scaffold learning experiences. For example, games may present players with authentic scenarios that require critical thinking and decision-making skills, mirroring real-world challenges. By aligning game mechanics with pedagogical principles, developers create immersive environments that promote active learning and knowledge transfer.

7.1.6 Accessibility and Inclusivity

Another fundamental principle of educational games design is ensuring accessibility and inclusivity for all learners. Design considerations should accommodate diverse learning styles, abilities, and preferences, allowing every player to engage meaningfully with the game. This may involve providing multiple pathways to success, incorporating audiovisual cues for learners with sensory impairments, or offering customizable difficulty settings. By fostering an inclusive learning environment, educational games promote equity and diversity, enabling learners from various backgrounds to succeed.

7.1.7 Promoting Collaboration and Social Interaction

Educational games have the potential to foster collaboration and social interaction among players, enriching the learning experience. Incorporating multiplayer features or collaborative challenges encourages teamwork and communication skills development.

Moreover, social elements such as leaderboards, achievements, and online communities provide opportunities for peer interaction and competition, motivating players to excel and support one another. By leveraging the power of social learning, educational games extend beyond individual skill mastery to promote collaborative problem-solving and collective achievement.

7.1.8 Ethical Considerations and Responsible Design

Ethical considerations are integral to the design and implementation of educational games, particularly concerning data privacy, content appropriateness, and player well-being. Developers must prioritize the safety and privacy of players, implementing robust security measures and adhering to data protection regulations. Moreover, ensuring that game content is age-appropriate and culturally sensitive is essential for creating a positive and inclusive learning environment. Responsible design practices also involve promoting balanced gameplay habits, avoiding addictive mechanics, and providing resources for managing screen time effectively.

7.1.9 Continuous Evaluation and Iterative Improvement

The final principle of educational games design emphasizes the importance of continuous evaluation and iterative improvement. Even after release, games should undergo rigorous assessment to gauge their effectiveness in achieving learning objectives. Collecting feedback from players and educators allows developers to identify areas for enhancement and refine gameplay mechanics accordingly. Furthermore, updates and expansions can introduce new content and features, keeping the gaming experience fresh and relevant over time. By embracing a cycle of evaluation and iteration, developers ensure that educational games remain responsive to evolving educational needs and technological advancements.

7.2 STORYTELLING IN EDUCATIONAL GAMES

Storytelling has been an integral part of human culture since ancient times, serving as a powerful medium for communication, entertainment, and education. In the realm of educational games, storytelling plays a crucial role in engaging learners, contextualizing learning content, and fostering emotional connections with the subject matter.

Storytelling is a potent tool for creating immersive, engaging, and effective educational games that inspire curiosity, foster empathy, and promote meaningful learning experiences. By integrating narratives with learning objectives, character development, emotional engagement, structural elements, interactivity, assessment, feedback mechanisms, ethical considerations, and representation, developers can harness the transformative power of storytelling to enhance learning outcomes and empower learners of all ages and backgrounds. As technology continues to evolve and storytelling techniques evolve, educational games remain at the forefront of innovation, shaping the future of education and entertainment in the digital age.

Storytelling, intertwined with the development of mythologies, predates writing. The earliest forms of storytelling were usually oral, combined with gestures and expressions. Some archaeologists believe that rock art, in addition to a role in religious rituals, may have served as a form of storytelling for many ancient cultures. The Australian aboriginal people painted symbols which also appear in stories on cave walls as a means of helping the storyteller remember the story. The story was then told using a combination of oral narrative, music, rock art and dance, which bring understanding and meaning to human existence through the remembrance and enactment of stories. People have used the carved trunks of living trees and ephemeral media (such as sand and leaves) to record folktales in pictures or with writing. Complex forms of tattooing may also represent stories, with information about genealogy, affiliation and social status.

Folktales often share common motifs and themes, suggesting possible basic psychological similarities across various human cultures. Other stories, notably fairy tales, appear to have spread from place to place, implying memetic appeal and popularity.

Groups of originally oral tales can coalesce over time into story cycles (like the *Arabian Nights*), cluster around mythic heroes (like King Arthur), and develop into the narratives of the deeds of the gods and saints of various religions. The results can be episodic (like the stories about Anansi), epic (as with Homeric tales), inspirational (note the tradition of *vitae*) and/or instructive (as in many Buddhist or Christian scriptures).

With the advent of writing and the use of stable, portable media, storytellers recorded, transcribed and continued to share stories over wide regions of the world. Stories have been carved, scratched, painted, printed or inked onto wood or bamboo, ivory and other bones, pottery, clay tablets, stone, palm-leaf books, skins (parchment), bark cloth, paper, silk, canvas and other textiles, recorded on film and stored electronically in digital form. Oral stories continue to be created, improvisationally by impromptu and professional storytellers, as well as committed to memory and passed from generation to generation, despite the increasing popularity of written and televised media in much of the world.

Modern storytelling has a broad purview. In addition to its traditional forms (fairytales, folktales, mythology, legends, fables etc.), it has extended itself to representing history, personal narrative, political commentary and evolving cultural norms. Contemporary storytelling is also widely used to address educational objectives. New forms of media are creating new ways for people to record, express and consume stories. Tools for asynchronous group communication can provide an environment for individuals to reframe or recast individual stories into group stories. Games and other digital platforms, such as those used in interactive fiction or interactive storytelling, may be used to position the user as a character within a bigger world. Documentaries, including interactive web documentaries, employ storytelling narrative techniques to communicate information about their topic.

Self-revelatory stories, created for their cathartic and therapeutic effect, are growing in their use and application, as in Psychodrama, Drama Therapy and Playback Theatre. Storytelling is also used as a means by which to precipitate psychological and social change in the practice of transformative arts.

Some people also make a case for different narrative forms being classified as storytelling in the contemporary world. For example, digital storytelling, online and dice-and-paper-based role-playing games. In traditional role-playing games, storytelling is done by the person who controls the environment and the non-playing fictional characters, and moves the story elements along for the players as they interact with the storyteller. The game is advanced by mainly verbal interactions, with dice roll determining random events in the fictional universe, where the players interact with each other and the storyteller. This type of game has many genres, such as sci-fi and fantasy, as well as alternate-reality worlds based on the current reality, but with different setting and beings such as werewolves, aliens, daemons, or hidden societies. These oral-based role-playing games were very popular in the 1990s among circles of youth in many countries before computer and console-based online MMORPG's took their place. Despite the prevalence of computer-based MMORPGs, the dice-and-paper RPG still has a dedicated following.

Oral traditions of storytelling are found in several civilizations; they predate the printed and online press. Storytelling was used to explain natural phenomena, bards told stories of creation and developed a pantheon of gods and myths. Oral stories passed from one generation to the next and storytellers were regarded as healers, leaders, spiritual guides, teachers, cultural secrets keepers and entertainers. Oral storytelling came in various forms including songs, poetry, chants and dance.

Albert Bates Lord examined oral narratives from field transcripts of Yugoslav oral bards collected by Milman Parry in the 1930s, and the texts of epics such as the Odyssey. Lord found that a large part of the stories consisted of text which was improvised during the telling process.

Lord identified two types of *story vocabulary*. The first he called "formulas": "Rosy-fingered Dawn", "the wine-dark sea" and other specific set phrases had long been known of in Homer and other oral epics. Lord, however, discovered that across many story traditions, fully 90% of an oral epic is assembled from lines which are repeated verbatim or which use one-for-one word substitutions. In other words, oral stories are built out of set phrases which have been stockpiled from a lifetime of hearing and telling stories.

The other type of story vocabulary is theme, a set sequence of story actions that structure a tale. Just as the teller of tales proceeds line-by-line using formulas, so he proceeds from event-to-event using themes. One near-universal theme is repetition, as evidenced in Western folklore with the "rule of three": Three brothers set out, three attempts are made, three riddles are asked. A theme can be as simple as a specific set sequence describing the arming of a hero, starting with shirt and trousers and ending with headdress and weapons. A theme can be large enough to be a plot component. For example: a hero proposes a journey to a dangerous place / he disguises himself / his disguise fools everybody / except for a common person of little account (a crone, a tavern maid or a woodcutter) / who immediately recognizes him / the commoner becomes the hero's ally, showing unexpected resources of skill or initiative. A theme does not belong to a specific story, but may be found with minor variation in many different stories.

The story was described by Reynolds Price, when he wrote:

- A need to tell and hear stories is essential to the species Homo sapiens – second in necessity apparently after nourishment and before love and shelter. Millions survive without love or home, almost none in silence; the opposite of silence leads quickly to narrative, and the sound of story is the dominant sound of our lives, from the small accounts of our day›s events to the vast incommunicable constructs of psychopaths.

In contemporary life, people will seek to fill "story vacuums" with oral and written stories. "In the absence of a narrative, especially in an ambiguous and/or urgent situation, people will seek out and consume plausible stories like water in the desert. It is our innate nature to connect the dots. Once an explanatory narrative is adopted, it's extremely hard to undo," whether or not it is true.

Folklorists sometimes divide oral tales into two main groups: *Märchen* and *Sagen*. These are German terms for which there are no exact English equivalents, however we have approximations:

Märchen, loosely translated as "fairy tale(s)" or little stories, take place in a kind of separate "once-upon-a-time" world of nowhere-in-particular, at an indeterminate time in the past. They are clearly not intended to be understood as true. The stories are full of clearly defined incidents, and peopled by rather flat characters with little or no interior life. When the supernatural occurs, it is presented matter-of-factly, without surprise. Indeed, there is very little effect, generally; bloodcurdling events may take place, but with little call for emotional response from the listener.

Sagen, translated as "legends", are supposed to have actually happened, very often at a particular time and place, and they draw much of their power from this fact. When the supernatural intrudes (as it often does), it does so in an emotionally fraught manner. Ghost and Lovers' Leap stories belong in this category, as do many UFO stories and stories of supernatural beings and events.

Another important examination of orality in human life is Walter J. Ong's *Orality and Literacy: The Technologizing of the Word* (1982). Ong studies the distinguishing characteristics of oral traditions, how oral and written cultures interact and condition one another, and how they ultimately influence human epistemology.

Storytelling is a means for sharing and interpreting experiences. Peter L. Berger says human life is narratively rooted, humans construct their lives and shape their world into homes in terms of these groundings and memories. Stories are universal in that they can bridge cultural, linguistic and age-related divides. Storytelling can be adaptive for all ages, leaving out the notion of age segregation. Storytelling can be used as a method to teach ethics, values and cultural norms and differences. Learning is most effective when it takes place in social environments that provide authentic social cues about how knowledge is to be applied. Stories function as a tool to pass on knowledge in a social context. So, every story has 3 parts. First, The setup (The Hero's world before the adventure starts). Second, The Confrontation (The hero's world turned upside down). Third, The Resolution (Hero conquers villain, but it is not enough for Hero to survive. The Hero or World must be transformed). Any story can be framed in such format.

Human knowledge is based on stories and the human brain consists of cognitive machinery necessary to understand, remember and tell stories. Humans are storytelling organisms that both individually and socially, lead storied lives. Stories mirror human thought as humans think in narrative structures and most often remember facts in story form. Facts can be understood as smaller versions of a larger story, thus storytelling can supplement analytical thinking. Because storytelling requires auditory and visual senses from listeners, one can learn to organize their mental representation of a story, recognize structure of language and express his or her thoughts.

Stories tend to be based on experiential learning, but learning from an experience is not automatic. Often a person needs to attempt to tell the story of that experience before realizing its value. In this case, it is not only the listener who learns, but the teller who also becomes aware of his or her own unique experiences and background. This process of storytelling is empowering as the teller effectively conveys ideas and, with practice, is able to demonstrate the potential of human accomplishment. Storytelling taps into existing knowledge and creates bridges both culturally and motivationally toward a solution.

Stories are effective educational tools because listeners become engaged and therefore remember. Storytelling can be seen as a foundation for learning and teaching. While the story listener is engaged, they are able to imagine new perspectives, inviting a transformative and empathetic experience. This involves allowing the individual to actively engage in the story as well as observe, listen and participate with minimal guidance. Listening to a storyteller can create lasting personal connections, promote innovative problem solving and foster a shared understanding regarding future ambitions. The listener can then activate knowledge and imagine new possibilities. Together a storyteller and listener can seek best practices and invent new solutions. Because stories often have multiple layers of meanings, listeners have to listen closely to identify the underlying knowledge in the story. Storytelling is used as a tool to teach children the importance of respect through the practice of listening. As well as connecting children with their environment, through the theme of the stories, and give them more autonomy by using repetitive statements, which improve their learning to learn competence. It is also used to teach children to have respect for all life, value inter-connectedness and always work to overcome adversity. To teach this a Kinesthetic learning style would be used, involving the listeners through music, dream interpretation, or dance.

For indigenous cultures of the Americas, storytelling is used as an oral form of language associated with practices and values essential to developing one's identity. This is because everyone in the community can add their own touch and perspective to the narrative collaboratively – both individual and culturally shared perspectives have a place in the co-creation of the story. Oral storytelling in indigenous communities differs from other forms of stories because they are told not only for entertainment, but for teaching values. For example, the Sto:lo community in Canada focuses on reinforcing children's identity by telling stories about the land to explain their roles.

Furthermore, Storytelling is a way to teach younger members of indigenous communities about their culture and their identities. In Donna Eder's study, Navajos were interviewed about storytelling practices that they have had in the past and what changes they want to see in the future. They notice that storytelling makes an impact on the lives of the children of the Navajos. According to some of the Navajos that were interviewed, storytelling is one of many main practices that teaches children the important principles to live a good life. In indigenous communities, stories are a way to pass knowledge on from generation to generation.

For some indigenous people, experience has no separation between the physical world and the spiritual world. Thus, some indigenous people communicate to their children through ritual, storytelling, or dialogue. Community values, learned through storytelling, help to guide future generations and aid in identity formation.

In the Quechua community of Highland Peru, there is no separation between adults and children. This allows for children to learn storytelling through their own interpretations of the given story. Therefore, children in the Quechua community are encouraged to listen to the story that is being told in order to learn about their identity and culture. Sometimes, children are expected to sit quietly and listen actively. This enables them to engage in activities as independent learners.

This teaching practice of storytelling allowed children to formulate ideas based on their own experiences and perspectives. In Navajo communities, for children and adults, storytelling is one of the many effective ways to educate both the young and old about their cultures, identities and history. Storytelling help the Navajos know who they are, where they come from and where they belong.

Storytelling in indigenous cultures is sometimes passed on by oral means in a quiet and relaxing environment, which usually coincides with family or tribal community gatherings and official events such as family occasions, rituals, or ceremonial practices. During the telling of the story, children may act as participants by asking questions, acting out the story, or telling smaller parts of the story. Furthermore, stories are not often told in the same manner twice, resulting in many variations of a single myth. This is because narrators may choose to insert new elements into old stories dependent upon the relationship between the storyteller and the audience, making the story correspond to each unique situation.

Indigenous cultures also use instructional ribbing— a playful form of correcting children's undesirable behavior— in their stories. For example, the Ojibwe (or Chippewa) tribe uses the tale of an owl snatching away misbehaving children. The caregiver will often say, "The owl will come and stick you in his ears if you don't stop crying!" Thus, this form of teasing serves as a tool to correct inappropriate behavior and promote cooperation.

There are various types of stories among many indigenous communities. Communication in Indigenous American communities is rich with stories, myths, philosophies and narratives that serve as a means to exchange information. These stories may be used for coming of age themes, core values, morality, literacy and history. Very often, the stories are used to instruct and teach children about cultural values and lessons. The meaning within the stories is not always explicit, and children are expected to make their own meaning of the stories. In the Lakota Tribe of North America, for example, young girls are often told the story of the White Buffalo Calf Woman, who is a spiritual figure that protects young girls from the whims of men. In the Odawa Tribe, young boys are often told the story of a young man who never took care of his body, and as a result, his feet fail to run when he tries to escape predators. This story serves as an indirect means of encouraging the young boys to take care of their bodies.

Narratives can be shared to express the values or morals among family, relatives, or people who are considered part of the close-knit community. Many stories in indigenous American communities all have a "surface" story, that entails knowing certain information and clues to unlocking the metaphors in the story. The underlying message of the story being told, can be understood and interpreted with clues that hint to a certain interpretation. In order to make meaning from these stories, elders in the Sto:lo community for example, emphasize the importance in learning how to listen, since it requires the senses to bring one's heart and mind together. For instance, a way in which children learn about the metaphors significant for the society they live in, is by listening to their elders and participating in rituals where they respect one another.

Stories in indigenous cultures encompass a variety of values. These values include an emphasis on individual responsibility, concern for the environment and communal welfare.

Stories are based on values passed down by older generations to shape the foundation of the community. Storytelling is used as a bridge for knowledge and understanding allowing the values of "self" and "community" to connect and be learned as a whole. Storytelling in the Navajo community for example allows for community values to be learned at different times and places for different learners. Stories are told from the perspective of other people, animals, or the natural elements of the earth. In this way, children learn to value their place in the world as a person in relation to others. Typically, stories are used as an informal learning tool in Indigenous American communities, and can act as an alternative method for reprimanding children's bad behavior. In this way, stories are non-confrontational, which allows the child to discover for themselves what they did wrong and what they can do to adjust the behavior.

Parents in the Arizona Tewa community, for example, teach morals to their children through traditional narratives. Lessons focus on several topics including historical or "sacred" stories or more domestic disputes. Through storytelling, the Tewa community emphasizes the traditional wisdom of the ancestors and the importance of collective as well as individual identities. Indigenous communities teach children valuable skills and morals through the actions of good or mischievous stock characters while also allowing room for children to make meaning for themselves. By not being given every element of the story, children rely on their own experiences and not formal teaching from adults to fill in the gaps.

When children listen to stories, they periodically vocalize their ongoing attention and accept the extended turn of the storyteller. The emphasis on attentiveness to surrounding events and the importance of oral tradition in indigenous communities teaches children the skill of keen attention. For example, Children of the Tohono O'odham American Indian community who engaged in more cultural practices were able to recall the events in a verbally presented story better than those who did not engage in cultural practices. Body movements and gestures help to communicate values and keep stories alive for future generations. Elders, parents and grandparents are typically involved in teaching the children the cultural ways, along with history, community values and teachings of the land.

Children in indigenous communities can also learn from the underlying message of a story. For example, in a nahuatl community near Mexico City, stories about ahuaques or hostile water dwelling spirits that guard over the bodies of water, contain morals about respecting the environment. If the protagonist of a story, who has accidentally broken something that belongs to the ahuaque, does not replace it or give back in some way to the ahuaque, the protagonist dies. In this way, storytelling serves as a way to teach what the community values, such as valuing the environment.

Storytelling also serves to deliver a particular message during spiritual and ceremonial functions. In the ceremonial use of storytelling, the unity building theme of the message becomes more important than the time, place and characters of the message. Once the message is delivered, the story is finished. As cycles of the tale are told and retold, story units can recombine, showing various outcomes for a person's actions.

Storytelling has been assessed for critical literacy skills and the learning of theatre-related terms by the nationally recognized storytelling and creative drama organization, Neighborhood Bridges, in Minneapolis. Another storyteller researcher in the UK proposes that the social space created preceding oral storytelling in schools may trigger sharing (Parfitt, 2014).

Storytelling has also been studied as a way to investigate and archive cultural knowledge and values within indigenous American communities. Iseke's study (2013) on the role of storytelling in the Metis community, showed promise in furthering research about the Metis and their shared communal atmosphere during storytelling events. Iseke focused on the idea of witnessing a storyteller as a vital way to share and partake in the Metis community, as members of the community would stop everything else they were doing in order to listen or "witness" the storyteller and allow the story to become a "ceremonial landscape", or shared reference, for everyone present.

This was a powerful tool for the community to engage and teach new learner shared references for the values and ideologies of the Metis. Through storytelling, the Metis cemented the shared reference of personal or popular stories and folklore, which members of the community can use to share ideologies. In the future, Iseke noted that Metis elders wished for the stories being told to be used for further research into their culture, as stories were a traditional way to pass down vital knowledge to younger generations.

For the stories we read, the "neuro-semantic encoding of narratives happens at levels higher than individual semantic units and that this encoding is systematic across both individuals and languages." This encoding seems to appear most prominently in the default mode network.

Storytelling in serious application contexts, as e.g. therapeutics, business, serious games, medicine, education, or faith can be referred to as serious storytelling. Serious storytelling applies storytelling "outside the context of entertainment, where the narration progresses as a sequence of patterns impressive in quality... and is part of a thoughtful progress".

Some approaches treat narratives as politically motivated stories, stories empowering certain groups and stories giving people agency. Instead of just searching for the main point of the narrative, the political function is demanded through asking, "Whose interest does a personal narrative serve"? This approach mainly looks at the power, authority, knowledge, ideology and identity; "whether it legitimates and dominates or resists and empowers". All personal narratives are seen as ideological because they evolve from a structure of power relations and simultaneously produce, maintain and reproduce that power structure".

Political theorist, Hannah Arendt argues that storytelling transforms private meaning to public meaning. Regardless of the gender of the narrator and what story they are sharing, the performance of the narrative and the audience listening to it is where the power lies.

Therapeutic storytelling is the act of telling one's story in an attempt to better understand oneself or one's situation. Oftentimes, these stories affect the audience in a therapeutic sense as well, helping them to view situations similar to their own through a different lens. Noted author and folklore scholar, Elaine Lawless states, "...this process provides new avenues for understanding and identity formation.

Language is utilised to bear witness to their lives". Sometimes a narrator will simply skip over certain details without realizing, only to include it in their stories during a later telling. In this way, that telling and retelling of the narrative serves to "reattach portions of the narrative". These gaps may occur due to a repression of the trauma or even just a want to keep the most gruesome details private. Regardless, these silences are not as empty as they appear, and it is only this act of storytelling that can enable the teller to fill them back in.

Psychodrama uses re-enactment of a personal, traumatic event in the life of a psychodrama group participant as a therapeutic methodology, first developed by psychiatrist, J.L. Moreno, M.D. This therapeutic use of storytelling was incorporated into Drama Therapy, known in the field as "Self Revelatory Theater". In 1975 Jonathan Fox and Jo Salas developed a therapeutic, improvisational storytelling form they called Playback Theatre. Therapeutic storytelling is also used to promote healing through transformative arts, where a facilitator helps a participant write and often present their personal story to an audience.

7.2.1 The Power of Narrative

Narrative serves as the backbone of storytelling in educational games, providing a cohesive structure that guides players through the learning experience. By weaving together characters, settings, conflicts, and resolutions, narratives create immersive worlds that captivate players' imagination and curiosity. Whether exploring historical events, scientific phenomena, or mathematical concepts, narratives contextualize learning content within relatable and meaningful contexts, making abstract concepts more accessible and engaging. Furthermore, narratives evoke emotional responses, fostering empathy and investment in the learning journey, which can enhance retention and understanding of educational concepts.

7.2.2 Integration of Learning Objectives

Effective storytelling in educational games integrates seamlessly with learning objectives, reinforcing key concepts and skills within the narrative framework. Before embarking on the design process, developers must identify the educational goals they aim to achieve and craft narratives that align with these objectives. Whether through quest-based adventures, interactive simulations, or branching storylines, narratives should present challenges and opportunities that encourage players to apply their knowledge and problem-solving skills in meaningful contexts. By embedding learning objectives within the narrative structure, educational games ensure that gameplay remains focused and relevant to educational outcomes.

7.2.3 Character Development and Player Agency

Character development is a central aspect of storytelling in educational games, allowing players to immerse themselves in the roles of protagonists who drive the narrative forward. Well-developed characters possess distinct personalities, motivations, and goals, creating opportunities for players to empathize with their struggles and triumphs. Moreover, player agency—a sense of autonomy and control over the game world—enhances engagement and immersion by allowing players to make meaningful choices that shape the course of the narrative. Branching storylines, multiple endings, and dialogue options provide avenues for player agency, empowering learners to explore different paths and consequences based on their actions.

7.2.4 Emotional Engagement and Immersion

Emotional engagement is a hallmark of effective storytelling in educational games, eliciting a range of feelings—from excitement and curiosity to empathy and reflection—that enrich the learning experience. Through compelling narratives, players become emotionally invested in the game world and its characters, forging connections that transcend mere intellectual engagement. Emotional resonance enhances memory retention and cognitive processing, as learners recall and internalize educational content within the context of their emotional experiences. Furthermore, immersion— the sense of being fully absorbed in the game world—heightens emotional engagement by blurring the boundaries between reality and fiction, creating an optimal environment for learning and exploration.

7.2.5 Structural Elements of Narrative Design

Narrative design encompasses a variety of structural elements that contribute to the effectiveness of storytelling in educational games. These include plot development, pacing, character arcs, dialogue, world-building, and thematic cohesion. Plot development involves crafting a compelling sequence of events that propel the narrative forward, maintaining players' interest and momentum throughout the game. Pacing refers to the rhythm and tempo at which the story unfolds, balancing moments of action, exposition, and reflection to sustain engagement. Character arcs involve the growth and transformation of protagonists over the course of the narrative, providing opportunities for character development and emotional investment. Dialogue serves as a means of character interaction and storytelling, conveying information, emotion, and personality traits through spoken or written exchanges. World-building entails creating rich, immersive environments that reflect the setting, culture, and themes of the narrative, enhancing players' sense of immersion and believability. Thematic cohesion ensures that all elements of the narrative—from plot twists to visual aesthetics—align cohesively with the overarching themes and messages of the educational content.

7.2.6 Interactivity and Nonlinear Storytelling

Interactivity is a defining feature of educational games that distinguishes them from passive forms of media such as books or films. In educational games, interactivity allows players to actively participate in the storytelling process, influencing the direction and outcome of the narrative through their actions and decisions. Nonlinear storytelling structures, such as branching narratives or open-world exploration, offer players greater freedom and agency to explore the game world at their own pace and in their own way. This nonlinearity promotes player engagement and replayability, as players discover new story paths, outcomes, and hidden content with each playthrough. Moreover, interactivity fosters active learning by encouraging players to experiment, problem-solve, and collaborate with others, thus deepening their understanding and mastery of educational concepts.

7.2.7 Assessment and Feedback Mechanisms

Assessment and feedback mechanisms are essential components of storytelling in educational games, providing opportunities for formative assessment and learning reinforcement. Throughout the narrative, players encounter challenges, puzzles, and quizzes that assess their understanding and application of educational content. Feedback mechanisms, such as immediate responses, progress indicators, and performance metrics, inform players of their strengths and areas for improvement, guiding their learning journey and motivating them to persevere through challenges. Moreover, narrative-driven assessments integrate seamlessly with the overarching story, contextualizing learning tasks within the game world and reinforcing their relevance to the narrative objectives.

7.2.8 Ethical Considerations and Representation

Ethical considerations and representation are critical aspects of storytelling in educational games, ensuring that narratives reflect diverse perspectives, cultures, and experiences in a respectful and authentic manner. Developers must be mindful of stereotypes, biases, and cultural sensitivities when crafting narratives, avoiding harmful or offensive portrayals that perpetuate stereotypes or marginalize underrepresented groups. Moreover, inclusive representation fosters empathy and understanding among players, promoting diversity and social justice within the gaming community. By prioritizing ethical considerations and representation, educational games can create inclusive and empowering storytelling experiences that resonate with learners from all backgrounds.

7.3 BALANCING FUN AND LEARNING

Balancing fun and learning is a perennial challenge in educational design, particularly in the realm of digital games and interactive media. While traditional educational approaches often prioritize academic rigor at the expense of engagement, educational games seek to bridge the gap by integrating learning objectives with entertaining gameplay experiences.

Balancing fun and learning is a complex yet essential endeavor in educational game design, requiring careful consideration of gameplay mechanics, learning objectives, player engagement, and pedagogical principles.

By aligning learning objectives with gameplay mechanics, creating compelling gameplay experiences, fostering intrinsic motivation and autonomy, balancing challenge and support, integrating formative assessment, and promoting collaboration and social interaction, developers can create engaging educational experiences that captivate learners' interest while fostering meaningful learning outcomes.

As educational games continue to evolve and innovate, the quest to balance fun and learning remains a dynamic and ongoing journey that holds the promise of transforming education in the digital age.

7.3.1 Game Balance

Game balance is a branch of game design with the intention of improving gameplay and user experience by balancing difficulty and fairness. Game balance consists of adjusting rewards, challenges, and/or elements of a game to create the intended player experience.

Overview and Development

Game balance is generally understood as introducing a level of fairness for the players. This includes adjusting difficulty, win-loss conditions, game states, economy balancing, and so on to work in tandem with each other. The concept of game balance depends on the game genre. Most game designers agree that game balancing serves towards providing an engaging player experience, especially through a meta. Game balance is commonly discussed among game designers, some of whom include Ernest Adams, Jeannie Novak, Ian Schreiber, David Sirlin, and Jesse Schell. The topic is also featured in many YouTube channels specializing in game design topics, including Extra Credits, GMTK and Adam Millard.

Terms Specific to Game Balance

PvP, PvE and Co-Op Games

- Player versus player (PvP) describes games that feature a competition between players. PvE is an acronym for player versus environment, where players instead compete with the environment and non-player characters (NPCs).
- Co-op is short for "cooperative" and refers to PvE and PvP games where you can work with other players.

Game Elements

Game elements are things that appear within a video game that contribute to the gameplay experience. In most game design frameworks, game elements are categorized into groups to help describe their roles in the games. A game element refers to anything ranging from a player's special ability to the relations between different game mechanics in a game.

Game Mechanics

Game mechanics are constructs that let the player interact with the game world. They define the goal, how players can achieve them and how they cannot, and what happens when they try. These would include challenges, competitive or cooperative gameplay, win-loss conditions and states, feedback loops, and how they relate to one another. Like game balance, the terminology behind game mechanics can vary depending on the designer or the resource's author.

Buffs and Nerfs

Buffs are changes to a game which increase the utility of game elements, items, environments, mechanics and so on, while nerfs are changes that decrease the utility of said game elements and alike. Buffs and nerfs are common methods for adjusting the challenge for the player. Both can be achieved indirectly by changing other elements and mechanics or introducing new ones. Both terms can also be used as verbs for the act of making such a change. The first established use of the term "nerf" was in *Ultima Online*, as a reference to the Nerf brand of toys due to their soft toy bullets. However, there is no concrete evidence to show where the term "buff" came from. It has been perceived that the term came from bodybuilding culture, where it is a slang term which refers to an individual's large musculature as a result of strength-based exercises.

The most popular use of these terms is found in most MMORPGs, where game designers use buffs and nerfs to maintain game balance shortly after introducing a new feature that may cause significant changes to the game's mechanics. This is sometimes due to a method of using or acquiring the object that was not considered by the developers. The frequency and scale of nerfing vary widely from game to game, but almost all MMOs have engaged in nerfing at some point.

Nerfs in various online games, such as *Anarchy Online*, have spurred in-world protests. Since many items in virtual worlds are sold or traded among players, a nerf may have an outsized impact on the virtual economy. As players respond, the nerf may cause prices to fluctuate before settling down in a different equilibrium. This impact on the economy, along with the original impact of the nerf, can cause large player resentment for even a small change. In particular, in the case of items or abilities which have been nerfed, players can become upset over the perceived wasted efforts in obtaining the now nerfed features. For games where avatars and items represent significant economic value, this may bring up legal issues over the lost value.

Overpowered and Underpowered

The terms "overpowered" (OP) and "underpowered" (UP) are used on game elements and mechanics that are too good or bad to describe a lack of game balance. More precisely, if a game element is too strong even with the highest possible cost, it is overpowered. If it is too weak even with the lowest possible cost, it is underpowered. On the other hand, a game element might simply be too expensive or not expensive enough for the benefit it provides.

Colloquially, overpowered is often used when describing a specific class in an RPG, a specific faction in strategic games, or a specific tactic, ability, weapon or unit in various games. For something to be deemed overpowered, it is either the best choice in a disproportionate number of situations (marginalizing other choices) and/or excessively hard to counter by the opponent compared to the effort required to use it.

Underpowered often refers to when describing a specific class in an RPG, a specific faction in strategic games, or a specific tactic, ability, weapon or unit in various games as far weaker than average, resulting in it being always one of the worst options to pick in most situations. In such way, it is often marginalized by other choices because it's inherently weaker than similar options or it's much more easily countered by opponents.

Gimp

A gimp is a character, character class or character ability that is underpowered in the context of the game (e.g. a close range warrior class equipping a full healing boosting armor set, despite having no healing abilities). Gimped characters lack effectiveness compared to other characters at a similar level of experience. A player may gimp a character by assigning skills and abilities that are inappropriate for the character class, or by developing the character inefficiently. However, this is not always the case, as some characters are purposely "gimped" by the game's developers in order to provide an incentive for raising their level, or to give the player an early head-start. An example of this is *Final Fantasy*'s Mystic Knight class, which starts out weak, but is able to become the most powerful class if brought to a very high level. Gimps may also be accidental on the part of the developer, and may require a software patch to balance.

Sometimes, especially in MMORPGs, gimp is used as a synonym for nerf to describe a rule modification that weakens the affected target. Unlike the connotatively neutral term nerf, gimp in this usage often implies that the rule change unfairly disadvantages the target.

Revamp

A revamp (or *rework*) is a significant change to a game that is designed to improve (or balance out) the game's overall quality. This can include changes to the game's mechanics, art style, storyline, or any other aspect of the game. Revamps are often done in response to player feedback or to address problems that have been identified with the game. They can also be done simply to refresh the game and keep it feeling fresh for players. Revamps can happen at any time during a game's development or after its release. The difference between a revamp and a remaster is that a remaster is simply an updated version of the game with better graphics and maybe some new content, while a revamp is a completely new game built on the foundation of the original. Revamps may be optional and may happen if something is not properly nerfed.

Essential Concepts of Balancing

Chance

While the optimal ratio between skill and chance are dependent on the target group, the outcome should be more influenced by skill. Chance and skill are viewed as partial opposites. Chance allows a weaker player to beat a stronger one. Generally, it is advised to favor many small random elements with little influence over a few with large effects to make results, that differ highly from average, less likely. The player should also receive a certain degree of information and control over random elements.

Difficulty

Difficulty is especially important for PvE-games, but has at least some significance for PvP-games regarding the usability of game elements. The perception of the difficulty depends on mechanics and numbers, but also on the players abilities and expectations.

The ideal difficulty therefore depends on individual player and should put the player in a state of flow. Consequently, for the development, it can be useful or even necessary to focus on a certain target group. Difficulty should increase throughout the game since players get better and usually unlock more power. Achieving all those goals is problematic since, among other things, skill cannot be measured objectively and testers also get continuously better. In any case, difficulty should be adjustable for or by the player in some way.

Dynamic and Static Balance

Game balance can be divided into a dynamic and a static component. Static balance is mostly concerned with a game's rules and elements, everything, that is set before a game or match starts. An example would be like player health and ammo left. Dynamic balance conversely describes the balance between players, environment and computer opponents and how it changes throughout the game. An example would be moving objects in a game environment

Economies

Within a game, everything that has an owner or is provided to a player can be called a resource. This includes commodities, units, tokens, but also information or time, for example. Those resource systems are similar to real economies, especially in regards to trading resources. There are some distinctions for video games though: There are open economies, that receive additional resources, but also closed ones that do not. Additionally, economies might provide indefinite resources, or all players have to share a set amount instead. Especially for online games, it therefore is important to design economies to make them "fun" and sustainable.

Fairness

A game is fair if all players have roughly the same chance of winning at the start independent of which offered options they choose. This makes fairness especially important for PvP games. Fairness also means, even for PvE games, that the player never feels like the opponents were unbeatable. Early appearances of the term "fairness":

- Any good computer game must be totally fair. It must be possible for the player to reach the objective and win. This is not to say the game cannot be complicated or random or *appear* unfair.—*Tim Barry of InfoWorld, 1981*
- An important trait of any game is the illusion of winnability. If a game is to provide a continuing challenge to players, it must also provide a continuing motivation to play. The game must appear to be winnable to all players, beginners and experts, but it must never truly be winnable or it will lose its appeal.—*Chris Crawford, 1982*
- Dani Bunten was once asked how to play-balance a game. Her one word answer was "Cheat." Asked what to do if gamers complained, she said, "Lie!"—*Johnny L. Wilson of Computer Gaming World, 1994*

Chris Crawford wrote in 1982 of the importance of a game's "illusion of winnability"; *Pac-Man* is popular because it "appears winnable to most players, yet is never quite winnable". When defeated "the player must perceive", *Computer Gaming World* wrote in 1984, "that failure was the player's fault (not the game's) but can be corrected by playing better the next time". The illusion of winnability, Crawford said, "is very difficult to maintain. Some games maintain it for the expert but never achieve it for the beginner; these games intimidate all but the most determined players", citing *Tempest* as an example.

A fair game is winnable but, *InfoWorld* stated in 1981, can be "complicated or random or *appear* unfair". Fairness does not necessarily mean that a game is balanced. This is particularly true of action games: Jaime Griesemer, design lead at Bungie, states that "every fight in *Halo* is unfair". This potential for unfairness creates uncertainty, leading to the tension and excitement that action games seek to deliver. In these cases balancing is instead the management of unfair scenarios, with the ultimate goal of ensuring that all of the strategies which the game intends to support are viable. The extent to which those strategies are equal to one another defines the character of the game in question.

Simulation games can be balanced unfairly in order to be true to life. A wargame may cast the player into the role of a general who was defeated by an overwhelming force, and it is common for the abilities of teams in sports games to mirror those of the real-world teams they represent regardless of the implications for players who pick them.

Player perception can also affect the appearance of fairness. Sid Meier stated that he omitted multiplayer alliances in *Civilization* because he found that the computer was almost as good as humans in exploiting them, which caused players to think that the computer was cheating.

Meaningful Decisions

Meaningful decisions are decisions whose alternatives are neither without any effect nor is one alternative clearly the best. This would make, for example, choosing between the numbers of a dice meaningless if 6 always gives the greatest benefit.

This example is a dominant strategy, the most damaging type of meaningless decision, since it doesn't leave a reason to choose any alternative. Meaningful decisions consequently are a central part of the interactive medium games. Meaningless decisions, also called trivial decisions, do not add anything desirable to a game.

They might actually harm the game by unnecessarily making it more complex. Additionally, a higher number of meaningful decisions can also make a game just more complex. Offered decisions should always be meaningful though. However, for the balancing irrelevant decisions might still influence the players experience, e.g. a decision between cosmetic alternatives like skins.

Strategies:

- Strategies are specific combinations of actions to achieve a certain goal. Classic examples for this are a rush or focusing on economy in a real-time strategy game. Not only elementary decisions within a strategy, e.g. between game elements, also the decision between strategies should remain meaningful.

Dominant strategies:

- A dominant strategy is a strategy that is always the most likely to lead to success, making it objectively the best strategy. This therefore renders all related decisions meaningless. Even if a strategy does not always win, but clearly is the best, it can be called (almost) dominant. Dominant strategies damage games and should strongly be avoided when possible. However, there is no objective border when a slightly better strategy becomes dominant.

Metagame

Metagame describes a game around the actual game, including discussions, like in forums, interactions between players, e.g. on local tournaments, but also the influence of extrinsic factors like finances. The "Meta", as it is also called, can act as a self-balancing force, since counters to popular strategies become widely known and lead to players changing their play behavior appropriately. This self-balancing force should not prevent developers from intervening in extreme cases of imbalance though.

Positive and Negative Feedback

Positive and negative feedback, also called positive and negative feedback loop, essentially describes game mechanics that reward or punish playing (usually well or bad) with power or the loss of it. Therefore, success leads to more power within a positive loop and therefore accelerates progress further, while a negative loop decreases power or adds additional costs to it. Feedback loops should be implemented carefully to only target the correct player, or otherwise they might determine the outcome too early or achieve nothing but simply delay the end of the game.

Many games become more challenging if the player is successful. For instance, real-time strategy games often feature "upkeep", a resource tax that scales with the number of units under a player's control. Team games which challenge players to invade their opponents' territory (football, capture the flag) have a negative feedback loop by default: the further a player pushes, the more opponents they are likely to face.

Many games also feature positive feedback loops – where success (for example capturing an enemy territory) leads to greater resources or capabilities, and hence greater scope for further successes (for example further conquests or economic investments). The overall dynamic balance of the game will depend on the comparative strength of positive and negative feedback processes, and therefore decreasing the power of positive feedback processes has the same effect as introducing negative feedback processes. Positive feedback processes may be limited by making capabilities some concave function of a measure of raw success. For example:

- In RPG (role-playing games) using a level structure, the level attained is usually a concave transformation of experience points – as the character becomes more proficient, they can defeat more powerful adversaries, and hence can earn more experience points in a given period of playtime – but conversely more experience points are required to 'level up'. In this case, the players level and perhaps also power does not improve exponentially, but approximately linearly in playing time.
- In many military strategy games, the conquest of new territory only gives a marginal increase in power – for example the 'home province' may be exceptionally productive, whereas new territories open to

acquisition might only have by comparison slight resources, or may be prone to revolts or public order penalties which reduce their ability to provide significant net resources, after resources are allocated to adequately suppressing revolts. In this case, a player with initially impressive successes may become 'overextended' attempting to hold may regions which provide only marginal increases in resources.

- In many games there is little or no advantage in acquiring a large horde of some particular item. For example, having a large and varied cache of equipment or weapons is an advantage, but only weakly over a somewhat smaller horde with a similar degree of diversity - for example only one weapon can be used at a time, and having another in an inventory with very similar capabilities offers only marginal gain. In more general terms, capabilities may depend on some bottleneck where there is no or only weak positive feedback.

Strongly net negative feedback loops can lead to frequent ties. Conversely, if there is on net a strong positive feedback loop, early successes can multiply very rapidly, leading to the player eventually attaining a commanding position from which losing is almost impossible.

Power and Costs

Power is everything that provides an advantage, while costs are essentially everything that is a disadvantage. Therefore, power and costs can be viewed as positive and negative values of the same scale. This allows calculations with both of them at the same time.

Sometimes, it is only a matter of perspective if something is an advantage or a disadvantage: Is it a benefit to have bonus damage against dragons? Or is it a drawback not to receive it against other targets? A crucial part of game balancing consists in relating power and costs to each other and find a suitable relation in the first place, e.g. a power curve. In addition to that, costs might not be explicitly quantified: Spending gold on something from any finite amount limits future purchases.

Also, certain investments might have prerequisites before they even become available. Sometimes, a game does not even show disadvantages. All of this can be referred to as shadow costs.

Rewards

Every player desires rewards, e.g. new game content or a simple compliment. Rewards should get bigger as the playtime increases. They give a player the feeling of doing something right and can enhance progress. A little bit of uncertainty about rewards makes them more desirable for many players.

Solvability

Colloquially speaking, solving a game refers to winning it or reaching its end. Ian Schreiber calls a game solvable if, for every situation, there is a recognizable best action. Generally, it is undesirable if a game can easily be solved, since this makes decisions meaningless, and games become boring faster. There are multiple tiers of solvability: A game might be trivial to solve, but it might also be solvable only in theory with a lot of computing effort. Even games with random elements are solvable since a best action can be found using expected values. Besides high complexity, hidden information and the influence of other human players are what makes it impossible for a human to completely solve a game.

Symmetry and Asymmetry

Symmetric games offer all players identical starting conditions and are therefore automatically fair in the above stated sense. While they are easier to balance, they still must be balanced, e.g. regarding their game elements. Most modern games are asymmetric though, while the grade of asymmetry can vary greatly. Fairness becomes even more important for those.

Giving each player identical resources is the simplest game balancing technique. Most competitive games feature some level of symmetry; some (such as *Pong*) are completely symmetric, but those in which players alternate turns (such as chess) can never achieve total symmetry as one player will always have a first-move advantage or disadvantage.

Symmetry is unappealing in games because both sides can and will use any effective strategy simultaneously, or success depends on a very small advantage such as one pawn in chess. An alternative is to offer symmetry with restrictions. Players in *Wizard's Quest* and *Catan* have the same number of territories, but choose them in alternating order; the differing combination of territories causes asymmetry. Symmetry can be undone by human psychology; the advantage of players wearing red over players wearing blue is a well-documented example of this.

Systems and Subsystems

In general, games can be viewed as systems of numbers and relations that typically consist of multiple subsystems. All numbers within a game only have a meaning in their given context. Subsystems can be dealt with separately and they might even have different balancing goals, but they also influence each other more or less. It is therefore crucial to consider how changes can affect the balance as a whole.

Transitivity and Intransitivity

(In-)transitivity is a term used for logical relations. In games, this usually refers to relations between game elements, e.g. between the element A, B and C: In case of transitivity given A beats B and B beats C, A beats C. This means that A is the best element of those three. A transitive relation is especially useful as rewards for the player to receive more and more useful game elements. In case of intransitivity given A beats B and B beats C, A does not automatically beat C. On the contrary, it might even be the case that C beats A, like in rock-paper-scissors. Intransitive relations can be assessed within the properties of game elements instead of just defining the outcome. This helps to create variety and prevent dominant strategies.

Balancing Process

Balancing always includes changing quantifiable values and relations between them, directly or indirectly; this is done as an iterative process and partially dependent on the genre, during development and also afterwards (e.g. by rule changes, addons or software-updates). However, it cannot be completely solved by algorithms since aesthetics are also important and a perfect balance might actually achieve the opposite of fun. Ideally, simple rules deliver complex results. This is also referred to as "emergence".

Firstly, a balanced basis should be created, so most later work consists in merely changing numbers and introducing new content becomes much easier. This makes it important for a designer to adjust numbers easily and they should always know how changes affect the overall system. Sight of the bigger picture should never be lost to create a positive experience for the player.

Extremely powerful game elements and dominant strategies are dangerous to the latter goal and should therefore be identified and corrected. Game elements that provide a highly situational use but have a fixed cost value, that is comparable to less situational elements, are particularly difficult to balance. Another priority is providing multiple viable options. Generally, players react better to buffing something than nerfing it.

It is possible, however, to achieve those indirectly by changing another part of the system, since most content, if not everything is connected and related to each other.

Goals of Balancing

The highest goal of balancing is always preserving or increasing the fun or engagement. This, however, can highly depend on the individual game and its audience and might even consist in great imbalance or turn into the opposite of fun: Especially in games with in game purchases or in-game advertising, the developer or publisher has an interest to monetize the game, even if it is detrimental to the fun. Such games may frequently interrupt the experience with advertisements or provide low chances (e.g. in loot boxes) to intentionally frustrate the player but keep engagement high to encourage spending money to skip frustrating parts.

Otherwise, the player may face huge disadvantages (imbalances) even against other paying players.

In general, though, there is a consensus that huge imbalances are bad for a game, even if the game still is fun to play – a better balance would make it even more fun. Opinions on exactly what should be balanced, how well-balanced a game should ideally be and even if perfect balance is achievable or even a good thing vary. In some cases, it is even stated that a slight imbalance is actually beneficial.

A crucial goal of balancing a is preventing any of its component systems from being ineffective or otherwise undesirable when compared to their peers. An unbalanced system represents wasted development resources at the very least, and at worst can undermine the game's entire ruleset by making important roles or tasks impossible to perform.

One balancing approach is to set strategies as the goal, so all offered strategies have roughly equal chances of success. Strategies can only be affected by changing underlying game elements, but the balance between game elements is not the focus here. Strategies should offer a deep gaming experience.

The balance can depend on player skill. Therefore, one level of skill should be chosen as the goal of all development efforts. This might be professional or casual players, for example. On all other levels, that do not fit the prime audience, more imbalances can be accepted.

Preserving strategies and game elements from becoming irrelevant also is emphasized: Every given option should have at least some use and should be viable. To achieve this, strategies and game elements should be compared within all contexts they compete in, e.g. combat or resource investments. Extremely powerful ("broken") strategies and elements are viewed as especially damaging since they devalue all their competitors.

Beyond all of that, there is an argument for some imbalances within a game, since that constantly encourages players to find new solution, e.g. by interacting in the metagame. This especially applies to frequently updated games. On the opposite end, (nearly) perfectly balanced games would result in mere execution of proven strategies, with only top players being able to create new successful strategies. Also, giving all game elements the exact same amount of power would make all decisions meaningless, since everything is equally powerful anyway.

Another approach emphasizes that balance between game elements, strategies and actions is not the most important factor, but providing counters against any situation that may arise. This always allows players to find them together and they never face unsolvable problems. At least, there is the idea to include players in the balancing regarding their skills and other prerequisites. Matchmaking and handicaps can help achieving that. This might also decrease the influence of imbalance since players are more equally matched. In addition to that, the players' perception of balance should be considered: Player behavior can affect success rates of strategies and game elements. Therefore, all changes should be communicated accordingly.

Characteristics of a Well-balanced Game

Despite not all goals of balancing are clear, many characteristics of well-balanced games are usually not disagreed on: Decisions should be meaningful. The player should still have a chance to win in most situations and no stalemates should arise, in which nobody can win or lose. Leading player or computer controlled opponents should never get an irretrievable advantage until they almost won. Early mistakes and chance should not make a game unwinnable. Also, the game should provide the player with enough information and control to avoid those errors, so the player always feels responsible for his or her actions. Measuring the state of balance is another matter though, since it requires interpretation of data. Sheer win rates of strategies or game elements do not have a great significance without considering other factors like player skill and pick rates. Making correct conclusions is therefore crucial to find causes for imbalance.

Methods and Tools

The following paragraphs present a collection of tools and methods used to balance a game or to measure its state. Not mathematical perfection, but fun, engagement or a mix of both is the main goal and human evaluation still is the only known measurement for successfully achieving those, especially fun. Also, balancing is an intricate process and typically needs many iterations.

Aesthetics and Narration

The visual impression of a game should not contradict with its balancing. On the contrary: Especially real models, e.g. historic facts, can serve as inspiration for mechanics, counters, orthogonal unit differences or intransitive relations.

Balancing Strategies

One approach is to move the balancing goal to strategies instead of game elements. Strategies typically include multiple elements and decisions. This makes sure that all game elements have at least some use and decisions stay meaningful. Also, seemingly fine game elements might become too powerful only in certain combinations. A difficulty of this is though that strategies can only be influenced by changing the game elements and mechanics they include.

Ban

Banning certain game elements or strategies is a way to remove dominant strategies from otherwise well-balanced games, especially in the competitive sector. This should be avoided when possible, however.

Central Resource

A chosen value, this may be an attribute of a game elements, costs or an additionally calculated value like power, can be nominated as a benchmark for all other values. Every change of one of them means another one must change as well. It can affect the central resource but also any other value to still fit the same budget.

Counter

There should be a counter to every action, game element strategy that beats those in a direct competition. This does not only make dominant strategies unlikelier to develop, it also allows players to find new solutions for current challenges.

Ideally, a counter relation is assessed within properties of game elements rather than simply defined. Also, decisions that are made at the beginning of a game that cannot be revised by the player should not determine the outcome right away.

Difficulty Level

Video games often allow players to influence their balance by offering a choice of "difficulty levels". These affect how challenging the game is to play, and usually run on a general scale of "easy", "medium", and "hard".

Sometimes, the difficulty is set once for the entirety of a game, while in other games it can be changed freely at any point. Modern games, e.g. *Horizon Zero Dawn*, may also feature a difficulty setting called "Story" for players who want to focus on the narrative rather than interactive parts like combat. There are also other terms. *The Last of Us*, for example, offers two settings above "hard", called "survivor" and "grounded".

In addition to altering the game's rules, difficulty levels can be used to alter what content is presented to the player. This usually takes the form of adding or removing challenging locations or events, but some games also change their narrative to reward players who play them on higher difficulty levels or end early as punishment for playing on easy. Difficulty selection is not always presented bluntly, particularly in competitive games where all players are affected equally, and the standard "easy/hard" terminology no longer applies. Sometimes veiled language is used (*Mario Kart* offers "CC select"), while at other times there may be an array of granular settings instead of an overarching difficulty option. An alternative approach to difficulty levels is catering to players of all abilities at the same time, a technique that has been called "subjective difficulty". This requires a game to provide multiple solutions or routes, each offering challenges appropriate to players of different skill levels (*Super Mario Galaxy*, *Sonic Generations*).

Feedback

While tester feedback is important when developing and updating a game, there are certain things to be kept in mind: Skill and the ability to explain do not necessarily correlate with each other. There are typically more players than developers, so they are better at solving it. Additionally, new testers should be added from time to time since practice effects emerge.

Gamemaster

A game can be balanced dynamically by a gamemaster who observes players and adjusts the game in response to their actions, emotional state, etc., or even proactively changes the direction of the game to create certain experiences. Although gamemasters have historically been humans, some videogames now feature artificial intelligence (AI) systems that perform a similar role by monitoring player ability and inferring emotional state from input. Such systems are often referred to as having dynamic difficulty. One notable example is *Left 4 Dead* and its sequel *Left 4 Dead 2*, cooperative games that have the players fight through hordes of zombie-like creatures including unique creatures with special abilities. Both games use an AI Director which not only generates random events but tries to create tension and fear by spawning-in creatures to specific rule sets based on how players are progressing, specifically penalizing players through more difficult challenges for not working together. Research into biofeedback peripherals is set to greatly improve the accuracy of such systems.

Game Theory

Game theory focuses more on theoretical modeling of competing players and their decision making and therefore is only for limited use in game design. However, it does offer knowledge and tools like a Net Payoff Matrix that can be helpful to measure power and understand player reasoning.

Handicaps

Handicaps may create a competitive situation between players of different skill level, but they might also go too far and render skill irrelevant. Handicaps are disadvantages that sometimes are deliberately self-inflicted.

Intuition

Games can be complex systems. Since development resources are limited, relying on intuition can sometimes be useful or even necessary. The designer should always keep in mind how changes affect other parts of the game and guesses should always rely on evidence or proof.

Matchmaking and Ranking

An approach to avoid some balancing problems all together is ranking players depending on their skill. Ideally, the ranking system predicts the outcome almost perfectly and every player (in a PvP game) has roughly the same win rate, even considering factors that lie outside the game, like the gaming device. In any case, good match making benefits a game greatly, since, for example, newbies are not matched against experienced players who leave them with no chance of winning and the challenge of stronger opponents rises together with each player's skills.

Observation

Some obvious problems become clear through sheer observation of the game and player behavior. This includes mathematical superiority of game elements or strategies but also extremely high or low usage of those. In any case, statistics do not necessarily represent causalities and that there are typically multiple factors.

Orthogonal Unit Differences

Orthogonal unit differences describes properties of game elements that cannot be compared by inherent numbers. Ideally, every game element has at least one unique trait. This also helps creating intransitivity and counters.

Pacing

Player versus environment games are usually balanced to tread the fine line of regularly challenging players' abilities without ever producing insurmountable or unfair obstacles. This turns balancing into the management of dramatic structure, generally referred to by game designers as "pacing". Pacing is also a consideration in competitive games, but the autonomy of players makes it harder to control.

Power Curve

A power curve is a relation that reflects the ratio between power and costs. It is especially useful when dealing with multiple game elements that provide varying benefits depending on different values of the same cost, e.g. when using a central resource. While a power curve always shows an order, it does not necessarily represent exact relations, depending on the level of measurement.

Randomization

Randomization of starting conditions is a technique common in board games, card games, and also experimental research, which fights back against the human tendency to optimize patterns in one's favor. The downside of randomization is that it takes control away from the player, potentially leading to frustration. Methods of overcoming this include giving the player a selection of random results within which they can optimize (*Scrabble, Magic: The Gathering*) and making each game session short enough to encourage multiple attempts in one play session

(Klondike, *Strange Adventures in Infinite Space*).

Statistical Analysis

Statistics can help collecting empiric data of player behavior, success rates, etc., to identify unbalanced areas and make corrections. Ideally, a game gathers this data automatically. Statistics can only support a designers' abilities and intuition and are therefore only one part of making design decisions, together with, for example, tester- or user feedback. Statistics and their interpretation should also consider factors like skill and pick-rates.

Tier List

A tier list orders game elements according to their power in multiple categories. This ranking can be achieved using feedback, empiric data or subjective impressions. While the number and names of tiers can vary, a list typically goes from "god tier" through multiple tiers in between to "garbage tier". While balancing, all elements within the god tier should be nerfed first. Too powerful elements make many other elements worse if not useless. After this, all elements within the garbage tier should be buffed until they are no longer useless. In the end, the power differences between all other tiers can be adjusted until a satisfying state is reached. A tier list is especially useful when working with game elements that have exactly the same cost, e.g. characters in a Fighting game.

7.3.2 Understanding Learning

Learning is the process of acquiring new understanding, knowledge, behaviors, skills, values, attitudes, and preferences. The ability to learn is possessed by humans, non-human animals, and some machines; there is also evidence for some kind of learning in certain plants. Some learning is immediate, induced by a single event (e.g. being burned by a hot stove), but much skill and knowledge accumulate from repeated experiences. The changes induced by learning often last a lifetime, and it is hard to distinguish learned material that seems to be "lost" from that which cannot be retrieved.

Human learning starts at birth (it might even start before in terms of an embryo's need for both interaction with, and freedom within its environment within the womb.) and continues until death as a consequence of ongoing interactions between people and their environment. The nature and processes involved in learning are studied in many established fields (including educational psychology, neuropsychology, experimental psychology, cognitive sciences, and pedagogy), as well as emerging fields of knowledge (e.g. with a shared interest in the topic of learning from safety events such as incidents/accidents, or in collaborative learning health systems). Research in such fields has led to the identification of various sorts of learning. For example, learning may occur as a result of habituation, or classical conditioning, operant conditioning or as a result of more complex activities such as play, seen only in relatively intelligent animals. Learning may occur consciously or without conscious awareness. Learning that an aversive event cannot be avoided or escaped may result in a condition called learned helplessness. There is evidence for human behavioral learning prenatally, in which habituation has been observed as early as 32 weeks into gestation, indicating that the central nervous system is sufficiently developed and primed for learning and memory to occur very early on in development.

Play has been approached by several theorists as a form of learning. Children experiment with the world, learn the rules, and learn to interact through play. Lev Vygotsky agrees that play is pivotal for children's development, since they make meaning of their environment through playing educational games. For Vygotsky, however, play is the first form of learning language and communication, and the stage where a child begins to understand rules and symbols. This has led to a view that learning in organisms is always related to semiosis, and is often associated with representational systems/activity.

Types

There are various functional categorizations of memory which have developed. Some memory researchers distinguish memory based on the relationship between the stimuli involved (associative vs non-associative) or based to whether the content can be communicated through language (declarative/explicit vs procedural/implicit). Some of these categories can, in turn, be parsed into sub-types. For instance, declarative memory comprises both episodic and semantic memory.

Non-associative Learning

Non-associative learning refers to "a relatively permanent change in the strength of response to a single stimulus due to repeated exposure to that stimulus." This definition exempt the changes caused by sensory adaptation, fatigue, or injury. Non-associative learning can be divided into habituation and sensitization.

- **Habituation:** *Habituation* is an example of non-associative learning in which one or more components of an innate response (e.g., response probability, response duration) to a stimulus diminishes when the stimulus is repeated. Thus, habituation must be distinguished from extinction, which is an associative process. In operant extinction, for example, a response declines because it is no longer followed by a reward. An example of habituation can be seen in small song birds—if a stuffed owl (or similar predator) is put into the cage, the birds initially react to it as though it were a real predator. Soon the birds react less, showing habituation. If another stuffed owl is introduced (or the same one removed and re-introduced), the birds react to it again as though it were a predator, demonstrating that it is only a very specific stimulus that is habituated to (namely, one particular unmoving owl in one place). The habituation process is faster for stimuli that occur at a high rather than for stimuli that occur at a low rate as well as for the weak and strong stimuli, respectively. Habituation has been shown in essentially every species of animal, as well as the sensitive plant *Mimosa pudica* and the large protozoan *Stentor coeruleus*. This concept acts in direct opposition to sensitization.

- **Sensitization:** *Sensitization* is an example of non-associative learning in which the progressive amplification of a response follows repeated administrations of a stimulus. This is based on the notion that a defensive reflex to a stimulus such as withdrawal or escape becomes stronger after the exposure to a different harmful or threatening stimulus. An everyday example of this mechanism is the repeated tonic stimulation of peripheral nerves that occurs if a person rubs their arm continuously. After a while, this stimulation creates a warm sensation that can eventually turn painful. This pain results from a progressively amplified synaptic response of the peripheral nerves. This sends a warning that the stimulation is harmful. Sensitization is thought to underlie both adaptive as well as maladaptive learning processes in the organism.

Active Learning

Active learning occurs when a person takes control of his/her learning experience. Since understanding information is the key aspect of learning, it is important for learners to recognize what they understand and what they do not. By doing so, they can monitor their own mastery of subjects. Active learning encourages learners to have an internal dialogue in which they verbalize understandings. This and other meta-cognitive strategies can be taught to a child over time. Studies within metacognition have proven the value in active learning, claiming that the learning is usually at a stronger level as a result. In addition, learners have more incentive to learn when they have control over not only how they learn but also what they learn. Active learning is a key characteristic of student-centered learning. Conversely, passive learning and direct instruction are characteristics of teacher-centered learning (or traditional education).

Associative Learning

Associative learning is the process by which a person or animal learns an association between two stimuli or events. In classical conditioning, a previously neutral stimulus is repeatedly paired with a reflex-eliciting stimulus until eventually the neutral stimulus elicits a response on its own. In operant conditioning, a behavior that is reinforced or punished in the presence of a stimulus becomes more or less likely to occur in the presence of that stimulus.

Operant conditioning:

- *Operant conditioning* is a way in which behavior can be shaped or modified according to the desires of the trainer or head individual. Operant conditioning uses the thought that living things seek pleasure and avoid pain, and that an animal or human can learn through receiving either reward or punishment at a specific time called trace conditioning. Trace conditioning is the small and ideal period of time between the subject performing the desired behavior, and receiving the positive reinforcement as a result of their performance. The reward needs to be given immediately after the completion of the wanted behavior.
- Operant conditioning is different from classical conditioning in that it shapes behavior not solely on bodily reflexes that occur naturally to a specific stimulus, but rather focuses on the shaping of wanted behavior that requires conscious thought, and ultimately requires learning.
- Punishment and reinforcement are the two principal ways in which operant conditioning occurs. Punishment is used to reduce unwanted behavior, and ultimately (from the learner's perspective) leads to avoidance of the punishment, not necessarily avoidance of the unwanted behavior. Punishment is not an appropriate way to increase wanted behavior for animals or humans. Punishment can be divided into two subcategories, positive punishment and negative punishment. Positive punishment is when an aversive aspect of life or thing is added to the subject, for this reason it is called positive punishment. For example, the parent spanking their child would be considered a positive punishment, because a spanking was added to the child. Negative punishment is considered the removal of something loved or desirable from the subject. For example, when a parent puts his child in time out, in reality, the child is losing the opportunity to be with friends, or to enjoy the freedom to do as he pleases. In this example, negative punishment is the removal of the child's desired rights to play with his friends etc.
- Reinforcement on the other hand is used to increase a wanted behavior either through negative reinforcement or positive reinforcement. Negative reinforcement is defined by removing an undesirable aspect of life, or thing. For example, a dog might learn to sit as the trainer

scratches his ears, which ultimately is removing his itches (undesirable aspect). Positive reinforcement is defined by adding a desirable aspect of life or thing. For example, a dog might learn to sit if he receives a treat. In this example the treat was added to the dog's life.

Classical conditioning:

- The typical paradigm for *classical conditioning* involves repeatedly pairing an unconditioned stimulus (which unfailingly evokes a reflexive response) with another previously neutral stimulus (which does not normally evoke the response). Following conditioning, the response occurs both to the unconditioned stimulus and to the other, unrelated stimulus (now referred to as the "conditioned stimulus"). The response to the conditioned stimulus is termed a *conditioned response*. The classic example is Ivan Pavlov and his dogs. Pavlov fed his dogs meat powder, which naturally made the dogs salivate—salivating is a reflexive response to the meat powder. Meat powder is the unconditioned stimulus (US) and the salivation is the unconditioned response (UR). Pavlov rang a bell before presenting the meat powder. The first time Pavlov rang the bell, the neutral stimulus, the dogs did not salivate, but once he put the meat powder in their mouths they began to salivate. After numerous pairings of bell and food, the dogs learned that the bell signaled that food was about to come, and began to salivate when they heard the bell. Once this occurred, the bell became the conditioned stimulus (CS) and the salivation to the bell became the conditioned response (CR). Classical conditioning has been demonstrated in many species. For example, it is seen in honeybees, in the proboscis extension reflex paradigm. It was recently also demonstrated in garden pea plants.
- Another influential person in the world of classical conditioning is John B. Watson. Watson's work was very influential and paved the way for B.F. Skinner's radical behaviorism. Watson's behaviorism (and philosophy of science) stood in direct contrast to Freud and other accounts based largely on introspection. Watson's view was that the introspective method was too subjective and that we should limit the study of human development to directly observable behaviors. In 1913, Watson published the article "Psychology as the Behaviorist Views", in which he argued that laboratory studies should serve psychology best as a science. Watson's most famous, and controversial, experiment was "Little Albert", where he demonstrated how psychologists can account for the learning of emotion through classical conditioning principles.

Observational learning:

- *Observational learning* is learning that occurs through observing the behavior of others. It is a form of social learning which takes various forms, based on various processes. In humans, this form of learning seems to not need reinforcement to occur, but instead, requires a social model such as a parent, sibling, friend, or teacher with surroundings.

Imprinting:

- *Imprinting* is a kind of learning occurring at a particular life stage that is rapid and apparently independent of the consequences of behavior. In filial imprinting, young animals, particularly birds, form an association with another individual or in some cases, an object, that they respond to as they would to a parent. In 1935, the Austrian Zoologist Konrad Lorenz discovered that certain birds follow and form a bond if the object makes sounds.

Play

Play generally describes behavior with no particular end in itself, but that improves performance in similar future situations. This is seen in a wide variety of vertebrates besides humans, but is mostly limited to mammals and birds. Cats are known to play with a ball of string when young, which gives them experience with catching prey. Besides inanimate objects, animals may play with other members of their own species or other animals, such as orcas playing with seals they have caught. Play involves a significant cost to animals, such as increased vulnerability to predators and the risk of injury and possibly infection. It also consumes energy, so there must be significant benefits associated with play for it to have evolved. Play is generally seen in younger animals, suggesting a link with learning. However, it may also have other benefits not associated directly with learning, for example improving physical fitness. Play, as it pertains to humans as a form of learning is central to a child's learning and development. Through play, children learn social skills such as sharing and collaboration. Children develop emotional skills such as learning to deal with the emotion of anger, through play activities. As a form of learning, play also facilitates the development of thinking and language skills in children.

Types of play:

- Sensorimotor play aka functional play, characterized by the repetition of an activity
- Roleplay occurs starting at the age of three
- Rule-based play where authoritative prescribed codes of conduct are primary

- Construction play involves experimentation and building
- Movement play aka physical play

These five types of play are often intersecting. All types of play generate thinking and problem-solving skills in children. Children learn to think creatively when they learn through play. Specific activities involved in each type of play change over time as humans progress through the lifespan. Play as a form of learning, can occur solitarily, or involve interacting with others.

Enculturation

Enculturation is the process by which people learn values and behaviors that are appropriate or necessary in their surrounding culture. Parents, other adults, and peers shape the individual's understanding of these values. If successful, enculturation results in competence in the language, values, and rituals of the culture.

This is different from acculturation, where a person adopts the values and societal rules of a culture different from their native one. Multiple examples of enculturation can be found cross-culturally. Collaborative practices in the Mazahua people have shown that participation in everyday interaction and later learning activities contributed to enculturation rooted in nonverbal social experience. As the children participated in everyday activities, they learned the cultural significance of these interactions. The collaborative and helpful behaviors exhibited by Mexican and Mexican-heritage children is a cultural practice known as being "acomedido". Chillihuani girls in Peru described themselves as weaving constantly, following behavior shown by the other adults.

Episodic Learning

Episodic learning is a change in behavior that occurs as a result of an event. For example, a fear of dogs that follows being bitten by a dog is episodic learning. Episodic learning is so named because events are recorded into episodic memory, which is one of the three forms of explicit learning and retrieval, along with perceptual memory and semantic memory. Episodic memory remembers events and history that are embedded in experience and this is distinguished from semantic memory, which attempts to extract facts out of their experiential context or – as some describe – a timeless organization of knowledge. For instance, if a person remembers the Grand Canyon from a recent visit, it is an episodic memory. He would use semantic memory to answer someone who would ask him information such as where the Grand Canyon is. A study revealed that humans are very accurate in the recognition of episodic memory even without deliberate intention to memorize it. This is said to indicate a very large storage capacity of the brain for things that people pay attention to.

E-learning and Augmented Learning

Electronic learning or e-learning is computer-enhanced learning. A specific and always more diffused e-learning is mobile learning (m-learning), which uses different mobile telecommunication equipment, such as cellular phones. When a learner interacts with the e-learning environment, it is called augmented learning. By adapting to the needs of individuals, the context-driven instruction can be dynamically tailored to the learner's natural environment. Augmented digital content may include text, images, video, audio (music and voice). By personalizing instruction, augmented learning has been shown to improve learning performance for a lifetime. Moore (1989) purported that three core types of interaction are necessary for quality, effective online learning:

- Learner–learner (i.e., communication between and among peers with or without the teacher present),
- Learner–instructor (i.e., student-teacher communication), and
- Learner–content (i.e., intellectually interacting with content that results in changes in learners' understanding, perceptions, and cognitive structures).

In his theory of transactional distance, Moore (1993) contented that structure and interaction or dialogue bridge the gap in understanding and communication that is created by geographical distances (known as transactional distance).

Rote Learning

Rote learning is memorizing information so that it can be recalled by the learner exactly the way it was read or heard. The major technique used for rote learning is *learning by repetition*, based on the idea that a learner can recall the material exactly (but not its meaning) if the information is repeatedly processed. Rote learning is used in diverse areas, from mathematics to music to religion.

Meaningful Learning

Meaningful learning is the concept that learned knowledge (e.g., a fact) is fully understood to the extent that it relates to other knowledge. To this end, meaningful learning contrasts with rote learning in which information is acquired without regard to understanding. Meaningful learning, on the other hand, implies there is a comprehensive knowledge of the context of the facts learned.

Evidence-based Learning

Evidence-based learning is the use of evidence from well designed scientific studies to accelerate learning. Evidence-based learning methods such as spaced repetition can increase the rate at which a student learns.

Formal Learning

Formal learning is a deliberate way attaining of knowledge, which takes place within a teacher-student environment, such as in a school system or work environment. The term formal learning has nothing to do with the formality of the learning, but rather the way it is directed and organized. In formal learning, the learning or training departments set out the goals and objectives of the learning and oftentimes learners will be awarded with a diploma, or a type of formal recognition.

Non-formal Learning

Non-formal learning is organized learning outside the formal learning system. For example, learning by coming together with people with similar interests and exchanging viewpoints, in clubs or in (international) youth organizations, and workshops. From the organizer's point of reference, non-formal learning does not always need a main objective or learning outcome. From the learner's point of view, non-formal learning, although not focused on outcomes, often results in an intentional learning opportunity.

Informal Learning

Informal learning is less structured than "non-formal learning". It may occur through the experience of day-to-day situations (for example, one would learn to look ahead while walking because of the possible dangers inherent in not paying attention to where one is going). It is learning from life, during a meal at the table with parents, during play, and while exploring etc.. For the learner, informal learning is most often an experience of happenstance, and not a deliberately planned experience.

Thus this does not require enrolment into any class. Unlike formal learning, informal learning typically does not lead to accreditation. Informal learning begins to unfold as the learner ponders his or her situation. This type of learning does not require a professor of any kind, and learning outcomes are unforeseen following the learning experience.

Informal learning is self-directed and because it focuses on day-to-day situations, the value of informal learning can be considered high. As a result, information retrieved from informal learning experiences will likely be applicable to daily life. Children with informal learning can at times yield stronger support than subjects with formal learning in the topic of mathematics. Daily life experiences take place in the workforce, family life, and any other situation that may arise during one's lifetime.

Informal learning is voluntary from the learner's viewpoint, and may require making mistakes and learning from them. Informal learning allows the individual to discover coping strategies for difficult emotions that may arise while learning. From the learner's perspective, informal learning can become purposeful, because the learner chooses which rate is appropriate to learn and because this type of learning tends to take place within smaller groups or by oneself.

Nonformal Learning and Combined Approaches

The educational system may use a combination of formal, informal, and nonformal learning methods. The UN and EU recognize these different forms of learning. In some schools, students can get points that count in the formal-learning systems if they get work done in informal-learning circuits. They may be given time to assist international youth workshops and training courses, on the condition they prepare, contribute, share, and can prove this offered valuable new insight, helped to acquire new skills, a place to get experience in organizing, teaching, etc.

To learn a skill, such as solving a Rubik's Cube quickly, several factors come into play at once:

- Reading directions helps a player learn the patterns that solve the Rubik's Cube.
- Practicing the moves repeatedly helps build "muscle memory" and speed.
- Thinking critically about moves helps find shortcuts, which speeds future attempts.
- Observing the Rubik's Cube's six colors help anchor solutions in the mind.
- Revisiting the cube occasionally helps retain the skill.

Tangential Learning

Tangential learning is the process by which people self-educate if a topic is exposed to them in a context that they already enjoy. For example, after playing a music-based video game, some people may be motivated to learn how to play a real instrument, or after watching a TV show that references Faust and Lovecraft, some people may be inspired to read the original work. Self-education can be improved with systematization. According to experts in natural learning, self-oriented learning training has proven an effective tool for assisting independent learners with the natural phases of learning.

Extra Credits writer and game designer James Portnow was the first to suggest games as a potential venue for "tangential learning". Mozelius *et al.* points out that intrinsic integration of learning content seems to be a crucial design factor, and that games that include modules for further self-studies tend to present good results. The built-in encyclopedias in the *Civilization* games are presented as an example - by using these modules gamers can dig deeper for knowledge about historical events in the gameplay. The importance of rules that regulate learning modules and game experience is discussed by Moreno, C., in a case study about the mobile game Kiwaka. In this game, developed by Landka in collaboration with ESA and ESO, progress is rewarded with educational content, as opposed to traditional education games where learning activities are rewarded with gameplay.

Incidental Learning

In *incidental teaching* learning is not planned by the instructor or the student, it occurs as a byproduct of another activity — an experience, observation, self-reflection, interaction, unique event (e.g. in response to incidents/accidents), or common routine task. This learning happens in addition to or apart from the instructor's plans and the student's expectations. An example of incidental teaching is when the instructor places a train set on top of a cabinet. If the child points or walks towards the cabinet, the instructor prompts the student to say "train". Once the student says "train", he gets access to the train set.

Steps most commonly used in incidental teaching:

- An instructor will arrange the learning environment so that necessary materials are within the student's sight, but not within his reach, thus impacting his motivation to seek out those materials.
- An instructor waits for the student to initiate engagement.
- An instructor prompts the student to respond if needed.
- An instructor allows access to an item/activity contingent on a correct response from the student.
- The instructor fades out the prompting process over a period of time and subsequent trials.

Incidental learning is an occurrence that is not generally accounted for using the traditional methods of instructional objectives and outcomes assessment. This type of learning occurs in part as a product of social interaction and active involvement in both online and onsite courses. Research implies that some un-assessed aspects of onsite and online learning challenge the equivalency of education between the two modalities. Both onsite and online learning have distinct advantages with traditional on-campus students experiencing higher degrees of incidental learning in three times as many areas as online students. Additional research is called for to investigate the implications of these findings both conceptually and pedagogically.

Domains

Benjamin Bloom has suggested three domains of learning in his taxonomy which are:

- **Cognitive:** To recall, calculate, discuss, analyze, problem solve, etc.
- **Psychomotor:** To dance, swim, ski, dive, drive a car, ride a bike, etc.

- **Affective:** To like something or someone, love, appreciate, fear, hate, worship, etc.

These domains are not mutually exclusive. For example, in learning to play chess, the person must learn the rules (cognitive domain)—but must also learn how to set up the chess pieces and how to properly hold and move a chess piece (psychomotor). Furthermore, later in the game the person may even learn to love the game itself, value its applications in life, and appreciate its history (affective domain).

Transfer

Transfer of learning is the application of skill, knowledge or understanding to resolve a novel problem or situation that happens when certain conditions are fulfilled. Research indicates that learning transfer is infrequent; most common when "... cued, primed, and guided..." and has sought to clarify what it is, and how it might be promoted through instruction.

Over the history of its discourse, various hypotheses and definitions have been advanced. First, it is speculated that different types of transfer exist, including: near transfer, the application of skill to solve a novel problem in a similar context; and far transfer, the application of skill to solve a novel problem presented in a different context. Furthermore, Perkins and Salomon (1992) suggest that positive transfer in cases when learning supports novel problem solving, and negative transfer occurs when prior learning inhibits performance on highly correlated tasks, such as second or third-language learning. Concepts of positive and negative transfer have a long history; researchers in the early 20th century described the possibility that "...habits or mental acts developed by a particular kind of training may inhibit rather than facilitate other mental activities". Finally, Schwarz, Bransford and Sears (2005) have proposed that transferring knowledge into a situation may differ from transferring knowledge out to a situation as a means to reconcile findings that transfer may both be frequent and challenging to promote.

A significant and long research history has also attempted to explicate the conditions under which transfer of learning might occur. Early research by Ruger, for example, found that the "level of attention", "attitudes", "method of attack" (or method for tackling a problem), a "search for new points of view", a "careful testing of hypothesis" and "generalization" were all valuable approaches for promoting transfer. To encourage transfer through teaching, Perkins and Salomon recommend aligning ("hugging") instruction with practice and assessment, and "bridging", or encouraging learners to reflect on past experiences or make connections between prior knowledge and current content.

Factors Affecting Learning

- **Genetics:** Some aspects of intelligence are inherited genetically, so different learners to some degree have different abilities with regard to learning and speed of learning.
- **Socioeconomic and Physical Conditions:** Problems like malnutrition, fatigue, and poor physical health can slow learning, as can bad ventilation or poor lighting at home, and unhygienic living conditions. The design, quality, and setting of a learning space, such as a school or classroom, can each be critical to the success of a learning environment. Size, configuration, comfort—fresh air, temperature, light, acoustics, furniture—can all affect a student's learning. The tools used by both instructors and students directly affect how information is conveyed, from the display and writing surfaces (blackboards, markerboards, tack surfaces) to digital technologies. For example, if a room is too crowded, stress levels rise, student attention is reduced, and furniture arrangement is restricted. If furniture is incorrectly arranged, sightlines to the instructor or instructional material are limited and the ability to suit the learning or lesson style is restricted. Aesthetics can also play a role, for if student morale suffers, so does motivation to attend school.

Psychological Factors and Teaching Style

Intrinsic motivation, such as a student's own intellectual curiosity or desire to experiment or explore, has been found to sustain learning more effectively than extrinsic motivations such as grades or parental requirements. Rote learning involves repetition in order to reinforce facts in memory, but has been criticized as ineffective and "drill and kill" since it kills intrinsic motivation. Alternatives to rote learning include active learning and meaningful learning.

The speed, accuracy, and retention, depend upon aptitude, attitude, interest, attention, energy level, and motivation of the students. Praising students who answer a question properly or give good results should be praised. This encouragement increases their ability and helps them produce better results. Certain attitudes, such as always finding fault in a student's answer or provoking or embarrassing the student in front of a class are counterproductive.

Certain techniques can increase long-term retention:

- The spacing effect means that lessons or studying spaced out over time (spaced repetition) are better than cramming
- Teaching material to other people

- "Self-explaining" (paraphrasing material to oneself) rather than passive reading
- Low-stakes quizzing

Epigenetic Factors

The underlying molecular basis of learning appears to be dynamic changes in gene expression occurring in brain neurons that are introduced by epigenetic mechanisms. Epigenetic regulation of gene expression involves, most notably, chemical modification of DNA or DNA-associated histone proteins. These chemical modifications can cause long-lasting changes in gene expression. Epigenetic mechanisms involved in learning include the methylation and demethylation of neuronal DNA as well as methylation, acetylation and deacetylation of neuronal histone proteins. During learning, information processing in the brain involves induction of oxidative modification in neuronal DNA followed by the employment of DNA repair processes that introduce epigenetic alterations. In particular, the DNA repair processes of non-homologous end joining and base excision repair are employed in learning and memory formation.

General Cognition-related Factors

The nervous system continues to develop during adulthood until brain death. For example:

- physical exercise has neurobiological effects;
- the consumption of foods (or nutrients), obesity, alterations of the microbiome, drinks, dietary supplements, recreational drugs and medications may possibly also have effects on the development of the nervous system;
- various diseases, such as COVID-19, have effects on the development of the nervous system;
- psychological events such as mental trauma and resilience-building;
- exposure to environmental pollution and toxins such as air pollution may have effects on the further development of the nervous system;
- other activities may also have effects on the development of the nervous system, such as lifelong learning, retraining, and types of media- and economic activities; and
- broadly, brain aging.

Adult Learning vs. Children's Learning

Learning is often more efficient in children and takes longer or is more difficult with age. A study using neuroimaging identified rapid neurotransmitter GABA boosting as a major potential explanation-component for why that is.

Children's brains contain more "silent synapses" that are inactive until recruited as part of neuroplasticity and flexible learning or memories. Neuroplasticity is heightened during critical or sensitive periods of brain development, mainly referring to brain development during child development.

What humans learn at the early stages, and what they learn to apply, sets humans on course for life or has a disproportional impact. Adults usually have a higher capacity to select what they learn, to what extent and how. For example, children may learn the given subjects and topics of school curricula via classroom blackboard-transcription handwriting, instead of being able to choose specific topics/skills or jobs to learn and the styles of learning. For instance, children may not have developed consolidated interests, ethics, interest in purpose and meaningful activities, knowledge about real-world requirements and demands, and priorities.

7.3.3 Understanding the Importance of Engagement

At the heart of balancing fun and learning lies the concept of engagement—the extent to which learners are actively involved and invested in the educational experience. Engagement encompasses cognitive, emotional, and behavioral dimensions, reflecting learners' motivation, interest, and enjoyment of the learning process. Research has shown that engaged learners demonstrate higher levels of attention, participation, and retention, leading to more positive learning outcomes. Therefore, fostering engagement is essential for creating effective educational experiences that resonate with learners and inspire a lifelong love of learning.

7.3.4 The Role of Fun in Learning

Fun is a powerful catalyst for engagement, providing learners with intrinsic motivation to explore, experiment, and persist in their learning endeavors. In educational games, fun manifests through interactive gameplay mechanics, compelling narratives, immersive environments, and rewarding challenges. By tapping into players' natural curiosity and desire for mastery, fun enhances motivation and enjoyment, making learning feel like a rewarding and enjoyable pursuit rather than a chore. Moreover, fun fosters a positive emotional state that promotes cognitive flexibility, creativity, and resilience, facilitating deeper engagement and learning.

7.3.5 Aligning Learning Objectives with Gameplay

Balancing fun and learning begins with aligning educational objectives with gameplay mechanics to ensure that both elements complement and reinforce each other. Before designing an educational game, developers must clearly define the learning goals they aim to achieve and identify the most effective ways to integrate them into the gameplay experience. Whether teaching mathematics, science, language arts, or social studies, every game mechanic should serve a dual purpose: advancing the narrative and promoting the acquisition of knowledge or skills. By seamlessly weaving learning objectives into the fabric of gameplay, developers create cohesive and immersive experiences that captivate learners' interest while facilitating meaningful learning outcomes.

7.3.6 Creating Compelling Gameplay Experiences

Compelling gameplay experiences are essential for balancing fun and learning, capturing players' attention and sustaining their engagement throughout the learning journey. Educational games employ a variety of gameplay mechanics, including exploration, problem-solving, collaboration, competition, and customization, to cater to diverse learning preferences and interests. Whether embarking on epic quests, solving challenging puzzles, conducting virtual experiments, or building and managing virtual worlds, gameplay experiences should be interactive, dynamic, and responsive, offering players a sense of agency and autonomy over their learning experience. Moreover, well-designed game mechanics provide clear goals, feedback, and progression pathways that motivate players to persist in their learning efforts and strive for mastery.

7.3.7 Fostering Intrinsic Motivation and Autonomy

Intrinsic motivation and autonomy are key drivers of engagement in educational games, empowering learners to take ownership of their learning journey and pursue their interests and goals autonomously. Intrinsic motivation arises from within the individual, driven by curiosity, interest, and a sense of competence and mastery. Educational games nurture intrinsic motivation by providing meaningful choices, challenges, and rewards that align with learners' interests and aspirations. Moreover, fostering autonomy— the freedom to explore, experiment, and make decisions—enhances engagement by empowering learners to take control of their learning process and pursue personalized learning pathways. By cultivating intrinsic motivation and autonomy, educational games create a sense of ownership and investment in the learning experience, leading to deeper engagement and more enduring learning outcomes.

7.3.8 Balancing Challenge and Support

Balancing challenge and support is essential for maintaining a dynamic and rewarding gameplay experience that strikes the right balance between engagement and frustration.

Educational games should provide challenges that are challenging yet achievable, stimulating learners' cognitive abilities and promoting skill development without overwhelming them. Moreover, games should offer appropriate levels of support, including hints, tutorials, scaffolding, and adaptive difficulty adjustments, to help learners navigate challenges and overcome obstacles effectively. By balancing challenge and support, developers create an optimal learning environment that promotes growth, resilience, and perseverance while minimizing feelings of frustration and discouragement.

7.3.9 Integration of Formative Assessment

Formative assessment is an integral component of educational games, providing ongoing feedback and opportunities for reflection and improvement throughout the learning process. By embedding assessment seamlessly into gameplay mechanics, developers can gauge learners' understanding and mastery of educational content in real time, identifying areas of strength and areas needing further development. Feedback mechanisms, such as immediate responses, progress indicators, and performance metrics, inform players of their progress and guide their learning efforts effectively. Moreover, formative assessment fosters metacognitive skills—the ability to monitor, evaluate, and regulate one's learning process—empowering learners to become self-directed and reflective learners.

7.3.10 Promoting Collaboration and Social Interaction

Collaboration and social interaction are powerful catalysts for engagement and learning in educational games, fostering communication, cooperation, and collective problem-solving skills. Multiplayer features, cooperative challenges, and online communities provide opportunities for learners to collaborate with peers, share knowledge and resources, and learn from each other's perspectives and experiences. Moreover, social elements such as leaderboards, achievements, and interactive discussions promote a sense of belonging and camaraderie among players, motivating them to excel and support one another. By promoting collaboration and social interaction, educational games extend beyond individual skill mastery to cultivate a collaborative learning culture that celebrates collective achievement and mutual support.

CHAPTER 8

TYPES OF EDUCATIONAL GAMES

8.1 SERIOUS GAMES FOR LEARNING

Serious games have emerged as a powerful tool for fostering learning across various domains, from education and training to healthcare and corporate learning. These games combine entertainment with educational content, leveraging the engaging nature of gaming to promote deep learning and skill acquisition.

Serious games for learning represent a dynamic and transformative approach to education and training, harnessing the power of gaming to engage, motivate, and empower learners across diverse domains. By combining entertainment with educational content, serious games offer immersive and interactive learning experiences that promote engagement, retention, transferability, and collaboration. Despite facing challenges and considerations, serious games hold promise as a versatile tool for addressing the evolving needs of learners and educators in the digital age. As technology continues to advance and new trends emerge, the future of serious games for learning is ripe with opportunities for innovation, collaboration, and impact in the educational landscape.

8.1.1 Defining Serious Games

Serious games are interactive digital experiences designed with a primary purpose other than entertainment, such as education, training, simulation, or behavior change. Unlike traditional entertainment games, serious games prioritize learning objectives and real-world applications, using game mechanics, narratives, and simulations to engage players in meaningful and immersive learning experiences. Serious games encompass a wide range of formats, including simulations, role-playing games, interactive narratives, and virtual environments, tailored to specific learning goals and target audiences.

History

The use of games in educational circles has been practiced since at least the twentieth century. Use of paper-based educational games became popular in the 1960s and 1970s, but waned under the Back to Basics teaching movement. (The Back to Basics teaching movement is a change in teaching style that started in the 1970s after student scores declined on standardized tests and students were alleged to be exploring too many electives. This movement wanted to focus students on reading, writing and arithmetic and intensify the curriculum.) Clark C. Abt is credited for coining the term "serious games" in the 1970s, defined as games that have an "explicit and carefully thought-out educational purpose and are not intended to be played primarily for amusement." Abt also recognized that this "does not mean that serious games are not, or should not be, entertaining."

The early 2000s saw a surge in different types of educational games, especially those designed for the younger learner. Many of these games were not computer-based but took on the model of other traditional gaming systems both in the console and hand-held formats. In 1999, LeapFrog Enterprises introduced the LeapPad, which combined an interactive book with a cartridge and allowed kids to play games and interact with a paper-based book. Based on the popularity of traditional hand-held gaming systems like Nintendo's Game Boy, they also introduced their hand-held gaming system called the Leapster in 2003. This system was cartridge-based and integrated arcade–style games with educational content.

Also in the 2000s, educational games saw an expanse into sustainable development with titles such as Learning Sustainable Development in 2000 and Climate Challenge in 2006.

Other directions for serious video games beyond education began to emerge in the early 2000s, with *America's Army* in 2002 as an early example. The game was a first-person shooter developed by the United States Army as a recruitment tool, and later used as an early training tool for new recruits.

By 2010, serious games had evolved to incorporate actual economies like *Second Life*, in which users can create actual businesses that provide virtual commodities and services for Linden dollars, which are exchangeable for US currency. In 2015, Project Discovery was launched as a serious game. Project Discovery was launched as a vehicle by which geneticists and astronomers with the University of Geneva could access the cataloging efforts of the gaming public via a mini-game contained within the *Eve Online* massively multiplayer online role-playing game (MMORPG). Players acting as citizen scientists categorize and assess actual genetic samples or astronomical data. This data was then utilized and warehoused by researchers. Any data flagged as atypical was further investigated by scientists.

Applications

Health

On the one hand, the health sector includes digital games for the professional area of doctor training, e.g. to train an operation or to impart specialist knowledge, and on the other hand they address the private end user who uses them, for example, as motivation tools for a healthier lifestyle, nutrition or for rehabilitation purposes. In addition, Serious Games can be used as a training measure for patients who acquire knowledge about their clinical pictures and possible therapy options. There is also an increasing use of serious games in health education programs. On 15 June 2020, the Food and Drug Administration approved the first video game treatment, a game for children aged 8–12 with certain types of ADHD called *EndeavorRx*. It can be downloaded with a prescription onto a mobile device, and is intended for use in tandem with other treatments. Patients play it for 30 minutes a day, 5 days a week, over a month-long treatment plan.

Scientific Tool

In 2021, Heather R. Campbell, a graduate student at the University of Kentucky, published her doctoral dissertation, *Towards a Holistic Risk Model For Safeguarding the Pharmaceutical Supply Chain: Capturing the Human-Induced Risk to Drug Quality*. In this work, Campbell developed a virtual pharmaceutical manufacturing plant and used the flexibility of video games to develop various real-life scenarios. The scenarios were then played by humans under different motivating objectives through a series of experiments. The results allowed Campbell to gather useful information on what might be the next threat to the pharmaceutical supply chain. The results showed promise for video games' future as a scientific data collection tool and was featured in a Bloomberg Prognosis Article. BeamNG.tech is used by various automotive vendors to simulate driving and collision mechanics.

Exercise Therapy

These include serious games that animate the player to sport and movement. For example, hand-eye coordination and upper body muscles can be trained using *Wii Sports*, regardless of age and physical disabilities, alone or with others. Even simple Jump-'n'-Run games can have an educational purpose, depending on the user. They are partly used in rehabilitation therapies to restore the user's finger mobility, reaction speed and eye-finger coordination.

Politics, Culture and Advertising

Persuasive games are developed for advertisers, policy makers, news organizations and cultural institutions. They are politically and socially motivated games that serve social communication. They cover areas such as politics, religion, environment, urban planning and tourism. The aim is to lead to create a demand for product due to a generated positive exposure to the product in the game or introduce new ways of thinking through experience.

Security

Serious games in the field of security are aimed at disaster control, the defense sector and recruitment. Public, private and municipal institutions, such as fire brigades, police, Federal Agency for Technical Relief (Technisches Hilfswerk - Germany THW), DRK as well as crisis centres and NGOs benefit from them. Scenarios such as natural disasters, acts of terrorism, danger prevention and emergency care are simulated. Challenges such as acting under time and pressure to succeed can thus be realistically tested with fewer resources and costs. This area formed the second focal point. An example of serious games from this sector is the *Emergency* game series or the possibility to explore the response of communities in a game in disaster management. Psychological effect that exist in real life-threatening situation are not realistic in a serious game but the training in a serious game and exposure to the requirements and constraints in disaster management can prepare to a better response of the teams in a real disaster management case and lead to an improved risk mitigation strategies.

Military Games

Games like America's Army are training simulations that are used in the training and recruitment of soldiers. The games try to represent warfare as realistically as possible in order to familiarize users with the dangers, strategies, weapons, tactics and vehicles.

Recruitment Games

This type of serious games is intended to bring the user closer to tasks that would otherwise be less in the limelight. Companies try to present and profile themselves through such games in order to attract apprentices and applicants. Future tasks will be presented and carried out in a large context, for example "TechForce", in which various technical areas are combined into an end product with the aim of winning a race.

Product Creation Games

The aim here is to give the user an understanding of a company's products. The user can test the products in a simulation under real conditions and convince themselves of their functionality. Technical basics, handling and security risks can be taught to the user.

Adult Education

Real simulations and simulation games provide the user with the opportunity to gain experience. Actions generated from knowledge can be tested here according to the trial and error principle. Theoretical knowledge can either be acquired beforehand or imparted during the game, which can then be tested in a virtual practice. There is an educational policy interest in the professionalisation of such offers. With the research project NetEnquiry, the Federal Ministry of Education and Research supports a corresponding research project for education and training, implemented here with the focus on mobile learning. In addition, there is an increasing incorporation of serious games within university curricula which students can use to consolidate learning or enhance knowledge. *The News Game*, with 100 headlines and stories, you guess if real or fake news, testing deduction and current affairs knowledge.

Youth Education

The user is given tasks and missions that they can only solve with the knowledge that they will gradually discover during the game. The theoretical aspects of the game are always taught in small quantities at the right time to be able to solve the next task and thus test the theoretical approaches in practice.

Art Games

An *art game* uses the medium of computer games to create interactive and multimedia art. For the first time, the term was described scientifically in 2002 to emphasize games that attach more importance to art than to game mechanics. Mostly they convince by a special aesthetics and atmosphere and use the interactivity for creativity and the thought stimulation of the player. Art created by or through computer games are also called art games.

8.1.2 Applications of Serious Games

Serious games find applications across diverse domains, serving as versatile tools for learning, training, and skill development. In education, serious games are used to teach academic subjects such as mathematics, science, language arts, and history, as well as social and emotional skills such as empathy, communication, and problem-solving. In corporate training, serious games are employed to simulate real-world scenarios, such as customer service interactions, sales negotiations, and leadership development, allowing employees to practice and refine their skills in a safe and immersive environment. In healthcare, serious games are utilized for medical education, patient rehabilitation, therapeutic interventions, and health behavior change, addressing a wide range of medical conditions and health-related challenges.

8.1.3 Benefits of Serious Games for Learning

Serious games offer a multitude of benefits for learning and skill development, making them a compelling tool for educators, trainers, and learners alike. One of the key benefits is engagement: serious games captivate learners' interest and motivation by leveraging the inherent appeal of gaming, fostering active participation and sustained attention. Moreover, serious games provide opportunities for experiential learning, allowing players to apply theoretical knowledge and skills in realistic contexts, thus enhancing retention and transferability. Additionally, serious games offer personalized learning experiences, adapting to learners' individual needs, preferences, and learning styles, thus promoting autonomy and self-directed learning. Furthermore, serious games promote collaboration and social interaction, facilitating peer learning, teamwork, and communication skills development. Overall, serious games offer a dynamic and immersive learning environment that promotes engagement, retention, transferability, and collaboration, making them a valuable asset in the educational landscape.

8.1.4 Challenges and Considerations

Despite their potential benefits, serious games face several challenges and considerations that warrant careful attention from developers, educators, and policymakers. One challenge is ensuring the alignment of game content with educational objectives, as serious games must strike a delicate balance between entertainment and learning to be effective. Moreover, serious games require careful design to maintain engagement and motivation throughout the learning experience, avoiding pitfalls such as cognitive overload, repetitive gameplay, or lack of challenge. Additionally, serious games must be accessible and inclusive, accommodating diverse learning styles, abilities, and preferences to ensure equitable learning opportunities for all players. Furthermore, serious games must address ethical considerations, such as data privacy, content appropriateness, and representation, to create a safe and respectful learning environment. Finally, serious games require adequate infrastructure and support, including technical resources, training for educators and trainers, and integration into existing curricula and training programs, to maximize their impact and scalability.

8.1.5 Future Prospects and Emerging Trends

The future of serious games for learning holds promise as technology continues to evolve and new trends emerge. One emerging trend is the integration of augmented reality (AR) and virtual reality (VR) technologies into serious games, offering immersive and interactive learning experiences that blur the boundaries between the physical and digital worlds. Moreover, gamification— the use of game elements and mechanics in non-game contexts— is gaining traction as a way to enhance engagement and motivation in learning and training activities. Additionally, adaptive learning technologies are being incorporated into serious games to personalize learning experiences and provide targeted support and feedback to learners. Furthermore, the rise of mobile and cloud computing enables anytime, anywhere access to serious games, making them more accessible and convenient for learners. Overall, the future of serious games for learning is bright, with continued innovation and collaboration driving the development of new technologies, methodologies, and applications to enhance educational outcomes and empower learners worldwide.

8.2 SIMULATION GAMES IN EDUCATION

Simulation games have gained widespread recognition as effective tools for education, offering immersive and interactive experiences that allow learners to explore complex concepts, scenarios, and skills in a virtual environment.

Simulation games in education represent a dynamic and transformative approach to teaching and learning, offering immersive and interactive experiences that allow learners to explore, experiment, and problem-solve in virtual environments. By combining realism with interactivity, simulation games provide opportunities for experiential learning, critical thinking, collaboration, and personalization across diverse educational domains. Despite facing challenges and considerations, simulation games hold promise as a versatile tool for addressing the evolving needs of learners and educators in the digital age. As technology continues to advance and new trends emerge, the future of simulation games in education is ripe with opportunities for innovation, collaboration, and impact in the educational landscape.

8.2.1 Defining Simulation Games

Simulation games are interactive digital experiences that replicate real-world systems, processes, or environments, allowing players to explore and interact with them in a dynamic and immersive manner. Unlike traditional entertainment games, simulation games prioritize realism and authenticity, striving to accurately represent the complexities and nuances of the subject matter being simulated. Simulation games encompass a wide range of genres and formats, including business simulations, flight simulators, medical simulations, city-building games, and scientific simulations, tailored to specific educational objectives and target audiences.

History

The Sumerian Game (1964), a text-based early mainframe game designed by Mabel Addis, based on the ancient Sumerian city-state of Lagash, was the first economic simulation game. Another early economic sim by Danielle Bunten Berry, *M.U.L.E.*, released in 1983.

In the 1980s, it became a trend for arcade video games to use hydraulic motion simulator arcade cabinets. The trend was sparked by Sega's "taikan" games, with "taikan" meaning "body sensation" in Japanese. Sega's first game to use a motion simulator cabinet was *Space Tactics* (1981), a space combat simulator that had a cockpit cabinet where the screen moved in sync with the on-screen action. The "taikan" trend later began when Yu Suzuki's team at Sega (later known as Sega AM2) developed *Hang-On* (1985), a racing video game where the player sits on and moves a motorbike replica to control the in-game actions. Suzuki's team at Sega followed it with hydraulic motion simulator cockpit cabinets for rail shooters such as *Space Harrier* (1985), racing games such as *Out Run* (1986), and combat flight simulators such as *After Burner* (1987) and *G-LOC: Air Battle* (1990). One of the most sophisticated motion simulator cabinets in arcades was Sega's R360 (1990), which simulated the full 360-degree rotation of an aircraft. Sega have since continued to manufacture motion simulator cabinets for arcade games through to the 2010s.

In the mid-1980s, Codemasters and the Oliver Twins released a number of games with "Simulator" in the title, including *BMX Simulator* (1986), *Grand Prix Simulator* (1986), and *Pro Boxing Simulator* (1988). Richard and David Darling of Codemasters were inspired by Concertmaster's best-selling games, which were based on real sports such as football and BMX racing, which had a pre-existing popularity. In a parody of the established "simulator" cliche, *Your Sinclair* released a game titled *Advanced Lawnmower Simulator* in 1988.

The introduction of the city-building simulation subgenre is closely associated with the 1989 release of *SimCity* by developer Will Wright. However, earlier city-building titles had been published, including the 1984 Colecovision title *Fortune Builder*. Later games published by Wright's company Maxis, including *SimLife* and *SimEarth*, simulated worlds at a broader scale, including recreations of genetics and global ecosystems.

A study of adolescents who played *SimCity 2000* found that those players had a greater appreciation and expectation of their government officials after playing.

Subgenres

Construction and Management Simulation

Construction and management simulation (CMS) is a type of simulation game in which players build, expand or manage fictional communities or projects with limited resources. Strategy games sometimes incorporate CMS aspects into their game economy, as players must manage resources while expanding their projects. Pure CMS games differ from strategy games in that "the player's goal is not to defeat an enemy, but to build something within the context of an ongoing process." Games in this category are sometimes also called "management games".

Life Simulation

Life simulation games (or artificial life games) are a subgenre of simulation video games in which the player lives or controls one or more artificial lifeforms. A life simulation game can revolve around "individuals and relationships, or it could be a simulation of an ecosystem". Social simulation games are one of its subgenres.

Sports

Some video games simulate the playing of sports. Most sports have been recreated by video games, including team sports, athletics and extreme sports. Some games emphasize playing the sport (such as the *Madden NFL* series), whilst others emphasize strategy and organization (such as *Football Manager*). Some, such as *Arch Rivals*, satirize the sport for comic effect. This genre has been popular throughout the history of video games, and is competitive, just like real-world sports. A number of game series feature the names and characteristics of real teams and players, and are updated continuously to reflect real-world changes.

Other Types

- In medical simulation games, the player takes the role of a surgeon. Examples include the *Trauma Center* and *LifeSigns* series.
- In photography simulation games, players take photographs of animals or people. This includes games such as *Pokémon Snap* and *Afrika*.
- Military simulation games are wargames with higher degrees of realism than other wargames set in a fantasy or science fiction environment. These attempt to simulate real warfare at either a tactical or strategic level.

19. Some simulators, like *GeoCommander* by Intelligence Gaming, are designed for the US military to help new officers learn how to handle situations in a game setting before taking command in the field.
20. Certain tactical shooters have higher degrees of realism than other shooters. Sometimes called "soldier sims", these games try to simulate the feeling of being in combat. This includes games such as *Arma*.

- Vehicle simulation game:

21. Flight simulators, including amateur flight simulators, combat flight simulators and space flight simulators
22. Racing video games, including sim racing
23. Submarine simulator games
24. Train simulator games
25. Truck simulator games

- Immersive sims are typically played from the first-person perspective in a simulates a consistent lived-in world, and include elements of numerous gameplay systems that the player can use to complete objectives in many different manners, creating a sense of player agency and emergent gameplay.
- "Blue collar" games that include both realistic and hyper-realistic presentation of blue collar jobs in a game setting. These can include

some of the vehicle simulation games including the flight, train and truck simulator titles, hunting games like *TheHunter* series, other job simulation games like *House Flipper* or *PowerWash Simulator*, and games themed around these types of jobs like *Overcooked*.

- Digital card games simulating blackjack and poker (including video poker)
- Video games designed to simulate mechanical or other real-world games. These may include simulations of pinball games and casino games such as slot machines, pachinko, and roulette.

In Education

Because Simulation games make learning a matter of direct experience, they may relieve the tedium associated with more conventional modes of instruction, as they demand increased participation rather than merely reading about or discussing concepts and ideas (like discrimination, culture, stratification, and norms). Students will experience them by actually ''living'' the experiences. Therefore, the use of simulation games may increase students' motivation and interest in learning.

Simulation games can provide increased insights into how the world is seen, like the moral and intellectual idiosyncrasies of others. They may also increase empathy for others and help develop awareness of personal and interpersonal values by allowing players to see moral and ethical implications of the choices they make. As such, they can be used to change and improve students attitudes toward self, environment, and classroom learning.

Many games are designed to change and develop specific skills of decision making, problem solving and critical thinking (such as those involved in survey sampling, perception and communication).

8.2.2 Applications of Simulation Games in Education

Simulation games find applications across various domains of education, serving as powerful tools for teaching and learning in formal and informal settings. In STEM education, simulation games are used to teach scientific principles, engineering concepts, mathematical modeling, and computer programming, allowing learners to experiment with simulations of physical phenomena, chemical reactions, and technological systems.

In social studies and humanities, simulation games are employed to simulate historical events, cultural contexts, political systems, and ethical dilemmas, enabling learners to explore different perspectives, make informed decisions, and understand the consequences of their actions. In vocational education and professional training, simulation games are utilized to simulate workplace scenarios, practical skills training, and decision-making exercises, preparing learners for real-world challenges and responsibilities.

8.2.3 Benefits of Simulation Games in Education

Simulation games offer a multitude of benefits for teaching and learning, making them a valuable asset in the educational toolkit. One of the key benefits is experiential learning: simulation games provide learners with opportunities to engage in hands-on exploration, experimentation, and problem-solving in a risk-free environment, thus enhancing retention and transferability of knowledge and skills. Moreover, simulation games promote critical thinking and decision-making skills by presenting players with complex scenarios, dilemmas, and uncertainties that require analysis, synthesis, and evaluation. Additionally, simulation games foster collaboration and teamwork by enabling players to work together to achieve common goals, share resources, and solve challenges collectively. Furthermore, simulation games offer personalized learning experiences, allowing learners to explore at their own pace, follow their interests, and receive immediate feedback and guidance tailored to their needs. Overall, simulation games provide a dynamic and interactive learning environment that promotes engagement, autonomy, and skill development across diverse educational domains.

8.2.4 Challenges and Considerations

Despite their potential benefits, simulation games face several challenges and considerations that warrant careful attention from developers, educators, and policymakers. One challenge is the complexity of designing and implementing realistic simulations that accurately represent the subject matter while remaining accessible and engaging for learners. Moreover, simulation games require robust technical infrastructure and resources, including high-quality graphics, realistic physics engines, and scalable cloud-based platforms, to deliver seamless and immersive experiences. Additionally, simulation games must address ethical considerations, such as data privacy, content appropriateness, and representation, to create a safe and respectful learning environment. Furthermore, simulation games may face resistance from educators and administrators who are skeptical of their effectiveness or perceive them as a distraction from traditional instructional methods. Finally, simulation games require ongoing evaluation and refinement to ensure their educational effectiveness, scalability, and sustainability in diverse educational contexts.

8.2.5 Future Prospects and Emerging Trends

The future of simulation games in education holds promise as technology continues to advance and new trends emerge. One emerging trend is the integration of artificial intelligence (AI) and machine learning algorithms into simulation games, enabling adaptive learning experiences that personalize content, provide targeted feedback, and optimize gameplay based on learners' performance and preferences. Moreover, the rise of augmented reality (AR) and virtual reality (VR) technologies offers new opportunities for immersive and interactive simulation experiences that blur the boundaries between the physical and digital worlds. Additionally, gamification— the use of game elements and mechanics in non-game contexts— is gaining traction as a way to enhance engagement and motivation in simulation-based learning activities. Furthermore, the democratization of game development tools and platforms empowers educators and learners to create their own simulation games, fostering creativity, collaboration, and innovation in educational game design. Overall, the future of simulation games in education is bright, with continued innovation and collaboration driving the development of new technologies, methodologies, and applications to enhance learning outcomes and empower learners worldwide.

8.3 EDUCATIONAL GAME GENRES

Educational games come in various genres, each offering unique experiences and opportunities for learning. From adventure and puzzle games to simulations and quizzes, educational game genres cater to diverse interests, preferences, and learning objectives.

Educational game genres offer a diverse array of experiences and opportunities for learning, catering to diverse interests, preferences, and learning objectives. From adventure and puzzle games to simulations and trivia games, each genre provides unique benefits and applications in educational settings. By leveraging the engaging and immersive nature of gaming, educational game genres promote active learning, critical thinking, collaboration, and personalization, making them valuable tools for educators, trainers, and learners alike. As technology continues to advance and new trends emerge, the potential of educational game genres to transform teaching and learning in the digital age is boundless, offering endless possibilities for innovation, creativity, and impact in education.

8.3.1 Adventure Games

Adventure games place players in immersive narratives and environments, where they embark on quests, solve puzzles, and interact with characters to progress through the story. In educational settings, adventure games offer opportunities to explore historical events, scientific phenomena, or literary works while engaging in problem-solving and critical thinking. Examples include "Oregon Trail," which teaches history and survival skills, and "Where in the World is Carmen Sandiego?" which teaches geography and cultural awareness.

8.3.2 Puzzle Games

Puzzle games challenge players to solve puzzles, riddles, and brainteasers through logic, spatial reasoning, and creative thinking. In educational contexts, puzzle games promote problem-solving skills, pattern recognition, and perseverance. Examples include "Portal," which teaches physics and spatial reasoning, and "Lumosity," which offers a collection of brain-training puzzles to improve cognitive abilities.

Puzzle Solving

Solutions of puzzles often require the recognition of patterns and the adherence to a particular kind of order. People with a high level of inductive reasoning aptitude may be better at solving such puzzles compared to others. But puzzles based upon inquiry and discovery may be solved more easily by those with good deduction skills. Deductive reasoning improves with practice. Mathematical puzzles often involve BODMAS. BODMAS is an acronym which stands for Bracket, Of, Division, Multiplication, Addition and Subtraction. In certain regions, PEMDAS (Parentheses, Exponents, Multiplication, Division, Addition and Subtraction) is the synonym of BODMAS. It explains the order of operations to solve an expression. Some mathematical puzzles require Top to Bottom convention to avoid the ambiguity in the order of operations. It is an elegantly simple idea that relies, as sudoku does, on the requirement that numbers appear only once starting from top to bottom as coming along.

Puzzle Makers

Puzzle makers are people who make puzzles. In general terms of occupation, a *puzzler* is someone who composes and/or solves puzzles. Some notable creators of puzzles are:

- Ernő Rubik
- Sam Loyd
- Henry Dudeney
- Boris Kordemsky
- David J. Bodycombe
- Will Shortz
- Oskar van Deventer
- Lloyd King
- Martin Gardner
- Raymond Smullyan

History of Jigsaw and other Puzzles

Jigsaw puzzles are perhaps the most popular form of puzzle. Jigsaw puzzles were invented around 1760, when John Spilsbury, a British engraver and cartographer, mounted a map on a sheet of wood, which he then sawed around the outline of each individual country on the map. He then used the resulting pieces as an aid for the teaching of geography.

After becoming popular among the public, this kind of teaching aid remained the primary use of jigsaw puzzles until about 1820.

The largest puzzle (40,320 pieces) is made by a German game company Ravensburger. The smallest puzzle ever made was created at LaserZentrum Hannover. It is only five square millimeters, the size of a sand grain.

The puzzles that were first documented are riddles. In Europe, Greek mythology produced riddles like the riddle of the Sphinx. Many riddles were produced during the Middle Ages, as well.

By the early 20th century, magazines and newspapers found that they could increase their readership by publishing puzzle contests, beginning with crosswords and in modern days sudoku.

8.3.3 Simulation Games

Simulation games simulate real-world systems, processes, or environments, allowing players to experience and interact with them in a virtual setting. In education, simulation games provide opportunities for experiential learning, experimentation, and skill development. Examples include "SimCity," which teaches urban planning and management, and "Flight Simulator," which teaches aviation principles and piloting skills.

8.3.4 Strategy Games

Strategy games require players to plan, strategize, and make decisions to achieve specific goals or objectives. In educational contexts, strategy games promote critical thinking, decision-making, and resource management skills. Examples include "Civilization," which teaches history, politics, and diplomacy, and "Chess," which teaches strategic thinking and problem-solving.

Strategy games are also seen as a descendant of war games, and define strategy in terms of the context of war, but this is more partial. A strategy game is a game that relies primarily on strategy, and when it comes to defining what strategy is, two factors need to be taken into account: its complexity and game-scale actions, such as each placement in a Total War series.

The definition of a strategy game in its cultural context should be any game that belongs to a tradition that goes back to war games, contains more strategy than the average video game, contains certain gameplay conventions, and is represented by a particular community. Although war is dominant in strategy games, it is not the whole story.

History

The history of turn-based strategy games goes back to the times of ancient civilizations found in places such as Rome, Greece, Egypt, the Levant, and India. Many were played widely through their regions of origin, but only some are still played today. One such game is mancala, which may have originated in Samaria approximately 5000 years ago and has since diversified into scores of varieties worldwide. One form challenges two opposing players to clear their side of a board of mancala pieces while adding them into their opponent's side and thereby preventing the opponent from clearing their side. At each end of the game board in this version there is a larger pit in which each player must try to deposit the pieces to try to gain points. When one side is cleared the other side of the board's pieces are added to the cleared side's pile. This version of mancala can be played quite casually, but still presents strategy demands, e.g. to interfere in the opponent's playing area while clearing one's own.

Another game that has stood the test of time is chess, believed to have originated in India around the sixth century CE. The game spread to the west by trade, but chess gained social status and permanence more strongly than many other games. Chess became a game of skill and tactics often forcing the players to think two or three moves ahead of their opponent just to keep up. This game also became accepted by many as a proxy for intelligence; people who became grand masters were considered smart. The game portrays foot soldiers, knights, kings, queens, bishops, and rooks. Several portray actual positions in the historical European military. Each piece has a unique movement pattern. For example, the knight is constricted to moving in an L-shape two squares long and one square to the side, the rook can only move in a straight line vertically or horizontally, and bishops can move diagonally on the board.

Types

Abstract Strategy

In abstract strategy games, the game is only loosely tied to a thematic concept, if at all. The rules do not attempt to simulate reality, but rather serve the internal logic of the game. A purist's definition of an abstract strategy game requires that it cannot have random elements or hidden information. This definition includes such games as chess and Go. However, many games are commonly classed as abstract strategy games which do not meet these criteria: games such as backgammon, Octiles, *Can't Stop*, Sequence and Mentalis have all been described as "abstract strategy" games despite having a chance element. A smaller category of non-perfect abstract strategy games incorporate hidden information without using any random elements; for example, Stratego.

Team Strategy

One of the most focused team strategy games is contract bridge. This card game consists of two teams of two players, whose offensive and defensive skills are continually in flux as the game's dynamic progresses. Some argue that the benefits of playing this team strategy card game extend to those skills and strategies used in business and that the playing of these games helps to automate strategic awareness.

Eurogames

Eurogames, or German-style boardgames, are a relatively new genre that sit between abstract strategy games and simulation games. They generally have simple rules, short to medium playing times, indirect player interaction and abstract physical components. The games emphasize strategy, play down chance and conflict, lean towards economic rather than military themes, and usually keep all the players in the game until it ends.

Simulation

This type of game is an attempt to simulate the decisions and processes inherent to some real-world situation. Most of the rules are chosen to reflect what the real-world consequences would be of each player's actions and decisions. Abstract games cannot be completely divided from simulations and so games can be thought of as existing on a continuum of almost pure abstraction (like *Abalone*) to almost pure simulation (like *Diceball!* or *Strat-o-Matic Baseball*).

Wargame

Wargames are simulations of military battles, campaigns, or entire wars. Players will have to consider situations that are analogous to the situations faced by leaders of historical battles. As such, wargames are usually heavy on simulation elements, and while they are all "strategy games", they can also be "strategic" or "tactical" in the military jargon sense. Its creator, H. G. Wells, stated how "much better is this amiable miniature [war] than the real thing".

Traditionally, wargames have been played either with miniatures, using physical models of detailed terrain and miniature representations of people and equipment to depict the game state; or on a board, which commonly uses cardboard counters on a hex map. Popular miniature wargames include *Warhammer 40,000* or its fantasy counterpart *Warhammer Fantasy*. Popular strategic board wargames include *Risk*,

Axis and Allies, *Diplomacy*, and *Paths of Glory*. *Advanced Squad Leader* is a successful tactical scale wargame.

It is instructive to compare the *Total War* series to the *Civilization* series, where moving troops to a specific tile is a tactic because there are no short-range decisions. But in *Empire: Total War (2009)*, every encounter between two armies activates a real-time mode in which they must fight and the same movement of troops is treated as a strategy. Throughout the game, the movement of each army is at a macro scale, because the player can control each battle at a micro scale. However, as an experience, the two types of military operations are quite similar and involve similar skills and thought processes. The concept of micro scale and macro scale can well describe the gameplay of a game; however, even very similar games can be difficult to integrate into a common vocabulary. In this definition, strategy does not explicitly describe the player's experience; it is more appropriate to describe different formal game components. The similarity of the actions taken in two different games does not affect our definition of them as strategy or tactics: we will only rely on their scale in their respective games.

Strategy Video Games

Strategy video games are categorized based on whether they offer the continuous gameplay of real-time strategy (RTS), or the discrete phases of turn-based strategy (TBS). Often the computer is expected to emulate a strategically thinking "side" similar to that of a human player (such as directing armies and constructing buildings), or emulate the "instinctive" actions of individual units that would be too tedious for a player to administer (such as for a peasant to run away when attacked, as opposed to standing still until otherwise ordered by the player); hence there is an emphasis on artificial intelligence.

8.3.5 Role-Playing Games (RPGs)

Role-playing games immerse players in fictional worlds and narratives, where they assume the roles of characters and embark on adventures, quests, and quests. In educational settings, RPGs offer opportunities for storytelling, character development, and moral decision-making. Examples include "The Elder Scrolls V: Skyrim," which teaches history and literature through its rich narrative, and "DragonBox," which teaches mathematics through its engaging gameplay mechanics.

A role-playing game (sometimes spelled roleplaying game, or abbreviated as RPG) is a game in which players assume the roles of characters in a fictional setting. Players take responsibility for acting out these roles within a narrative, either through literal acting or through a process of structured decision-making regarding character development. Actions taken within many games succeed or fail according to a formal system of rules and guidelines.

There are several forms of role-playing games. The original form, sometimes called the tabletop role-playing game (TRPG or TTRPG), is conducted through discussion, whereas in live action role-playing (LARP), players physically perform their characters' actions. In both of these forms, an arranger called a game master (GM) usually decides on the rules and setting to be used, while acting as the referee; each of the other players takes on the role of a single character.

Several varieties of RPG also exist in electronic media, such as multiplayer text-based Multi-User Dungeons (MUDs) and their graphics-based successors, massively multiplayer online role-playing games (MMORPGs). Role-playing games also include single-player role-playing video games in which players control a character, or team of characters, who undertake(s) quests and may include player capabilities that advance using statistical mechanics. These electronic games sometimes share settings and rules with tabletop RPGs, but emphasize character advancement more than collaborative storytelling.

This type of game is well-established, so some RPG-related game forms, such as trading/collectible card games (CCGs) and wargames, may not be included under the definition. Some amount of role-playing activity may be present in such games, but it is not the primary focus. The term *role-playing game* is also sometimes used to describe games involving roleplay simulation and exercises used in teaching, training, and academic research.

Purpose

Both authors and major publishers of tabletop role-playing games consider them to be a form of interactive and collaborative storytelling. Events, characters, and narrative structure give a sense of a narrative experience, and the game need not have a strongly-defined storyline. Interactivity is the crucial difference between role-playing games and traditional fiction. Whereas a viewer of a television show is a passive observer, a player in a role-playing game makes choices that affect the story. Such role-playing games extend an older tradition of storytelling games where a small party of friends collaborate to create a story.

While simple forms of role-playing exist in traditional children's games of make believe, role-playing games add a level of sophistication and persistence to this basic idea with additions such as game facilitators and rules of interaction. Participants in a role-playing game will generate specific characters and an ongoing plot. A consistent system of rules and a more or less realistic campaign setting in games aids suspension of disbelief. The level of realism in games ranges from just enough internal consistency to set up a believable story or credible challenge up to full-blown simulations of real-world processes.

Tabletop role-playing games may also be used in therapy settings to help individuals develop behavioral, social, and even language skills. Beneficiaries commonly include young people with learning difficulties such as Autism spectrum disorders, attention-deficit hyperactive disorder (ADHD), and dyslexia.

Varieties

Role-playing games are played in a wide variety of formats, ranging from discussing character interaction in tabletop form, physically acting out characters in LARP to playing characters virtually in digital media. There is also a great variety of systems of rules and game settings. Games that emphasize plot and character interaction over game mechanics and combat sometimes prefer the name storytelling game. These types of games tend to reduce or eliminate the use of dice and other randomizing elements. Some games are played with characters created before the game by the GM, rather than those created by the players. This type of game is typically played at gaming conventions, or in standalone games that do not form part of a campaign.

Tabletop

Tabletop and *pen-and-paper* (PnP) RPGs are conducted through discussion in a small social gathering. The GM describes the game world and its inhabitants. The other players describe the intended actions of their characters, and the GM describes the outcomes. Some outcomes are determined by the game system, and some are chosen by the GM.

This is the format in which role-playing games were first popularized. The first commercially available RPG, *Dungeons & Dragons* (*D&D*), was inspired by fantasy literature and the wargaming hobby and was published in 1974. The popularity of *D&D* led to the birth of the tabletop role-playing game industry, which publishes games with many different themes, rules, and styles of play. The popularity of tabletop games has decreased since the modern releases of online MMO RPGs.

This format is often referred to simply as a *role-playing game.* To distinguish this form of RPG from other formats, the retronyms *tabletop role-playing game* or *pen and paper role-playing game* are sometimes used, though neither a table nor pen and paper are strictly necessary.

Live Action

A LARP is played more like improvisational theatre. Participants act out their characters' actions instead of describing them, and the real environment is used to represent the imaginary setting of the game world. Players are often costumed as their characters and use appropriate props, and the venue may be decorated to resemble the fictional setting. Some live-action role-playing games use rock paper scissors or comparison of attributes to resolve conflicts symbolically, while other LARPs use physical combat with simulated arms such as airsoft guns or foam weapons.

LARPs vary in size from a handful of players to several thousand, and in duration from a couple of hours to several days. Because the number of players in a LARP is usually larger than in a tabletop role-playing game, and the players may be interacting in separate physical spaces, there is typically less of an emphasis on tightly maintaining a narrative or directly entertaining the players, and game sessions are often managed in a more distributed manner.

Electronic Media

Tabletop role-playing games have been translated into a variety of electronic formats. As early as 1974, the same year as the release of Dungeons & Dragons, unlicensed versions of it were developed on mainframe university systems under titles such as *dnd* and *Dungeon.* These early computer RPGs influenced all of electronic gaming, as well as spawning the role-playing video game genre. Some authors divide digital role-playing games into two intertwined groups: single-player games using RPG-style mechanics, and multiplayer games incorporating social interaction.

- **Single-player:** Single-player role-playing video games form a loosely defined genre of computer and console games with origins in role-playing games such as *Dungeons & Dragons,* on which they base much of their terminology, settings, and game mechanics. This translation changes the experience of the game, providing a visual representation of the world but emphasizing statistical character development over collaborative, interactive storytelling.
- **Multiplayer:** Online text-based role-playing games involve many players using some type of text-based interface and an Internet connection to play an RPG. Games played in a real-time way include MUDs, MUSHes, and other varieties of MU*. Games played in a turn-based fashion include play-by-mail games and play-by-post games.

Massively multiplayer online role-playing games (MMORPGs) combine the large-scale social interaction and persistent world of MUDs with graphic interfaces. Most MMORPGs do not actively promote in-character role-playing, however, players can use the games' communication functions to role-play so long as other players cooperate. The majority of players in MMORPGs do not engage in role-playing in this sense. Computer-assisted gaming can be used to add elements of computer gaming to in-person tabletop role-playing, where computers are used for record-keeping and sometimes to resolve combat, while the participants generally make decisions concerning character interaction.

People

Gamemaster

One common feature of many RPGs is the role of a gamemaster, a participant who has special duties to present the fictional setting, arbitrate the results of character actions, and maintain the narrative flow. In tabletop and live-action RPGs the GM performs these duties in person. In video RPGs, many of the functions of a GM are fulfilled by the game engine. However, some multi-player video RPGs also allow for a participant to take on a GM role through a visual interface called a *GM toolkit*, albeit with abilities limited by the available technology.

Player Character

Another standard concept in RPGs is the player character, a character in the fictional world of the game whose actions the player controls. Typically each player controls a separate player character, sometimes more, each of whom acts as a protagonist in the story.

Non-player Character

In contrast to player characters, non-player characters (NPCs) are controlled by the gamemaster or game engine, or by people assisting the gamemaster. Non-player characters fill out the population of the fictional setting and can act as antagonists, bystanders, or allies of the player characters.

8.3.6 Trivia and Quiz Games

Trivia and quiz games challenge players to answer questions on various topics, ranging from general knowledge to specific subject areas. In educational contexts, trivia and quiz games reinforce learning objectives, assess knowledge retention, and promote memory recall. Examples include "Trivia Crack," which offers trivia questions on a wide range of topics, and "Kahoot," which allows educators to create and customize quiz-based learning activities for their students.

8.3.7 Music and Rhythm Games

Music and rhythm games require players to synchronize their actions with musical beats, rhythms, and melodies. In educational settings, music and rhythm games promote auditory processing, rhythm recognition, and coordination skills. Examples include "Rock Band," which allows players to simulate playing musical instruments in a band setting, and "Just Dance," which encourages physical activity and movement while following dance routines.

8.3.8 Augmented Reality (AR) Games

Augmented reality games blend digital content with the real-world environment, overlaying virtual elements onto the physical world through mobile devices or wearable technology. In educational contexts, AR games provide immersive and interactive learning experiences that bridge the gap between virtual and real-world learning. Examples include "Pokemon Go," which encourages exploration and discovery of real-world landmarks, and "Zombies, Run!," which combines storytelling and fitness challenges in an immersive zombie apocalypse setting. This experience is seamlessly interwoven with the physical world such that it is perceived as an immersive aspect of the real environment. In this way, augmented reality alters one's ongoing perception of a real-world environment, whereas virtual reality completely replaces the user's real-world environment with a simulated one.

Augmented reality is largely synonymous with mixed reality. There is also overlap in terminology with extended reality and computer-mediated reality.

The primary value of augmented reality is the manner in which components of the digital world blend into a person's perception of the real world, not as a simple display of data, but through the integration of immersive sensations, which are perceived as natural parts of an environment. The earliest functional AR systems that provided immersive mixed reality experiences for users were invented in the early 1990s, starting with the Virtual Fixtures system developed at the U.S. Air Force's Armstrong Laboratory in 1992. Commercial augmented reality experiences were first introduced in entertainment and gaming businesses. Subsequently, augmented reality applications have spanned commercial industries such as education, communications, medicine, and entertainment. In education, content may be accessed by scanning or viewing an image with a mobile device or by using markerless AR techniques.

Augmented reality can be used to enhance natural environments or situations and offers perceptually enriched experiences. With the help of advanced AR technologies (e.g. adding computer vision, incorporating AR cameras into smartphone applications, and object recognition) the information about the surrounding real world of the user becomes interactive and digitally manipulated. Information about the environment and its objects is overlaid on the real world. This information can be virtual. Augmented Reality is any experience which is artificial and which adds to the already existing reality. or real, e.g. seeing other real sensed or measured information such as electromagnetic radio waves overlaid in exact alignment with where they actually are in space. Augmented reality also has a lot of potential in the gathering and sharing of tacit knowledge. Augmentation techniques are typically performed in real-time and in semantic contexts with environmental elements. Immersive perceptual information is sometimes combined with supplemental information like scores over a live video feed of a sporting event. This combines the benefits of both augmented reality technology and heads up display technology (HUD).

Comparison with Virtual Reality

In virtual reality (VR), the users' perception of reality is completely based on virtual information. In augmented reality (AR) the user is provided with additional computer- generated information within the data collected from real life that enhances their perception of reality. For example, in architecture, VR can be used to create a walk-through simulation of the inside of a new building; and AR can be used to show a building's structures and systems super-imposed on a real-life view. Another example is through the use of utility applications. Some AR applications, such as Augment, enable users to apply digital objects into real environments, allowing businesses to use augmented reality devices as a way to preview their products in the real world. Similarly, it can also be used to demo what products may look like in an environment for customers, as demonstrated by companies such as Mountain Equipment Co-op or Lowe's who use augmented reality to allow customers to preview what their products might look like at home through the use of 3D models.

Augmented reality (AR) differs from virtual reality (VR) in the sense that in AR part of the surrounding environment is 'real' and AR is just adding layers of virtual objects to the real environment. On the other hand, in VR the surrounding environment is completely virtual and computer generated. A demonstration of how AR layers objects onto the real world can be seen with augmented reality games. WallaMe is an augmented reality game application that allows users to hide messages in real environments, utilizing geolocation technology in order to enable users to hide messages wherever they may wish in the world. Such applications have many uses in the world, including in activism and artistic expression.

Hardware

Hardware components for augmented reality are: a processor, display, sensors and input devices. Modern mobile computing devices like smartphones and tablet computers contain these elements, which often include a camera and microelectromechanical systems (MEMS) sensors such as an accelerometer, GPS, and solid state compass, making them suitable AR platforms. There are two technologies used in augmented reality: diffractive waveguides and reflective waveguides.

Display

Various technologies are used in augmented reality rendering, including optical projection systems, monitors, handheld devices, and display systems, which are worn on the human body.

A head-mounted display (HMD) is a display device worn on the forehead, such as a harness or helmet-mounted. HMDs place images of both the physical world and virtual objects over the user's field of view. Modern HMDs often employ sensors for six degrees of freedom monitoring that allow the system to align virtual information to the physical world and adjust accordingly with the user's head movements. HMDs can provide VR users with mobile and collaborative experiences. Specific providers, such as uSens and Gestigon, include gesture controls for full virtual immersion.

- **Eyeglasses:** AR displays can be rendered on devices resembling eyeglasses. Versions include eyewear that employs cameras to intercept the real world view and re-display its augmented view through the eyepieces and devices in which the AR imagery is projected through or reflected off the surfaces of the eyewear lens pieces.
- **HUD:** A head-up display (HUD) is a transparent display that presents data without requiring users to look away from their usual viewpoints. A precursor technology to augmented reality, heads-up displays were first developed for pilots in the 1950s, projecting simple flight data into their line of sight, thereby enabling them to keep their "heads up" and not look down at the instruments. Near-eye augmented reality devices can be used as portable head-up displays as they can show data, information, and images while the user views the real world. Many definitions of augmented reality only define it as overlaying the information. This is basically what a head-up display does; however, practically speaking, augmented reality is expected to include registration and tracking between the superimposed perceptions, sensations, information, data, and images and some portion of the real world.
- **Contact Lenses:** Contact lenses that display AR imaging are in development. These bionic contact lenses might contain the elements for display embedded into the lens including integrated circuitry, LEDs and an antenna for wireless communication. The first contact lens display was patented in 1999 by Steve Mann and was intended to work in combination with AR spectacles, but the project was abandoned, then 11 years later in 2010–2011. Another version of contact lenses, in development for the U.S. military, is designed to function with AR spectacles, allowing soldiers to focus on close-to-the-eye AR images on the spectacles and distant real world objects at the same time. At CES 2013, a company called Innovega also unveiled similar contact lenses that required being combined with AR glasses to work. The futuristic short film *Sight* features contact lens-like augmented reality devices. Many scientists have been working on contact lenses capable of different technological feats. A patent filed by Samsung describes an

AR contact lens, that, when finished, will include a built-in camera on the lens itself. The design is intended to control its interface by blinking an eye. It is also intended to be linked with the user's smartphone to review footage, and control it separately. When successful, the lens would feature a camera, or sensor inside of it. It is said that it could be anything from a light sensor, to a temperature sensor. The first publicly unveiled working prototype of an AR contact lens not requiring the use of glasses in conjunction was developed by Mojo Vision and announced and shown off at CES 2020.

- **Virtual Retinal Display:** A virtual retinal display (VRD) is a personal display device under development at the University of Washington's Human Interface Technology Laboratory under Dr. Thomas A. Furness III. With this technology, a display is scanned directly onto the retina of a viewer's eye. This results in bright images with high resolution and high contrast. The viewer sees what appears to be a conventional display floating in space. Several of tests were done to analyze the safety of the VRD. In one test, patients with partial loss of vision—having either macular degeneration (a disease that degenerates the retina) or keratoconus—were selected to view images using the technology. In the macular degeneration group, five out of eight subjects preferred the VRD images to the cathode-ray tube (CRT) or paper images and thought they were better and brighter and were able to see equal or better resolution levels. The Keratoconus patients could all resolve smaller lines in several line tests using the VRD as opposed to their own correction. They also found the VRD images to be easier to view and sharper. As a result of these several tests, virtual retinal display is considered safe technology. Virtual retinal display creates images that can be seen in ambient daylight and ambient room light. The VRD is considered a preferred candidate to use in a surgical display due to its combination of high resolution and high contrast and brightness. Additional tests show high potential for VRD to be used as a display technology for patients that have low vision.
- **EyeTap:** The EyeTap (also known as Generation-2 Glass) captures rays of light that would otherwise pass through the center of the lens of the wearer's eye, and substitutes synthetic computer-controlled light for each ray of real light. The Generation-4 Glass (Laser EyeTap) is similar to the VRD (i.e. it uses a computer-controlled laser light source) except that it also has infinite depth of focus and causes the eye itself to, in effect, function as both a camera and a display by way of exact

alignment with the eye and resynthesis (in laser light) of rays of light entering the eye.

- **Handheld:** A Handheld display employs a small display that fits in a user's hand. All handheld AR solutions to date opt for video see-through. Initially handheld AR employed fiducial markers, and later GPS units and MEMS sensors such as digital compasses and six degrees of freedom accelerometer–gyroscope. Today simultaneous localization and mapping (SLAM) markerless trackers such as PTAM (parallel tracking and mapping) are starting to come into use. Handheld display AR promises to be the first commercial success for AR technologies. The two main advantages of handheld AR are the portable nature of handheld devices and the ubiquitous nature of camera phones. The disadvantages are the physical constraints of the user having to hold the handheld device out in front of them at all times, as well as the distorting effect of classically wide-angled mobile phone cameras when compared to the real world as viewed through the eye. Games such as *Pokémon Go* and *Ingress* utilize an Image Linked Map (ILM) interface, where approved geotagged locations appear on a stylized map for the user to interact with.
- **Projection Mapping:** Projection mapping augments real-world objects and scenes, without the use of special displays such as monitors, head-mounted displays or hand-held devices. Projection mapping makes use of digital projectors to display graphical information onto physical objects. The key difference in projection mapping is that the display is separated from the users of the system. Since the displays are not associated with each user, projection mapping scales naturally up to groups of users, allowing for collocated collaboration between users. Examples include shader lamps, mobile projectors, virtual tables, and smart projectors. Shader lamps mimic and augment reality by projecting imagery onto neutral objects. This provides the opportunity to enhance the object's appearance with materials of a simple unit—a projector, camera, and sensor. Other applications include table and wall projections. One innovation, the Extended Virtual Table, separates the virtual from the real by including beam-splitter mirrors attached to the ceiling at an adjustable angle. Virtual showcases, which employ beam splitter mirrors together with multiple graphics displays, provide an interactive means of simultaneously engaging with the virtual and the real. Many more implementations and configurations make spatial augmented reality display an increasingly attractive interactive alternative. A projection mapping system can display

on any number of surfaces in an indoor setting at once. Projection mapping supports both a graphical visualization and passive haptic sensation for the end users. Users are able to touch physical objects in a process that provides passive haptic sensation.

Tracking

Modern mobile augmented-reality systems use one or more of the following motion tracking technologies: digital cameras and/or other optical sensors, accelerometers, GPS, gyroscopes, solid state compasses, radio-frequency identification (RFID). These technologies offer varying levels of accuracy and precision. These technologies are implemented in the ARKit API by Apple and ARCore API by Google to allow tracking for their respective mobile device platforms.

Networking

Mobile augmented reality applications are gaining popularity because of the wide adoption of mobile and especially wearable devices. However, they often rely on computationally intensive computer vision algorithms with extreme latency requirements. To compensate for the lack of computing power, offloading data processing to a distant machine is often desired. Computation offloading introduces new constraints in applications, especially in terms of latency and bandwidth. Although there are a plethora of real-time multimedia transport protocols, there is a need for support from network infrastructure as well.

Input Devices

Techniques include speech recognition systems that translate a user's spoken words into computer instructions, and gesture recognition systems that interpret a user's body movements by visual detection or from sensors embedded in a peripheral device such as a wand, stylus, pointer, glove or other body wear. Products which are trying to serve as a controller of AR headsets include Wave by Seebright Inc. and Nimble by Intugine Technologies.

Computer

The computer analyzes the sensed visual and other data to synthesize and position augmentations. Computers are responsible for the graphics that go with augmented reality. Augmented reality uses a computer-generated image which has a striking effect on the way the real world is shown. With the improvement of technology and computers, augmented reality is going to lead to a drastic change on ones perspective of the real world. According to *Time*, in about 15–20 years it is predicted that augmented reality and virtual reality are going to become the primary use for computer interactions. Computers are improving at a very fast rate, leading to new ways to improve other technology. The more that computers progress, augmented reality will become more flexible and more common in society. Computers are the core of augmented reality. The computer receives data from the sensors which determine the relative position of an objects' surface. This translates to an input to the computer which then outputs to the users by adding something that would otherwise not be there. The computer comprises memory and a processor. The computer takes the scanned environment then generates images or a video and puts it on the receiver for the observer to see. The fixed marks on an object's surface are stored in the memory of a computer. The computer also withdraws from its memory to present images realistically to the onlooker.

Projector

Projectors can also be used to display AR contents. The projector can throw a virtual object on a projection screen and the viewer can interact with this virtual object. Projection surfaces can be many objects such as walls or glass panes.

Software and Algorithms

A key measure of AR systems is how realistically they integrate augmentations with the real world. The software must derive real world coordinates, independent of camera, and camera images. That process is called image registration, and uses different methods of computer vision, mostly related to video tracking. Many computer vision methods of augmented reality are inherited from visual odometry. An augogram is a computer generated image that is used to create AR. Augography is the science and software practice of making augograms for AR.

Usually those methods consist of two parts. The first stage is to detect interest points, fiducial markers or optical flow in the camera images. This step can use feature detection methods like corner detection, blob detection, edge detection or thresholding, and other image processing methods. The second stage restores a real world coordinate system from the data obtained in the first stage. Some methods assume objects with known geometry (or fiducial markers) are present in the scene. In some of those cases the scene 3D structure should be calculated beforehand. If part of the scene is unknown simultaneous localization and mapping (SLAM) can map relative positions.

If no information about scene geometry is available, structure from motion methods like bundle adjustment are used. Mathematical methods used in the second stage include: projective (epipolar) geometry, geometric algebra, rotation representation with exponential map, kalman and particle filters, nonlinear optimization, robust statistics.

In augmented reality, the distinction is made between two distinct modes of tracking, known as *marker* and *markerless*. Markers are visual cues which trigger the display of the virtual information. A piece of paper with some distinct geometries can be used. The camera recognizes the geometries by identifying specific points in the drawing. Markerless tracking, also called instant tracking, does not use markers. Instead, the user positions the object in the camera view preferably in a horizontal plane. It uses sensors in mobile devices to accurately detect the real-world environment, such as the locations of walls and points of intersection.

Augmented Reality Markup Language (ARML) is a data standard developed within the Open Geospatial Consortium (OGC), which consists of Extensible Markup Language (XML) grammar to describe the location and appearance of virtual objects in the scene, as well as ECMAScript bindings to allow dynamic access to properties of virtual objects.

To enable rapid development of augmented reality applications, some software development applications such as Lens Studio from Snapchat and Spark AR from Facebook were launched including Software Development kits (SDKs) from Apple and Google have emerged.

Development

The implementation of augmented reality in consumer products requires considering the design of the applications and the related constraints of the technology platform. Since AR systems rely heavily on the immersion of the user and the interaction between the user and the system, design can facilitate the adoption of virtuality. For most augmented reality systems, a similar design guideline can be followed. The following lists some considerations for designing augmented reality applications:

Environmental/Context Design

Context Design focuses on the end-user's physical surrounding, spatial space, and accessibility that may play a role when using the AR system. Designers should be aware of the possible physical scenarios the end-user may be in such as:

- Public, in which the users use their whole body to interact with the software
- Personal, in which the user uses a smartphone in a public space
- Intimate, in which the user is sitting with a desktop and is not really moving
- Private, in which the user has on a wearable.

By evaluating each physical scenario, potential safety hazards can be avoided and changes can be made to greater improve the end-user's immersion. UX designers will have to define user journeys for the relevant physical scenarios and define how the interface reacts to each.

Another aspect of context design involves the design of the system's functionality and its ability to accommodate user preferences. While accessibility tools are common in basic application design, some consideration should be made when designing time-limited prompts (to prevent unintentional operations), audio cues and overall engagement time. It is important to note that in some situations, the application's functionality may hinder the user's ability. For example, applications that is used for driving should reduce the amount of user interaction and use audio cues instead.

Interaction Design

Interaction design in augmented reality technology centers on the user's engagement with the end product to improve the overall user experience and enjoyment. The purpose of interaction design is to avoid alienating or confusing the user by organizing the information presented. Since user interaction relies on the user's input, designers must make system controls easier to understand and accessible. A common technique to improve usability for augmented reality applications is by discovering the frequently accessed areas in the device's touch display and design the application to match those areas of control. It is also important to structure the user journey maps and the flow of information presented which reduce the system's overall cognitive load and greatly improves the learning curve of the application.

In interaction design, it is important for developers to utilize augmented reality technology that complement the system's function or purpose. For instance, the utilization of exciting AR filters and the design of the unique sharing platform in Snapchat enables users to augment their in-app social interactions. In other applications that require users to understand the focus and intent, designers can employ a reticle or raycast from the device.

Visual Design

In general, graphic design is the appearance of the developing application that engages the user. To improve the graphic interface elements and user interaction, developers may use visual cues to inform the user what elements of UI are designed to interact with and how to interact with them. Since navigating in an AR application may appear difficult and seem frustrating, visual cue design can make interactions seem more natural.

In some augmented reality applications that use a 2D device as an interactive surface, the 2D control environment does not translate well in 3D space making users hesitant to explore their surroundings. To solve this issue, designers should apply visual cues to assist and encourage users to explore their surroundings.

It is important to note the two main objects in AR when developing VR applications: 3D volumetric objects that are manipulated and realistically interact with light and shadow; and animated media imagery such as images and videos which are mostly traditional 2D media rendered in a new context for augmented reality. When virtual objects are projected onto a real environment, it is challenging for augmented reality application designers to ensure a perfectly seamless integration relative to the real-world environment, especially with 2D objects. As such, designers can add weight to objects, use depths maps, and choose different material properties that highlight the object's presence in the real world. Another visual design that can be applied is using different lighting techniques or casting shadows to improve overall depth judgment. For instance, a common lighting technique is simply placing a light source overhead at the 12 o'clock position, to create shadows on virtual objects.

In Education and Training

In educational settings, AR has been used to complement a standard curriculum. Text, graphics, video, and audio may be superimposed into a student's real-time environment. Textbooks, flashcards and other educational reading material may contain embedded "markers" or triggers that, when scanned by an AR device, produced supplementary information to the student rendered in a multimedia format.

The 2015 Virtual, Augmented and Mixed Reality: 7th International Conference mentioned Google Glass as an example of augmented reality that can replace the physical classroom.

First, AR technologies help learners engage in authentic exploration in the real world, and virtual objects such as texts, videos, and pictures are supplementary elements for learners to conduct investigations of the real-world surroundings.

As AR evolves, students can participate interactively and interact with knowledge more authentically. Instead of remaining passive recipients, students can become active learners, able to interact with their learning environment. Computer-generated simulations of historical events allow students to explore and learning details of each significant area of the event site.

In higher education, Construct3D, a Studierstube system, allows students to learn mechanical engineering concepts, math or geometry. Chemistry AR apps allow students to visualize and interact with the spatial structure of a molecule using a marker object held in the hand. Others have used HP Reveal, a free app, to create AR notecards for studying organic chemistry mechanisms or to create virtual demonstrations of how to use laboratory instrumentation. Anatomy students can visualize different systems of the human body in three dimensions. Using AR as a tool to learn anatomical structures has been shown to increase the learner knowledge and provide intrinsic benefits, such as increased engagement and learner immersion.

AR has been used to develop different safety training application for several types of disasters such as, earthquakes and building fire. Further, several AR solutions have been proposed and tested to navigate building evacuees towards safe places in both large scale and small scale disasters. Further, AR applications can have several overlapping with many other digital technologies, such as BIM, internet of things and artificial intelligence, to generate smarter safety training and navigation solutions.

Concerns

Reality Modifications

In a paper titled "Death by Pokémon GO", researchers at Purdue University's Krannert School of Management claim the game caused "a disproportionate increase in vehicular crashes and associated vehicular damage, personal injuries, and fatalities in the vicinity of locations, called PokéStops, where users can play the game while driving." Using data from one municipality, the paper extrapolates what that might mean nationwide and concluded "the increase in crashes attributable to the introduction of Pokémon GO is 145,632 with an associated increase in the number of injuries of 29,370 and an associated increase in the number of fatalities of 256 over the period of 6 July 2016, through 30 November 2016." The authors extrapolated the cost of those crashes and fatalities at between $2bn and $7.3 billion for the same period. Furthermore, more than one in three surveyed advanced Internet users would like to edit out disturbing elements around them, such as garbage or graffiti. They would like to even modify their surroundings by erasing street signs, billboard ads, and uninteresting shopping windows. So it seems that AR is as much a threat to companies as it is an opportunity. Although, this could be a nightmare to numerous brands that do not manage to capture consumer imaginations it also creates the risk that the wearers of augmented reality glasses may become unaware of surrounding dangers. Consumers want to use augmented reality glasses to change their surroundings into something that reflects their own personal opinions. Around two in five want to change the way their surroundings look and even how people appear to them.

Next, overload and over-reliance issues are the biggest danger of AR. For the development of new AR-related products, this implies that the user-interface should follow certain guidelines as not to overload the user with information while also preventing the user from over-relying on the AR system such that important cues from the environment are missed. This is called the virtually-augmented key. Once the key is ignored, people might not desire the real world anymore.

Privacy Concerns

The concept of modern augmented reality depends on the ability of the device to record and analyze the environment in real time. Because of this, there are potential legal concerns over privacy. While the First Amendment to the United States Constitution allows for such recording in the name of public interest, the constant recording of an AR device makes it difficult to do so without also recording outside of the public domain. Legal complications would be found in areas where a right to a certain amount of privacy is expected or where copyrighted media are displayed.

In terms of individual privacy, there exists the ease of access to information that one should not readily possess about a given person. This is accomplished through facial recognition technology. Assuming that AR automatically passes information about persons that the user sees, there could be anything seen from social media, criminal record, and marital status.

The Code of Ethics on Human Augmentation, which was originally introduced by Steve Mann in 2004 and further refined with Ray Kurzweil and Marvin Minsky in 2013, was ultimately ratified at the virtual reality Toronto conference on 25 June 2017.

8.3.9 Benefits of Educational Game Genres

Educational game genres offer a multitude of benefits for teaching and learning, making them valuable tools for educators, trainers, and learners alike. One of the key benefits is engagement: educational game genres captivate learners' interest and motivation by leveraging the inherent appeal of gaming, fostering active participation and sustained attention. Moreover, educational game genres provide opportunities for experiential learning, problem-solving, and critical thinking, allowing learners to apply theoretical knowledge and skills in realistic contexts. Additionally, educational game genres promote collaboration and social interaction, enabling players to work together to achieve common goals, share resources, and solve challenges collectively. Furthermore, educational game genres offer personalized learning experiences, allowing learners to explore at their own pace, follow their interests, and receive immediate feedback and guidance tailored to their needs.

CHAPTER 9

INTEGRATING GAME INTO THE CURRICULUM

9.1 INCORPORATING GAMES INTO LESSON PLANS

Incorporating games into lesson plans is a dynamic approach to education that engages students in interactive and immersive learning experiences. Games have long been recognized as effective tools for promoting engagement, motivation, and retention of information. Integrating games into lesson plans allows educators to create dynamic learning environments that cater to diverse learning styles and foster critical thinking, collaboration, and problem-solving skills.

Incorporating games into lesson plans is a dynamic and effective approach to education that engages students in interactive and immersive learning experiences. By identifying appropriate games, designing game-based learning activities, promoting active learning and collaboration, assessing learning outcomes, providing differentiation and support, and fostering reflection and metacognition, educators can create dynamic learning environments that cater to diverse learning styles and promote academic growth.

As technology continues to evolve and new educational games emerge, the potential for incorporating games into lesson plans to enhance learning outcomes is limitless. By embracing game-based learning, educators can inspire curiosity, creativity, and lifelong learning in their students.

9.1.1 The Benefits of Games in Education

Before delving into the specifics of incorporating games into lesson plans, it's crucial to understand the benefits they offer in educational settings. Games are inherently engaging and motivating, capturing students' attention and encouraging active participation in the learning process. Through gameplay, students are immersed in interactive experiences that promote exploration, experimentation, and discovery, leading to deeper understanding and retention of concepts. Additionally, games provide opportunities for collaboration and social interaction, fostering teamwork, communication, and empathy among students. Moreover, games offer immediate feedback, allowing students to assess their progress and adjust their strategies accordingly, thus promoting a growth mindset and resilience.

9.1.2 Identifying Appropriate Games for Lesson Plans

The first step in incorporating games into lesson plans is identifying appropriate games that align with the learning objectives and content of the curriculum. Educators should consider factors such as the subject area, grade level, learning goals, and students' interests and preferences when selecting games. There is a wide variety of educational games available, ranging from digital games and board games to outdoor activities and simulations. Educators should choose games that are age-appropriate, culturally relevant, and pedagogically sound, ensuring they enhance the learning experience and promote academic growth. Additionally, educators can leverage educational game platforms and resources to discover and evaluate games that meet their instructional needs.

9.1.3 Integrating Games across Curriculum Areas

Games can be integrated into lesson plans across various curriculum areas, including mathematics, science, language arts, social studies, and beyond. In mathematics, educators can use math games to reinforce concepts such as addition, subtraction, multiplication, and division, making abstract mathematical concepts more tangible and accessible to students. In science, educators can incorporate simulation games to explore scientific phenomena, conduct virtual experiments, and develop inquiry skills. In language arts, educators can use storytelling games to enhance literacy skills such as reading comprehension, vocabulary, and storytelling. In social studies, educators can use historical simulations and role-playing games to engage students in exploring historical events, cultures, and perspectives.

9.1.4 Designing Game-Based Learning Activities

Once appropriate games have been identified, educators can design game-based learning activities that align with their lesson objectives and instructional goals. Game-based learning activities can take many forms, including structured gameplay sessions, game-based assessments, gamified quizzes, and collaborative projects. Educators should provide clear instructions and guidelines for gameplay, establish learning goals and success criteria, and facilitate meaningful debrief discussions to reflect on the learning experience. Additionally, educators can incorporate elements of gamification, such as badges, rewards, and leaderboards, to enhance motivation and engagement.

9.1.5 Promoting Active Learning and Collaboration

Games promote active learning by encouraging students to take an active role in the learning process, rather than passively receiving information. During gameplay, students are actively engaged in problem-solving, decision-making, and critical thinking, thus developing essential 21st-century skills. Moreover, games promote collaboration and teamwork as students work together to achieve common goals, share knowledge and resources, and solve challenges collectively. Through collaborative gameplay, students learn to communicate effectively, listen to others' perspectives, and negotiate solutions, fostering a sense of community and belonging in the classroom.

9.1.6 Assessing Learning Outcomes

Assessing learning outcomes is an essential component of incorporating games into lesson plans to ensure that students are meeting the intended learning objectives. Educators can assess learning outcomes through a variety of methods, including formative assessments, summative assessments, and observations during gameplay. Formative assessments, such as quizzes, exit tickets, and group discussions, can provide insights into students' understanding and mastery of concepts during gameplay. Summative assessments, such as project-based assessments or written reflections, can evaluate students' overall learning and growth over time. Additionally, educators can observe students' engagement, collaboration, and problem-solving skills during gameplay to inform their assessment of learning outcomes.

9.1.7 Providing Differentiation and Support

Incorporating games into lesson plans allows educators to provide differentiation and support to meet the diverse needs of students in the classroom. Educators can adapt game-based learning activities to accommodate students with varying learning styles, abilities, and preferences. For example, educators can provide scaffolding and support to struggling learners by offering additional guidance, resources, or modifications to the gameplay experience. Similarly, educators can provide enrichment opportunities for advanced learners by challenging them with more complex tasks, extensions, or alternative game formats. Additionally, educators can leverage technology tools and resources to provide personalized learning experiences that cater to individual students' needs and interests.

9.1.8 Fostering Reflection and Metacognition

Reflection and metacognition are essential components of game-based learning that promote students' self-awareness, self-regulation, and critical thinking skills. Educators can facilitate reflection activities before, during, and after gameplay to help students make connections between their gameplay experiences and their learning objectives. Before gameplay, educators can activate students' prior knowledge, set learning goals, and discuss strategies for success. During gameplay, educators can encourage students to reflect on their decision-making process, analyze their performance, and identify areas for improvement. After gameplay, educators can facilitate debrief discussions to discuss key learning insights, challenges, and strategies for applying their learning to real-world contexts.

9.2 GAME-BASED LEARNING ACROSS SUBJECTS

Game-based learning is a versatile and effective approach to education that transcends traditional subject boundaries, offering immersive and interactive experiences that engage students in meaningful learning across diverse disciplines. By leveraging the inherent appeal of games, educators can create dynamic learning environments that foster critical thinking, collaboration, and problem-solving skills while reinforcing academic content.

Game-based learning offers a versatile and effective approach to education that transcends traditional subject boundaries, offering immersive and interactive experiences that engage students in meaningful learning across diverse disciplines. By integrating games into instruction, educators can create dynamic learning environments that foster critical thinking, collaboration, and problem-solving skills while reinforcing academic content. Whether teaching mathematics, science, language arts, social studies, or the arts, game-based learning provides students with opportunities to explore, experiment, and learn in a fun and engaging way. As technology continues to evolve and new educational games emerge, the potential for game-based learning to enhance education across subjects is limitless. By embracing game-based learning, educators can inspire curiosity, creativity, and lifelong learning in their students.

9.2.1 Mathematics

Game-based learning in mathematics has emerged as a powerful pedagogical approach to engage students in meaningful and interactive learning experiences. By leveraging the intrinsic motivation and engagement inherent in games, educators can create dynamic environments where students actively explore mathematical concepts, develop problem-solving skills, and build mathematical fluency.

Game-based learning in mathematics offers a dynamic and effective approach to engage students in meaningful and interactive learning experiences. By leveraging the intrinsic motivation and engagement inherent in games, educators can create dynamic environments where students actively explore mathematical concepts, develop problem-solving skills, and build mathematical fluency. Through effective strategies, educators can harness the educational potential of math games to enhance learning outcomes and foster a positive attitude towards mathematics. As technology continues to evolve and new trends emerge, the future of game-based learning in mathematics is ripe with opportunities for innovation, collaboration, and impact in mathematics education. By embracing game-based learning, educators can inspire curiosity, creativity, and lifelong learning in their students, thus preparing them for success in an increasingly complex and interconnected world.

Benefits of Game-Based Learning in Mathematics

Game-based learning in mathematics offers a myriad of benefits for students at all levels of education. One of the key benefits is increased engagement and motivation. Games captivate students' attention by providing immediate feedback, clear goals, and meaningful challenges, thus fostering a positive attitude towards learning mathematics. Moreover, game-based learning promotes active learning as students become actively involved in problem-solving, critical thinking, and decision-making processes. Through gameplay, students develop mathematical fluency and problem-solving skills by applying mathematical concepts in context, thus enhancing retention and transferability of knowledge. Additionally, game-based learning promotes collaboration and social interaction as students work together to solve problems, share strategies, and achieve common goals, fostering a sense of community and camaraderie in the classroom.

Applications of Game-Based Learning in Mathematics

Game-based learning in mathematics can be applied across various topics and concepts, ranging from basic arithmetic operations to advanced mathematical principles. Educators can use math games to reinforce fundamental skills such as addition, subtraction, multiplication, division, and fractions, making abstract mathematical concepts more tangible and accessible to students. Additionally, educators can incorporate problem-solving games, logic puzzles, and mathematical simulations to develop students' critical thinking skills and mathematical reasoning abilities. Moreover, educators can use math games to explore advanced topics such as algebra, geometry, statistics, and calculus, providing opportunities for students to apply mathematical concepts in real-world contexts.

Effective Strategies for Game-Based Learning in Mathematics

Several effective strategies can enhance the implementation of game-based learning in mathematics. First and foremost, educators should align game-based learning activities with learning objectives and curriculum standards to ensure coherence and relevance. By selecting games that address specific mathematical concepts and skills, educators can maximize the educational value of gameplay experiences. Additionally, educators should provide clear instructions and guidelines for gameplay, establish learning goals and success criteria, and facilitate meaningful debrief discussions to reflect on the learning experience. Moreover, educators can incorporate elements of gamification, such as badges, rewards, and leaderboards, to enhance motivation and engagement. Furthermore, educators should provide differentiation and support to meet the diverse needs of students in the classroom, adapting game-based learning activities to accommodate students with varying learning styles, abilities, and preferences.

Digital and Non-Digital Math Games

Math games come in both digital and non-digital formats, offering educators a diverse range of options to suit their instructional needs and preferences. Digital math games, such as educational apps, online platforms, and computer-based simulations, provide interactive and immersive experiences that leverage technology to engage students in gameplay. These games often feature dynamic graphics, sound effects, and animation, enhancing the sensory experience and increasing student engagement. Non-digital math games, such as board games, card games, and manipulative-based activities, offer hands-on learning experiences that promote tactile exploration and social interaction. These games provide opportunities for students to collaborate, communicate, and problem-solve together, thus fostering a sense of camaraderie and teamwork in the classroom. Both digital and non-digital math games have their unique strengths and advantages, and educators can leverage a combination of both to create dynamic and engaging learning experiences for their students.

Challenges and Considerations

Despite the many benefits of game-based learning in mathematics, educators may encounter challenges and considerations in its implementation. One challenge is selecting appropriate games that align with learning objectives and curriculum standards. With the abundance of math games available, educators must critically evaluate games to ensure they meet educational goals and provide meaningful learning experiences. Additionally, educators may face challenges in integrating game-based learning into existing instructional practices and classroom routines. Educators must carefully plan and scaffold game-based learning activities to ensure they complement and enhance traditional teaching methods rather than replace them. Moreover, educators may encounter logistical challenges, such as limited access to technology or insufficient resources, which may hinder the implementation of digital math games. Furthermore, educators must consider ethical considerations, such as data privacy, content appropriateness, and representation, to create a safe and respectful learning environment for all students.

Future Directions in Game-Based Learning in Mathematics

The future of game-based learning in mathematics is bright, with continued innovation and collaboration driving the development of new technologies, methodologies, and applications. One emerging trend is the integration of artificial intelligence (AI) and machine learning algorithms into math games, enabling adaptive learning experiences that personalize content, provide targeted feedback, and optimize gameplay based on students' performance and preferences.

Moreover, the rise of augmented reality (AR) and virtual reality (VR) technologies offers new opportunities for immersive and interactive math learning experiences that blur the boundaries between the physical and digital worlds. Additionally, the gamification of mathematics education is gaining traction as a way to enhance motivation and engagement through the use of game elements and mechanics in non-game contexts. Overall, the future of game-based learning in mathematics holds promise as a dynamic and innovative approach to mathematics education that inspires curiosity, creativity, and lifelong learning in students.

9.2.2 Science

Game-based learning in science has emerged as a dynamic and effective approach to engage students in hands-on exploration, inquiry, and discovery. By harnessing the power of games, educators can create immersive and interactive learning experiences that promote scientific literacy, critical thinking, and problem-solving skills.

Game-based learning in science offers a dynamic and effective approach to engage students in hands-on exploration, inquiry, and discovery. By harnessing the power of games, educators can create immersive and interactive learning experiences that promote scientific literacy, critical thinking, and problem-solving skills.

As technology continues to evolve and new trends emerge, the future of game-based learning in science is ripe with opportunities for innovation, collaboration, and impact in science education.

By embracing game-based learning, educators can inspire curiosity, creativity, and lifelong learning in their students, thus preparing them for success in an increasingly complex and interconnected world.

Benefits of Game-Based Learning in Science

Game-based learning in science offers a multitude of benefits for students at all levels of education. One of the key benefits is increased engagement and motivation. Games captivate students' attention by providing clear goals, meaningful challenges, and immediate feedback, thus fostering a positive attitude towards learning science.

Moreover, game-based learning promotes active learning as students become actively involved in inquiry-based exploration, experimentation, and problem-solving. Through gameplay, students develop scientific inquiry skills, such as observation, hypothesis testing, data analysis, and conclusion drawing, thus enhancing their understanding of scientific concepts and processes. Additionally, game-based learning promotes collaboration and social interaction as students work together to solve problems, share resources, and achieve common goals, fostering a sense of community and teamwork in the classroom.

Applications of Game-Based Learning in Science

Game-based learning in science can be applied across various scientific disciplines, including biology, chemistry, physics, earth science, and environmental science. Educators can use science games to explore scientific phenomena, conduct virtual experiments, and simulate real-world scenarios, providing students with opportunities to apply scientific concepts in context. Moreover, educators can incorporate problem-solving games, simulations, and virtual labs to develop students' critical thinking skills and scientific reasoning abilities. Additionally, educators can use science games to explore complex topics such as climate change, biodiversity, and genetics, allowing students to engage with current scientific issues and develop informed opinions.

Effective Strategies for Game-Based Learning in Science

Several effective strategies can enhance the implementation of game-based learning in science. First and foremost, educators should align game-based learning activities with learning objectives and curriculum standards to ensure coherence and relevance. By selecting games that address specific scientific concepts and skills, educators can maximize the educational value of gameplay experiences. Additionally, educators should provide clear instructions and guidelines for gameplay, establish learning goals and success criteria, and facilitate meaningful debrief discussions to reflect on the learning experience. Moreover, educators can incorporate elements of gamification, such as badges, rewards, and leaderboards, to enhance motivation and engagement. Furthermore, educators should provide differentiation and support to meet the diverse needs of students in the classroom, adapting game-based learning activities to accommodate students with varying learning styles, abilities, and preferences.

Digital and Non-Digital Science Games

Science games come in both digital and non-digital formats, offering educators a diverse range of options to suit their instructional needs and preferences. Digital science games, such as educational apps, online simulations, and computer-based games, provide interactive and immersive experiences that leverage technology to engage students in gameplay. These games often feature dynamic graphics, realistic simulations, and interactive features, enhancing the sensory experience and increasing student engagement. Non-digital science games, such as board games, card games, and hands-on activities, offer tactile learning experiences that promote exploration and experimentation. These games provide opportunities for students to collaborate, communicate, and problem-solve together, thus fostering a sense of community and teamwork in the classroom. Both digital and non-digital science games have their unique strengths and advantages, and educators can leverage a combination of both to create dynamic and engaging learning experiences for their students.

Challenges and Considerations

Despite the many benefits of game-based learning in science, educators may encounter challenges and considerations in its implementation. One challenge is selecting appropriate games that align with learning objectives and curriculum standards. With the abundance of science games available, educators must critically evaluate games to ensure they meet educational goals and provide meaningful learning experiences.

Additionally, educators may face challenges in integrating game-based learning into existing instructional practices and classroom routines. Educators must carefully plan and scaffold game-based learning activities to ensure they complement and enhance traditional teaching methods rather than replace them. Moreover, educators may encounter logistical challenges, such as limited access to technology or insufficient resources, which may hinder the implementation of digital science games. Furthermore, educators must consider ethical considerations, such as data privacy, content appropriateness, and representation, to create a safe and respectful learning environment for all students.

Future Directions in Game-Based Learning in Science

The future of game-based learning in science is bright, with continued innovation and collaboration driving the development of new technologies, methodologies, and applications. One emerging trend is the integration of augmented reality (AR) and virtual reality (VR) technologies into science games, offering immersive and interactive learning experiences that blur the boundaries between the physical and digital worlds.

Moreover, the rise of artificial intelligence (AI) and machine learning algorithms enables adaptive learning experiences that personalize content, provide targeted feedback, and optimize gameplay based on students' performance and preferences. Additionally, the gamification of science education is gaining traction as a way to enhance motivation and engagement through the use of game elements and mechanics in non-game contexts. Overall, the future of game-based learning in science holds promise as a dynamic and innovative approach to science education that inspires curiosity, creativity, and lifelong learning in students.

9.2.3 Language Arts

Game-based learning in language arts has revolutionized the way educators engage students in literacy development, communication skills, and critical thinking. By integrating games into language arts instruction, educators can create immersive and interactive learning experiences that inspire creativity, foster collaboration, and enhance language proficiency.

Game-based learning in language arts offers a dynamic and effective approach to engage students in literacy development, communication skills, and critical thinking. By integrating games into language arts instruction, educators can create immersive and interactive learning experiences that inspire creativity, foster collaboration, and enhance language proficiency. As technology continues to evolve and new trends emerge, the future of game-based learning in language arts is ripe with opportunities for innovation, collaboration, and impact in literacy education. By embracing game-based learning, educators can inspire a love of reading, writing, and storytelling in their students, thus preparing them for success in school and beyond.

Benefits of Game-Based Learning in Language Arts

Game-based learning in language arts offers a multitude of benefits for students across all grade levels. One of the key benefits is increased engagement and motivation. Games captivate students' attention by providing clear goals, meaningful challenges, and immediate feedback, thus fostering a positive attitude towards reading, writing, and communication.

Moreover, game-based learning promotes active learning as students become actively involved in storytelling, vocabulary building, grammar practice, and literary analysis. Through gameplay, students develop language proficiency, fluency, and comprehension skills by engaging with authentic texts, exploring diverse genres, and interacting with characters and narratives. Additionally, game-based learning promotes collaboration and social interaction as students work together to solve puzzles, complete challenges, and create stories, fostering a sense of community and teamwork in the classroom.

Applications of Game-Based Learning in Language Arts

Game-based learning in language arts can be applied across various aspects of literacy development, including reading comprehension, writing skills, vocabulary acquisition, and grammar practice. Educators can use reading games to reinforce comprehension strategies such as summarizing, predicting, inferring, and analyzing text. Moreover, educators can incorporate writing games to inspire creativity, develop narrative skills, and practice various forms of writing, including storytelling, persuasive writing, and poetry. Additionally, educators can use vocabulary games to expand students' word knowledge, strengthen language skills, and enhance vocabulary retention. Furthermore, educators can integrate grammar games to reinforce grammatical concepts, practice sentence structure, and improve writing mechanics.

By leveraging games, educators can create dynamic and engaging learning experiences that cater to diverse learning styles and promote language proficiency.

Effective Strategies for Game-Based Learning in Language Arts

Several effective strategies can enhance the implementation of game-based learning in language arts. First and foremost, educators should align game-based learning activities with learning objectives and curriculum standards to ensure coherence and relevance. By selecting games that address specific language arts skills and concepts, educators can maximize the educational value of gameplay experiences. Additionally, educators should provide clear instructions and guidelines for gameplay, establish learning goals and success criteria, and facilitate meaningful debrief discussions to reflect on the learning experience. Moreover, educators can incorporate elements of gamification, such as badges, rewards, and leaderboards, to enhance motivation and engagement. Furthermore, educators should provide differentiation and support to meet the diverse needs of students in the classroom, adapting game-based learning activities to accommodate students with varying language proficiency levels, learning styles, and interests.

Digital and Non-Digital Language Arts Games

Language arts games come in both digital and non-digital formats, offering educators a diverse range of options to suit their instructional needs and preferences. Digital language arts games, such as educational apps, online platforms, and interactive eBooks, provide immersive and interactive experiences that leverage technology to engage students in gameplay. These games often feature dynamic graphics, sound effects, and animation, enhancing the sensory experience and increasing student engagement. Non-digital language arts games, such as board games, card games, and storytelling activities, offer hands-on learning experiences that promote creativity and collaboration. These games provide opportunities for students to engage in imaginative play, explore narrative structures, and develop storytelling skills. Both digital and non-digital language arts games have their unique strengths and advantages, and educators can leverage a combination of both to create dynamic and engaging learning experiences for their students.

Challenges and Considerations

Despite the many benefits of game-based learning in language arts, educators may encounter challenges and considerations in its implementation. One challenge is selecting appropriate games that align with learning objectives and curriculum standards. With the abundance of language arts games available, educators must critically evaluate games to ensure they meet educational goals and provide meaningful learning experiences. Additionally, educators may face challenges in integrating game-based learning into existing instructional practices and classroom routines. Educators must carefully plan and scaffold game-based learning activities to ensure they complement and enhance traditional teaching methods rather than replace them. Moreover, educators may encounter logistical challenges, such as limited access to technology or insufficient resources, which may hinder the implementation of digital language arts games. Furthermore, educators must consider ethical considerations, such as data privacy, content appropriateness, and representation, to create a safe and respectful learning environment for all students.

Future Directions in Game-Based Learning in Language Arts

The future of game-based learning in language arts is bright, with continued innovation and collaboration driving the development of new technologies, methodologies, and applications. One emerging trend is the integration of artificial intelligence (AI) and natural language processing (NLP) technologies into language arts games, enabling adaptive learning experiences that personalize content, provide targeted feedback, and optimize gameplay based on students' language proficiency and learning needs. Moreover, the rise of augmented reality (AR) and virtual reality (VR) technologies offers new opportunities for immersive and interactive storytelling experiences that blur the boundaries between the physical and digital worlds. Additionally, the gamification of language arts education is gaining traction as a way to enhance motivation and engagement through the use of game elements and mechanics in non-game contexts. Overall, the future of game-based learning in language arts holds promise as a dynamic and innovative approach to literacy development that inspires creativity, communication, and lifelong learning in students.

9.2.4 Social Studies

Game-based learning in social studies has transformed the way educators engage students in the study of history, geography, civics, and culture. By integrating games into social studies instruction, educators can create immersive and interactive learning experiences that inspire curiosity, critical thinking, and empathy.

Game-based learning in social studies offers a dynamic and effective approach to engage students in the study of history, geography, civics, and culture. By integrating games into social studies instruction, educators can create immersive and interactive learning experiences that inspire curiosity, foster collaboration, and enhance critical thinking skills. As technology continues to evolve and new trends emerge, the future of game-based learning in social studies is ripe with opportunities for innovation, collaboration, and impact in social studies education. By embracing game-based learning, educators can inspire a love of learning about the world and empower students to become informed and engaged citizens.

Benefits of Game-Based Learning in Social Studies

Game-based learning in social studies offers a multitude of benefits for students across all grade levels. One of the key benefits is increased engagement and motivation. Games captivate students' attention by providing clear goals, meaningful challenges, and immediate feedback, thus fostering a positive attitude towards learning history, geography, and civics. Moreover, game-based learning promotes active learning as students become actively involved in exploring historical events, analyzing primary sources, and engaging with cultural artifacts. Through gameplay, students develop historical thinking skills, such as sourcing, contextualization, corroboration, and interpretation, thus enhancing their understanding of historical events and perspectives. Additionally, game-based learning promotes collaboration and social interaction as students work together to solve problems, make decisions, and explore complex issues, fostering a sense of community and civic responsibility in the classroom.

Applications of Game-Based Learning in Social Studies

Game-based learning in social studies can be applied across various topics and themes, including ancient civilizations, world wars, political systems, and global issues. Educators can use historical simulation games to recreate historical events, simulate political processes, and explore alternative historical scenarios, providing students with opportunities to engage with historical content in a dynamic and interactive way. Moreover, educators can incorporate geography games to explore maps, regions, and landscapes, allowing students to develop spatial awareness and geographic literacy skills. Additionally, educators can use civics games to explore concepts such as democracy, citizenship, and social justice, empowering students to become informed and engaged members of society. Furthermore, educators can integrate cultural games to explore diverse cultures, traditions, and perspectives, fostering empathy and appreciation for cultural diversity.

Effective Strategies for Game-Based Learning in Social Studies

Several effective strategies can enhance the implementation of game-based learning in social studies. First and foremost, educators should align game-based learning activities with learning objectives and curriculum standards to ensure coherence and relevance. By selecting games that address specific social studies concepts and skills, educators can maximize the educational value of gameplay experiences. Additionally, educators should provide clear instructions and guidelines for gameplay, establish learning goals and success criteria, and facilitate meaningful debrief discussions to reflect on the learning experience. Moreover, educators can incorporate elements of gamification, such as badges, rewards, and leaderboards, to enhance motivation and engagement. Furthermore, educators should provide differentiation and support to meet the diverse needs of students in the classroom, adapting game-based learning activities to accommodate students with varying interests, abilities, and backgrounds.

Digital and Non-Digital Social Studies Games

Social studies games come in both digital and non-digital formats, offering educators a diverse range of options to suit their instructional needs and preferences. Digital social studies games, such as educational apps, online simulations, and virtual reality experiences, provide immersive and interactive experiences that leverage technology to engage students in gameplay. These games often feature dynamic graphics, realistic simulations, and interactive features, enhancing the sensory experience and increasing student engagement. Non-digital social studies games, such as board games, card games, and role-playing activities, offer hands-on learning experiences that promote collaboration and critical thinking. These games provide opportunities for students to engage in interactive storytelling, decision-making, and problem-solving, thus fostering a deeper understanding of social studies concepts and themes. Both digital and non-digital social studies games have their unique strengths and advantages, and educators can leverage a combination of both to create dynamic and engaging learning experiences for their students.

Challenges and Considerations

Despite the many benefits of game-based learning in social studies, educators may encounter challenges and considerations in its implementation. One challenge is selecting appropriate games that align with learning objectives and curriculum standards. With the abundance of social studies games available, educators must critically evaluate games to ensure they meet educational goals and provide meaningful learning experiences. Additionally, educators may face challenges in integrating game-based learning into existing instructional practices and classroom routines. Educators must carefully plan and scaffold game-based learning activities to ensure they complement and enhance traditional teaching methods rather than replace them. Moreover, educators may encounter logistical challenges, such as limited access to technology or insufficient resources, which may hinder the implementation of digital social studies games. Furthermore, educators must consider ethical considerations, such as data privacy, content appropriateness, and representation, to create a safe and respectful learning environment for all students.

Future Directions in Game-Based Learning in Social Studies

The future of game-based learning in social studies is bright, with continued innovation and collaboration driving the development of new technologies, methodologies, and applications. One emerging trend is the integration of augmented reality (AR) and virtual reality (VR) technologies into social studies games, offering immersive and interactive learning experiences that blur the boundaries between the physical and digital worlds. Moreover, the rise of artificial intelligence (AI) and machine learning algorithms enables adaptive learning experiences that personalize content, provide targeted feedback, and optimize gameplay based on students' performance and preferences. Additionally, the gamification of social studies education is gaining traction as a way to enhance motivation and engagement through the use of game elements and mechanics in non-game contexts. Overall, the future of game-based learning in social studies holds promise as a dynamic and innovative approach to social studies education that inspires curiosity, critical thinking, and civic engagement in students.

9.2.5 Art and Music

Game-based learning in art and music has revolutionized the way educators engage students in creative expression, aesthetic appreciation, and musical literacy. By integrating games into art and music instruction, educators can create immersive and interactive learning experiences that inspire curiosity, foster collaboration, and enhance artistic and musical skills.

Game-based learning in art and music offers a dynamic and effective approach to engage students in creative expression, aesthetic appreciation, and musical literacy. By integrating games into art and music instruction, educators can create immersive and interactive learning experiences that foster creativity, collaboration, and self-expression. As technology continues to evolve and new trends emerge, the future of game-based learning in art and music is ripe with opportunities for innovation, collaboration, and impact in artistic and musical education. By embracing game-based learning, educators can inspire a love of art, music, and creativity in their students, thus preparing them for success in an increasingly complex and interconnected world.

Benefits of Game-Based Learning in Art and Music

Game-based learning in art and music offers a multitude of benefits for students of all ages. One of the key benefits is increased engagement and motivation. Games captivate students' attention by providing clear goals, meaningful challenges, and immediate feedback, thus fostering a positive attitude towards artistic and musical exploration. Moreover, game-based learning promotes active learning as students become actively involved in creating, composing, and performing artistic and musical works. Through gameplay, students develop creativity, problem-solving skills, and self-expression by engaging with diverse artistic styles, techniques, and genres. Additionally, game-based learning promotes collaboration and social interaction as students work together to create, share, and critique artwork and music, fostering a sense of community and artistic identity in the classroom.

Applications of Game-Based Learning in Art and Music

Game-based learning in art and music can be applied across various aspects of artistic and musical development, including visual art, digital art, painting, drawing, sculpture, music composition, music theory, and performance. Educators can use art games to explore artistic concepts such as color theory, perspective, composition, and art history, allowing students to experiment with different mediums and techniques. Moreover, educators can incorporate music games to explore musical concepts such as rhythm, melody, harmony, form, and style, providing students with opportunities to compose, improvise, and perform music. Additionally, educators can integrate digital art and music software to create multimedia projects, interactive installations, and collaborative performances, enabling students to explore the intersection of art, music, and technology. By leveraging games, educators can create dynamic and engaging learning experiences that foster creativity, expression, and artistic and musical literacy.

Effective Strategies for Game-Based Learning in Art and Music

Several effective strategies can enhance the implementation of game-based learning in art and music. First and foremost, educators should align game-based learning activities with learning objectives and curriculum standards to ensure coherence and relevance. By selecting games that address specific artistic and musical concepts and skills, educators can maximize the educational value of gameplay experiences. Additionally, educators should provide clear instructions and guidelines for gameplay, establish learning goals and success criteria, and facilitate meaningful debrief discussions to reflect on the learning experience. Moreover, educators can incorporate elements of gamification, such as badges, rewards, and leaderboards, to enhance motivation and engagement. Furthermore, educators should provide differentiation and support to meet the diverse needs of students in the classroom, adapting game-based learning activities to accommodate students with varying artistic and musical interests, abilities, and backgrounds.

Digital and Non-Digital Art and Music Games

Art and music games come in both digital and non-digital formats, offering educators a diverse range of options to suit their instructional needs and preferences. Digital art and music games, such as educational apps, software programs, and online platforms, provide immersive and interactive experiences that leverage technology to engage students in gameplay. These games often feature dynamic graphics, sound effects, and animation, enhancing the sensory experience and increasing student engagement. Non-digital art and music games, such as drawing games, music notation games, and improvisation activities, offer hands-on learning experiences that promote creativity and collaboration. These games provide opportunities for students to experiment, explore, and express themselves through artistic and musical creation. Both digital and non-digital art and music games have their unique strengths and advantages, and educators can leverage a combination of both to create dynamic and engaging learning experiences for their students.

Challenges and Considerations

Despite the many benefits of game-based learning in art and music, educators may encounter challenges and considerations in its implementation. One challenge is selecting appropriate games that align with learning objectives and curriculum standards. With the abundance of art and music games available, educators must critically evaluate games to ensure they meet educational goals and provide meaningful learning experiences. Additionally, educators may face challenges in integrating game-based learning into existing instructional practices and classroom routines. Educators must carefully plan and scaffold game-based learning activities to ensure they complement and enhance traditional teaching methods rather than replace them. Moreover, educators may encounter logistical challenges, such as limited access to technology or insufficient resources, which may hinder the implementation of digital art and music games. Furthermore, educators must consider ethical considerations, such as copyright, intellectual property, and cultural appropriation, to create a respectful and inclusive learning environment for all students.

Future Directions in Game-Based Learning in Art and Music

The future of game-based learning in art and music is bright, with continued innovation and collaboration driving the development of new technologies, methodologies, and applications. One emerging trend is the integration of augmented reality (AR) and virtual reality (VR) technologies into art and music games, offering immersive and interactive learning experiences that blur the boundaries between the physical and digital worlds. Moreover, the rise of artificial intelligence (AI) and machine learning algorithms enables adaptive learning experiences that personalize content, provide targeted feedback, and optimize gameplay based on students' artistic and musical preferences and abilities. Additionally, the gamification of art and music education is gaining traction as a way to enhance motivation and engagement through the use of game elements and mechanics in non-game contexts. Overall, the future of game-based learning in art and music holds promise as a dynamic and innovative approach to artistic and musical development that inspires creativity, expression, and lifelong learning in students.

9.2.6 Physical Education

Game-based learning in physical education has transformed the way educators engage students in health promotion, fitness development, and lifelong physical activity. By integrating games into physical education instruction, educators can create dynamic and interactive learning experiences that inspire movement, teamwork, and skill development.

Game-based learning in physical education offers a dynamic and effective approach to engage students in health promotion, fitness development, and lifelong physical activity. By integrating games into physical education instruction, educators can create immersive and interactive learning experiences that inspire movement, teamwork, and skill development. As technology continues to evolve and new trends emerge, the future of game-based learning in physical education is ripe with opportunities for innovation, collaboration, and impact in health and physical education. By embracing game-based learning, educators can inspire a love of movement and fitness in their students, thus promoting lifelong health and well-being.

Benefits of Game-Based Learning in Physical Education

Game-based learning in physical education offers numerous benefits for students of all ages. One of the key benefits is increased engagement and motivation. Games captivate students' attention by providing clear objectives, meaningful challenges, and immediate feedback, thus fostering a positive attitude towards physical activity and fitness. Moreover, game-based learning promotes active participation as students become actively involved in movement-based activities, skill development, and team-based challenges. Through gameplay, students develop motor skills, coordination, balance, and spatial awareness, thus enhancing their physical literacy and overall fitness levels. Additionally, game-based learning promotes collaboration and social interaction as students work together to achieve common goals, fostering a sense of camaraderie and teamwork in the classroom.

Applications of Game-Based Learning in Physical Education

Game-based learning in physical education can be applied across various aspects of health and fitness development, including locomotor skills, manipulative skills, fitness components, sport-specific skills, and cooperative games. Educators can use locomotor skill games to reinforce fundamental movement patterns such as running, jumping, hopping, and skipping, providing students with opportunities to practice and refine their motor skills in a fun and engaging way. Moreover, educators can incorporate manipulative skill games to develop hand-eye coordination, throwing, catching, kicking, and striking skills, allowing students to explore a variety of sports and activities. Additionally, educators can use fitness-based games to improve cardiovascular endurance, muscular strength, flexibility, and body composition, providing students with opportunities to engage in physical challenges and fitness assessments. Furthermore, educators can integrate cooperative games to promote teamwork, communication, and sportsmanship, fostering a positive and inclusive learning environment for all students.

Effective Strategies for Game-Based Learning in Physical Education

Several effective strategies can enhance the implementation of game-based learning in physical education. First and foremost, educators should align game-based learning activities with learning objectives and curriculum standards to ensure coherence and relevance. By selecting games that address specific motor skills, fitness components, and health concepts, educators can maximize the educational value of gameplay experiences. Additionally, educators should provide clear instructions and guidelines for gameplay, establish safety rules and guidelines, and facilitate meaningful debrief discussions to reflect on the learning experience. Moreover, educators can incorporate elements of gamification, such as point systems, rewards, and challenges, to enhance motivation and engagement. Furthermore, educators should provide differentiation and support to meet the diverse needs of students in the classroom, adapting game-based learning activities to accommodate students with varying skill levels, abilities, and interests.

Digital and Non-Digital Physical Education Games

Physical education games come in both digital and non-digital formats, offering educators a diverse range of options to suit their instructional needs and preferences. Digital physical education games, such as exergames, interactive fitness apps, and virtual reality simulations, provide immersive and interactive experiences that leverage technology to engage students in movement-based activities. These games often feature dynamic graphics, motion tracking, and feedback mechanisms, enhancing the sensory experience and increasing student engagement. Non-digital physical education games, such as tag games, relay races, cooperative games, and sport drills, offer hands-on learning experiences that promote movement, teamwork, and skill development. These games provide opportunities for students to engage in active play, explore different movement patterns, and develop social skills. Both digital and non-digital physical education games have their unique strengths and advantages, and educators can leverage a combination of both to create dynamic and engaging learning experiences for their students.

Challenges and Considerations

Despite the many benefits of game-based learning in physical education, educators may encounter challenges and considerations in its implementation. One challenge is selecting appropriate games that align with learning objectives and curriculum standards. With the abundance of physical education games available, educators must critically evaluate games to ensure they meet educational goals and provide meaningful learning experiences. Additionally, educators may face challenges in integrating game-based learning into existing instructional practices and class routines. Educators must carefully plan and scaffold game-based learning activities to ensure they complement and enhance traditional teaching methods rather than replace them. Moreover, educators may encounter logistical challenges, such as limited access to equipment or space, which may hinder the implementation of physical education games. Furthermore, educators must consider safety considerations, such as injury prevention, supervision, and equipment maintenance, to create a safe and supportive learning environment for all students.

Future Directions in Game-Based Learning in Physical Education

The future of game-based learning in physical education is bright, with continued innovation and collaboration driving the development of new technologies, methodologies, and applications. One emerging trend is the integration of augmented reality (AR) and virtual reality (VR) technologies into physical education games, offering immersive and interactive learning experiences that blur the boundaries between the physical and digital worlds. Moreover, the rise of wearable technology and fitness trackers enables personalized learning experiences that monitor students' movement, performance, and health metrics, providing real-time feedback and motivation. Additionally, the gamification of physical activity and fitness is gaining traction as a way to enhance motivation and engagement through the use of game elements and mechanics in non-game contexts. Overall, the future of game-based learning in physical education holds promise as a dynamic and innovative approach to health promotion, fitness development, and lifelong physical activity.

9.3 INTERDISCIPLINARY APPROACHES

Interdisciplinary approaches in education have gained prominence as educators recognize the interconnectedness of knowledge across various disciplines. By integrating multiple subject areas into cohesive learning experiences, interdisciplinary approaches foster critical thinking, creativity, and problem-solving skills.

Interdisciplinary approaches in education offer a holistic and integrative approach to learning that fosters critical thinking, creativity, and problem-solving skills. By connecting concepts, skills, and perspectives from multiple disciplines, interdisciplinary approaches prepare students for success in an increasingly interconnected and complex world. As educators continue to explore and implement interdisciplinary approaches, they have the opportunity to create dynamic and engaging learning experiences that inspire curiosity, collaboration, and lifelong learning. By embracing interdisciplinary education, educators can empower students to become knowledgeable, adaptable, and ethical contributors to society.

Interdisciplinary approaches in education transcend traditional disciplinary boundaries, allowing students to explore complex topics and themes from multiple perspectives. Unlike multidisciplinary approaches, which involve studying separate subjects in isolation, interdisciplinary approaches emphasize the integration of knowledge, skills, and perspectives across disciplines. By connecting concepts, theories, and methodologies from different subject areas, interdisciplinary approaches promote holistic understanding and deeper learning experiences.

9.3.1 Benefits of Interdisciplinary Approaches

Interdisciplinary approaches offer numerous benefits for students, educators, and society as a whole. One key benefit is the promotion of critical thinking and problem-solving skills. By engaging with diverse perspectives and approaches, students develop the ability to analyze complex issues, synthesize information, and generate creative solutions. Moreover, interdisciplinary approaches foster a deeper understanding of real-world problems and issues by providing multiple lenses through which to examine them. Additionally, interdisciplinary learning promotes collaboration and teamwork as students work together to integrate knowledge from different disciplines and perspectives. Furthermore, interdisciplinary approaches prepare students for success in an increasingly interconnected and complex world by equipping them with the skills and competencies needed to navigate diverse contexts and challenges.

9.3.2 Applications of Interdisciplinary Approaches

Interdisciplinary approaches can be applied across various subject areas and topics, including STEM (science, technology, engineering, and mathematics), humanities, social sciences, and the arts. For example, educators can integrate science, technology, and engineering concepts into mathematics instruction through project-based learning activities that involve designing and building structures or conducting experiments. Similarly, educators can incorporate historical, cultural, and social perspectives into literature studies by exploring the historical context of literary works or analyzing the social issues they address. Moreover, educators can use interdisciplinary approaches to address complex societal challenges such as climate change, globalization, and social justice by drawing on knowledge and methods from multiple disciplines to develop innovative solutions.

9.3.3 Effective Strategies for Implementing Interdisciplinary Approaches

Several effective strategies can enhance the implementation of interdisciplinary approaches in education. First and foremost, educators should collaborate across disciplines to design cohesive learning experiences that integrate concepts, skills, and perspectives from multiple subject areas. By working together, educators can identify common themes, connections, and opportunities for interdisciplinary learning. Additionally, educators should provide scaffolding and support to help students make connections between different disciplines and understand how they relate to one another. Moreover, educators should incorporate active learning strategies such as project-based learning, problem-based learning, and inquiry-based learning to engage students in interdisciplinary exploration and inquiry. Furthermore, educators should create opportunities for reflection and metacognition to help students develop a deeper understanding of the interdisciplinary connections they are making and the implications of those connections for their learning and thinking.

9.3.4 Challenges and Considerations

Despite the many benefits of interdisciplinary approaches, educators may encounter challenges and considerations in their implementation. One challenge is the need for time, resources, and support to develop interdisciplinary curricula and instructional materials. Educators may also face resistance from traditional disciplinary structures and institutional barriers that prioritize subject specialization and compartmentalization. Additionally, educators must navigate the complexities of assessment and evaluation in interdisciplinary contexts, as traditional assessment methods may not adequately capture the breadth and depth of interdisciplinary learning. Furthermore, educators must ensure that interdisciplinary approaches are inclusive and equitable, taking into account diverse perspectives, backgrounds, and experiences.

9.3.5 Future Directions in Interdisciplinary Education

The future of interdisciplinary education is bright, with continued innovation and collaboration driving the development of new approaches, methodologies, and applications. One emerging trend is the integration of technology and digital tools to facilitate interdisciplinary learning experiences, such as virtual reality simulations, multimedia resources, and online collaboration platforms. Moreover, the rise of interdisciplinary research and scholarship is generating new insights and perspectives that can inform interdisciplinary teaching and learning practices. Additionally, the growing recognition of the importance of interdisciplinary skills and competencies in the workforce is driving demand for interdisciplinary education at all levels. Overall, the future of interdisciplinary education holds promise as a dynamic and innovative approach to preparing students for success in a rapidly changing world.

PART-IV

IMPLEMENTATION AND BEST PRACTICES

CHAPTER 10

TEACHER TRAINING AND SUPPORT

10.1 PREPARING EDUCATORS FOR GAME-BASED LEARNING

As game-based learning gains traction as a powerful educational tool, it becomes imperative to equip educators with the necessary knowledge, skills, and resources to effectively integrate games into their teaching practices.

Preparing educators for game-based learning involves providing professional development opportunities, fostering a supportive learning environment, and empowering teachers to leverage games as transformative tools for student engagement and learning.

Preparing educators for game-based learning is essential for unlocking its full potential as a transformative educational tool. By providing professional development opportunities, fostering a supportive learning environment, and empowering educators as champions of game-based learning, schools can ensure that teachers are equipped with the knowledge, skills, and resources to effectively integrate games into their teaching practices.

As technology continues to evolve and new trends emerge, the future of preparing educators for game-based learning holds promise for enhancing student engagement, promoting active learning, and fostering 21st-century skills. By embracing game-based learning, educators can empower their students to become critical thinkers, problem solvers, and lifelong learners in an increasingly complex and interconnected world.

10.1.1 Significance of Game-Based Learning

Before delving into preparing educators for game-based learning, it's crucial to understand the significance of this approach in education. Game-based learning offers a dynamic and interactive way to engage students, promote critical thinking, and enhance learning outcomes across various subject areas and grade levels. By integrating games into instruction, educators can create immersive learning experiences that foster collaboration, problem-solving, and creativity, thus preparing students for success in a rapidly changing world. Moreover, game-based learning aligns with the principles of active learning, student-centered instruction, and educational technology integration, making it a valuable tool for 21st-century education.

10.1.2 Challenges in Preparing Educators for Game-Based Learning

Despite the potential benefits of game-based learning, educators may encounter several challenges in its implementation. One challenge is a lack of awareness and familiarity with game-based learning principles, methodologies, and resources. Many educators may have limited experience with using games in educational settings and may be unsure how to effectively integrate them into their teaching practices. Additionally, educators may face logistical challenges, such as limited access to technology, time constraints, and institutional barriers, which may hinder their ability to implement game-based learning effectively. Moreover, educators may encounter resistance from colleagues, administrators, and parents who perceive games as distractions or trivial pursuits rather than valuable educational tools.

10.1.3 Strategies for Preparing Educators for Game-Based Learning

To address the challenges of preparing educators for game-based learning, several strategies can be implemented. First and foremost, professional development opportunities should be provided to educators to enhance their knowledge and skills in game-based learning. These opportunities can take various forms, including workshops, seminars, online courses, and peer collaboration groups, and should cover topics such as game design principles, pedagogical strategies, assessment methods, and technology integration. Moreover, educators should be encouraged to explore and experiment with different types of games, platforms, and resources to find what works best for their teaching context and student needs. Additionally, educators should be provided with ongoing support and resources, such as access to educational games, lesson plans, and technical assistance, to facilitate their implementation of game-based learning in the classroom. Furthermore, educators should be encouraged to collaborate with colleagues, share best practices, and reflect on their experiences to continuously improve their game-based learning practices.

10.1.4 Empowering Educators as Game-Based Learning Champions

In addition to providing professional development opportunities, educators should be empowered as champions of game-based learning within their schools and communities. Educators who have successfully implemented game-based learning in their classrooms can serve as mentors and advocates for their colleagues, sharing their experiences, successes, and challenges. Moreover, educators can collaborate with administrators, curriculum developers, and educational researchers to develop policies, guidelines, and resources to support game-based learning initiatives. Additionally, educators can engage with parents and stakeholders to communicate the benefits of game-based learning and address any concerns or misconceptions. By empowering educators as game-based learning champions, schools can foster a culture of innovation, collaboration, and continuous improvement in teaching and learning.

10.1.5 Future Directions in Preparing Educators for Game-Based Learning

Looking ahead, the future of preparing educators for game-based learning holds promise as new technologies, methodologies, and applications continue to emerge. One emerging trend is the integration of artificial intelligence (AI) and machine learning algorithms into educational games, enabling adaptive learning experiences that personalize content, provide targeted feedback, and optimize gameplay based on students' learning needs and preferences. Moreover, the rise of augmented reality (AR) and virtual reality (VR) technologies offers new opportunities for immersive and interactive learning experiences that blur the boundaries between the physical and digital worlds. Additionally, the gamification of professional development and teacher training is gaining traction as a way to enhance engagement and motivation among educators. By leveraging these advancements, educators can be better prepared to harness the power of game-based learning to engage and empower their students.

10.2 PROFESSIONAL DEVELOPMENT FOR GAMIFICATION

As gamification gains momentum as a powerful educational strategy, it becomes crucial to equip educators with the knowledge, skills, and resources to effectively implement gamified learning experiences in their classrooms. Professional development for gamification involves providing educators with training, support, and resources to integrate game elements and mechanics into their teaching practices.

Professional development for gamification is essential for unlocking its full potential as a transformative educational strategy. By providing educators with training, support, and resources, schools can ensure that teachers are equipped with the knowledge, skills, and confidence to effectively implement gamified learning experiences in their classrooms. As technology continues to evolve and new trends emerge, the future of professional development for gamification holds promise for enhancing student engagement, motivation, and learning outcomes. By embracing gamification, educators can create dynamic and immersive learning experiences that inspire curiosity, foster collaboration, and promote lifelong learning in students.

Before delving into professional development for gamification, it's essential to understand the significance of this approach in education. Gamification involves applying game design principles and mechanics to non-game contexts, such as education, to increase engagement, motivation, and learning outcomes. By incorporating elements such as points, badges, leaderboards, and challenges into learning experiences, gamification transforms traditional instruction into interactive and immersive experiences that motivate and inspire students. Moreover, gamification aligns with the principles of active learning, student-centered instruction, and educational technology integration, making it a valuable tool for promoting 21st-century skills.

10.2.1 Challenges in Professional Development for Gamification

Despite the potential benefits of gamification, educators may encounter several challenges in its implementation. One challenge is a lack of awareness and familiarity with gamification principles, methodologies, and resources. Many educators may have limited experience with using gamification in educational settings and may be unsure how to effectively integrate it into their teaching practices. Additionally, educators may face logistical challenges, such as limited access to technology, time constraints, and institutional barriers, which may hinder their ability to implement gamification effectively. Moreover, educators may encounter resistance from colleagues, administrators, and parents who perceive gamification as a superficial or gimmicky approach to education.

10.2.2 Strategies for Professional Development in Gamification

To address the challenges of professional development for gamification, several strategies can be implemented. First and foremost, professional development opportunities should be provided to educators to enhance their knowledge and skills in gamification. These opportunities can take various forms, including workshops, seminars, online courses, and peer collaboration groups, and should cover topics such as game design principles, pedagogical strategies, assessment methods, and technology integration. Moreover, educators should be encouraged to explore and experiment with different gamification platforms, tools, and resources to find what works best for their teaching context and student needs. Additionally, educators should be provided with ongoing support and resources, such as access to gamification frameworks, templates, and technical assistance, to facilitate their implementation of gamification in the classroom. Furthermore, educators should be encouraged to collaborate with colleagues, share best practices, and reflect on their experiences to continuously improve their gamification practices.

10.2.3 Empowering Educators as Gamification Champions

In addition to providing professional development opportunities, educators should be empowered as champions of gamification within their schools and communities. Educators who have successfully implemented gamification in their classrooms can serve as mentors and advocates for their colleagues, sharing their experiences, successes, and challenges. Moreover, educators can collaborate with administrators, curriculum developers, and educational researchers to develop policies, guidelines, and resources to support gamification initiatives. Additionally, educators can engage with parents and stakeholders to communicate the benefits of gamification and address any concerns or misconceptions.

By empowering educators as gamification champions, schools can foster a culture of innovation, collaboration, and continuous improvement in teaching and learning.

10.2.4 Future Directions in Professional Development for Gamification

Looking ahead, the future of professional development for gamification holds promise as new technologies, methodologies, and applications continue to emerge. One emerging trend is the integration of artificial intelligence (AI) and machine learning algorithms into gamified learning platforms, enabling adaptive learning experiences that personalize content, provide targeted feedback, and optimize engagement based on students' learning needs and preferences.

Moreover, the rise of augmented reality (AR) and virtual reality (VR) technologies offers new opportunities for immersive and interactive gamified learning experiences that blur the boundaries between the physical and digital worlds.

Additionally, the gamification of professional development itself is gaining traction as a way to enhance engagement and motivation among educators. By leveraging these advancements, educators can be better prepared to harness the power of gamification to engage and empower their students.

10.3 TEACHER COMMUNITIES AND RESOURCES

Teacher communities and resources play a vital role in supporting educators' professional development, collaboration, and well-being. These communities provide a platform for teachers to connect, share ideas, access resources, and collaborate on educational initiatives.

Teacher communities and resources play a vital role in supporting educators' professional growth, collaboration, and well-being. By providing a platform for educators to connect, share ideas, access resources, and collaborate on educational initiatives, teacher communities empower educators to continuously improve their practice and better meet the needs of their students.

As technology continues to evolve and new trends emerge, the future of teacher communities and resources holds promise for fostering innovation, collaboration, and impact in education. By embracing these communities and leveraging available resources, educators can cultivate a culture of lifelong learning, collaboration, and excellence in teaching and learning.

10.3.1 Significance of Teacher Communities and Resources

Teacher communities and resources serve as invaluable assets for educators in their professional journey. These communities provide a supportive network of peers who understand the challenges and joys of teaching, offering encouragement, advice, and camaraderie. Moreover, teacher communities offer opportunities for collaboration and knowledge sharing, allowing educators to exchange ideas, strategies, and best practices to enhance their teaching practices. Additionally, teacher resources, such as lesson plans, instructional materials, and professional development opportunities, provide educators with the tools and support they need to succeed in the classroom. By leveraging teacher communities and resources, educators can access a wealth of knowledge, expertise, and support to continuously improve their practice and better meet the needs of their students.

10.3.2 Benefits of Teacher Communities and Resources

Teacher communities and resources offer numerous benefits for educators, including:

- **Professional Growth:** Teacher communities provide opportunities for educators to engage in ongoing learning, reflection, and professional development. By participating in discussions, workshops, and collaborative projects, educators can expand their knowledge, skills, and expertise in teaching and learning.
- **Collaboration:** Teacher communities facilitate collaboration and teamwork among educators, allowing them to share ideas, resources, and experiences to support each other's growth and success. Collaboration enables educators to pool their collective expertise and creativity to address common challenges and achieve common goals.
- **Support and Encouragement:** Teacher communities offer a supportive network of peers who understand the joys and challenges of teaching. Educators can seek advice, share concerns, and celebrate successes with fellow teachers, fostering a sense of belonging and well-being.
- **Access to Resources:** Teacher resources, such as lesson plans, instructional materials, and professional development opportunities, provide educators with the tools and support they need to enhance their teaching practice. These resources save educators time and effort by providing access to high-quality, vetted materials and activities.

10.3.3 Challenges in Building and Sustaining Teacher Communities

Despite the many benefits of teacher communities and resources, educators may encounter several challenges in building and sustaining these communities:

- **Time Constraints:** Educators often face time constraints due to busy schedules, administrative duties, and personal responsibilities. Finding time to participate in teacher communities and engage with resources can be challenging, especially for educators with heavy teaching loads.
- **Access and Equity:** Not all educators have equal access to teacher communities and resources, particularly those in rural or underserved areas. Limited access to technology, internet connectivity, and professional development opportunities can exacerbate disparities in access and equity.
- **Engagement and Participation:** Building active and engaged teacher communities requires fostering a culture of participation, collaboration, and inclusivity. Educators may face challenges in motivating and engaging their peers to actively participate in discussions, share resources, and contribute to community initiatives.
- **Sustainability:** Sustaining teacher communities requires ongoing effort, leadership, and support from administrators, stakeholders, and community members. Without adequate resources, funding, and institutional support, teacher communities may struggle to maintain momentum and relevance over time.

10.3.4 Strategies for Building and Sustaining Teacher Communities

To address the challenges of building and sustaining teacher communities, several strategies can be implemented:

- **Providing Professional Development:** Offering professional development opportunities that focus on building community, fostering collaboration, and leveraging resources can help educators develop the skills and knowledge they need to engage in meaningful community participation.
- **Leveraging Technology:** Utilizing technology platforms, such as online forums, social media groups, and virtual meeting spaces, can facilitate communication, collaboration, and resource sharing among educators. Technology can also help overcome barriers related to geography and accessibility.
- **Promoting Leadership and Ownership:** Empowering educators to take on leadership roles within their communities can foster a sense

of ownership and investment in community initiatives. Providing opportunities for educators to lead discussions, organize events, and facilitate professional development activities can strengthen community cohesion and engagement.

- **Fostering Inclusivity:** Creating a welcoming and inclusive environment that respects diverse perspectives, experiences, and backgrounds is essential for building strong and vibrant teacher communities. Educators should actively work to promote equity, diversity, and inclusion within their communities, ensuring that all voices are heard and valued.

10.3.5 Future Directions in Teacher Communities and Resources

Looking ahead, the future of teacher communities and resources holds promise for continued innovation, collaboration, and impact. Emerging technologies, such as artificial intelligence (AI), machine learning, and data analytics, offer new opportunities for personalized learning experiences, community engagement, and resource sharing. Moreover, the rise of global networks and partnerships enables educators to connect and collaborate with peers from around the world, expanding their perspectives and opportunities for growth. Additionally, the growing recognition of the importance of social-emotional learning (SEL) and well-being in education is driving demand for supportive and inclusive teacher communities that prioritize holistic educator development and self-care.

CHAPTER 11

OVERCOMING CHALLENGES AND CONCERNS

11.1 ADDRESSING EQUITY AND ACCESS

As game-based learning gains popularity as an effective educational tool, it's essential to address equity and access concerns to ensure that all students have equal opportunities to benefit from this approach. Equity and access in game-based learning involve providing all students, regardless of background or circumstance, with the resources, support, and opportunities needed to engage in meaningful learning experiences.

Addressing equity and access concerns in game-based learning is essential for ensuring that all students have equal opportunities to engage in meaningful learning experiences. By recognizing and addressing barriers related to technology, cost, representation, and accessibility, educators and game developers can create more inclusive and equitable learning environments. Through strategic investments in technology, resources, and professional development, schools and districts can ensure that all students have the tools, support, and opportunities they need to succeed in game-based learning. By promoting diversity, inclusion, and accessibility in educational games, educators can create more engaging and empowering learning experiences that meet the needs of all students, regardless of their background or circumstance.

11.1.1 Equity and Access in Game-Based Learning

Equity in game-based learning refers to providing all students with the resources, support, and opportunities they need to succeed, regardless of their background, socioeconomic status, or ability level. Access, on the other hand, involves ensuring that all students have the physical, technological, and instructional resources needed to participate fully in game-based learning activities. Equity and access are essential principles in education, as they help to level the playing field and address disparities in learning opportunities and outcomes.

11.1.2 Challenges and Concerns

Several challenges and concerns exist regarding equity and access in game-based learning:

- **Technological Barriers:** Not all students have access to the technology and devices needed to participate in game-based learning activities. Students from low-income families or underserved communities may lack access to computers, tablets, or high-speed internet, limiting their ability to engage in digital learning experiences.
- **Cost of Games and Software:** Some educational games and software programs come with a price tag, making them inaccessible to students from low-income families or under-resourced schools. The cost of purchasing licenses or subscriptions for game-based learning platforms can create disparities in access to quality educational resources.
- **Representation and Diversity:** Many educational games lack diversity and representation, failing to reflect the experiences, cultures, and backgrounds of all students. This lack of representation can alienate students from marginalized communities and perpetuate stereotypes and biases in educational settings.
- **Learning Disabilities and Special Needs:** Students with learning disabilities or special needs may face barriers to participation in game-based learning activities. Some games may not be designed with accessibility features or accommodations for students with disabilities, making it challenging for these students to engage fully in the learning experience.

11.1.3 Strategies for Overcoming Challenges

To address equity and access concerns in game-based learning, several strategies can be implemented:

- **Providing Technology and Devices:** Schools and districts can provide students with access to technology and devices needed for game-based learning activities. This may involve distributing laptops, tablets, or internet hotspots to students who lack access to these resources at home.
- **Investing in Open-Source and Free Resources:** Educators can explore open-source and free educational games and software programs that are accessible to all students, regardless of their socioeconomic status. By leveraging free resources, educators can ensure that all students have equal opportunities to engage in game-based learning activities.

- **Promoting Diversity and Inclusion:** Educators and game developers can work to promote diversity and inclusion in educational games by creating games that represent a variety of cultures, backgrounds, and perspectives. By incorporating diverse characters, settings, and storylines, games can become more inclusive and engaging for all students.
- **Providing Professional Development:** Educators can receive professional development and training on how to integrate accessibility features and accommodations into game-based learning activities. By learning how to modify games and instructional materials to meet the needs of students with disabilities, educators can ensure that all students can participate fully in the learning experience.

11.2 DEALING WITH TECHNOLOGY ISSUES

Game-based learning offers exciting opportunities to engage students in immersive and interactive educational experiences. However, like any technology-driven approach, game-based learning comes with its own set of challenges and concerns, particularly related to technical issues.

Technology issues can pose significant challenges in game-based learning environments, impacting student engagement, learning outcomes, and overall effectiveness. However, by implementing proactive strategies for addressing these issues, educators can minimize disruptions and create a more seamless and productive learning experience for students. Through technical support, preparation, training, collaboration, and feedback, educators can overcome technology challenges and unlock the full potential of game-based learning to enhance student learning and achievement.

11.2.1 Technology Issues in Game-Based Learning

Technology issues in game-based learning encompass a wide range of challenges that can disrupt the learning process and hinder student engagement. These issues may arise from hardware malfunctions, software glitches, network connectivity issues, or compatibility problems. Common technology issues include:

- **Hardware Malfunctions:** Problems with computers, tablets, or gaming consoles, such as crashes, freezes, or hardware failures, can disrupt gameplay and impede learning progress.
- **Software Glitches:** Bugs, errors, or glitches within the game software itself can cause gameplay to be unstable or inconsistent, leading to frustration and disengagement among students.

- **Network Connectivity Problems:** Poor internet connectivity or network issues can prevent students from accessing online games or multiplayer features, limiting their ability to participate fully in game-based learning activities.
- **Compatibility Issues:** Compatibility issues between different devices, operating systems, or software versions can result in games not running properly or displaying incorrectly, creating barriers to participation for students.

11.2.2 Strategies for Overcoming Technology Issues

To address technology issues in game-based learning, educators can implement several strategies to minimize disruptions and ensure a smooth learning experience:

- **Technical Support and Troubleshooting:** Provide students with access to technical support resources, such as help desks, troubleshooting guides, or online forums, where they can seek assistance in resolving hardware or software issues independently.
- **Preparation and Testing:** Before implementing game-based learning activities in the classroom, thoroughly test the technology infrastructure, including hardware, software, and network connectivity, to identify and address any potential issues proactively.
- **Backup Plans and Alternatives:** Develop backup plans and alternative activities in case of technical difficulties or disruptions, allowing for seamless transitions between different learning modalities to minimize disruptions to the learning process.
- **Regular Maintenance and Updates:** Ensure that hardware and software systems are regularly maintained, updated, and patched to address security vulnerabilities, optimize performance, and prevent compatibility issues that could impact gameplay.
- **Student Training and Orientation:** Provide students with training and orientation sessions on how to use the technology tools and platforms required for game-based learning activities, including instructions on troubleshooting common issues and accessing technical support resources.
- **Flexible Learning Environments:** Design flexible learning environments that accommodate different devices, operating systems, and software platforms, allowing students to access game-based learning activities using their preferred devices or tools.

- **Collaboration with IT Professionals:** Collaborate with IT professionals or technology specialists to address complex technical issues, leverage expertise, and implement best practices for technology integration in game-based learning environments.
- **Feedback and Continuous Improvement:** Solicit feedback from students and educators on their experiences with game-based learning technology, including any technical issues encountered, and use this feedback to inform continuous improvement efforts and future planning.

11.3 GAMEFICATION ETHICS AND CONCERNS

As game-based learning continues to gain traction in educational settings, it brings to light various ethical considerations and concerns. Gamification, while offering innovative and engaging learning experiences, also raises questions about equity, privacy, and ethical use of data.

Gamification in education holds great potential for engaging students, enhancing motivation, and promoting learning outcomes. However, it also raises important ethical considerations and concerns that must be addressed to ensure responsible and equitable implementation.

By designing gamified learning experiences with equity, privacy, transparency, and inclusivity in mind, educators and developers can create positive and impactful learning environments that prioritize students' well-being, autonomy, and success. Through collaboration, professional development, and ethical reflection, stakeholders can navigate the complexities of gamification ethics and build a future where gamified learning experiences empower all students to thrive and succeed.

11.3.1 Gamification Ethics

Gamification ethics encompasses principles and guidelines for the responsible design, implementation, and use of gamified learning experiences. Key ethical concerns in gamification include:

- **Equity and Access:** Ensuring that all students, regardless of background or circumstance, have equal opportunities to participate in and benefit from gamified learning experiences.
- **Privacy and Data Security:** Protecting students' privacy and personal data from unauthorized access, use, or disclosure and ensuring compliance with relevant privacy laws and regulations.
- **Fairness and Transparency:** Designing gamified systems and mechanics that are fair, transparent, and free from bias or discrimination, and

providing clear explanations of how points, rewards, and progression systems work.

- **Inclusivity and Representation:** Promoting diversity, inclusivity, and representation in game content, characters, and narratives to reflect the experiences and identities of all students.
- **Engagement and Motivation:** Balancing the use of gamification techniques to enhance student engagement and motivation with considerations for intrinsic motivation, autonomy, and well-being.

11.3.2 Ethical Concerns in Gamification

Several ethical concerns arise in the context of gamification in education:

- **Inequitable Access:** Gamified learning experiences may exacerbate existing disparities in access to technology, resources, and support, creating barriers for students from underserved or marginalized communities.
- **Data Privacy and Security:** Collecting and storing student data in gamified systems raises concerns about privacy, security, and the potential misuse or unauthorized access to sensitive information.
- **Manipulative Design:** Gamification techniques, such as points, badges, and leaderboards, may inadvertently promote extrinsic motivation and reward-driven behavior, undermining intrinsic motivation and genuine interest in learning.
- **Bias and Stereotypes:** Gamified content and narratives may perpetuate stereotypes, biases, and cultural representations that marginalize or exclude certain groups of students.
- **Commercialization and Monetization:** Some gamified learning platforms may prioritize profit motives over educational goals, leading to commercialization, advertising, or monetization strategies that exploit students' attention and data.

11.3.3 Strategies for Addressing Ethical Concerns

To address ethical concerns in gamification, educators and developers can implement several strategies:

- **Equitable Design and Access:** Design gamified learning experiences with equity and accessibility in mind, ensuring that all students have equal opportunities to participate and succeed, regardless of their background or circumstance.

- **Privacy by Design:** Embed privacy protections into the design and development of gamified systems, including data encryption, anonymization, and user consent mechanisms, to safeguard student privacy and data security.
- **Transparency and Consent:** Provide clear explanations of how gamified systems work, including the collection, use, and sharing of student data, and obtain informed consent from students and parents for participation in gamified activities.
- **Inclusive Content and Representation:** Incorporate diverse perspectives, cultures, and identities into gamified content and narratives to promote inclusivity, representation, and cultural sensitivity.
- **Balanced Motivation and Engagement:** Strike a balance between extrinsic rewards and intrinsic motivation in gamified learning experiences, fostering genuine interest, autonomy, and mastery in students' learning journeys.
- **Educational Value and Assessment:** Ensure that gamified activities are aligned with educational goals, standards, and curriculum requirements and use valid and reliable assessment methods to measure learning outcomes and progress.
- **Professional Development and Training:** Provide educators with training and support on ethical considerations in gamification, including best practices for designing, implementing, and evaluating gamified learning experiences.

PART-V

FUTURE DIRECTION AND INNOVATIONS

CHAPTER 12

EMERGING TRENDS AND TECHNOLOGIES

12.1 VIRTUAL REALITY AND AUGMENTED REALITY IN EDUCATION

Virtual Reality (VR) and Augmented Reality (AR) are immersive technologies that hold tremendous promise for revolutionizing education. By providing immersive and interactive learning experiences, VR and AR have the potential to engage students, enhance comprehension, and foster deeper learning across various subjects and disciplines.

Virtual Reality and Augmented Reality offer transformative opportunities to enhance teaching and learning experiences in education. By providing immersive, interactive, and engaging learning experiences, VR and AR have the potential to engage students, deepen understanding, and foster collaboration and creativity. However, challenges such as cost, accessibility, technical complexity, and ethical considerations must be addressed to ensure responsible and equitable implementation.

Through continued research, innovation, and collaboration, VR and AR have the potential to revolutionize education and empower learners to thrive in a rapidly changing world.

12.1.1 Virtual Reality and Augmented Reality

- **Virtual Reality (VR):** VR refers to a simulated environment that immerses users in a completely digital or computer-generated environment, typically through the use of headsets or goggles. In VR environments, users can interact with virtual objects, explore virtual spaces, and engage in simulated activities in a highly immersive and interactive manner.
- **Augmented Reality (AR):** AR overlays digital information, such as images, videos, or 3D models, onto the real-world environment, typically through the use of smartphones, tablets, or AR glasses. AR enhances the real-world environment with additional digital content, allowing users to interact with virtual objects or information in a contextualized and spatially-aware manner.

12.1.2 Applications of VR and AR in Education

- **Immersive Learning Experiences:** VR and AR offer immersive and interactive learning experiences that engage students' senses and promote active learning. Students can explore virtual environments, manipulate virtual objects, and interact with digital content in ways that are not possible in traditional classroom settings.
- **Virtual Field Trips:** VR allows students to embark on virtual field trips to distant locations, historical landmarks, or inaccessible environments, providing them with firsthand experiences and opportunities for exploration and discovery.
- **Simulation-Based Learning:** VR and AR simulations enable students to engage in hands-on learning experiences, such as scientific experiments, medical procedures, or engineering simulations, in a safe and controlled environment.
- **Visualizations and 3D Modeling:** AR enables students to visualize complex concepts, such as anatomical structures, geological formations, or architectural designs, in three-dimensional space, enhancing comprehension and spatial reasoning skills.
- **Interactive Storytelling:** VR and AR can be used to create immersive storytelling experiences that transport students to fictional worlds, historical events, or narrative-driven scenarios, fostering empathy, creativity, and critical thinking.

12.1.3 Benefits of VR and AR in Education

- **Engagement and Motivation:** VR and AR captivate students' attention and spark curiosity by providing immersive and interactive learning experiences that are inherently engaging and enjoyable.
- **Experiential Learning:** VR and AR enable students to engage in experiential learning activities that simulate real-world contexts and situations, allowing for hands-on exploration, experimentation, and problem-solving.
- **Personalized Learning:** VR and AR can be customized to accommodate students' individual learning styles, preferences, and needs, providing personalized and adaptive learning experiences that cater to diverse learners.
- **Enhanced Comprehension:** VR and AR facilitate deeper understanding and comprehension of complex concepts by providing visual, spatial, and interactive representations that reinforce learning and memory retention.

- **Collaborative Learning:** VR and AR support collaborative learning experiences by allowing students to interact with virtual objects and environments together, fostering teamwork, communication, and collaboration skills.

12.1.4 Challenges and Considerations

- **Cost and Accessibility:** VR and AR technologies can be expensive to acquire and implement, posing challenges for schools and educators with limited resources. Additionally, access to VR and AR devices may be unevenly distributed, leading to disparities in access and opportunities for students.
- **Technical Complexity:** Implementing VR and AR in educational settings requires technical expertise, infrastructure, and support, including hardware setup, software integration, and troubleshooting capabilities.
- **Content Creation:** Developing high-quality VR and AR content requires specialized skills and resources, including 3D modeling, programming, and instructional design expertise, which may be lacking in educational settings.
- **Safety and Ethical Concerns:** VR and AR raise ethical considerations related to privacy, data security, and digital citizenship, particularly when collecting and storing student data or exposing students to potentially sensitive or controversial content.
- **Health and Well-being:** Prolonged use of VR and AR devices may lead to issues such as eye strain, motion sickness, and fatigue, necessitating careful consideration of usage guidelines and best practices for mitigating health risks.

12.1.5 Future Directions and Opportunities

- **Advancements in Technology:** Continued advancements in VR and AR technologies, including improvements in hardware capabilities, software development tools, and content creation platforms, will drive innovation and expansion in educational applications.
- **Integration with Artificial Intelligence:** Integration of VR and AR with artificial intelligence (AI) technologies, such as natural language processing and machine learning, will enable personalized and adaptive learning experiences that respond to students' individual needs and preferences.
- **Expanded Access and Equity:** Efforts to reduce costs, improve accessibility, and broaden distribution channels for VR and AR devices

will expand access and opportunities for students from diverse backgrounds and underserved communities.

- **Research and Evaluation:** Continued research and evaluation of VR and AR applications in education will generate empirical evidence of their effectiveness and impact on student learning outcomes, informing best practices and guiding future development efforts.
- **Global Collaboration and Partnerships:** Collaboration and partnerships between educators, developers, researchers, and policymakers will drive innovation, knowledge sharing, and capacity building in the field of VR and AR in education, fostering a global community of practice and advancing the collective understanding of their potential and limitations.

12.2 GAMIFIEID LEARNING ENVIRONMENTS

Gamified learning environments have emerged as a powerful educational tool, leveraging game elements and mechanics to create engaging and interactive learning experiences. By integrating elements such as points, badges, leaderboards, and challenges into educational activities, gamified learning environments aim to motivate students, promote learning, and foster a sense of achievement.

Gamified learning environments offer a promising approach to engaging students, enhancing motivation, and promoting learning outcomes in education. By leveraging game elements and mechanics to create immersive, interactive, and rewarding learning experiences, gamified environments empower students to take ownership of their learning and develop essential skills for success in the digital age.

Gamified learning environments are educational settings or platforms that incorporate game elements, mechanics, and principles to engage students in learning activities. Unlike traditional classrooms, which often rely on passive instruction and rote memorization, gamified learning environments emphasize active participation, exploration, and problem-solving. By tapping into the motivational power of games, gamified learning environments aim to increase student engagement, promote intrinsic motivation, and enhance learning outcomes.

12.2.1 Elements of Gamified Learning Environments

- **Points:** Points are a common game element used in gamified learning environments to track students' progress, accomplishments, and contributions. Points are awarded for completing tasks, answering questions correctly, or achieving specific milestones, providing students with immediate feedback and reinforcement.

- **Badges:** Badges are visual symbols or icons awarded to students for mastering skills, demonstrating proficiency, or reaching predetermined goals. Badges serve as tangible representations of achievement and progress, motivating students to strive for excellence and recognition.
- **Leaderboards:** Leaderboards display rankings of students based on their performance, scores, or achievements within a gamified learning environment. Leaderboards promote competition, social comparison, and goal setting, encouraging students to excel and outperform their peers.
- **Challenges and Quests:** Challenges and quests are structured tasks or activities designed to engage students in problem-solving, critical thinking, and creativity. Challenges may involve solving puzzles, completing missions, or overcoming obstacles, providing students with opportunities to apply knowledge and skills in authentic and meaningful contexts.

12.2.2 Benefits of Gamified Learning Environments

- **Increased Engagement:** Gamified learning environments capture students' attention and interest by making learning fun, interactive, and rewarding. By incorporating game elements such as points, badges, and leaderboards, gamified environments motivate students to actively participate and stay engaged in learning activities.
- **Enhanced Motivation:** Gamified learning environments leverage intrinsic and extrinsic motivators to encourage students to set goals, overcome challenges, and persist in their learning efforts. By providing clear objectives, feedback, and rewards, gamified environments foster a sense of achievement and progress, motivating students to invest time and effort in their learning.
- **Improved Learning Outcomes:** Research has shown that gamified learning environments can lead to improved learning outcomes, including increased knowledge retention, comprehension, and skill acquisition. By promoting active learning, problem-solving, and collaboration, gamified environments help students develop critical thinking, creativity, and communication skills essential for success in the 21st century.
- **Promotion of Collaboration:** Gamified learning environments foster collaboration and teamwork among students through features such as leaderboards, challenges, and cooperative quests. By working together to achieve common goals, students learn to communicate effectively, share ideas, and support each other's learning.

12.2.3 Challenges and Considerations

- **Design Complexity:** Designing effective gamified learning environments requires careful consideration of instructional goals, learner characteristics, and game mechanics. Balancing game elements with educational content and pedagogical principles can be challenging, requiring collaboration between educators, instructional designers, and game developers.
- **Equity and Access:** Ensuring equitable access to gamified learning environments for all students, regardless of socioeconomic status or technological resources, is a key challenge. Schools and educators must address issues such as access to technology, internet connectivity, and digital literacy to prevent disparities in learning opportunities.
- **Overemphasis on Rewards:** Overreliance on extrinsic rewards such as points and badges can undermine intrinsic motivation and genuine interest in learning. Educators must strike a balance between providing meaningful feedback and incentives and avoiding the gamification of learning for its own sake.
- **Privacy and Data Security:** Collecting and storing student data in gamified learning environments raises concerns about privacy, security, and the ethical use of data. Schools and educators must adhere to relevant laws and regulations, such as the Family Educational Rights and Privacy Act (FERPA), and implement safeguards to protect students' personal information.

12.2.4 Design Principles for Gamified Learning Environments

- **Clear Objectives and Feedback:** Clearly communicate learning objectives, expectations, and criteria for success to students, providing regular feedback and reinforcement to guide their progress and performance.
- **Choice and Autonomy:** Empower students to make choices and decisions within the gamified learning environment, allowing them to customize their learning experience and pursue topics of interest or relevance to their goals.
- **Challenge and Mastery:** Design challenging and scaffolded learning activities that gradually increase in complexity and difficulty, promoting a sense of mastery, competence, and achievement.
- **Social Interaction and Collaboration:** Foster social interaction and collaboration among students through cooperative challenges, group projects, and peer feedback mechanisms, promoting a sense of belonging and community within the learning environment.

12.2.5 Future Directions in Gamified Learning Environments

- **Personalization and Adaptivity:** Advances in artificial intelligence (AI) and machine learning (ML) technologies enable the development of personalized and adaptive gamified learning environments that tailor content, challenges, and feedback to individual students' needs, preferences, and learning styles.
- **Integration with Emerging Technologies:** Integration of gamified learning environments with emerging technologies such as virtual reality (VR), augmented reality (AR), and mixed reality (MR) holds promise for creating immersive and interactive learning experiences that transcend traditional boundaries of time and space.
- **Global Collaboration and Knowledge Sharing:** Collaboration between educators, researchers, and developers from around the world fosters knowledge sharing, innovation, and best practices in the design, implementation, and evaluation of gamified learning environments.
- **Ethical and Responsible Design:** Continued emphasis on ethical and responsible design principles ensures that gamified learning environments prioritize student well-being, equity, and inclusivity, while respecting privacy, data security, and ethical considerations.

12.3 GANIFICATION FOR SOFT SKILLS DEVELOPMENT

In today's rapidly changing world, success depends not only on academic knowledge but also on soft skills such as communication, collaboration, critical thinking, and adaptability. Gamification offers a promising approach to developing these essential skills by engaging learners in interactive and immersive experiences that simulate real-world scenarios.

Gamification offers a promising approach to developing essential soft skills such as communication, collaboration, critical thinking, creativity, and adaptability in learners of all ages. By incorporating game elements, mechanics, and principles into learning experiences, gamification engages learners, fosters motivation, and promotes active and experiential learning. While challenges such as design complexity, equity, and ethical considerations must be addressed, the future of gamification for soft skills development holds great potential for empowering learners to thrive in a rapidly changing world.

Soft skills, also known as interpersonal skills or transferable skills, refer to a set of personal attributes and abilities that enable individuals to interact effectively with others, navigate complex situations, and succeed in diverse environments. Key soft skills include:

- **Communication:** The ability to express ideas, thoughts, and feelings effectively through verbal, nonverbal, and written channels, and to listen actively and empathetically to others.
- **Collaboration:** The capacity to work cooperatively with others towards shared goals, contribute ideas, perspectives, and expertise, and resolve conflicts constructively.
- **Critical Thinking:** The skill of analyzing information, evaluating arguments, and making reasoned judgments or decisions based on evidence, logic, and reasoning.
- **Creativity:** The ability to generate novel ideas, solutions, or approaches, think outside the box, and adapt to new or challenging situations with imagination and ingenuity.
- **Adaptability:** The capacity to respond flexibly to changes, setbacks, or unexpected circumstances, and to learn from experiences, embrace uncertainty, and adjust course as needed.

12.3.1 Benefits of Gamification for Soft Skills Development

- **Engagement and Motivation:** Gamification makes learning enjoyable and rewarding by incorporating game elements such as points, badges, leaderboards, and challenges, motivating learners to actively participate and persevere in their efforts.
- **Contextualized Learning:** Gamification provides learners with opportunities to practice and apply soft skills in authentic and meaningful contexts, such as simulations, role-plays, or interactive scenarios, which enhances relevance and retention.
- **Immediate Feedback and Reflection:** Gamification offers immediate feedback and reflection opportunities, allowing learners to receive real-time feedback on their actions, decisions, and performance, and to reflect on their strengths, areas for improvement, and growth.
- **Collaborative Learning Experiences:** Gamification promotes collaboration and teamwork among learners through features such as cooperative challenges, group quests, and peer feedback mechanisms, fostering communication, cooperation, and shared learning.
- **Risk-Free Environment:** Gamification creates a safe and supportive environment for learners to take risks, make mistakes, and experiment with different approaches or strategies without fear of failure or negative consequences, which encourages exploration and innovation.

12.3.2 Challenges and Considerations

- **Design Complexity:** Designing effective gamified experiences for soft skills development requires careful consideration of learning objectives, audience needs, game mechanics, and assessment criteria, which can be challenging for educators and instructional designers.
- **Overemphasis on Competition:** Overreliance on competitive game elements such as leaderboards or rankings may foster unhealthy competition, anxiety, or disengagement among learners, particularly those who are less competitive or introverted.
- **Equity and Access:** Ensuring equitable access to gamified learning experiences for all learners, regardless of socioeconomic status, technological resources, or cultural backgrounds, poses challenges in terms of accessibility, inclusivity, and digital divide.
- **Integration with Curriculum:** Integrating gamification into existing curriculum and instructional practices requires alignment with educational standards, learning objectives, and assessment methods, as well as collaboration with educators and administrators.
- **Ethical and Responsible Design:** Ethical considerations related to privacy, data security, and student well-being must be addressed in the design and implementation of gamified experiences, including informed consent, data protection, and respectful representation.

12.3.3 Strategies for Effective Gamification for Soft Skills Development

- **Clear Learning Objectives:** Clearly define learning objectives, outcomes, and expectations for soft skills development, and align gamified experiences with curriculum standards, instructional goals, and assessment criteria.
- **Meaningful Game Mechanics:** Select game elements and mechanics that are meaningful, relevant, and supportive of soft skills development, such as collaboration, communication, problem-solving, and reflection.
- **Scaffolded Challenges:** Design scaffolded challenges and quests that gradually increase in complexity and difficulty, providing learners with opportunities to build and apply soft skills in incremental steps.
- **Choice and Autonomy:** Empower learners to make choices and decisions within gamified experiences, allowing for autonomy, self-direction, and personalization of learning pathways and strategies.
- **Feedback and Reflection:** Incorporate feedback mechanisms and reflection prompts into gamified experiences to provide learners with

opportunities for self-assessment, peer feedback, and metacognitive reflection on their progress and growth.

12.3.4 Future Directions in Gamification for Soft Skills Development

- **Personalized Learning Experiences:** Advances in artificial intelligence (AI) and machine learning (ML) enable the development of personalized and adaptive gamified experiences that tailor content, challenges, and feedback to individual learners' needs, preferences, and learning styles.
- **Virtual and Augmented Reality:** Integration of virtual reality (VR) and augmented reality (AR) technologies into gamified learning experiences offers opportunities for immersive and interactive simulations that enhance engagement, presence, and authenticity.
- **Global Collaboration and Knowledge Sharing:** Collaboration between educators, researchers, and developers from around the world fosters knowledge sharing, innovation, and best practices in the design, implementation, and evaluation of gamified experiences for soft skills development.
- **Ethical and Responsible Design:** Continued emphasis on ethical and responsible design principles ensures that gamified experiences prioritize learner well-being, equity, and inclusivity, while respecting privacy, data security, and ethical considerations.

CHAPTER 13

RESEARCH AND EVALUATION IN GAME-BASED LEARNING

13.1 RESEARCH FINDINGS AND IMPACT

Game-based learning has gained significant attention in educational research as a promising approach to engage students, enhance motivation, and improve learning outcomes. Over the years, numerous studies have investigated the effectiveness of game-based learning across various subjects, grade levels, and learning environments. In this exploration, we delve into key research findings and the impact of game-based learning on student engagement, learning outcomes, and educational practices.

- **Defining Game-Based Learning:** Game-based learning refers to the use of games, simulations, and interactive digital media to facilitate learning and instruction. Games can range from simple quiz-based applications to complex immersive simulations, and they can be designed for various educational purposes, including content delivery, skill development, and assessment.
- **Research Methods:** Research on game-based learning employs a variety of quantitative and qualitative methods, including experimental studies, surveys, interviews, case studies, and classroom observations. Researchers examine factors such as game design, engagement, motivation, learning outcomes, and transfer of learning to real-world contexts.

13.1.1 Impact of Game-Based Learning

- **Enhanced Engagement:** One of the key benefits of game-based learning is its ability to engage students in learning activities. Games provide interactive, immersive, and enjoyable experiences that capture students' attention and maintain their interest over time, leading to increased motivation and participation.
- **Improved Learning Outcomes:** Research suggests that game-based learning can lead to improved learning outcomes compared to

traditional instructional methods. Games promote active learning, problem-solving, critical thinking, and collaboration, which are associated with deeper understanding and retention of content.

- **Transfer of Learning:** Game-based learning has been found to promote the transfer of learning from virtual environments to real-world contexts. Skills and knowledge acquired through games can be applied to practical situations, tasks, and challenges, demonstrating the potential for long-term impact on students' academic and professional success.
- **Addressing Diverse Learning Needs:** Games can be tailored to accommodate diverse learning needs, preferences, and abilities. They provide opportunities for differentiated instruction, scaffolding, and individualized feedback, allowing students to learn at their own pace and level of proficiency.
- **Promoting 21st-Century Skills:** Game-based learning fosters the development of 21st-century skills such as communication, collaboration, creativity, and digital literacy. Games often require students to work together, communicate effectively, think critically, and adapt to changing circumstances, preparing them for success in the digital age.

13.1.2 Key Research Findings

- **Positive Effects on Academic Achievement:** Numerous studies have found positive effects of game-based learning on academic achievement, including increased test scores, grades, and subject mastery. Games that incorporate educational content in engaging and interactive ways have been particularly effective in improving learning outcomes.
- **Motivational Benefits:** Research consistently shows that game-based learning enhances student motivation and engagement. Games provide immediate feedback, clear goals, and rewards for progress, which motivate students to persist in their learning efforts and overcome challenges.
- **Retention and Transfer:** Game-based learning has been shown to improve retention and transfer of knowledge and skills. Games that include spaced repetition, retrieval practice, and real-world application of learning content facilitate deeper understanding and longer-term retention of information.
- **Inclusive Learning Environments:** Games can create inclusive learning environments that accommodate diverse learners, including students with disabilities, English language learners, and those from

underserved communities. Accessible design features, multiple modes of representation, and flexible learning pathways promote equitable participation and learning outcomes.

- **Positive Student Perceptions:** Research indicates that students have positive attitudes towards game-based learning and perceive it as enjoyable, challenging, and effective for learning. Games provide opportunities for autonomy, mastery, and social interaction, which contribute to positive learning experiences and attitudes towards learning.

13.1.3 Implications for Educational Practice

- **Integration into Curriculum:** Educators can integrate game-based learning into curriculum and instruction to enhance engagement, motivation, and learning outcomes. Games can be used as supplementary resources, enrichment activities, or formative assessment tools to support and reinforce instructional objectives.
- **Professional Development:** Educators may benefit from professional development opportunities to enhance their knowledge and skills in game-based learning pedagogy, design, and implementation. Training workshops, online courses, and collaborative learning communities can provide educators with the tools and support they need to effectively integrate games into their teaching practices.
- **Research-Informed Design:** Game developers and instructional designers can draw on research findings and best practices to inform the design and development of educational games. Incorporating evidence-based strategies, feedback mechanisms, and assessment tools can enhance the effectiveness and impact of game-based learning experiences.
- **Collaboration and Partnerships:** Collaboration between researchers, educators, game developers, and policymakers can facilitate knowledge sharing, innovation, and scale-up of game-based learning initiatives. Partnerships with industry, academia, and government agencies can support the development and dissemination of high-quality games and resources for educational purposes.

13.1.4 Future Directions in Game-Based Learning Research

- **Emerging Technologies:** Advances in virtual reality (VR), augmented reality (AR), and artificial intelligence (AI) offer new opportunities for research and development in game-based learning. Studies exploring the impact of immersive and adaptive technologies on student engagement, learning outcomes, and transfer of learning are needed to inform future practice and policy.

- **Contextual Factors:** Research on the contextual factors that influence the effectiveness of game-based learning, such as student demographics, school culture, and instructional support, can inform the design and implementation of tailored interventions for diverse populations and settings.
- **Meta-Analyses and Syntheses:** Meta-analyses and systematic reviews of existing research can synthesize findings across studies, identify trends, and determine the overall effectiveness of game-based learning interventions. Meta-analytic techniques can provide robust evidence to guide policy decisions and educational practices.

13.2 DESIGNING EFFECTIVE RESEARCH STUDIES

Conducting rigorous research studies in game-based learning is crucial for understanding its effectiveness, identifying best practices, and informing educational practice and policy. Designing effective research studies requires careful consideration of research questions, methodologies, variables, and ethical considerations.

13.2.1 Identifying Research Questions

- **Clear and Specific Objectives:** Research questions in game-based learning should be clear, specific, and aligned with the goals of the study. They should address relevant aspects of game design, learning outcomes, student engagement, or instructional practices.
- **Theoretical Framework:** Research questions should be grounded in theoretical frameworks from educational psychology, cognitive science, or game design theory. They should aim to test hypotheses, explore relationships, or generate new knowledge within the context of existing theoretical perspectives.

13.2.2 Choosing Experimental Designs

- **Experimental vs. Quasi-Experimental Designs:** Researchers can use experimental designs, such as randomized controlled trials (RCTs), or quasi-experimental designs, such as pretest-posttest designs, depending on the research question and practical constraints. RCTs offer stronger causal inference, while quasi-experimental designs may be more feasible in educational settings.
- **Controlled Variables:** Effective experimental designs control for extraneous variables that may confound the results, such as student demographics, prior knowledge, or instructional conditions. Random assignment, matching, or statistical techniques can help minimize the influence of confounding variables.

13.2.3 Selecting Data Collection Methods

- **Quantitative Data:** Quantitative data collection methods, such as surveys, assessments, or behavioral observations, provide numerical data that can be analyzed statistically to test hypotheses and measure effects. Standardized instruments, such as achievement tests or engagement scales, can ensure reliability and validity of measurements.
- **Qualitative Data:** Qualitative data collection methods, such as interviews, focus groups, or observations, offer insights into participants' experiences, perceptions, and attitudes towards game-based learning. Open-ended questions, probing techniques, and thematic analysis can capture rich and nuanced data for deeper understanding.

13.2.4 Ethical Considerations

- **Informed Consent:** Researchers must obtain informed consent from participants, including students, parents, and educators, prior to their involvement in the study. Informed consent forms should clearly outline the purpose, procedures, risks, and benefits of participation, and ensure voluntary participation and confidentiality.
- **Privacy and Confidentiality:** Researchers should protect the privacy and confidentiality of participants' data, including personal information, responses, and performance data. Data should be anonymized, encrypted, and stored securely to prevent unauthorized access or disclosure.
- **Beneficence and Non-maleficence:** Researchers should prioritize the well-being and safety of participants, ensuring that research procedures do not cause harm or distress. Risks should be minimized, and appropriate safeguards should be in place to mitigate potential harms, such as adverse effects on learning or emotional well-being.
- **Respect for Diversity and Inclusion:** Researchers should respect diversity and inclusion in participant recruitment, data collection, and interpretation of findings. They should ensure equitable representation of diverse populations, including students from different backgrounds, cultures, and abilities.

13.2.5 Analyzing and Interpreting Results

- **Quantitative Analysis:** Quantitative data analysis involves statistical techniques, such as t-tests, ANOVA, or regression analysis, to examine relationships, differences, or trends in the data. Effect sizes, confidence intervals, and significance levels can help interpret the strength and significance of findings.

- **Qualitative Analysis:** Qualitative data analysis involves coding, categorizing, and interpreting textual or visual data to identify themes, patterns, or insights. Techniques such as thematic analysis, content analysis, or grounded theory can help uncover meanings, perspectives, and experiences embedded in the data.

13.2.6 Reporting and Disseminating Findings

- **Clear and Transparent Reporting:** Researchers should report their findings accurately, transparently, and comprehensively in research papers, conference presentations, or publications. They should provide detailed descriptions of methods, procedures, results, and interpretations, along with limitations and implications for practice.
- **Open Access and Sharing:** Researchers should promote open access to research findings and data, making them available to the broader academic community, educators, policymakers, and the public. Open access journals, repositories, and platforms facilitate dissemination, replication, and collaboration in the field of game-based learning.

13.2.7 Future Directions in Research

- **Longitudinal Studies:** Longitudinal research designs can provide insights into the long-term effects and sustainability of game-based learning interventions. Studies tracking students' academic achievement, career pathways, and lifelong learning habits can shed light on the lasting impact of games on educational outcomes and success.
- **Mixed-Methods Research:** Combining quantitative and qualitative approaches in mixed-methods research can provide a comprehensive understanding of the complex relationships and mechanisms underlying game-based learning. Integration of multiple sources of data and perspectives enriches the validity and reliability of findings.
- **Replication Studies:** Replication studies can validate and extend existing research findings, ensuring their generalizability and robustness across different contexts, populations, and methodologies. Replication efforts contribute to the cumulative knowledge base in game-based learning and promote transparency and accountability in research practices.

13.3 ADVANCING THE FIELD OF GAME-BASED LEARNING

As game-based learning continues to evolve, educators, researchers, and developers are exploring new frontiers to advance the field and maximize its potential for educational impact. From emerging technologies to interdisciplinary collaborations, various avenues are shaping the future of game-based learning.

Advancing the field of game-based learning requires a multifaceted approach that leverages emerging technologies, promotes inclusive design, fosters interdisciplinary collaboration, supports educator professional development, advocates for policy and funding support, and engages stakeholders and communities. By embracing innovation, collaboration, and evidence-based practice, the field of game-based learning can continue to evolve and thrive, driving positive educational outcomes and opportunities for learners around the world.

13.3.1 Leveraging Emerging Technologies

Virtual Reality (VR) and Augmented Reality (AR)

Virtual reality (VR) and augmented reality (AR) technologies offer immersive and interactive experiences that enhance engagement and learning outcomes. By creating virtual environments and overlays that simulate real-world contexts, VR and AR games provide opportunities for experiential learning and exploration across diverse subjects and disciplines.

Artificial Intelligence (AI) and Adaptive Learning

Artificial intelligence (AI) and adaptive learning technologies personalize and optimize game-based learning experiences based on individual learner needs, preferences, and performance data. AI algorithms analyze learner interactions, assess proficiency levels, and adapt game content and challenges in real-time, ensuring tailored and responsive instruction.

13.3.2 Promoting Inclusive and Accessible Design

Universal Design for Learning (UDL)

Universal design for learning (UDL) principles guide the development of game-based learning experiences that accommodate diverse learners, including students with disabilities, English language learners, and those with varying learning styles or preferences. UDL emphasizes multiple means of representation, engagement, and expression to ensure equitable access and participation for all students.

Accessible Design Features

Incorporating accessible design features, such as adjustable difficulty levels, alternative input methods, and customizable interfaces, enhances the usability and inclusivity of game-based learning experiences. Accessible design practices ensure that games are playable and beneficial for learners with diverse needs and abilities.

13.3.3 Fostering Interdisciplinary Collaboration

Educator-Developer Partnerships

Collaboration between educators, researchers, and game developers fosters the co-design and implementation of game-based learning experiences that align with educational goals and pedagogical practices. Educator-developer partnerships leverage expertise from both domains to create innovative and effective learning solutions.

Cross-Disciplinary Research

Interdisciplinary research initiatives bring together experts from fields such as education, psychology, computer science, and game design to investigate complex phenomena and address pressing challenges in game-based learning. Cross-disciplinary collaborations enrich the theoretical frameworks, methodologies, and practical applications of game-based learning research.

13.3.4 Supporting Educator Professional Development

Training and Resources

Providing educators with training, resources, and support for integrating game-based learning into their teaching practice enhances their confidence, competence, and effectiveness in using games for instruction. Professional development opportunities include workshops, courses, communities of practice, and online repositories of educational games and materials.

Research-Informed Practices

Promoting research-informed practices in game-based learning empowers educators to make evidence-based decisions about game selection, implementation strategies, and assessment methods. Access to research findings, best practices, and case studies informs educators' pedagogical approaches and instructional design choices.

13.3.5 Advocating for Policy and Funding Support

Policy Advocacy

Advocating for policies that support the integration of game-based learning in educational settings promotes awareness, adoption, and investment in game-based learning initiatives. Policy efforts may include curriculum standards, funding incentives, professional development mandates, and research priorities related to game-based learning.

Funding Opportunities

Securing funding support for game-based learning research, development, and implementation initiatives accelerates innovation and scalability in the field. Public and private funding sources, such as government grants, philanthropic organizations, and industry partnerships, provide resources for research projects, pilot programs, and infrastructure investments.

13.3.6 Engaging Stakeholders and Communities

Student Involvement

Engaging students as co-designers, testers, and advocates for game-based learning promotes student agency, ownership, and enthusiasm for learning. Students' input and feedback inform the development and improvement of educational games, ensuring relevance, authenticity, and engagement.

Parent and Community Engagement

Involving parents and community members in discussions about game-based learning fosters understanding, support, and collaboration in educational settings. Parent workshops, community forums, and outreach events provide opportunities to showcase the benefits of game-based learning and address concerns or misconceptions.

CONCLUSION

SUMMER OF KEY POINTS

- **Understanding Gamification and Game-Based Learning:** Picture yourself delving into the depths of gamification, unraveling its intricacies, and discovering how games can be powerful tools for learning.
- **The Psychology of Play and Learning:** Dive into the fascinating psychology behind play and learning, exploring how games engage our minds and foster deeper understanding.
- **The Role of Technology in Game-Based Learning:** Feel the warmth of technological advancements as they illuminate the path towards innovative game-based learning experiences.
- **Gamification Principles and Strategies:** Like the gentle breeze guiding a sailboat, learn the principles and strategies that navigate the seas of gamification.
- **Gamification in Different Educational Settings:** Wander through diverse educational landscapes, witnessing how gamification flourishes in various settings, from classrooms to online platforms.
- **Assessment and Evaluation in Gamification:** As the sun sets, casting a reflective glow over the day's adventures, reflect on the methods and tools for assessing and evaluating the effectiveness of gamification.
- **Designing Educational Games:** Feel the creative energy flowing as you immerse yourself in the art of designing educational games, crafting experiences that captivate and educate.
- **Types of Educational Games:** Explore the vast spectrum of educational games, from immersive simulations to interactive quizzes, each offering unique opportunities for learning.
- **Integrating Games into the Curriculum:** Like pieces of a puzzle coming together, discover how games seamlessly integrate into the curriculum, enhancing learning experiences across subjects.

- **Teacher Training and Support:** As a guiding light in the world of education, empower teachers with the knowledge and support they need to harness the potential of game-based learning.
- **Overcoming Challenges and Concerns:** Navigate through the challenges and concerns that may arise on this journey, finding solutions and forging ahead with resilience.
- **Emerging Trends and Technologies:** Ride the wave of emerging trends and technologies, staying ahead of the curve and embracing new possibilities for game-based learning.
- **Research and Evaluation in Game-Based Learning:** Delve into the realm of research and evaluation, uncovering insights that drive continuous improvement and innovation in game-based learning.

THE FUTURE OF GAMIFICATION AND GAME-BASED LEARNING

In recent years, gamification and game-based learning have emerged as powerful tools in education, training, and various other fields. This trend is expected to evolve and expand significantly in the coming years as technology continues to advance and our understanding of human behavior deepens. The future of gamification and game-based learning holds immense potential to revolutionize how we engage, learn, and interact in both virtual and real-world settings.

The future of gamification and game-based learning holds tremendous promise in transforming education, training, and personal development. Technological advancements will drive innovation, enabling personalized, adaptive, and immersive learning experiences across various domains and industries.

By integrating gamified elements into traditional education systems, fostering lifelong learning opportunities, and promoting social collaboration, we can unlock the full potential of gamification and game-based learning to empower learners and shape a brighter future.

However, it's essential to approach this future with ethical considerations and responsible practices to ensure that gamification and game-based learning benefit society as a whole.

Before delving into the future, it's crucial to grasp the concepts of gamification and game-based learning. Gamification involves applying game design elements and principles to non-game contexts to enhance user engagement, motivation, and participation. This could range from incorporating point systems, badges, and leaderboards into educational platforms to incentivize learning and progress.

On the other hand, game-based learning involves using games as educational tools themselves. These games are specifically designed to teach certain concepts, skills, or behaviors while keeping players immersed and entertained. Examples include educational video games, simulation exercises, and virtual reality experiences tailored to specific learning objectives.

Technological Advancements Driving the Future

The future of gamification and game-based learning is deeply intertwined with technological advancements. Emerging technologies such as augmented reality (AR), virtual reality (VR), artificial intelligence (AI), and blockchain are poised to revolutionize how games are designed, delivered, and experienced.

AR and VR technologies will offer immersive and interactive learning environments, allowing learners to engage with content in three-dimensional spaces. AI algorithms will enable personalized learning experiences by adapting game mechanics and content to individual preferences and proficiency levels. Blockchain technology will provide transparent and secure platforms for tracking achievements, verifying credentials, and rewarding participants.

Personalized Learning and Adaptive Experiences

One of the most significant trends in the future of gamification and game-based learning is the shift towards personalized and adaptive experiences. By leveraging data analytics and AI algorithms, educational games can dynamically adjust difficulty levels, pacing, and content based on learners' performance and preferences.

Personalization enhances engagement and motivation by ensuring that learners are appropriately challenged without feeling overwhelmed or bored. Adaptive experiences cater to diverse learning styles and abilities, accommodating individual differences and maximizing learning outcomes.

Integration with Traditional Education

As gamification and game-based learning become more sophisticated and mainstream, they will increasingly integrate with traditional education systems. Educational institutions, from K-12 schools to universities, will adopt gamified platforms and game-based curricula to supplement traditional teaching methods.

Teachers and instructors will serve as facilitators and guides, leveraging gamified elements to enhance classroom activities, assessments, and homework assignments. Students will have access to interactive learning modules, educational games, and collaborative virtual environments that complement traditional lectures and textbooks.

Lifelong Learning and Professional Development

Beyond formal education, the future of gamification and game-based learning will extend to lifelong learning and professional development. Employers will utilize gamified training programs and simulations to onboard new employees, develop specific skills, and foster a culture of continuous learning within organizations.

Online platforms and mobile apps will offer gamified experiences for upskilling, reskilling, and pursuing certifications in various industries and domains. Gamification will incentivize participation, track progress, and provide instant feedback, making learning more accessible and enjoyable for learners of all ages.

Social and Collaborative Gaming Experiences

Another aspect of the future of gamification and game-based learning is the emphasis on social and collaborative gaming experiences. Multiplayer games and collaborative challenges will promote teamwork, communication, and problem-solving skills, mirroring real-world collaboration in professional settings.

Social features such as leaderboards, group competitions, and virtual communities will foster a sense of belonging and camaraderie among learners. Peer-to-peer interactions and cooperative gameplay will enhance motivation and engagement, encouraging learners to support and learn from each other.

Ethical Considerations and Concerns

As gamification and game-based learning evolve, it's essential to address ethical considerations and potential concerns. Designing ethical games involves ensuring inclusivity, diversity, and cultural sensitivity to avoid reinforcing stereotypes or promoting discriminatory behaviors. Moreover, developers must prioritize data privacy and security to protect users' personal information and prevent exploitation. Balancing the addictive nature of games with responsible usage and healthy habits is crucial to prevent excessive screen time and potential negative impacts on mental health.

FINAL THOUGHTS AND REFLECTION

As we conclude our exploration of gamification and game-based learning, it's evident that these approaches hold immense potential to revolutionize education, training, and personal development. From enhancing engagement and motivation to fostering collaboration and critical thinking skills, games offer a dynamic and immersive medium for learning and growth. Gamification and game-based learning represent not just a technological innovation, but a paradigm shift in how we approach education, training, and personal development. By embracing the power of play, personalization, collaboration, and lifelong learning, we can create a future where learning knows no bounds and every individual has the opportunity to unlock their full potential. Reflecting on the journey through the world of gamification and game-based learning, several key insights emerge:

Engagement through Play

At the heart of gamification and game-based learning lies the concept of play. By tapping into the inherent human desire for challenge, achievement, and social interaction, games captivate learners' attention and drive active participation. Whether through virtual simulations, educational quests, or competitive challenges, play serves as a powerful catalyst for learning and discovery.

Personalized Pathways to Learning

The future of education is personalized, adaptive, and learner-centric. Gamification and game-based learning offer tailored pathways for individuals to pursue their educational goals at their own pace and according to their unique preferences. Through data-driven insights and adaptive algorithms, learners can receive personalized feedback, recommendations, and support, maximizing their potential for success.

Collaboration and Community

Learning is inherently social, and games provide fertile ground for collaboration, communication, and community building. Multiplayer experiences, cooperative challenges, and virtual environments enable learners to connect with peers, share knowledge, and collectively solve problems. By fostering a sense of belonging and mutual support, games create rich learning ecosystems where every participant has the opportunity to contribute and thrive.

Lifelong Learning and Continuous Improvement

In a rapidly evolving world, the journey of learning never truly ends. Gamification and game-based learning offer pathways for lifelong learning and continuous improvement, empowering individuals to adapt to new challenges, acquire new skills, and pursue their passions throughout their lives. Whether in formal education, professional development, or personal enrichment, games provide a dynamic and engaging platform for growth and exploration.

Ethical Considerations and Responsible Design

As we embrace the power of gamification and game-based learning, it's crucial to approach their design and implementation with ethical considerations and responsible practices. Ensuring inclusivity, diversity, and cultural sensitivity, protecting users' privacy and security, and promoting healthy usage habits are essential priorities. By prioritizing ethical considerations, we can harness the transformative potential of games while mitigating potential risks and pitfalls.

APPENDICES

APPENDIX A: EXAMPLES OF GAMIFICATION IN EDUCATION

- **Kahoot!**: A popular platform that allows educators to create interactive quizzes, surveys, and discussions for students. It employs gamified elements such as points, leaderboards, and instant feedback to enhance engagement and learning outcomes.
- **Classcraft**: This platform gamifies the classroom experience by turning learning into a role-playing game. Students create avatars, form teams, and earn points for academic achievements, collaboration, and positive behavior.
- **Duolingo**: A language-learning app that incorporates gamified features such as levels, streaks, and rewards to motivate users to practice regularly. Learners progress through lessons while earning virtual currency and unlocking new content.
- **Mathletics**: An online math program for students that offers interactive activities, games, and competitions to reinforce mathematical concepts and skills. It tracks individual progress and provides instant feedback to support personalized learning.

APPENDIX B: RESEARCH STUDIES ON GAME-BASED LEARNING

- **"The Effectiveness of Educational Games: A Literature Review and Discussion"**: This meta-analysis examines the impact of educational games on learning outcomes across various subjects and age groups. It highlights the positive effects of game-based learning on motivation, engagement, and knowledge retention.
- **"Game-Based Learning: Latest Evidence and Future Directions"**: A comprehensive review of recent research on game-based learning, focusing on its effectiveness in improving academic performance, problem-solving skills, and collaboration among students.
- **"The Role of Gamification in Higher Education: A Systematic Literature Review"**: This study investigates the use of gamification in higher education settings, analyzing its effects on student motivation, engagement, and satisfaction with learning experiences.

- **"Game-Based Learning in Virtual Reality: A Review of Current Research and Applications"**: A survey of studies exploring the potential of virtual reality games for educational purposes. It discusses the benefits and challenges of using VR technology in game-based learning environments.

APPENDIX C: TOOLS AND PLATFORMS FOR CREATING EDUCATIONAL GAMES

- **Unity**: A powerful game development platform that allows users to create 2D, 3D, and AR/VR games. It offers a wide range of tools and resources for designing educational games with interactive features and immersive environments.
- **Twine**: An open-source tool for creating interactive fiction and branching narratives. Educators can use Twine to develop text-based adventure games that engage students in storytelling and decision-making activities.
- **Scratch**: A beginner-friendly programming environment that enables users to create animations, games, and interactive stories. It provides a visual interface and drag-and-drop coding blocks, making it suitable for teaching programming concepts to young learners.
- **Roblox Studio**: A game creation platform that allows users to design and publish multiplayer games across various genres. Educators can leverage Roblox Studio to engage students in collaborative game development projects and coding challenges.

APPENDIX D: CHALLENGES AND CONSIDERATIONS IN IMPLEMENTING GAMIFICATION AND GAME-BASED LEARNING

- **Technology Access and Equity**: Ensuring that all students have access to the necessary technology devices and internet connectivity to participate in gamified learning experiences.
- **Teacher Training and Support**: Providing professional development opportunities and resources for educators to effectively integrate gamification and game-based learning into their teaching practices.
- **Assessment and Evaluation**: Developing valid and reliable methods for assessing learning outcomes and measuring the effectiveness of gamified educational interventions.
- **Sustainability and Long-Term Engagement**: Designing gamified systems and learning activities that sustain learners' interest and motivation over time, avoiding the pitfalls of novelty and short-term engagement.

- **Ethical and Social Implications:** Addressing concerns related to data privacy, inclusivity, and the potential for addictive behaviors associated with gamification and gaming experiences.

APPENDIX E: FUTURE DIRECTIONS AND OPPORTUNITIES FOR GAMIFICATION AND GAME-BASED LEARNING

- **Integration with Emerging Technologies:** Exploring the potential of augmented reality, virtual reality, artificial intelligence, and blockchain to enhance gamified learning experiences and create innovative educational solutions.
- **Cross-Disciplinary Collaboration:** Fostering collaboration between educators, game developers, researchers, and policymakers to co-design gamified learning environments that address diverse learning needs and preferences.
- **Globalization and Cultural Adaptation:** Adapting gamified educational content and experiences to different cultural contexts and languages to ensure relevance, accessibility, and inclusivity for learners worldwide.
- **Research and Evidence-Based Practice:** Conducting rigorous research studies and evaluations to generate empirical evidence on the effectiveness and impact of gamification and game-based learning across various educational settings and populations.
- **Community Engagement and Advocacy:** Engaging stakeholders, including students, parents, educators, and policymakers, in discussions about the value and potential of gamification and game-based learning to drive positive change in education.

GLOSSARY OF TERMS

Gamification: The application of game design elements, mechanics, and principles in non-game contexts to engage and motivate users towards specific goals or behaviors.

Game-Based Learning: An educational approach that utilizes games as teaching tools to facilitate learning and skill development in various subjects and disciplines.

Points: Virtual currency or rewards earned by users for completing tasks, achieving goals, or demonstrating desired behaviors within a gamified system.

Badges: Digital symbols or icons awarded to users as visual representations of accomplishments, achievements, or milestones in gamified experiences.

Leaderboard: A visual display of rankings or scores that highlights the performance of users relative to one another, often used to foster competition and motivation in gamified environments.

Quests/Missions: Structured challenges or tasks presented to users within a game-based learning environment, typically aligned with learning objectives or curriculum standards.

Experience Points (XP): Units of progress or advancement earned by users as they engage in activities, complete quests, or achieve objectives within a game or gamified system.

Levels: Stages or tiers of progression within a game or gamified experience, often associated with increasing difficulty, complexity, or rewards as users advance.

Avatars: Digital representations or characters created by users to interact with virtual environments, other players, or learning content in game-based learning platforms.

Interactive Fiction: Text-based narratives or stories in which readers/player's choices influence the outcome and progression of the story, often used in educational game design to promote critical thinking and decision-making skills.

Branching Narratives: Storytelling structures in which the plot or storyline diverges based on the choices made by the reader/player, allowing for multiple possible outcomes or paths through the narrative.

Simulation: A digital representation or model of real-world processes, systems, or environments that allows users to interact with and explore various scenarios, often used for experiential learning in game-based learning.

Augmented Reality (AR): Technology that overlays digital content or information onto the physical world, enhancing users' perception and interaction with their environment, often used to create immersive learning experiences.

Virtual Reality (VR): Immersive technology that transports users to computer-generated environments, providing a sense of presence and interaction within virtual worlds, commonly used for experiential learning and simulations in game-based learning.

Artificial Intelligence (AI): Technology that enables machines or computer systems to perform tasks that typically require human intelligence, such as learning, reasoning, and problem-solving, often used to personalize learning experiences and provide adaptive feedback in game-based learning environments.

RESOURCES FOR FURTHER READING

A Theory of Fun for Game Design by Raph Koster (Published: 2004)

Actionable Gamification: Beyond Points, Badges, and Leaderboards by Yu-kai Chou (Published: 2015)

Digital Game-Based Learning edited by Marc Prensky (Published: 2007)

Digital Games and Learning: Research and Theory edited by Nicola Whitton and Alex Moseley (Published: 2012)

Engaging Learning: Designing e-Learning Simulation Games by Clark Aldrich (Published: 2003)

Fun Inc.: Why Gaming Will Dominate the Twenty-First Century by Tom Chatfield (Published: 2010)

Game Design Workshop: A Playcentric Approach to Creating Innovative Games by Tracy Fullerton (Published: 2014)

Game Design: Theory and Practice by Richard Rouse III (Published: 2001)

Game On: Energize Your Business with Social Media Games by Jon Radoff (Published: 2011)

Game On: Engaging Teachers in Gameful Learning by Kevin Bell (Published: 2019)

Game-Based Learning: How to Delight and Instruct in the 21st Century by Marc Prensky (Published: 2001)

Gamification and Education: A Critical Review by Lei Hao and Zhenhui Jiang (Published: 2014)

Gamification and Game Mechanics in Human Resources Management: Emerging Research and Opportunities by Monica Beltrametti and Stefano Tardini (Published: 2017)

Gamification and the Enterprise by Mario Herger (Published: 2014)

Gamification by Design: Implementing Game Mechanics in Web and Mobile Apps by Gabe Zichermann and Christopher Cunningham (Published: 2011)

Gamification for Development: Enabling Learning and Innovation by Brian Burke and Karen Tinio (Published: 2014)

Gamification for Human Factors Integration: Social, Education, and Psychological Issues by Nathaniel Osgood and Mihaela Ulieru (Published: 2014)

Gamification for Learning by Anmol Madan and Vineet Sinha (Published: 2017)

Gamification for Training and Education by Janaki Mythily Kumar and Mario Herger (Published: 2013)

Gamification in Business: Designing Motivating Solutions to Problem Situations by Michael Hugos (Published: 2014)

Gamification in Education and Business by Torsten Reiners and Lincoln C. Wood (Published: 2014)

Gamification in Education: Breakthroughs in Research and Practice edited by Information Resources Management Association (Published: 2019)

Gamification in Learning and Education: Enjoy Learning Like Gaming by Sangkyun Kim and Toshiyuki Kaneda (Published: 2018)

Gamification with Unity 5.x by Lauren S. Ferro (Published: 2016)

Gamification: Concepts, Methodologies, Tools, and Applications edited by Information Resources Management Association (Published: 2015)

Gamification: Using Game Elements in Serious Contexts edited by Minhua Ma, Andreas Oikonomou, and Lakhmi C. Jain (Published: 2017)

Gamify: How Gamification Motivates People to Do Extraordinary Things by Brian Burke (Published: 2014)

Learning by Playing: Game-based Education System Design and Development by Jannicke Baalsrud Hauge and Huy Ngoc Nguyen (Published: 2017)

Learning in a Digital World: Reflections on Gamification and Education by David Williamson Shaffer (Published: 2015)

Learning in a Digitalized Age: Plugged in, Turned on, Totally Engaged? by Karen D. Schrier (Published: 2016)

Learning Online with Games, Simulations, and Virtual Worlds: Strategies for Online Instruction by Clark Aldrich (Published: 2009)

Learning Through Digital Game Design and Building in a Participatory Culture by Elisabeth R. Hayes and Sean C. Duncan (Published: 2012)

Learning with Digital Games: A Practical Guide to Engage Students in Higher Education by Nicola Whitton (Published: 2010)

Playful Design: Creating Game Experiences in Everyday Interfaces by John Ferrara (Published: 2018)

Playful Learning: An Integrated Gameful Design Approach by David McHugh and John O'Flynn (Published: 2020)

Power Play: How Video Games Can Save the World by Asi Burak and Laura Parker (Published: 2017)

Reality is Broken: Why Games Make Us Better and How They Can Change the World by Jane McGonigal (Published: 2011)

Rethinking Gamification by Mathias Fuchs and Sonia Fizek (Published: 2014)

Serious Game Design and Development: Technologies for Training and Learning edited by Jan Cannon-Bowers and Clint Bowers (Published: 2010)

Serious Games: Mechanisms and Effects by Ralf Dörner and Stefan Göbel (Published: 2017)

The Gameful Life: Improve Your Mind, Body, and Relationships with the Science of Games by Steve Kamb (Published: 2020)

The Gameful World: Approaches, Issues, Applications edited by Steffen P. Walz and Sebastian Deterding (Published: 2015)

The Gamification of Learning and Instruction Fieldbook: Ideas into Practice by Karl M. Kapp (Published: 2013)

The Gamification of Learning and Instruction: Game-Based Methods and Strategies for Training and Education by Karl M. Kapp (Published: 2012)

The Gamification of Work: The Use of Games in the Workplace by Nigel P. Cook (Published: 2016)

The Gamification Toolkit: Dynamics, Mechanics, and Components for the Win by Kevin Werbach and Dan Hunter (Published: 2015)

The Multiplayer Classroom: Designing Coursework as a Game by Lee Sheldon (Published: 2011)

Understanding Minecraft: Essays on Play, Community, and Possibilities edited by Nate Garrelts (Published: 2014)

INDEX

www.ingramcontent.com/pod-product-compliance
Lightning Source LLC
LaVergne TN
LVHW062113200926
848484LV00007B/1657